D0329366

automated educational systems

ENOCH HAGA, editor

THE BUSINESS PRESS
Elmhurst, Illinois, U.S.A.
1967

automated educational systems

Printed in the United States of America

Library of Congress Catalog Card Number: 67-22351

DEDICATION
TO
ROBERT WILSON SIMS, JR., EdD
from his colleagues
in the
State of Florida
Department of Education

FOR THOSE WHO KNEW HIM, *there is a deep sense of inadequacy in attempting to express the personal and professional loss in the passing of Bob Sims. Pioneering the cause of Information Systems at all levels, he left a clearly marked path into the future for those who are to follow.*

His unusual ability to unite diverse opinions, while directing thought and discussion into the heart of real issues, continues to be an inspiration to all. He was wholeheartedly dedicated to the educational profession, and he exemplified the inherent goodness in all mankind. We can all say, "I am a better man for having known him."

INTRODUCTION

WE LIVE IN A WORLD OF TOMORROWS. Everywhere around us is a bustling creative society literally bursting with new knowledge and looking for a way to apply that knowledge for the betterment of mankind. The field of education, sadly enough, continues to lag behind progress being made in industry. There are many bright and creative people in education, many whose works are to be found in the following pages, yet the fruits of their labors are not often to be found in school district operations or instructional programs.

A vast gulf exists between what we know about automated educational systems and our ability to implement this "know-how" in an operational setting. Local school district superintendents are, in general, not ready to accept total systems concepts, programmed instruction, and a host of technically oriented improvements to education.

It is my hope that a publication such as this will help educators to understand the technology of our times and serve as a bridge between our world of pedagogy and the science of the space age. The world of data processing has much to offer education. It is my hope that we take advantage of it.

Max Rafferty

MAX RAFFERTY
Superintendent of Public Instruction
State of California
January 1967

PREFACE

The aim of this book is to present to school administrators, educators, and students in colleges of education, an overview of where we stand today in planning and implementing automated systems for both administrative and instructional applications. The purpose is to delineate the topography—not to examine it thoroughly. Hence, this volume is intended for those who wish to become acquainted with the vast potentialities and possibilities for improvement of administration and instruction which are inherent in the process of automating educational systems. There are gaps and rough spots in this book. I do not apologize for them. Instead, I urge all readers to continually scan the literature (which is added to, month after month, without cessation), for new information.

If the written word could bring about direct action, education would long since have been revolutionized. Only people in action can bring about dynamic and living improvements, and my hope is that you, the readers of this book, will be instrumental in bringing about long overdue reforms in both administrative processes and methods and techniques of instruction. There will be many roads to these ends, but let us hope that the day will soon come when we will expend as much money and effort on educational improvement as we do today for death-dealing and destruction.

Part I, Concepts and Patterns, consists of eight chapters designed to introduce the reader to some of the concepts and potential applications for education of systems, including the use of computers. Chapters 5 to 8 show possibilities in local, regional, state, and national educational data centers or information systems. *Part II, Applications and Techniques,* runs the gamut with its selection of administrative and instructional applications and computerized techniques. The ten chapters give a good outline of what can be achieved in such areas as student accounting and scheduling, computerized sectioning and class scheduling, and computer-assisted instruction.

This book doesn't have everything, but I believe that it is possibly the best book that could have been put together by anyone, given the realistic working constraints. The book couldn't be too small, nor too big; it must try to cover the field in a reasonable way; and the chapters must be authoritative—written by people who are working experts in their respective fields. Unfortunately, the doers and the thinkers aren't always ready and willing to write at pushbutton command. The fact that these authors *did* speaks well for them; it has been my experience that the really competent person is always ready to do "a little bit more" in helping others with their problems.

Acknowledgments. And so I commend this book to you, pausing only to thank those who, in addition to the chapter authors, helped with this project, as well as those who wished to help, but due to circumstances of one sort or another were unable to participate. These people include Robert P. Beynon, Don D. Bushnell, Sylvia Charp, Robert A. Edberg, John F. Flowers, W. G. Katzenmeyer, Paul C. Libassi, Gerald L. McManis, Claude Simpson, Murray Tondow, Warren C. Vogt, and Karl L. Zinn. Special thanks are due to James J. Fast, Jr., executive secretary, Association for Educational Data Systems (AEDS) for his early cooperation; to Walter S. Lennartson, director, The Business Press, for his faith in this project; and to my wife, Elna, for her assistance, patience, and understanding during the preparation of this work.

ENOCH HAGA

Livermore, California
January 1967

ABOUT THE EDITOR

Enoch J. Haga received his MA in Business Education from Sacramento State College in 1958, and his BA in Social Science from the same institution in 1955.

His teaching experience has ranged from junior high school mathematics to high school business education to university graduate-level business administration. He was formerly assistant professor of business at Stanislaus State College (Turlock, California), where he taught graduate and upper division courses in business administration, including statistics and systems and procedures. His business experience includes work as an engineering writer, senior publications engineer, and procedures analyst for such companies as Hughes Aircraft Co., Librascope (General Precision, Inc.), Lockheed Missiles & Space Co., and Holmes & Narver, Inc.

Mr. Haga's numerous publications include several professional articles and a book, *Understanding Automation: A Data Processing Curriculum Guide and Reference Text* (Elmhurst, Illinois: The Business Press, 1965). For several years he has been a contributing editor of *The Journal of Business Education,* for whom he conducts a monthly column, "Automation and You" (formerly called "Understanding Automation"). He was co-founder of the Society for Automation in Business Education (SABE), and was first editor of the *SABE Data Processor.* He is a reviewer for ACM's *Computing Reviews.* As education editor of *Business Automation Magazine,* he is editor of the *Automation Educator* section, which is published as an insert six times a year.

TABLE OF CONTENTS

PART I — CONCEPTS AND PATTERNS

PART II — APPLICATIONS AND TECHNIQUES

LIST OF ILLUSTRATIONS

part I
CONCEPTS AND PATTERNS

1 systems concepts and practices in education

ROBERT W. SIMS

The late DR. ROBERT W. SIMS *received his EdD from Florida State University and his MA and BS from the University of Southern Mississippi.*

His extensive experience included service as a mathematics teacher, athletic coach, and principal. Since 1956 he served with the Florida State Department of Education, first as a specialist in educational research, and later in the area of information systems development and implementation.

Dr. Sims was a charter member of AEDS and of the Florida Association for Educational Data Systems; he served FAEDS as secretary-treasurer and on the board of directors. He was associate editor of the Florida Journal of Educational Research, *and was a contributor to various professional publications.*

TRADITIONAL PRACTICES

Educational information has traditionally been classified in terms of functional areas of administrative control within the educational organization, such as payroll, attendance, scheduling, testing, purchasing, etc. Information handling in each of these areas is under the direct supervision and control of an administrator responsible to the superintendent or president for all matters directly relating to that function. Therefore, each such administrator is primarily responsible for defining his own information needs, gathering the necessary raw data, and manipulating the data to provide the desired reports. Data processing then, like most other functions, is carried on in relative independence of the activities of other administrators. In fact, personnel in one division usually have little if any knowledge of the information needs of any of the other divisions, and no one in the organization has an adequate conception of the overall information needs of the organization. Among the major weaknesses of the traditional approach are:

1. The duplication of effort required by those furnishing the raw data.

2. Unmanageable collections of paper work in each administrative area resulting in the preparation of management reports so out of date that they provide little help to the decision makers. Most educators have seen *estimated* figures for a given school year that were published two years or more after the close of the school year.
3. Inability to adequately mechanize processing activities due to excessive annual cost of equipment needed for handling large masses of data during rush periods, with resulting idle time during the the off-season.

INTRODUCTION OF HIGH SPEED DATA PROCESSING EQUIPMENT

When high speed data processing equipment is introduced into an educational organization, attempts to utilize the equipment usually fall into one of three general categories:

Job-by-Job Conversion

A job-by-job conversion of existing procedures is made with no attempt to integrate the data "belonging to" the various subdivisions of the organization. This approach tends to intensify the problem of duplication of effort on the part of those furnishing the raw data and those preparing data for input to the data processing machines. The cost of these activities has usually been prohibitive under such conditions.

The job-by-job conversion approach is said to be much like building a family dwelling one room at a time, while assuring that no two rooms share the same wall. This approach to home building has one definite advantage. Each member of the family has a self-contained unit to call his very own. Likewise, this approach to information handling retains for each administrator exclusive control of his own data files and procedures—an advantage dear to the hearts of many administrators who fear both the loss of control of "my" data and that "outsiders" will upset comfortable and familiar routines. Perhaps we in the data processing field have contributed to this feeling of fear by allowing to stand unchallenged many popular but unreasonable claims as to the magic powers of our machines, or allowing key administrators who lack technical knowledge to expect machines to solve systems or organizational problems. *We know* that application of machines to faulty systems within an inadequate organizational structure will only call attention to these problems, and that it will then appear that machines and machine people are at fault.

Modification and Improvement

A second approach to conversion is to combine and/or coordinate inputs and outputs of the procedures serving various administrators in order to eliminate some of the duplication of effort inherent in free-standing procedures. This method brings about an early partial integration of information systems in certain areas, but fails to benefit from insights and advantages that may be gained from a fresh approach, a thorough appraisal of information needs, and evaluation of alternate solutions to systems problems.

The modification and improvement approach also raises some difficult problems in regard to "ownership and control of data" as well as the management of the development and maintenance of procedures which cross conventional administrative lines. Such problems are most often solved, if at all, through persuasion and compromise on each issue as it arises rather than through well established policies and a clear chain of command. This approach will ultimately lead to a coordinated information system, if a workable body of policy and a clear-cut chain of command can be evolved before key systems personnel or administrators are overwhelmed by the pressures inherent in the unstable climate which result from a lack of centralized authoritative direction of the significant changes occurring in procedures and responsibilities.

The organization choosing the modification and improvement approach must be willing to live with such disadvantages as:

1. Continuous redefinition and redesign of the system, which lends an aura of firefighting to all systems work and limits the efficiency of the work of the programing staff as well as the efficient use of the machines.
2. Frustration of area administrators because certain needed operational reports are delayed by changes in some other segment of the system which, although controlled by another administrator, provides inputs required to prepare the needed report.
3. An unusual degree of reliance upon the diplomatic and persuasive powers of key systems personnel to guide area administrators toward sound systems decisions, even when such action appears, to one or more of the administrators involved, to be inconsistent with his own immediate needs. This is a particularly crucial area, since the management of the development and maintenance of the information system is one of the most exacting functions of the organization which, by the very nature of the function, requires strict adherence to defined procedures as well as production time schedules established well in advance.
4. The necessity to direct the efforts of personnel toward the achievement of two essential and sometimes temporarily diver-

> gent objectives, i.e., to meet the immediate vital information needs of the various operational units of the organization, and to design and implement an information system which more nearly approaches the ideal. If undue emphasis is placed on the latter, immediate information needs will not be met and operational units of the organization will come to question the efficacy of the information systems function. On the other hand, if the latter is neglected the continuing immediate information needs will never be met in an orderly manner and the information system will collapse from the dead weight of progressive inefficiency. Some reasonable balance must be maintained, despite the fact that many of the efforts toward the achievement of one objective do not necessarily contribute to the attainment of the other.

The modification and improvement approach just described may well be the most progressive alternative open to educational management. It has, in fact, been the approach most often taken in practice, even by those who subscribe in theory to the total systems approach, but who lack either the courage or the resources to come to grips with the problems involved in establishing the prerequisites of a total systems approach.

Total Systems Approach

The total systems approach requires the . . . . .

> acceptance of newer systems concepts which recognize an organization as an organic system composed of many interdependent subsystems; concepts which call for the determination of the real management information needs, and which will utilize fully the unique capabilities of the computer and other new tools to produce better, more integrated administrative (and educational) processes.[1]

This approach to information systems recognizes and emphasizes the fact that the nature of "data processing" is such that it cannot function in isolation from other subunits of the organization. Data processing is more appropriately conceived as only one of the major functions of an information system which is dependent upon people, materials, procedures, and information, as well as machines.

It is only during the last few years that organizations have made significant progress toward the optimum use of computers and other electronic equipment in the information system. Recent developments in the machine area have been so dramatic that attention of users has been drawn away from other elements of the informa-

---

[1] N. L. Senensieb, "Systems and Procedures," *The Encyclopedia of Management*, Vol. II (Carl Heyel, ed.). New York: Reinhold Publishing Corporation, 1963, p. 967.

tion system and concentrated on the machines. A certain amount of concentration on machines is, of course, necessary, but successful use of data processing machines in the information system requires equal attention to other elements.

Since the information system of any organization is interwoven throughout the organization, practically all of its functions are affected by the introduction of high speed data processing equipment. Therefore, commitment to a total systems approach and the effective utilization of computers in an educational organization demand that the superintendent or president recognize, in the beginning, that the administrative structure and organizational policies, to which information system personnel (as well as others) relate, must be such as to make possible the orderly development, maintenance, and control of procedures which will promote the free flow of information throughout the organization: horizontally across conventional administrative lines, and vertically between the highest and lowest level of users, whether administrators, researchers, teachers or students.

There must be a readiness throughout the organization to accept change in the method of performing daily operations—even change in the nature of operations to be performed. Such readiness can be inspired only through the leadership of a superintendent or president who is committed to the principle of optimum use of both machines and men in the educational enterprise.

In order for the information system to adequately serve the needs of the organization, top-level coordination of the development and implementation of the system is essential.

Once adequate organizational structure and policies have been established, a nucleus of information system specialists should be recruited or identified from among existing staff. Each segment of the system must be planned to make a contribution to the establishment and maintenance of a data bank which may be accessed for use in other segments. Such planning assumes comprehensive knowledge on the part of key planners concerning current contents of the data bank, as well as the design of files and procedures for future storage of data. It is unreasonable to expect that any administrator of an operating division of the organization will have time or the inclination to gain such knowledge. Unless provision is made in the beginning for use of one or more competent information system specialists in key planning roles, the total systems approach should probably not be attempted.

When key information system specialists are on site, their energies should be turned to a study of the information needs of the organization. This begins with an analysis of information structures ranging from the complex of data underlying the operation of the educational institution, to the principles which underlie the collecting, coding, storage, retrieval, processing, and transformation of data and a consideration of the most appropriate modes of presenting information to the users.

The next step is the acquisition of the appropriate processing equipment and the full staffing of the technical support necessary to accomplish defined goals within a realistic time frame.

As yet, to my knowledge, no educational organization has dared venture so far from tradition as to attempt full scale adoption of a total systems approach *in practice!* Perhaps the current national emphasis on quality education and on the scientific assessment of the degree to which educational objectives are attained in our country will provide for educators both the motivation and the financial resources required to take the bold strides necessary to actually develop and implement a total information system for education.

It may occur in our time!

2 the concept of total systems in education

BRUCE KEITH ALCORN

DR. BRUCE K. ALCORN received his PhD from the University of Iowa in Educational Psychology and Measurement; his MS from New York State College of Education (Oneonta, N.Y.) is in Elementary Education; and his BRE is from the Baptist Bible Seminary (Johnson City, N.Y.).

Since joining the faculty of Bowling Green University, Dr. Alcorn has taught in the areas of educational data processing, measurement, statistics, and research methodology; in addition to his teaching assignments, he has served as a consultant to schools as well as to the university, and recently his work was instrumental in reorganizing the university's data processing system.

Dr. Alcorn has served as president of the Association for Educational Data Systems (AEDS) in Ohio, and as a department editor (Administrative Data Systems in Higher Education) for the AEDS Monitor. *Dr. Alcorn's numerous professional publications include work on a standardized achievement test.*

THE CONCEPT IN GENERAL

"Total systems" is a phrase which is subject to a great deal of misunderstanding, semantic war, and indiscriminate use. In spite of such problems, it is a topic worth serious consideration by educators at all levels.

The total information system as a concept is not new, but its implementation had to await the arrival of tools which could handle data quickly, efficiently, and meaningfully.

Most of the development work relative to this concept has been done by the leaders in the field of management science; they have, however, drawn upon the work of others. For example, when Ludwig von Bertalanffy, a biologist, discussed general system theory, he stated that:

> A "system" can be defined as a complex of elements standing in interaction. There are general principles holding for systems, irrespective of the nature of the component elements and of the relations or forces between them.[1]

[1] Ludwig von Bertalanffy, *Problems of Life.* New York: Harper & Brothers (Harper Torchbook Edition), 1960, p. 176.

Another example comes from the work of the late Norbert Wiener, who coined the word "cybernation" to cover the scientific field dealing with the *control* and *communication* of information.

From management science itself we find men such as Richards and Greenlaw, who take a basic approach in *Management Decision Making* which they call the "information decision system." In defining this approach they state:

> Although many managerial and organizational processes have not yet been adequately conceptualized in terms of their dynamic interaction with other facets of the organizational system, we nonetheless believe that the most broadly based integrative conception of managerial and organizational behavior existing at this time is one in which organizations are viewed in cybernetic and systems terms.[2]

Two others at the management level have stated that:

> By total we mean that the paper work needs of the whole organization are considered, without omitting any part of it. The word integrated implies the same idea. Nothing is segregated. The existing organizational lines won't stop us from making combinations which improve efficiency.[3]
>
> Thus, integrated data processing and total systems convey the idea that the area of interest takes in the recording work of all departments of the company, with particular reference to the relationships among similar or similarly used information.[4]

Numerous labels have been used with reference to the concept under discussion such as "total system," "information-decision system," "integrated information system," etc. In connection with the latter it is interesting to note that some have vigorously argued for the use of "integrated" rather than "total" on the basis that a *total* information system can never be attained. The idea behind the choice of "total" here is more one of attitude than of semantics. The goal is total information even though in practice it may be only degrees of total. This situation is analogous to a recent advertising approach of the Burlington Railroad in which the president, Louis Menk, stressed the point that his railroad was not in the railroad business. According to Menk, they are in the distribution business to serve the total distribution needs of the shipper.

It cannot be emphasized too strongly that the word "computer" was left out of the title of this chapter purposely. Granted, computers and other equipment are vital to the fulfillment of the goals and

---

[2] Max D. Richards and Paul S. Greenlaw. *Management Decision Making.* Homewood, Illinois: Richard D. Irwin, Inc., 1966, p. 22.

[3] Alan D. Meacham and Van B. Thompson (eds.), and Enoch J. Haga and Maurice F. Ronayne (coordinating eds.). *Total Systems.* Detroit: American Data Processing, Inc., 1962, p. 81.

[4] *Ibid.,* p. 16.

aspirations of those advocating total systems; they are nonetheless only tools. The concept of a total information system transcends the domain of computers. In fact, "system" and "cybernetics" also go beyond equipment per se. It has been said, in reference to defining a total management system, that it is:

> . . ."a corporate program to increase profits through the systematic collection and effective use of available facts and figures." Unfortunately, most companies have attempted to cope with the information problem through the relatively simple but entirely inadequate expedient of authorizing their data processing organizations to procure hardware that could store a given number of times more data and print out countless variations of the old familiar reports at amazing speed. The nature, scope, and complexity of the problem does not lend itself to a simple "hardware" solution.[5]

We can talk about total systems beyond the machine level because the new technology of the so-called "Second Industrial Revolution" now makes total information systems possible in practice as well as in principle. The following phrases are indicative of some of the advances which have made this possible. Most, if not all of them are described elsewhere in this book, so they are only mentioned here. They are: real-time, time-sharing, teleprocessing, CAI (computer-assisted instruction), document readers, computer-generated voice, information retrieval, data reduction, direct inquiry, visual display, communications switching, machine-independent languages, random-access, and unlimited "memories."

In fact, equipment considerations and the like should not enter into the theoretical discussion of the development of a total information system until the implementation implications must be dealt with. If this is not done the "cart-before-the-horse" condition will develop. A more detailed discussion of a related nature (educational specifications vs. systems) appears elsewhere and need not be repeated here.[6]

Before proceeding to specific application of these concepts to the field of education, it might be wise to bring out a few statistics relative to the "information explosion" for the reader who is not convinced of the need for a "system." For ages man has emphasized the need for more and new information about himself and the world in which he lives. This is still true and with added impetus, however, an additional stress has come to the fore. It is that of learning how to use more effectively the knowledge we now have.

---

[5] Charles W. Heuendorf, "The Total Systems Approach," *The Systems Approach to Personnel Management*. Management Bulletin 62. New York: American Management Association, 1965, p. 10.

[6] Bruce K. Alcorn, "Educational Specifications vs. Systems—Does the Tail Wag the Dog?" *Journal of Educational Data Processing*, Summer 1965, pp. 99-102.

Even though scientists today publish no more per man than those of the 17th century, more scientific information is published because the number of scientists has doubled about every ten years for three centuries. In fact, the director of research for a steel company recently said it was cheaper to risk duplication of information on a project if it cost less than $100,000.[7] The number of scientific journals alone doubled in the fifteen-year period following 1950. Progress in science and technology is documented by sixty million pages of government and private industrial reports, while the amount expended on research and development in documentation has increased seven-fold in approximately the last five years.[8] Scientific data doubles every 10–15 years (at the present rate) and new federal records are being created at a rate of 4.5 billion per year. In addition, U. S. businesses *store* an estimated trillion pieces of paper in file drawers, while federal, state, and local government accumulates twice that amount.[9]

Consideration of such facts as these and the interaction with "population explosion" leads one to realize that the problem is more one of control than of production. It is not too unlike the taming of a wild river in an effort to turn potential disaster into productive energy. During the first decade of the 19th century, Goethe, a German poet, reacted to all the new information which was a product of the Industrial Revolution as follows:

> The modern age has a false sense of superiority because of the great mass of data at its disposal. But the valid criterion of distinction is rather the extent to which man knows how to form and master the material at his command.[10]

This remark remains quite appropriate for today.

THE CONCEPT IN EDUCATION

There was a time in our country when a teacher was able to keep all the information he needed to do his job in a small desk drawer, a "class-book," and in his memory; a time when a school superintendent required no more than a ledger and some cards to do a "good" job of administration; a time when the college president knew each student and staff member personally as well as their immediate families. For example, the Annual Report of the Ohio State Commissioner of Common Schools (now called the State

[7] Bruce H. Frisch, "The Big Information Mess," *Science Digest,* Vol. 58, No. 3, 1965, pp. 24-5.

[8] Barbara Lee Hazeltine, "The Information Explosion," *The Science Teacher,* Vol. 32, No. 2, 1965, pp. 26-7.

[9] "Information Explosion in the Factory," *Dun's Review and Modern Industry,* March 1965, pp. 112-13.

[10] *Ibid.*

Superintendent of Public Instruction) for the 1879–1880 school year was contained on fifty 6″ x 9½″ pages. Of course, there were then only one million school-age children and 24,000 teachers in the state, whereas in 1965 there were almost 2.7 million students and 97,000 teachers. This means that in the last 85 years the number of students in Ohio has almost tripled and the number of teachers has more than quadrupled. The Ohio increase is typical of the nation as a whole.

When these figures are coupled with the increase in the numbers and kinds of information schools now acquire, the "mess" is evident. At the end of each school year the storage facilities are stuffed even more. The saddest factor of all comes to light when the utility of all the overflowing files and cumulative records is examined. Once again we are reminded of Goethe's statement and its applicability for today.

Educators have come a long way in developing new methods of obtaining more essential data about the learner and the learning process, and they have been successful in actually collecting such data. However, this information-seeking process will have to continue at an increasing rate, in both quality and quantity, if American education is to keep pace with the knowledge and population explosions. The key to being able to keep pace now depends upon a total information system, whose development must increase at an exponential rate—or else we will fall behind.

Just what then is a total information system for an educational institution? Grossman and Howe present a good definition to start with:

> An information system is nothing more than a planned method of collecting necessary data and converting it to summaries and other reports that serve some vital purpose in the educational program. All of these systems are powered either by hand (manual systems) or by machine (automated system).[11]

This definition was not intended as an exhaustive and definitive essay on information systems, so it purposely leaves many things unsaid. The "planning" of any such system is perhaps the most important phase. It is not to be taken lightly, as simple, skeletal, problem-free, nor easy. Nor can the "conversion" of data be underestimated. The whole area of data reduction (taking masses of related data which are too vast to assimilate and reducing them to a few relatively meaningful and useful bits of information for purposes of making decisions), is one of the most Herculean tasks

[11] Alvin Grossman and Robert L. Howe. *Data Processing for Educators.* Chicago: Educational Methods, Inc., 1965, p. 3.

before the educational researcher. The idea of such a system yielding "summaries and other reports" is limiting. Perhaps this is what most present systems produce—paper. Who here on earth knows just what the future holds? Perhaps we shall even have a system someday that produces students!

The system must be "total" in principle if not in practice. Today the system must also be automated or else it will not work except in the very smallest of units.

A total educational information system is a complex of procedures, methods, and instruments coordinated to collect and digest all factors involved in the educational process and to yield a product which is useful and meaningful in obtaining the goals of education.

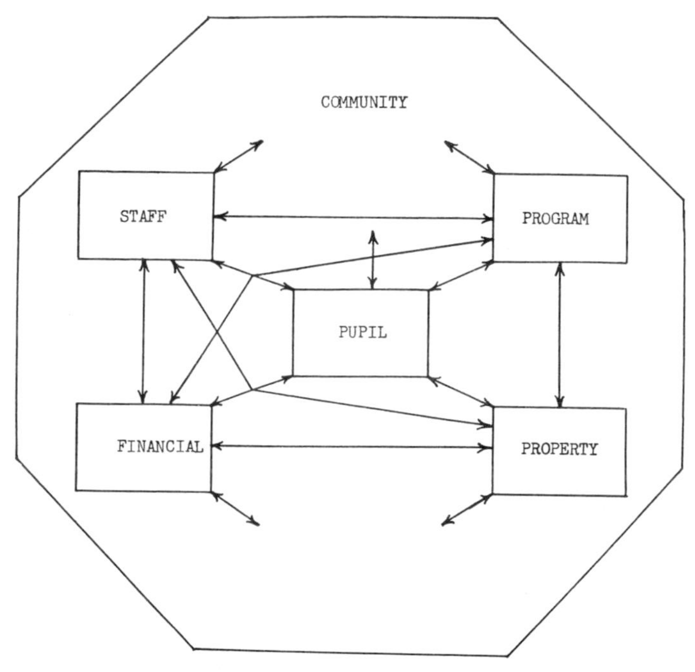

Fig. 1 — Categories of Educational Data.

What does "total" in this context encompass? This question cannot be completely answered since we have not discovered all of the factors affecting human behavior, and we probably never will. Nonetheless, we can point out many of the areas involved. At present, all available educational data can be classified into one or more of six categories. Figure 1 diagrammatically identifies these categories and illustrates the interrelatedness of the data.

Since a pupil does not exist in a vacuum, information about him is largely meaningless without being related to other elements. For example, a sixth-grade student is under the direction of a teacher (staff data), studying division of fractions (program data), using a desk in a classroom (property data), which all costs money (financial data). In addition, all of these operate interrelatedly in a community.

How many educational decisions have been made which turned out to be mistakes? How many such mistakes were never found out? How many of these errors were due to lack of total information? If a total information system had been working the etiology of that slow learner's correctable problem would have been discovered long before he reached the seventh grade.

When a total information system is working efficiently, the students will learn more and at a faster rate; and I do not mean the memory drum will simply turn faster. How much do we actually know about how a child learns to read? If we could "keep tabs" on all the responses involved we would be able to do a much better job.

How confident are we that our teacher certification requirements are sufficient? We have never really been able to examine the products of our teachers; that is, students with given characteristics are products of teachers possessing what traits? of what kind of schools?

The idea of "total" goes beyond the classroom and the school building; it extends nationally. If we are going to continuously evaluate and improve our educational system, we cannot be satisfied with an information system which is confined to school district lines. Even if we were degraded to the point where we had no concern about the status of educational systems other than our own, we would still need to look elsewhere for help in improving our own status. If you ever find a manufacturer who doesn't spend considerable time and money critically examining his competitors' products, you will have found a dying company or one which is too insignificant to be competitive.

An example of how information flow beyond school district lines can be beneficial to all comes from a recent bus maintenance problem in Ohio. Due to proper lines of communication, it was discovered that a certain make and model of school bus was experiencing the same type of brake failure. Because sufficient information was available in meaningful form, the manufacturer corrected the situation.

Figure 2 presents a diagram of "data banks" and channels of information flow for only a small sample of all the sources of educational data.

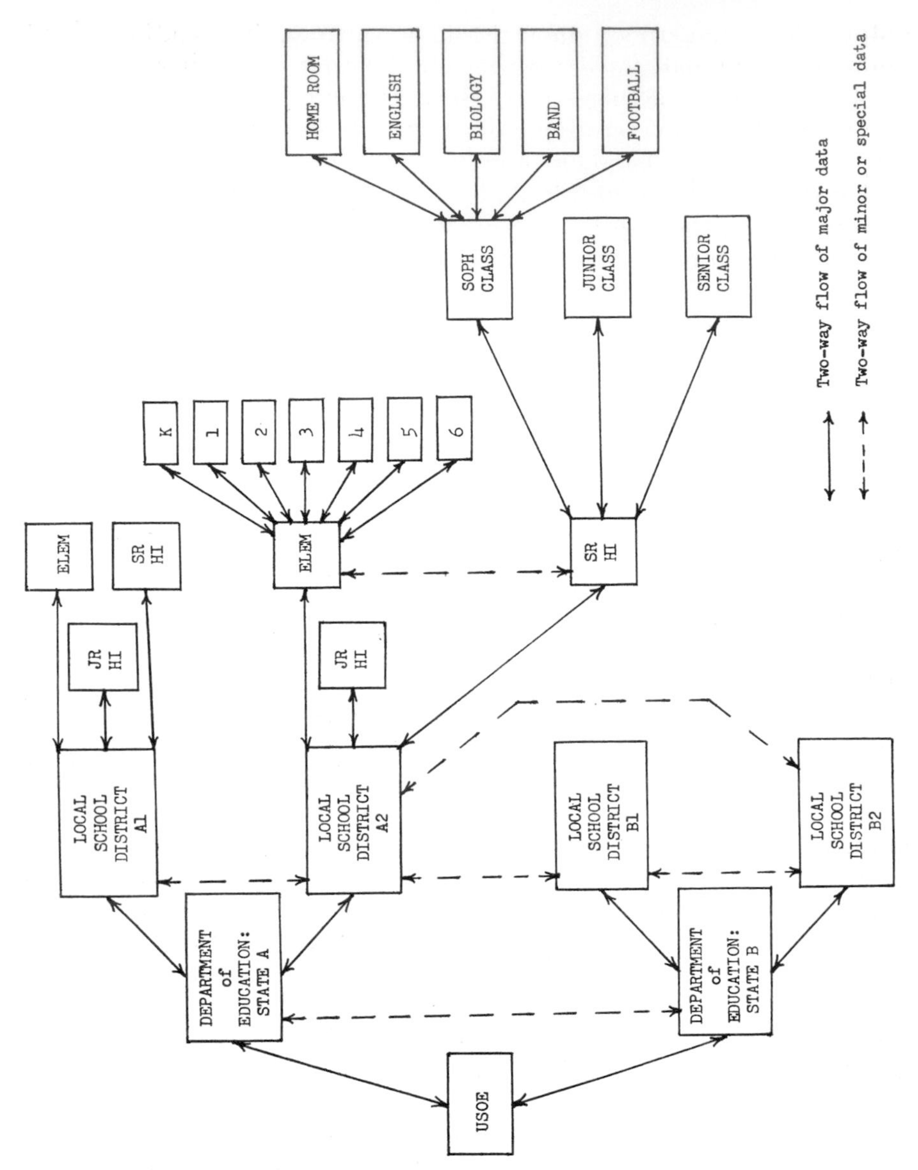

Fig. 2 — A System of Data Banks and Information Flow (A Partial Display).

Patrick stated that a data bank "consists of data and a means of access to data."[12] It is a place of data storage plus imput and

[12] R. L. Patrick and E. W. Frank. "Criteria Influencing Data Base Organization Design," *Proceedings of the Symposium, Development and Management of a Computer-Centered Data Base.* Santa Monica, California: System Development Corporation, 1964.

output. A kindergarten classroom is a data bank. Its teacher stores information and data flows out and into the class.

The solid lines indicate flow channels for the major data. "Major" is used here to indicate items of information which are needed at higher levels, or which are mutually agreed upon as essential for that level. For example, attendance figures constitute major information at the school district level. That is, each school would feed attendance data to the district office as a data bank.

The broken lines indicate flow channels for minor data. Minor data is that information which is not needed at higher levels nor mutually agreed upon as essential for that level, but still deemed essential for certain data banks. For example, religious affiliation is an item of information which at present probably would not be stored in many data banks. However, such information is often useful for educational research, and those who do use this data may need to communicate directly with each other. Storage of potentially desired data naturally enhances the value of the system.

Note that the arrows indicate the flow of information to be in both directions. This is essential for a total system.

Data Banks Concept Has Problems

This concept is not new. In fact, educators have been working with certain aspects of it for some time. Neither is it problem and emotion-free. The issue of security of personal data is a real "bomb." A great deal of study in this area has been initiated, but it will perhaps be the hardest hurdle to get over.

One of the earlier and continuing efforts in this direction is the handbook series sponsored by the U. S. Office of Education (USOE). The first handbook, *The Common Core of State Educational Information* (1953), was designed to serve as a dictionary and taxonomy of educational information. For example, what is a "secondary school?" Does it include grades 7–12, 8–12, 9–12 or just what? What is a part-time college student? Does this phrase include those taking less than 9 semester-hours, less than 10, or what? In addition to this original publication, others have been produced or are in the development stage. They now do or will cover financial, property, pupil, staff, program, and community data.

Related to this, the USOE has also inaugurated the BEDS Project. The title is quite descriptive: Basic Educational Data System. The role of the USOE has been one of coordination and leadership. The projects mentioned are utilizing the resources of professional educational organizations, state officials, and individual educators from across the country.

A PROPOSAL FOR A TOTAL SYSTEM FOR EDUCATIONAL INSTITUTIONS

A total information system does not just come into being; it must be created through careful planning and preparation. One of

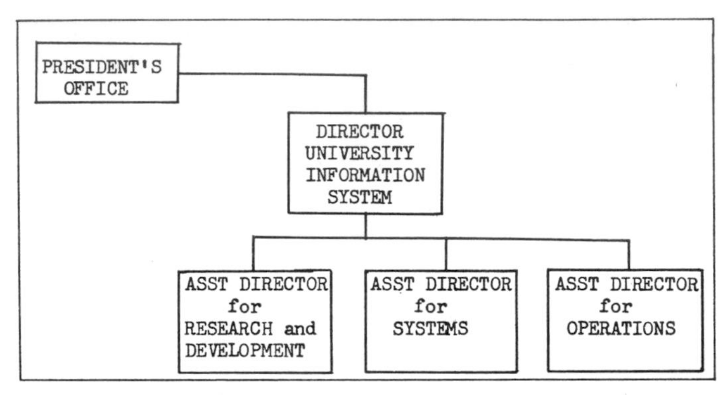

Fig. 3 — General Organizational Structure of a University Information System.

the requirements is the structuring or restructuring of the educational organization to facilitate such a system. Figure 3[13] presents

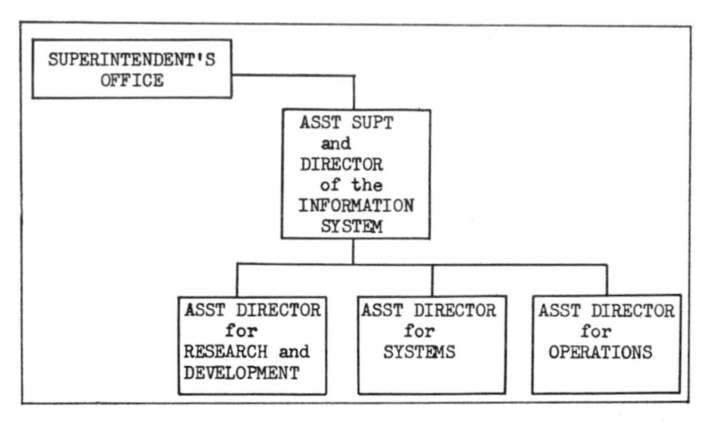

Fig. 4 — General Organizational Structure of a School Information System.

the structure of the top management for a university total information system and Figure 4 does the same for a large school system.

The director of such a system should be responsible directly to a top administrator. This need not interfere with the executive chain of command, because it can be a staff rather than a line

[13] Adapted from Bruce K. Alcorn, "A Proposal for a Total Information System for Educational Institutions," *Journal of Educational Data Processing*, Spring 1966, pp. 67-72.

relationship. In addition to giving the director the authority that goes with a position at this level, certain qualifications are implied. These will be discussed later.

Placing the top administrator of the information system next to the top executive of the educational institution is extremely important. Without this, the survival technique of "pleasing the boss first" will distort the priority setup. This also places the burden of serving all segments equally, and in an integrated manner, where it belongs. It is essential for a "total" system.

In a university, the director should report directly to the Office of the President. Figure 4 shows the director in that situation as an Assistant Superintendent, in an analogous position.

Next in the chain of command are the assistant directors. The function of the operations division is to collect, process, and dispense the data according to the specifications of systems. The work of this group might also be labeled "production."

The systems group develops the procedures for acquisition, processing, and dispensing of the data, basing its work on the educational specifications set up by research and development personnel, and tempering it with the limitations of operations. The educational specifications include, among other things, what to collect, where, when, etc.

Research and development is the starting point for the system—the innovators, one might say. The members of this staff deal with problems in the language of those needing and/or providing the data, whereas systems more or less prepares the way for the automated processors.

In spite of the fact that each area has its specific functions, they work very closely together, especially during the development of a given subsystem.

Suppose the coordinator of mathematics instruction of a local school system, along with his staff, decides to utilize some computer-assisted instruction (CAI) with a given course. After proceeding through the necessary academic channels, the director of the system would be consulted. The next step would involve the research and development staff, which would work with the math coordinator, instructors, perhaps the principal of the school involved, and other necessary academic personnel, to determine the educational specifications. Once it is determined what is going to be done, when, where and some of the hows, systems enters the picture. It aims at meeting all of the specifications, and takes them to operations for analysis and perhaps a pilot run.

Any conflicts have to be resolved jointly. If the particular time chosen by the mathematics staff should be in conflict with some other operation, the burden of solution lies first with operations. If it cannot be resolved there, systems attempts to work around the difficulty. Perhaps the particular educational specification may have to be changed, but that should be the last resort.

Once the program is running, it is simply a matter of continuing under the direction of operations. Few programs will run for extended periods without minor or even major changes. Such changes would start with research and development and work their way to operations. In view of this, eventually there might be staff in both systems and development spending most or all of their time on such programs as CAI.

Some jobs, such as the research projects of faculty members, may not get to the point of staying in operations. This would be especially true of "one-shot" studies. These programs would also start with the research and development staff and work through systems, with personnel competent in research procedures and systems carrying the load.

The examples thus far have referred to situations in which the request for assistance comes from outside the organization. The research and development staff would have the additional responsibility of developing new uses for their tools, as well as keeping the whole staff fully aware of all of the potentials involved, both old and new.

The personnel required below the assistant director level are not too different in type from those now employed or needed under existing structures, so the concern here is with the director and his assistants.

The director of the educational information system needs to be an educator who knows data processing, not the reverse. That is, he must basically be one who understands education, but who has data processing skills in addition.

Business management has learned from experience that the directors of total information systems need to be people who can view problems as a whole. They need to be able to see the "forest" and the integration rather than the "trees." They should not have allegiances to specific departments or only be experts in certain areas. Such men need not be machine operators or seasoned programers, but they must know how to apply the tools to the solution of problems. They must understand both the tools and the problems.

School districts which have automated their information systems generally find it more successful to train "schoolmen" in data processing, and let them direct the systems, than to bring in a former programer, systems analyst, etc., and acquaint him with the educational situation.

The most desirable holder of the title, "director," would be one with the following qualifications:

- Professional educator
- Successful experience as an educator (preferably at more than one level)
- In a university, qualified to hold academic rank (doctorate preferred)
- When in a dual role including research, additional competencies required in research methodology.
- An understanding of the principles of data processing and total systems (technically and educationally)
- Personality commensurate with the position

The assistant director for operations should be one who has had considerable experience in operating, that is, in "running a shop."

The assistant director for systems should also have systems experience, especially in education. These two assistants are easier than the third to find simply because such positions have existed longer. This does not make them less vital.

The third assistant needs to understand the problems of education and research methology and should have experience along these lines. He also must be able to develop new uses for the system as well as to stimulate the faculty and staff into using what is available.

Many educational institutions presently operate with both a data processing center and a computer center. This requires a larger operating budget than when the two centers are combined. However, present budgets are going up, and further, the capabilities of proposed systems far outstrip those of the present.

In looking only at the machine requirements of dual organizations vs. the proposed (one-computer) system, we can come up with some cost estimates for given capabilities. A comparison reveals two facts:

1. Holding cost approximately equal, a one-computer complex has far greater capabilities (speed, volume, versatility) than a dual complex.
2. Holding capability approximately equal, a one-computer complex is less costly than a dual complex.

In addition, under the proposed system the potential for additional funds should be greater and the ability to innovate and experiment will be profound.

CONCLUDING REMARKS

In closing here are some general remarks about the concept of a total educational information system:

The emphasis on "total" is more one of attitude than of reality.

A total information system is neither a panacea nor an end in itself.

Such a system goes far beyond machines, but they do make the system possible.

The organizational structure of the system must have the power to be total.

Very little innovation in education can be justified on the basis of saving funds, but rather on the assumption that education will be improved.

Taken with a "grain of salt," there is some wisdom in this anonymous comment: "If you worry about total systems too much, you will never get started."

REFERENCE

"The Office: The Era of 'Total' Information," *Dun's Review and Modern Industry,* September 1965.

3 ten values of the utilization of computers in education

ROBERT E. SMITH

DR. ROBERT E. SMITH *received his PhD from the University of Pittsburgh, and his BA from the University of Iowa. Dr. Smith entered the computer industry in 1956 after more than 20 years in the field of education.*

As a professional educator, he taught in public and private high schools in several states, then for 10 years on the college and university level at Duquesne University and the Carnegie Institute of Technology (Pittsburgh, Pennsylvania).

Dr. Smith joined Control Data Corporation during its first year; beginning as a mathematical analyst, he has held various administrative positions—all concerned with the rapid growth of the Corporation. In recent years, Dr. Smith has devoted considerable time to writing materials and designing applications for the use of computers in education. It is his opinion that most educators in general have not yet realized the tremendous potential of the computer as an academic tool.

Among Dr. Smith's most popular writings are: The Autotester *(a guide to learning basic Fortran), published by Wiley in 1961; and* The Teacher-Student Approach to Programming Concepts, *published by Control Data Corporation in 1964. His most recent text is* The Bases of Fortran, *a self-teaching text for students.*

Computer utilization in education affords teachers an opportunity to unite the practical with the theoretical—that which is approximate with that which is exact—and to analyze, synthesize, and test creative and effective techniques of logical problem solving and record keeping. The detail of these advantages are described in the ten "values" on the following pages.

VALUE 1: EMPHASIS IS DIRECTED TOWARD THE PRACTICAL

Somewhere in the distant past, the art of counting evolved into the art of logistics, and emphasis in practical education swung toward the theoretical. Recent events have reversed its arc and caused the world to look once more at the practical side. One such event has been the advent of the electronic digital computer.

Coming into its own, this marvel of calculating power has rapidly made itself known in many walks of life. Since it is a tremendous problem solver, the computer will affect the teaching of quantitative concepts and the learning processes involved. One of the primary values of computer utilization is:

IT EMPHASIZES THE PRACTICAL ASPECTS OF LEARNING

The search for that which can be used is a significant aspect in any learning process. It is closely tied to one's *desire* and the need to learn! In a similar vein, the introduction of the computer and its techniques into the classroom provides a practical base upon which the creative teacher can motivate students to want to learn.

This is not to claim that all learning will fall into the computer's sphere of influence. Nor is there any intent to place all practical aspects of learning at the computer's doorstep. Yet the fact remains that in the computer, and through computer concepts, the modern teacher has a unique opportunity to emphasize the practical viewpoint and to aptly demonstrate the usefulness of many of the quantitative concepts that are taught.

As an example, in junior high school mathematics, one of the first acquaintances with concepts which are related to computers is that of number bases. Two bases are very important in computer work: *binary,* base 2, and *octal*, base 8. The practicality of these two bases in computer work should be made known to students.

One of the first skills that many computer programers must master is the ability to work with *octal* and *binary* number bases. Actually, the octal base is important because it can be used to more conveniently express the binary base. Computer programers often have to perform simple arithmetic in the binary system. A typical example is the following:

Add the two binary numbers below:

```
 001 101 110 101
 010 110 010 100
 ---------------
 100 100 001 001
```

Another example is to *multiply* in binary.

```
    1011
    1101
    ----
    1011
   1011
  1011
--------
10001111
```

Students will enjoy multiplying in binary—there are no carries involved. In this discovery, some will uncover the reason why there *are* carries in multiplying with other bases! Likewise, the relationship between the number of bits in the product and the sum of the number of bits in multiplier and multiplicand is clearly evident.

The work in number bases is simply one small area of instruction for a teacher of arithmetic or algebra. More important are innumerable learning areas in education which provide topics and principles that are elegant computer utilization subjects.

VALUE 2: THE ART OF INDUCTION IS REVIVED

Induction involves the use of two of education's most neglected ingredients: *influence* and *inference*. During induction, learning develops as an incidental aspect of the inductive procedure. Learning becomes an aftereffect brought about by the natural flow of events or as a result of disclosures that are made through experimentation. The laboratory is not the only place where inductive learning can occur. Every classroom learning situation involves aspects which can be elegantly portrayed through this type of reasoning.

During induction, certain facts and information are evolved by nature of the activities and procedures carried out by the student. This data *influences* the student to *infer* basic doctrines, beliefs, and principles which might otherwise be totally neglected. The amount and rate of learning is directly related to the individual student's ability to discover, evaluate, and assimilate material or information that is available.

Induction involves student exploration and initiation. Consequently, since it involves relinquishing many of the traditional reins of education to the student, the teacher often finds it difficult to apply. Often teachers turn to deductive techniques which are more teacher-dominated. Here, the student is generally left to salvage those morsels of satisfaction which come from applying numerous parameters to a generalization discovered by someone else and passed on by the teacher—a "hand-me-down goodie"—to be sampled, tested, and validated!

As a direct result of the popularity of this method of reasoning, the problems and exercise material in many texts have only presented deductive stereotypes. As a consequence, many students who are good "memorizers" have gained reputations as successful problem solvers because they have been able to categorize problems into neatly bounded packages—each possessing its unique "tricks" or methods of solution. Even the task of categorization has often been eliminated, since many authors list the categories. Topic labels in text books of mathematics, for example, often list problems as the following:

- Time, Distance, Rate Problems
- River Current Problems
- Airplane-Wind Problems
- Percentage Problems
- Work Problems
- Age Problems
- Number Problems (reversing the tens and units digits) Etc.

One of the more distressing features of over-categorization is the fact that such categories have a tendency to confuse the student in the "real world" of problem solving. The simple "Time-Distance-Rate" category becomes rather meaningless and takes on unforeseen characteristics. The rate of speed of the modern jet is well known, the distance between two cities can be measured to the desired accuracy, yet the time of arrival can rarely be found by simply dividing the distance by the rate!

Similar situations occur if one attempts to use the standard deductive methods of calculating various aspects of his savings and checking accounts. One soon realizes it is necessary to consider several factors which never appear in the textbook approach!

Deduction then, is a subtractive process–it involves a removal or "taking away." It is an important part of the educational process and it should be an important element in every teacher's repertoire. Yet, to be effective, deduction must be supported from time to time by its opposite–the inductive process. The digital computer, more than any other machine yet invented, brings to the teacher the potential to exercise inductive procedures. Thus, the second great value of computer utilization in the education curriculum is:

IT PROVIDES AN INDUCTIVE APPROACH TO LEARNING

It is also important to note that the inductive approach is taken by most researchers in attempting to initiate and arrive at new principles. The natural powers of observation, insight, and creative thought are brought into play and the "learner learns while learning."

It is certainly true that with some subject matter it is inherently difficult to exploit the inductive method through computer utilization. This is particularly true when the principles involved are not closely related to numerical or quantitative elements. On the other hand, many subject areas in the natural, sociological, and abstract sciences abound with opportunities for induction based upon numerical concepts. In many of these, the computer is a remarkable device to enable teachers and students to carry out effective and efficient learning projects.

VALUE 3: DEDUCTION IS ADVANCED AND SYMBOLISM BECOMES DYNAMIC

Once a student has made his own discoveries, the deductive logic of the problem unfolds and leads to realistic conclusions. Deduction which occurs after induction also carries much greater impact, since the student has experienced and become knowledgeable in the relationships involved. It is no longer an exercise far removed from his concern; rather, it related directly to improving his basic understanding of the various facets involved.

What is deductive logic? Deduction, unlike induction, is a subtractive process. It "takes away" some part or parts of the larger concept. It concentrates and turns attention to specific elements and reasoning advances by emphasizing *particular* points of view. During the process, partial conclusions are formed and examination of parts indicate fundamental truths upon which the whole principle is based.

Deductive procedures are often best described by a language of symbols. Many students have a difficult time with symbols. Often they appear to be completely unrelated to the concepts they are studying. Yet, in many subject areas—particularly the abstract sciences—understanding the language of symbols is most important and essential.

On the other hand, the experimenter or researcher who has had practical experience which is related to the logic and who has had an opportunity to make observations based upon inductive thinking, finds symbols are both meaningful and helpful. Such a person is motivated to understand and use symbols himself, and significantly, to understand the symbolic language used by others.

Induction is not only a valuable technique in itself, it also compliments and advances the deductive processes. Consequently, the third value of computer utilization in education is:

IT COMPLEMENTS AND ADVANCES DEDUCTIVE PROCESSES AND SYMBOLISM BECOMES MORE DYNAMIC

One of logic's greatest strengths is its symbolism. Yet symbolism can become its greatest weakness. Too often, the inquiring student is not encouraged to look beyond or behind the symbols. Consequently, he learns to move symbols around quickly and efficiently; he learns the rules and laws which govern the treatment of symbols, and he learns how to manipulate symbols to prove numerous relationships. The one thing he may not learn—and perhaps it is more important—is the *numerical* significance of the symbol logic he is able to perform.

Since a computer is a calculator, it requires numbers to calculate upon. Thus, representation of symbolic concepts is hinged to numbers. For this reason, the student who uses a computer in educational applications is forced to think "behind" the symbols to existing numerical relationships. Once this step is taken, he is better able to understand and more fully appreciate the great value in the deductive approach.

VALUE 4: ORDER, SEQUENCE, AND DETAIL BECOME MOST IMPORTANT

A famous mathematician was once asked to propose the most important capability required for proficiency in mathematics.

"It is not memory," he said, "Some of our greatest mathematicians have not had exceptional memories. Likewise, speed of thought does not appear to be a priority qualification."

"I would have to place at the head of the list," he continued, "the ability to *anticipate*—that is, to logically consider, balance, and measure the steps of an unfolding sequence of events starting with initial conditions and ending with a possible solution."

That all experts would accept this analysis without some reservation is unlikely; yet there is general agreement among those who study and teach mathematics that order, sequence, and organization are essential characteristics in the logical treatment of a problem.

Teachers in all subject areas can name many students who were unsuccessful because of carelessness and disregard for the order of events. Furthermore, a close examination of the essential qualities involved in reasoning and decision-making indicates that order and sequence are of significant importance.

Computer utilization within the framework of the educational curricula provides numerous opportunities for the student to exercise and form habits of order and sequence. When one "programs" a problem, that is, when one determines the steps and procedures leading toward a solution, he must *think, design,* and *write* in a step-by-step (algorithmic) process. Consequently, the very nature of the process itself requires complete dedication and concentration to order, sequence, and step-by-step reasoning.

The teacher must not forget that algorithmic procedures are already deeply rooted in the habitual reasoning processes of students. The same claim can be made for adults. Everyone tends to solve problems one step at a time. Consequently, the algorithmic approach is one which is natural and practical. Its use is in harmony with students' habit patterns.

For many years, some of our more effective teachers have made use of the algorithmic approach to introduce new topics to the student. These master teachers have discovered that by building upon the previous knowledge of the student, advanced concepts are easier to grasp and they become more meaningful to the student.

Examining the importance of algorithmic processes further, one must also realize that much of the everyday reasoning performed by the student is algorithmic in nature! The simple flowchart that follows (Figure 5) indicates one example of this:

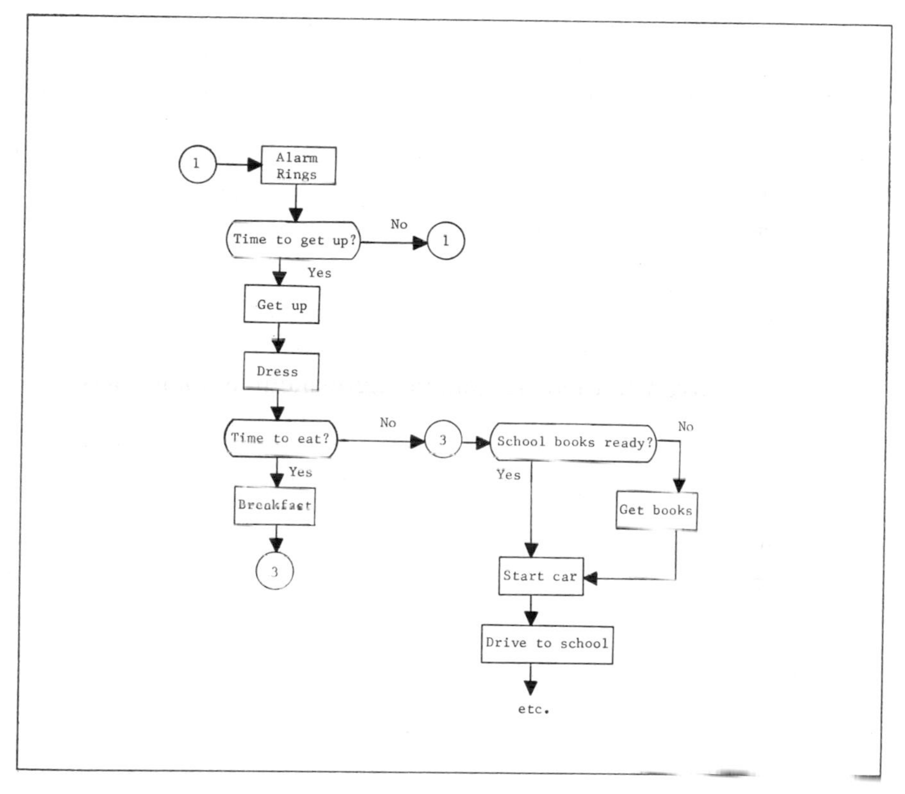

Fig. 5 – A Simple Flowchart.

The student who learns to use computer techniques soon discovers the importance of order and sequence. He soon realizes that interchanging the order of only two steps in a program generally leads to entirely different results than planned.

In addition to the great emphasis that must be placed upon

sequence, the student begins to realize the tremendous importance of *detail.* It is impossible for the student to omit symbols, to neglect writing complete statements, to disregard other organizational conventions, and be able to end with correct results.

The student quickly learns that he cannot expect the computer to compensate for errors or carelessness in planning and writing the program directions. Of even greater importance, the student *himself* must now be very sure of the exact form and detail of all rules and procedures that are used. Furthermore, he must anticipate and *plan for* contingency situations which may occur during the time the computer is executing the sequential instructions he has written.

Computer utilization in education requires dedicated concentration on planning, organization, and detail, far beyond similar efforts in other subject areas. In no other area are final successful results so dependent upon correct and accurate procedures. As a consequence, the characteristics of order, along with careful attention to detail, become necessary parts of a computer application.

VALUE 5: THE LONG OVERDUE CASE FOR APPROXIMATIONS

Several years ago, while teaching high school mathematics, the author had occasion to introduce the quantity:

$$9^{(9^9)}$$

The claim was made that this was the largest number that could be represented by three digits. In attempting to indicate the tremendous size of this number, various examples were given to show how long it would take a person to write down the result—assuming a result could be found; how many volumes would be required to contain the answer; etc. Finally, the author made the following statement, "Although the number of digits in this number can be found by using logarithms, there are too many digits to find the exact result."

Several days later, a student reported that her father refused to believe that the result could not be found. In the words of this student, "Father says that mathematics is an exact science and all problems can be solved."

This story is related to exemplify the misconception that is prevalent among many persons—that mathematics is completely deterministic and exact.

Two reasons, more than any others, can be advanced for the spread of this concept:

1. The typical mathematics textbook often presents topics and problem exercises with emphasis upon exact parameters and exact results!
2. Many teachers have emphasized problem applications in which exact quantities or integer amounts are used. At the same time, they have completely ignored applications involving approximations.

When the student leaves school he suddenly discovers the world of work is *not* built upon exactitude. Instead of deterministic philosophies and exact practices, he often finds a world based upon probabilistic philosophies and techniques which make use of approximations.

With the computer, there is no longer reason for the teacher to avoid problems or problem parameters involving approximations. In the subject area of geometry, for example, areas need not be related to isolated rectangles, squares, triangles, circles, etc. More often than not, the real world of areas involves irregularities—areas that must be approximated by means of trapezoids, parts of circles and combinations of triangles, rectangles, etc. Using the computer, this becomes a very rewarding problem. The student learns more about areas because of analyses he must perform. In addition, the tediousness and difficulty arising from using approximate parameters during computations is removed.

It is hardly possible to end this discussion without some reference to the calculus and the great role of approximations—at least in the fundamental concepts of that subject. The essential concepts involved in differentiation and integration are so closely tied to an understanding of approximations that one never completely understands either subject until he gains some experience and appreciation of the role of approximate quantities.

VALUE 6: IT ORIENTS AND EMPHASIZES RESEARCH PROCEDURES

There is often an important difference between a "knowing" man and a "thinking" man. One might argue that thinking depends upon knowledge, that one implies the other. Yet, this is not always true. "Knowing" may refer to the ability to recall important facts. If these facts are directly related to the problem at hand, the "knowing" man is often considered to be a "thinking" man. On the other hand, the known facts may not be directly related to the problem. In this case, a "thinking" man is required. Such a man must be able to use facts which he had learned—and which are not directly related—to derive and discover the new facts required to solve the problem.

If this latter situation occurs—and there is evidence to indicate it is the rule rather than the exception—"thinking" involves more than merely recalling facts. *Techniques, procedures, methods of attack* become very important! Without these, one may be at a complete loss to generate any action—and without action, there are no results.

If one agrees with this analysis, it appears that education should devote a significant portion of its philosophy and practice to training students in *procedures* and *techniques* of problem solving. These are often termed "research procedures."

Although there is logic in the argument that research should be delayed until the student has sufficient knowledge to establish a firm base of operation, the procedures and methods of research can be extracted from the total process. One can begin training students in *procedures* of problem solving very early in the game.

One of the great advantages offered by computer utilization in education is the fact that research procedures are indispensable to each application. Each computer application involves the following three phases:

Phase 1: The Analytical Phase

During this phase, the student must, first of all, *think* about the problem! He must develop a mental plan of attack which can lead to a solution. In order to do this, he must thoroughly understand and comprehend the varying conditions and parameters which are related to the problem situation.

During this phase, various plans will be contemplated, examined, and possibly discarded for one reason or another. This oscillating period of decision making is an important and critical part of the analytical phase.

During this phase, a plan of attack will emerge. It will be a distinct plan—one that has been fashioned by the background, experience, and knowledge of the individual student.

Phase 2: The Building or Synthesis Phase

During this phase, the chosen plan of attack must be translated into a step-by-step (algorithmic) program which the computer must follow in order to arrive at a solution. The sequence of these steps is most important; each is directly related to the steps which immediately precede and follow.

During this phase, the student will draw up a blueprint—or flowchart as in Fig. 5—of the algorithm he is building. This is simply a diagrammatic presentation which is an aid in building the program.

During this phase, the use of symbols, abbreviations, and coded phrases will be encouraged. If the student has a mathematical background, he will probably use symbolic characters; otherwise, short,

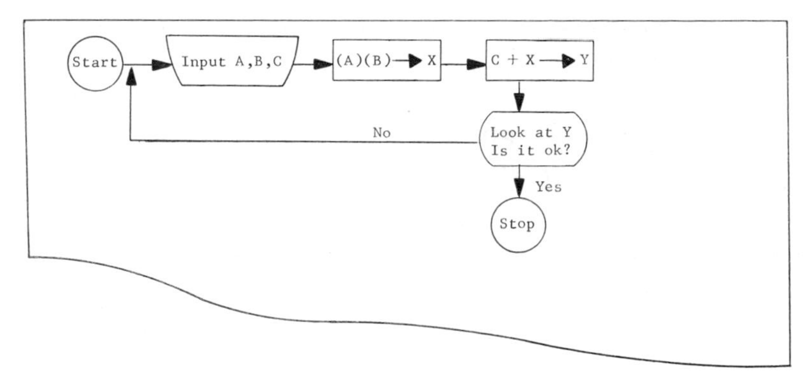

Fig. 6 – Use of Symbols in Flowcharting.

crisp phrases and coded words. A symbolic example is indicated in Fig. 6.

Phase 3: The Performance Phase
During this phase, the problem is taken to the computer, the plan of attack is executed, and the results are examined for validity and accuracy. If the written program does not work–that is, the computer is unable to give results, or results appear to be unreasonable–the student must thoroughly recheck his analysis and synthesis.

During this phase, results will disclose characteristics of the synthesis or analytical phases which the student will wish to change or remodel. Additions and deletions will be made. This period of the total process–when results predict changes in the preceding phases–is often referred to as "feedback." It is a most important phase of the process, since the student begins to realize that results are not final; instead, they are guideposts to improved performance.

In summary, there are three important phases which the student must perform to reach his goal:

- Analysis
- Synthesis
- Performance

These are identical procedures to those which this student will use in college, if required to conduct a research project, or in real life, if required to be a "thinking" man!

Computer utilization in education offers the opportunity for the teacher to teach research procedures *without* preparing a formal course of instruction on these procedures. The process of using the computer itself will force the student into these techniques. As a consequence, he will learn a method of attack and a problem-solving technique which will be invaluable to him after he leaves school. No other aspect of computer utilization in education is so intriguing or offers so many elegant possibilities!

VALUE 7: IT PROVIDES OPPORTUNITY FOR CREATIVITY AND PENETRATION IN DEPTH

Some educators insist that it is not possible to teach creativity. Rather, they state, creativity is a quality so closely tied to basic ability, imagination, and native intelligence that it cannot be learned. However, such a claim seems to be based upon a narrow definition of creativity. There is more to creativity than the potential to "bring into being that which has never before existed." Certainly, another important aspect of creativity is *production*—that is, the power and capability to produce. The fact that something already exists is not a deterrent to creating the same thing. The student who derives a solution through self-effort and knowledge is just as creative as the person who initially solved the problem.

Additional insight into creativity comes from the realization that all progress and innovations are based upon that which has been discovered before. Discovery is really re-discovery resulting from new techniques or different analyses.

A noted inventor once said, "the problems one discovers are just as important as the answers one finds." If this is true, the *opportunity to discover* is an important aspect of creativity. This leads to the premise that whether or not one believes creativity can be learned, it is important that opportunities be made available to develop and implement this potential.

Computer utilization in education offers many opportunities for students to be productive. Significantly, most of this productive effort is student-centered—that is, it is initiated, planned, and carried out by the student himself. Although many of the first exercises and projects will be limited and of relatively little importance from a creative standpoint, each is a self-contained and complete unit of student accomplishment, from the analysis stage through that of performance. In a larger sense, each of these units of production provide many opportunities to be creative.

Along with creativity, and perhaps a related part of it, is the opportunity to penetrate a subject in depth. The modern teacher seldom has a school environment which enables him to set horizons for each student able to progress beyond scheduled goals. "Individual attention," as it is termed, is a well meaning, but difficult practice to implement.

Computer utilization in the curricula provides opportunities for individual progress and study. Once the student becomes acquainted with the procedures and techniques of programing, his horizon of individual projects is expanded. Possibly for the first time in school, he is able to chart his own course and to follow his own interests in various aspects of subject matter. This is genuine progress in the educative process.

The type of creativity which students produce through computer applications will not be "earth-shaking" in scope or complexity. Actually, it may take a discerning teacher to even recognize the creative aspects of the programs produced. Yet, there will be creative elements in almost every program which is designed.

Two significant prerequisites for preparing a problem for the computer are freedom of choice and the requirement that decisions must be made! The person who can't make up his mind unless directed by someone else will not enjoy computer applications. Each problem contains a myriad of points where decisions have to be made—decisions which the student must make himself—and it is this characteristic which makes computer utilization both creative and educational.

Creating "Creative Experts"

In concluding this section, the author cannot resist the temptation to recall to the mind of the reader the events leading up to the creation of a space vehicle by the United States. Where did the "creative space experts" suddenly come from when they were needed? The government did not beat the bushes for inventors, super I.Q. people, and those born with a "touch of genius." Instead, intelligent persons from many walks of life, and trained in many different disciplines, were brought together and given the directive and the opportunity to work on the space problem.

These people—most of whom had never thought of creating a space vehicle—had to analyze, synthesize, and produce a new capability. In the course of their work, these people had to make many decisions—some involving *uncertainties of principles* as well as *uncertainties of practice.* In arriving at and making these decisions, these people produced a space vehicle and the space travel capability. Creative? Yes, these were creative people. Yet until the opportunity was provided, they were *not* creative as far as space travel is concerned! However, they were the type of people who could analyze a problem, arrive at possible solutions, and carry through planned actions.

Our educational systems want to turn out many individuals who have similar capabilities. Computer utilization in education has much to offer in assisting educators to meet this objective.

VALUE 8: COMPUTER PROGRAMS CAN SIMULATE UNIQUE SYSTEMS AND ENVIRONMENTS

Much of education is concerned with preparing students for eventual assimilation into some aspect of industrial, business, political, or professional activity. All of these can be considered as "systems" which include unique standards, laws, and techniques. Each system contains numerous subsystems, which in turn contain other smaller systems.

Economics, for example, can be considered a subsystem of the business community. Within economics it is possible to find other systems: credit, sales, savings, budgeting, debt, etc.

In preparing students for eventual participation in our economy, topics and subjects within the system are studied. The educator hopes that by integrating the knowledge gained in many topic areas, the student will acquire skill and understanding in the concepts comprising the total system. For many systems this philosophy is successful; yet for others, concepts are more distinguishable when it is possible to work with overall principles. In other areas, learning is more effective and occurs at a faster rate when it is possible to perform or experiment within the framework of the total system rather than to concentrate on some specific sub-area.

Until the advent of the modern computer many total system studies and activities were impractical since even a modestly scaled system required more information, computations, and detail than could be efficiently performed by hand.

The computer has made it possible to effectively and efficiently study overall systems. The technique which makes this possible is often referred to as "computer simulation."

In computer simulation, special computer programs are written (generally by experienced programers) which permit students to essentially duplicate or "simulate" the activities and procedures which are carried on in a real total system complex. This computer program, generally known as the "simulator", usually provides some judgment criteria whereby it is possible to determine the degree of success or failure of performance within the system.

An example, and one which is valuable in business education, is the "management game." This is a simulation program for teaching students how to encounter and make decisions in business systems where management decisions are required. Using the management game simulator program, the student is transformed into a manager of a thriving (or struggling) business enterprise who is faced with many of the problems commonly involved in success or failure in business. Acting either as an individual businessman or as a member of a management team, he must make decisions which immediately affect the profit or loss statement of the business. The computer monitors these decisions, makes evaluations by comparing them to decisions made under similar conditions occurring in real business enterprises, and notifies the student of the economic consequences of his decision.

The management game is only one of many such programs which have been designed to simulate systems. Several other programs have been developed.

Medical diagnosis is another area where computer simulation is being used to advantage. This program involves a comparison between diagnoses made by qualified physicians or students in medical school and those made by the computer. The computer can make these diagnoses since a cross-reference index of symptoms and all possible diagnoses are pre-stored in the computer memory. The memory is then searched to find all diagnoses for a given set of symptoms. These are then compared to diagnoses made by the physician or medical student.

Political and social sciences are other fertile areas for simulation activities. Election trends, population changes, and other effects can be analyzed and studied within the framework of larger political and social systems.

VALUE 9: THE COMPUTER AND PROGRAMED LEARNING

The concept of programed learning involves relatively concise and sequential instructional steps intermixed with testing procedures to determine the rate and amount of learning. The instructional steps are usually presented in a series of written lessons (often called "frames"). Each lesson contains a series of short explanations or descriptions of some aspect of the concept to be learned. These explanations are then generally followed by a question or a set of quiz questions which test the student's progress, and at the same time reinforce explanations already made. Sometimes, the individual lessons are presented to the student by means of a device or a machine which exposes one frame of instructions at a time, along with sufficient space for the student to respond to questions.

In some situations, all students use the same materials and study the same sequence of frames. For this reason, this method is often called *single-paths* instructional technique.

If a computer is adapted to the programed learning technique, *variable paths* are made possible. Under this philosophy, not all students study the same sequence of instructions. If a student knows a concept (as indicated by a correct response), he proceeds to the next concept in the material. If a mistake is made, or if the responses indicate uncertainty, additional descriptive and explanatory material is presented for study before the student can move on to the next concept. The computer constantly monitors the response of each student, selects the material to be presented, guides each student through the various sequential set of instructions, and performs various statistical calculations to determine rates of progress.

In the past decade there has been much controversy over the merits of programed learning in education. Initially, the move toward programed instruction was too rapid and many educators were disappointed and disillusioned by the results. Others feared and resisted the movement since it implied changes in staff functions and administration. As opposition increased, the acceptance and implementation of programed instruction diminished and appeared to vanish.

Recently, interest in this technique has been rekindled and educators are claiming significant advantages in applying this technique to selected areas of learning. Many factors have influenced this revival. Among these are:

1. Programed instruction is economical. There are evidences of economies in time, costs, and administration for many learning situations. Some universities, for example, can provide computer-monitored programed instruction to hundreds of class groups (basic courses, review sections, psychological tests) with decreasing commitments from faculty, administrators, and space allocations.
2. Programed instruction is a natural auxiliary for certain instructional media now is use. An example is the classroom television presentation. The addition of programed instruction, as part of the visual program, increases the effectiveness and efficiency of the visual display and augments the learning potential.
3. Programed learning has proved to be very effective in training students in unique skills or maintenance of specialized equipments. The United States Air Force, for example, along with many of the other services, have found programed learning techniques to be of great value in teaching skills related to operating and maintaining equipment components of varying complexities.
4. Psychologists and learning theorists have produced evidence to indicate that the experienced student who learns well from a standard textbook often improvises his own form of programed learning as he studies. He tends to ask himself questions, to review special topics, and to branch to supplementary aids when the

need arises. These practices have often been referred to, in past, as "good study habits."

5. Educators also realize that many students never acquire these "habits." In such cases, the student is unqualified to know which topics are most important to learn. He wastes time on reading details which are often relatively insignficant or irrelevant; his periods of concentration are relatively short in duration and his attention wanders from one item to another; much of his time is spent in trying to separate the critical aspects of the lesson from those of small concern.
6. For these students, programed learning offers substantial rewards. The bookkeeping functions involved in sifting the important items from the unimportant are performed by the computer or the programed text; the current progress of the student is monitored so that he is constantly aware of success or failure; and periodic motivators are presented to bolster his sagging powers of concentration and interest. Used in this way, the programed learning device becomes a "study crutch" enabling the slow, average, and even the gifted student to attain a preplanned level of achievement and knowledge in a more efficient manner.
7. Programed learning provides control features which are lacking in the traditional approach. A significant part of the success of education is the ability to recognize progress or lack of progress. A person can claim he has the perfect system but if he has no method of validating the claim, it is open to question. Many traditional educational techniques are extremely difficult to measure. They contain no built-in parameters or indicators which can measure the rate of progress or the degree of success attained. In most cases, success is a matter of having passed a test—one which in itself may be a very poor instrument.

In late years there has been a growing demand to place more educational functions on a profit-and-loss basis, that is, to attempt to measure—on a cost basis—the values of various educational techniques. Under this concept, an educational institution is similar to a business. Both are concerned with people; one measures its success on a dollar profit basis, the other should be able to measure its progress in the achievement of its students or upon some similar basis. The programed learning system offers many advantages under this concept. The program itself is built upon a philosophy that achievement can be measured. Likewise, the time required to meet various levels of performance is easily distinguishable. The computer-based system is even more attractive under this concept, since statistical measures and quality control parameters can be designed into the program without disturbing other factors of the system.

The effectiveness of computer-based programed instructional systems is entirely dependent upon the skill and knowledge of the experts who design the procedures and write the materials which make the system operable. In addition, several types of experts are required. Some of these are:

- Systematist
- Programer
- Engineer
- Psychologist
- Administrator
- Teacher
- Operator

These people, whose functions are partially revealed by their professions, must cooperate and coordinate their efforts to design and construct an instructional system that will produce a level of achievement for the "target population" (students for whom the system was designed) which is significantly higher than that produced by traditional educational systems.

Such a system is not easy to achieve. But it can be accomplished—and in fact, it already exists in varying degrees. More systems will appear in the near future. Possibly some of the larger universities possess the potential for this development. These institutions have the professional help required to build such a system. In addition, they contain increasing numbers of students who are in need of systems of this kind.

VALUE 10: THE COMPUTER AS A DATA AND INFORMATION PROCESSOR

The great increase in school populations has also brought new and increasing demands for information handling and processing in education. For example, class scheduling and grade reportings have become so complex and extensive that many schools could not perform these functions without the help of automated machinery. The computer has been called upon in increasing numbers to provide services of this kind in education.

The number and kinds of such services are very great. As computers have been acquired by schools for these purposes, administrators and teachers have found ever increasing uses for similar types of functions. The result, in many institutions, has been a work overload for some faculty personnel along with a possible overemphasis upon the computer as being solely a data processor.

Some institutions have attempted to solve this problem by acquiring more than one computer system. One system is then assigned the data processing and business chores; the other system is used for academic and research projects.

Some schools have attempted to share one computer for all functions by partitioning the total amount of available computer time among the various departments of the school. In the larger educational institutions, where demands from many departments are intense, this type of time sharing has not been satisfactory.

Recently, another kind of time-sharing philosophy has become popular among the larger universities. This is the attempt to share the computer (usually a very large-scale computer system) by using remote display devices, which are placed in various departments throughout the campus, and which are able to communicate with the computer. These time-sharing systems require extensive networks of communicating electronic devices. In addition, the programing system, which enables the various department functions to time-share the computer, is very complex and must be designed and written through the coordinated efforts of computer experts along with university administrators and faculty.

Certainly, the use of the computer to provide the various purchasing, accounting, recording, grading, scheduling, and planning reports required by a modern educational plant is of utmost importance. Administrators and teachers have been relieved of many of the tedious and time-consuming chores associated with these functions.

The problem is one of proper balance between academic and business values which accrue from computer utilization. Educators must face demands for emphasis on both in the years immediately ahead. Behind this conflict of influence is the student. Perhaps the answer can be found from the question: "Which values better serve the basic needs and interests of the student?"

There are many signs which indicate increasing demands for more emphasis upon the academic uses of computers in education. Many schools are insisting that business and recordkeeping functions be performed at a time which does not interfere with the academic uses of the computer by faculty and students. Still other schools are attempting to separate the two functions by using different computer systems under separate supervision and control. Both trends are examples of the determination of educators to exploit the computer as an academic device.

4 electronic data processing as a tool for research in education

JAMES W. WHITLOCK

DR. JAMES WILLIAM WHITLOCK *received his EdD and MA degrees from George Peabody College for Teachers (Nashville, Tennessee) in 1956 and 1952, respectively. In addition to his other duties, he now serves that institution as associate director, Center for Southern Education Studies, and as professor of education. He received his BS degree from the University of Tennessee (Knoxville) in 1949.*

Dr. Whitlock's professional experience has included service as a junior high school assistant principal and teacher, as a high school principal, and in a variety of administrative, staff, and consultive positions for state and local boards and departments of education, George Peabody College for Teachers, and the U.S. Office of Education (USOE). As a consultant, he has worked in the area of automatic data processing for numerous school systems, and he has served as director of a USOE Special Study on Automation and Its Implications for Education in the Nashville Metropolitan Area.

His published works include as author, Automatic Data Processing in Education, *and as co-author,* Jobs and Training for Southern Youth.

The first task in the discussion of the use of automatic data processing equipment as a tool for improving educational research is that of defining the terms involved. The reader should be clear at this point in this book as to the meaning of electronic data processing (EDP) equipment and systems. It is synonymous with the electronic computer. Only the need for defining "research in education" remains in completing this first task.

Research in the technical sense is the systematic, detailed, and relatively prolonged attempt to discover or confirm the facts that bear upon a certain problem or problems and the laws or principles that govern it. In the most liberal sense of this definition, all decision making in education, if based on an attempt to discover and confirm the facts, could be classified as research or, at least, as research implementation. But there are some who would argue that the definition of the technical sense does not import the essence of the term, and so research may be better described as a frame of mind rather than a set of techniques.

In the discussions which follow, research in education is used in its technical sense to encompass both the formal, highly organized attempts at discovering the facts essential to answering basic questions in education, and the day-to-day analysis of data for immediate decision making. It will be shown that EDP can be a valuable tool for improving educational research as defined in its technical sense. If space permitted, an equal case could probably be made for the tool in helping to stimulate a research state of mind—a "composer" mind instead of the "fiddler" mind and the "tomorrow" mind instead of the "yesterday" mind.

In the improvement of research, used in its technical sense, EDP equipment can make several major contributions. In the first place, the equipment can be used to do many of the various routine operations of educational management and control and thus free the school administrator, his central staff, and the teaching staff to participate in professional activities, including research activities. Second, it can serve as the calculating tool essential to handling mass data. Third, the equipment can be used to improve research instruments. Fourth, it will improve the adequacy of the data being used in research. Fifth, electronic equipment can be used to simulate an educational system.

USE IN ROUTINE CLERICAL AND MANAGEMENT OPERATIONS

Several major problems can be associated with the rapid increase of the nation's school enrollment. One of these problems has been the increasing need for efficient handling of pupil records and daily pupil accounting and the time-consuming task of scheduling classes and making reports to parents. To these functions must be combined the paper work of correspondence, duplication, testing, public relations, extracurricular activities, and guidance. Not only has the number of pupils increased the amount of data that must be processed, but there has also been a demand for a greater variety of information about each pupil. A variety of data has now become essential for planning and evaluating instruction, curriculum revision, planning for facilities and equipment, determining special services needed, financial planning, and the clear presentation of school costs and problems to the taxpayer.

Most of the activities concerned with the tabulating and processing of such data are primarily clerical in nature. Nevertheless, much of the increased burden of data processing has fallen to professional staff members with the corresponding detraction from their professional functions of teaching and planning.

This book discusses, in many other chapters, several applications of EDP in simplifying the day-to-day routine operations of educational management and control. In addition to the many uses in the business office and related staff personnel functions, it has been shown that with EDP equipment, the student recordkeeping can be centralized in one convenient location. The equipment can be used for school census; for pupil registration and student scheduling; for permanent cumulative recordkeeping; for analyzing and interpreting standardized and teacher-made test results; and for attendance accounting and the allied activities of reporting to parents, and local, state, and federal education agencies. Flexible student scheduling is being accomplished by computers during the week before school begins. This function is a particularly important aid to the new methods of individualizing instruction which have been hampered by the enormous task of arranging the complex schedule required for such programs.

Teachers are employed to teach, and principals are employed to supervise the various aspects of instruction and building administration. The reduction of the amount of time teachers and principals must spend doing simple routine clerical tasks is an Elysium dreamed of by school administrators and now being realized in many schools over the nation. The wealth of information collected relative to individual students and the total educational process lends itself to almost every type of interpretation and analysis. Therefore, in addition to reduction of clerical responsibilities, teachers, principals, and supervisors now can have access to information which previously was not considered because of its inaccessibility.

EDP equipment is the tool for simplifying many of the various routine operations of school management and control. This should provide a greater opportunity for the school administrator, his central staff, and the teaching staff to participate in organized research. Furthermore, the professional staff can now have access to the comprehensive data on all aspects of the school program which are essential for the day-to-day decision making and long-range planning, including the organized research activities essential to sound planning.

A TOOL FOR HANDLING MASS DATA

Closely related to the foregoing discussion, but treated in a separate section for point of emphasis, is the ability of the EDP system to handle mass data. The system's capability to correlate, compare, interrelate, and synthesize data is almost unlimited. School administrators now have available to them the necessary facility for taking the vast amount of educational data and correlating it with sociological and technological information to supply answers to a host of questions facing education today. In the area of calculation, the electronic computer is an amazing laborsaving statistical worker. It will not only simplify and facilitate the production of such research work now being done, but makes possible an entirely new brand of research work. For example, group classification analysis can now be done on a scale which would have been computationally prohibitive prior to the advent of the electronic computer. The problem of distinguishing among several groups on the basis of several variables involves only a few minutes of time on the latest computer.

But simply being able to compute more chi-squares or bigger correlation matrices, or t tests, and doing it faster and easier, may not in itself make much difference in the quality of the educational research being done. The value is that it should produce a movement away from the traditional univariate research design which proved fruitful for physical scientists, but which has had little payoff in education research. Experiments continue to fill the educational literature in which performance on some achievement test is compared for two groups—one taught by television or films, the other by conventional methods. This type of experimental design has had little impact. Human behavior and the objectives of education are too complex.

Multivariate statistical methods and the computer now permit the testing of any number of groups on multiple criteria. For example, Project Talent, conducted by Flanagan at the University of Pittsburgh, tested a sampling of 450,000 students from all parts of the country on more than 700 different items of information on achievement, aptitude, interests, personal characteristics, and biographical data. Specially developed electronic equipment scanned the answer sheets and converted responses to punched cards. The data were then processed on the IBM 7070 computer. The 10,000 word core storage memory of the IBM 7070 allows storage of half of a symmetrical 130 x 130 correlation matrix. A program has been developed to compute all of the 8,385 correlations in such a matrix efficiently with a single program. These intercorrelations can be determined in less than seven seconds per case; i.e., for a sample of 1,100 cases the 8,385 correlations could be computed in about two hours. This 130 x 130 matrix can than be inverted in about thirty minutes, thus making the multiple correlation between any one of the 130 variables and the remaining 129 immediately available. The partial correlations are also available from the inverted matrix.[1]

Predicting the implications of the new data processing techniques for research in education is difficult. The experience on projects such as Project Talent suggests some likely directions. In addition to the types of small exploratory studies which have been most common in educational research, increasing numbers of both large-scale and long-range definitive research projects can be expected in the future. Certainly new research studies do not have to be limited to the small number of variables feasible for older data processing methods.

Examples can be cited to support the above prediction. The Peabody College Center for Southern Education Studies has recently completed a comprehensive study of the programs and personnel in the approved high schools in eleven southern states—4,776 of them, enrolling 2,318,449 youth. The Center collected hundreds of items of quantifiable data on each high school and, through the use of the IBM 7070 computer, analysed these data on the basis of such variables as total enrollment in the school, size of graduating class, grade organizational pattern of the school and per pupil expenditure, and interpreted the data against a background of socioeconomic movements underway in the South.[2]

If we define research liberally to include the discovery and confirmation of facts essential to all sound decision making, we can expect improvements in the "quality control" aspects of educational research. In fact, such aspects of educational research (as distinguished from the so-called "pure" research) will not only be much improved, but, in many instances, are only now possible because of electronic data processing techniques. Once school data on all aspects of the school program—pupils, teachers, programs, buildings, buses, finances, and so on—are recorded on punched cards or magnetic tape, or on some other data processing system input medium, a variety of research operations are then feasible. For example, many school systems today conduct large-scale standardized testing programs and then do almost nothing with this potentially useful data. The Peabody College Division of Surveys and Field Services has developed computer techniques for analyzing standardized test data on a system-wide basis to identify

---

[1] J. C. Flanagan and others. *Designing the Study.* Project Talent Monograph Series, Monograph No. 1. Washington: Cooperative Research Program, U. S. Office of Education, 1960.

[2] *High Schools in the South: A Fact Book.* Nashville, Tennessee: Center for Southern Education Studies, George Peabody College for Teachers, 1966.

clues for needed curriculum changes. These analyses range from the complex to the simple and include the following:

1. Processing the results of a standardized survey test of achievement to furnish a diagnostic analysis of learning difficulties for a class, a grade, or an entire school system. The pupil's response to each test item can be marked for electrical sensing and conversion to punched card form. The computer can be instructed to store the correct response to each test item, to analyze each response for correctness, and on the basis of this analysis to classify and tabulate individuals according to the number of incorrect responses relating to a specific learning skill.
2. Coding the test results and other related data for each pupil, and using a computer program to show the mass picture of educational achievement in the school system in all grades and subjects. A simple printout might be a tabular summary for each grade in each school of the mean grade placement score on each subtest of a standardized achievement test. This summary enables the administrative and supervisory staff to see the range of achievement status of each grade in each school and to compare the average grade placement score on each subtest with national norms. Such comparisons help to identify points of need for administrative or supervisory assistance.

These comparisons have more meaning if some attempt is made to relate pupils' achievement levels to their potential levels; this attempt can be made through comparisons of actual achievement levels and levels suggested by intelligence test information. With the computer, the intelligence quotient and the chronological age of each pupil can be combined in computing an achievement level that may be expected at the time the achievement tests are taken.

"Quality control," however, should not be limited to pupil evaluation. School systems should adopt some techniques employed by industry, which has for years employed the "management by exception" principle. Certain limits or standards are established and the management staff concerns itself primarily with those situations which are exceptions to the established limits or standards of efficiency. The ability of EDP systems to handle a mass of data makes the "management by exception" principle equally applicable to the business of education. For example, in the area of attendance accounting, wouldn't it be helpful to have, as a by-product, an identification of the schools which have excessive absenteeism of either students or teachers? In the textbook program wouldn't it save a considerable amount of clerical time if the computer would identify excessive requests for books rather than having someone examine each request received? On the financial accounting side, reasonable unit cost standards could be established. The computer could identify those situations where unit costs are outside the range of reasonable expectations. Many other types of "exception" data can be obtained as a by-product of routine operations and used for the purpose of identifying situations requiring administrative decisions.

AN AID TO IMPROVING RESEARCH INSTRUMENTS

As shown in the preceding section, educational research is no longer limited in terms of statistical models or computational feasibility. It is limited, in part, however, by the lack of reliable instruments for making the multiple measurements which are now analyzable. The goals of education may need to be more operationally defined. But EDP equipment is useful here also. Item analysis, so important in the development of new tests, no longer need be the drudgery it once was. Computer programs are readily available for this task.

Another important tool in educational research is multiple factor analysis. This can now be done as it should be, but has not been done because of computational problems. These techniques are very useful in understanding human behavior and also can be useful in instrument development. Factor analysis of a large number of items poses no particular problem in computer computation.

IMPROVING THE ADEQUACY OF EDUCATIONAL DATA

One equipment manufacturer makes use of the term "gigo" to emphasize the importance of the quality of the input data in the EDP system. The use of the system imposes a tremendous responsibility on educational researchers to collect adequate data. For truly, "garbage in" the system means "garbage out" of the system, with the output at speeds many thousand times faster than manual methods. Adequate data in education must meet the following criteria: (1) accuracy, (2) timeliness, (3) comparability, and (4) comprehensiveness. Automatic data processing systems can contribute to the accomplishment of each of these criteria.

Accuracy of Data

Inaccurate data are worthless for research purposes, and may be highly detrimental to sound decision making. Educational information that is not accurate is worse than no data at all. While EDP equipment is not infallible, it is much more reliable for a sustained period of time than any manual operation. Certain controls and checks for accuracy can be programed into the data processing system to assure almost complete accuracy in the end product. Data can be collected in machine-usable form at the original source and can be passed through an intercommunicating data system from school to school district to state to federal levels. This should help to achieve the criterion of accuracy at each of these reporting levels.

One example should serve to illustrate this point. The Tennessee State Department of Education has, for many years, required local school systems to submit annually detailed information on the training, experience, and employment of each teacher in the system. With the installation of EDP equipment, the department now prints out the teacher information sheets for each school system based on the report for the preceding year, mails it to each school system, and the system reports by noting any exceptions to the listing. This procedure, with extensive reduction in local school system clerical time, influences the accuracy of the data.

Timeliness of Data

Sound decision making requires that the data bearing on a particular problem be available while the problem is current. Otherwise the data have historical value only. EDP can multiply the speed of the data collection, analysis, and dissemination processes many times that of any manual system. The contributions of the equipment to providing current data are evident.

Comparability of Data

Standard accounts and terminology are the foundation for accurate recording, reporting, and interpreting educational information. Only when basic items of educational information have the same meaning in all state departments of education and in all local school districts can they be used profitably for all purposes.

Educational data have been and will continue to be used extensively for comparative purposes. Any school, school system, or state can expect to have its program of public education evaluated on the basis of what other comparable schools, systems, or states are doing. It becomes imperative that all educational data be uniformly defined and collected.

Progress has been made toward achieving uniformity. A national yardstick of educational measurement is available in the form of five handbooks that identify and define standard educational terms. The handbooks, part of a series designed to help states and local school districts reach a high degree of comparability in their reporting of educational information, have been prepared by the Office of Education working with the Council of Chief State School

Officers and other national organizations. *Handbook I, the Common Core of State Educational Information,*[3] identifies and defines 516 items of educational information. *Handbook II, Financial Accounting for Local and State School Systems,*[4] contains standard receipt and expenditure accounts, classified and defined, and additional terminology necessary to use them effectively. *Handbook III, Property Accounting for Local and State Systems,*[5] classifies and defines the specific items of information about land, buildings, and equipment that need to be comparable among local school systems. *Handbook IV, Staff Accounting for Local and State School Systems,*[6] is a basic guide that identifies and defines those items of information about school staff members which need to be collected and maintained by local and state school systems in the United States. *Handbook V, Pupil Accounting for Local and State School Systems,*[7] serves as a guide for local and state school systems for items of information used in keeping records and making reports about pupils. It classifies and defines specific items of information about pupils and presents additional related terminology. In so doing, the handbook provides the basis for maintaining records about all pupils who are in elementary schools, secondary schools, junior colleges, and adult education programs under the jurisdiction of local boards of education.

Despite the progress in achieving comparability, there is still a long way to go. EDP systems can contribute to the goal. As the various states and the federal government plan intercommunicating systems for the flow of educational information from school to school system to state to federal levels, increased attention must be given to comparability of educational terms and definitions.

Comprehensive Educational Data Needed

The ever increasing complexity of the public education enterprise demands that decision making be based on the analysis of comprehensive data on all aspects of the school program. The

[3] Paul L. Reason, Emery M. Foster, and Robert F. Will. *The Common Core of State Educational Information.* Bulletin No. 8, U. S. Office of Education. Washington: Government Printing Office, 1953.

[4] Paul L. Reason and Alpheus L. White. *Financial Accounting for Local and State School Systems.* Bulletin No. 4, U. S. Office of Education. Washington: Government Printing Office, 1957.

[5] Paul L. Reason and George G. Tankard, Jr. *Property Accounting for Local and State School Systems.* Bulletin No. 22, U. S. Office of Education. Washington: Government Printing Office, 1959.

[6] Allan R. Lichtenberger and Richard J. Penrod. *Staff Accounting for Local and State School Systems.* Bulletin No. 18, U. S. Office of Education. Washington: Government Printing Office, 1965.

[7] John F. Putnam and George G. Tankard, Jr. *Pupil Accounting for Local and State School Systems.* Bulletin No. 39, U.S. Office of Education. Washington: Government Printing Office, 1964.

educational planner must have adequate information on the numbers to be educated, the scope of both present and needed programs of instruction, the teaching force, the physical facilities, the auxiliary services to the instructional program, the financial requirements of the enterprise, and the ability of the various governmental units to provide the necessary financial resources. More detailed cost analyses are essential if educational administration is to evaluate properly the varying demands for new programs and for innovations in the present program. Detailed classification of school expenditures is a prerequisite to these necessary cost analyses; and a coding system for classifying school expenditures in sufficient detail to meet these needs is more feasible with EDP equipment.

School expenditures can be coded by function (purpose served by the expenditure) and by object (what was purchased with the expenditure). The broad functions can then be divided into subfunctions and each subfunction can be further classified. For example, *instruction* is a function. Its subfunctions might be *supervision, principal, teaching,* and so on. Teaching might be further divided into *classroom teaching* and *other teaching. Classroom teaching* might be further divided into *program areas (elementary, junior high, or secondary).* The *secondary area* could then be classified by *subject areas.* Under each of these functions and subfunctions the particular expenditure could be classified by object. Object classifications might be *salaries professional, salaries clerical, other salaries, contracted services, supplies and materials, other expenses, principal and interest, land, buildings, and equipment.* Under this detailed coding, for example, the salary of all teachers teaching *French* at the secondary school level could be determined.

EDP systems enable millions of characters of educational information stored in "data banks" to be retrieved and analyzed at high speeds. The criterion of comprehensiveness in data used in long-range educational planning is, thereby, attainable.

SIMULATION OF AN EDUCATIONAL SYSTEM

EDP systems are far from being "electronic brains." They do only what they are told to do by a human operator. However, it may be erroneous to suppose that there will always be a wide gap between human and artificial intelligence. Scientists now look toward development of computers that will store experience as well as facts. When confronted with a problem, such machines would choose their own way of solving it. Such an accomplishment is easily believable when one views the present uses being made of the electronic systems.

For example military men are uneasy about the growing influence of computers on defense strategy. They complained as early as 1962 that a decision to hold back funds for a reconnaissance strike bomber was based on computer calculations. Computers in the Pentagon conduct elaborate war games and choose the best weapons and designs from hundreds of alternatives. Indeed, they may have reduced the need for some kinds of nuclear testing. To a large extent, battlefield performance of weapons can be predicted by computers while the weapons are still on the drawing board.

Computers already are used both in conduct of government and business. The Internal Revenue Service has opened regional computer centers to handle income tax returns. When fully developed, the computer network will process and, when necessary, audit every federal income tax return in the country.

Business concerns and financial institutions employ EDP systems in a variety of ways. The systems are used by banks to process checks and accounts; by insurance companies for premium billing, accounting, and actuarial forecasting; and by airline offices for ticketing and answering queries on availability of seating space.

The computer may be a godsend in certain chronically understaffed professions. For example, when fed data about a patient's case history, environment, symptoms, and laboratory test results, computers can come up with a remarkably accurate diagnosis of his ailment. Thus, they promise to give physicians more time to spend on treatment and research. The teaching process is also being simulated on the computer. In this usage the goal is the development of a flexible, automatic teaching machine that can release teachers from their roles as paper graders and drill masters. In this process of simulation, however, we may be able to learn more about the teaching and learning process.

It is possible to study new aircraft designs by computers without having to build expensive test models. And computers can predict what share of the market a new product will capture under varying sales budget, introduction times, advertising appeals, packaging, and pricing.

Many other examples of simulation by computers can be cited. A computer program can be made to mimic the behavior of many things. There is little doubt then that the computer can be programed to simulate an entire school organization. This permits advanced educational planning and decision making. By simulating an educational system for a given region and inserting such information as socioeconomic data, population trends, and other pertinent data, educational planners can cycle the program ahead and generate predictions about future educational needs. Facility planning, salary bill projections, and other problems are already being solved with the use of computers.

SOME PREREQUISITES TO EFFECTIVE USE OF ELECTRONIC DATA PROCESSING IN EDUCATIONAL RESEARCH

The preceding discussion has attempted to show the present and potential role of EDP equipment in improving educational research. However, the lag between the development of the new techniques and their application is a major problem to be overcome in realizing the potential of EDP systems in education. A major difficulty will be in familiarizing educational research workers with the techniques of modern data processing. This can best be accomplished through the instructional programs of institutions involved in training education leaders. This does not mean that all graduate students in education should be trained to be computer programers. However, a core of students thoroughly familiar with EDP techniques must be developed. These people are needed to develop the specific applications of these techniques to both pure educational research and the process of "quality control," and to guide their colleagues in data processing applications as the need arises. At least a one-semester laboratory-type course should be offered to teach students the necessary fundamentals of punched card equipment and digital computers and to acquaint them with both present and potential uses of the equipment in educational management and control. The regular instruction must be supplemented periodically with short-term workshops aimed at reaching teachers, administrators, and school supervisory personnel who are on the job. Stated another way, the time has come when we must have our school professional personnel trained in data processing. In accomplishing this task, it would be possible for each institution to "get on its horse and go off in a different direction." Coordination of training efforts is essential and the state department of education is in the best position to achieve the necessary coordination. The institutions of higher education, working through the state department of education, should reach agreement on basic needs to be met and the knowledge, skills, and understandings to be imparted in the training program.

Another major impediment to effective use of EDP equipment is the cost of preparing the so-called "software" of the system. The preparation of the program of instructions that will enable a person to control the equipment and make it do its job can be very expensive. Manufacturers are attempting to solve this cost problem through "packaged programs." A packaged program is a standard set of instructions broad enough to fit many situations without modification. This approach has many limitations, the most important of which is that it usually means modifying school system procedures to accommodate a program.

Teacher training institutions, working in close cooperation with state departments of education, need to attack the so-called "software" problem in achieving effective use of computer systems in education. Extensive study of data processing applications for schools should be conducted and the reports of new techniques published regularly. The problem of developing the "software" of educational applications is presently under limited attack at two or three university centers and in a few school systems which have pioneered in the use of computer equipment. More centers are needed and an effective means of collecting and disseminating new computer programs should be developed.

School Responsibilities More Than Instruction and Program

The responsibilities of institutions of higher education in the area of EDP are not limited to their instructional programs and the development of computer programs. University centers should establish installations to be used in field service activities with local school systems. The university staff should be able to provide consultative service to local school systems in the planning and installation of data processing equipment. University installations are needed to serve as service bureaus for school systems which cannot afford their own equipment and which could profitably utilize the equipment.

Obviously, a final problem to be overcome is the problem of availability of the computer to the local school system and more particularly to the educational researcher. The use of data processing equipment in educational management and control is limited primarily to punched card equipment. Only a few of the large metropolitan school systems have been able to afford the installation of computer systems. Certain developments are underway, however, which should improve the possibilities for computer utilization by local school systems. The number of commercial and university data processing centers is increasing. School systems within commuting distance to such centers can usually buy computer time on an hourly rate. School systems should be able to get computer time on industrial installations in the school district which may not be used to full capacity. Then too, small scale computers may now be secured by school districts on a reasonable rental basis.

SUMMARY

The potential of EDP equipment in the improvement of educational research and the subsequent decision making in education has many facets. Its use in the routine clerical chores of day-to-day management and control should free teachers, administrators, and other school personnel to participate more in on-going research programs. The possibility now exists for the use of large samples yielding a quantity of data which would have been previously unanalyzable. Basic data and research information on what is currently being done in the schools and how well it is being done can now be stored and retrieved at fantastic speeds. A new brand of research in education is possible and is now emerging. The computer is effecting improvements in the quality of research instruments and in the adequacy of educational information being used in educational decision making. And finally, the computer can be used to simulate the educational enterprise.

On the other hand, however, these improvements are not automatically assured. Serious obstacles must be overcome. These new developments must be communicated to workers in education. Computer "software" must be further developed. Then obviously, computer systems must be made available to educational workers.

5 a national educational information system

ALVIN GROSSMAN

Dr. Alvin Grossman received his EdD from the University of Washington in 1961, his master's from the University of Georgia in 1950, and his bachelor's in Psychology from the University of Illinois in 1947.

He has been a college professor, a state consultant in pupil personnel services, and a county office of education director of research and guidance. He is co-author of a text on educational data processing, and has been a contributor to numerous publications in the field of data processing. In addition, Dr. Grossman has served as editor of the Journal of Educational Data Processing, *as a board member of AEDS, as chairman of the California State Advisory Committee on Integrated Data Processing, and as a member of the Governor's task force on ADP.*

National attention is being focused on the strategic importance of education. The past decade has witnessed pressure on our schools of an intensity never before experienced. Because of these pressures, the continued use of antiquated information processing procedures in the face of the growing size and complexity of American education constitutes a gross anachronism. Next to national defense, education is the largest single enterprise in the United States. In 1964, expenditures for all levels of public education, including capital outlay, reached approximately 27 billion dollars. The nation's schools and colleges enrolled one-fourth of our population. With millions of people and billions of dollars to be accounted for, the American educational enterprise is in urgent need of a comprehensive management and information system with nationwide compatibility.

EDUCATION AS AN INFORMATION SYSTEM

Information problems are woven through the fabric of educational processes, from problems of collecting, storing, communicating, retrieving, and displaying information, to problems of receiving, learning, and using the information. Student, teacher, administrator, research and guidance worker, business manager, board member—all are directly concerned with transmission and utilization of information. Education is, in large measure, an information processing system. However, in the schools of today, momentous educational decisions concerning the lives and future careers of students and millions of dollars of the taxpayers' money are made with a dearth of information. Even when information is on hand, one is apt to find that little or no effort has been made to integrate that information and that it is almost totally unrelated. The status of information processing in education is all the more surprising when it has been a truism for years that "the right data at the right moment can give students, teachers, and administrators the edge they need for making calculated rather than uninformed decisions." For too long educators have attached relatively little importance to developing information systems that could provide the facility to generate "educational intelligence" (meaningful action-oriented reports based on the management-by-exception concept) and instead, virtually have continued to do things the way they were always done—because it was traditional.

There is an old saw about the distaff side of human relations that is meant to reassure the young man who thinks he might lose his girl: "Like the streetcar, another will be along soon." It may not be too far-fetched to identify a parallel to this in public education. Too often educators console themselves for not investigating and adopting educational innovations or for not incorporating new technological advances into their arsenal by rationalizing that, after all, another "gimmick" will be along soon.

Tradition Can Be an Impediment

It has been the nature of American schools to respond to a variety of appeals. This they have done, but ever so slowly. Change takes time, particularly when it is applied to education. And time today is the element that educators do not have. The age of the computer began in 1946, and the space age began in 1957 with the orbiting of Sputnik. Educators, after 100 years of relatively static curriculum, suddenly have been faced with a very—and perhaps terrifying—situation in which change must be brought about immediately. Students who have come through our traditional programs suddenly were unable to cope with the highly complex and technological world around them. The traditional time lapse between significant scientific, technological, and social changes and the need to accept and to adapt to them has become non-existent. These changes have come about not only in the scientific area, but also in the technological and social areas, as illustrated by the pressing problems of automation, unemployment, leisure time, and integration.

EDUCATIONAL INNOVATION

The entire nation looks to education for the solution to each of these problems, or at least as the agency best suited to provide a solution. Whether this is appropriate or good should be left to the philosophers and politicians to debate. The main point is that life is moving too rapidly; educators can no longer do nothing in the hope that solutions will come with time. This is the moment for bold and imaginative educational innovations that should not be thought of merely as curriculum changes, but should probe to the very heart of the unrest and change of our times. The status quo type of thinking has made educators captives of the written word. Since Gutenberg invented movable type in the middle of the 15th century, they have accepted the printed page as the best way to impart knowledge. To be sure, other aids and tools have been recognized—such as audio-visual aids, but their use is regarded as supplemental to the instructional program rather than as an integral part of it.

Probably the greatest roadblock to the acceptance of different ways of doing things is the fact that educators treasure the old seasoned methods and back off from new challenges. Almost everyone in a school district knows how its operations can be improved, but too often improvements are stillborn or not born at all. A variety of reasons, of course, are seized upon. No one is available to plan changes; new proposals may offend someone; there may not be any room in the budget, and so on.

It is now an established fact that while technological developments have fairly cascaded onto the American scene, the public schools have not kept pace. Most educators have failed to employ current innovations because they have adopted the traditional "next streetcar" attitude. When a new technology becomes available, they want to see if someone else has determined or demonstrated its feasibility. By the time its potential to the schools is widely accepted, another new development springs up on the horizon; we abandon trial of the prior one because now we must see if the newcomer will prove to be of greater value. While we wait for each new "streetcar" to come along and let each one go by, our students are being deprived of educational aids that could equip them to cope with the new and challenging space age.

It is hoped that the time has come when we as educators can begin to build and create an educational information system that will engender an intense, enthusiastic, three-dimensional study of ways in which public education can be tellingly improved. We need to develop a system that will touch off a fire of analysis and evaluation that will sweep across the land and create such excitement, such a passion for renewal, that all of us will be caught up in it. A revolution is what we need; a revolution in modernizing and streamlining the schools is what we must have if we are really to assume the right of educational leadership.

Our passivity, our love affair with the status quo, has led the citizenry and some state legislatures to feel that we have become drifters and that only a few in our profession can boast of realistic programs to educate today's youth. They have become increasingly tired of our lofty pronouncements, our seven cardinal precepts, our vague dreams of Utopia. On all sides they see a highly technological society; they also see the majority of our schools caught up in the backwash of an ancient time. Small wonder that lawmakers step in and mandate new rules to govern our behavior and our practices.

Like animals in the wild, weak men are prey for the strong. Let there be no dispute about it—we have been marked in society's book as the weak. It is not surprising that our publics refuse to give us additional financial support for "more of the same thing"; nor is it strange that before they will sanction new funds, they want us to demonstrate, individually as teachers and collectively as school systems, that we can do a far better job than we have done in the past.

Most educators are in agreement that there is an urgent need today for a cooperative national effort to develop and maintain a National Educational Information System which would give education the forward thrust it needs. The best approach to such a system would see the U. S. Office of Education, along with the 50 states, cooperatively set up a joint project to capitalize on what has already been accomplished in leading states and areas such as California, Iowa, New England, and Florida.

MANAGEMENT SYSTEMS

In order to accomplish its objectives, the U. S. Office of Education or its designated representatives must be able to give strong central direction to this effort. This is imperative if any comprehensive system is to survive. Notwithstanding the evident need for central systems direction, humans by nature are ruggedly independent, particularly those leaders in the various states who have risen to the management level in data processing. Therefore, recognizing the need for central direction is one thing, and voluntarily continuing cooperation is another.

To accomplish this mammoth undertaking, resources provided must be commensurate with the size of the task. Going one step further, however, the provision of various resource components will not in itself assure success. In order to apply available resources effectively, we must insure full coordination of the efforts of the various state departments, regional projects, and similar local activities. Unless we achieve a high degree of coordination, a considerable share of potential individual resources and capabilities will be dissipated.

The information system should be based on strong central direction of system development but allow operating units a paramount voice in determining the direction to be followed. Once the direction has been determined, compliance with these determinations should be required.

Regardless of the quality of the planning and the high quality of top management leadership, the potential of this program cannot be expeditiously or fully attained unless the proper resources are provided.

PLANNING FOR NATIONAL DEVELOPMENT

The plan for a national system is based upon the Lockheed report to the California state government titled, "The California Statewide Information System Study," July 1965.

The design of a developmental plan for a project as important and pervasive in its potential effect on education as this one is a task which deserves much care. It should involve many of the forward-looking states in the development and organization of a master plan. A major objective of the plan, perhaps the most significant, is to preserve and promote the drive toward EDP (electronic data processing) by the more advanced states, and offer coordination and guidance to any or all states only as far as is necessary for each state to reach a desired goal of an integrated statewide information system.

As shown in Figure 7, the developmental plan of a national information system will probably cover a ten-year period. The initial development plan for a long-term project must identify and develop two basic elements:

1. Broad strategy for reaching a goal
2. Insight into the necessary steps of implementation

With respect to the second item, it is recognized that major emphasis must be placed on the early phases of the plan. This provides the necessary insight and understanding to advance the project to its next phase, and also illuminates the immediate course of action.

The detailed structure of individual steps in the development must be sufficiently flexible to allow modification as the project

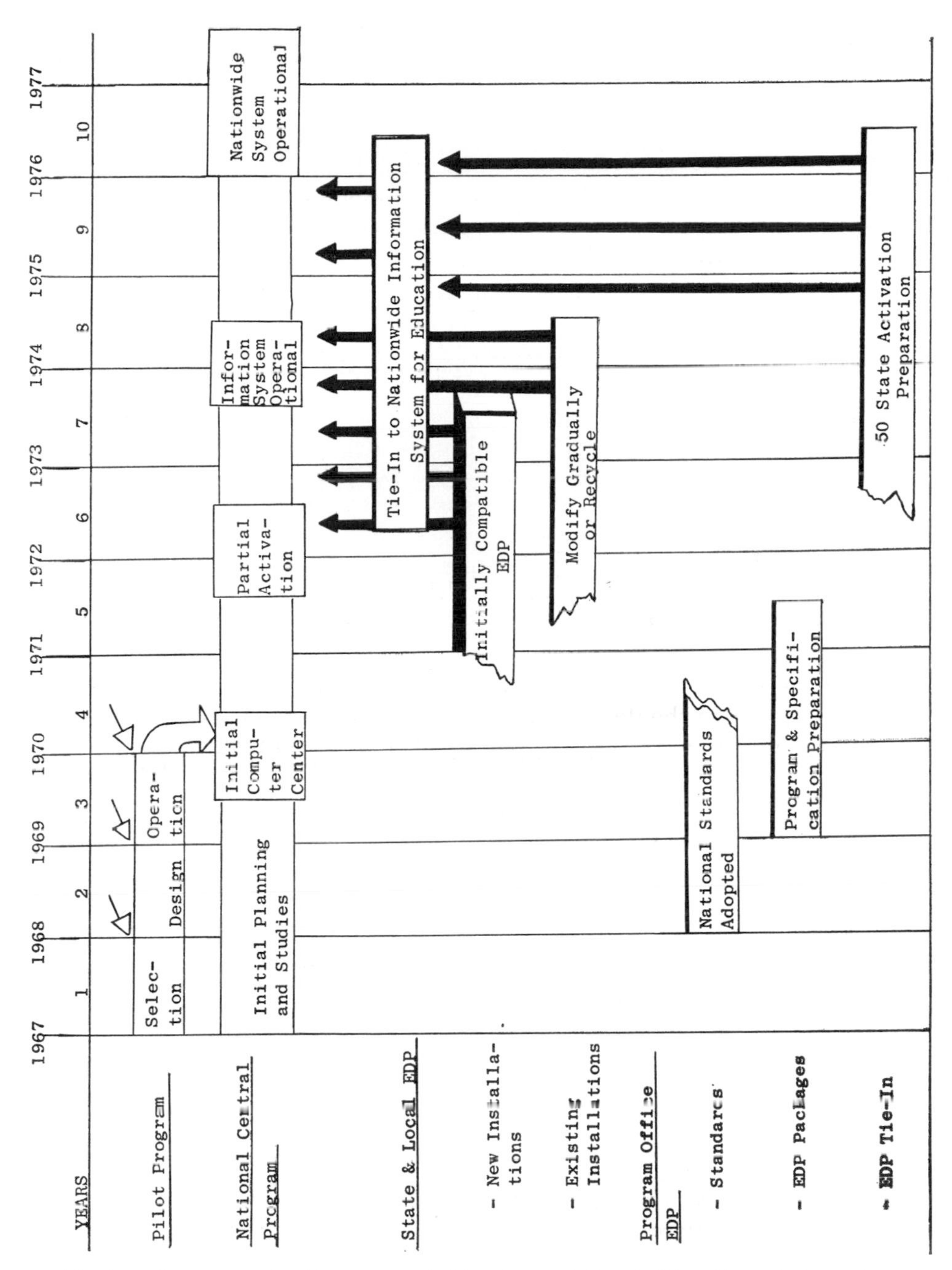

Fig. 7. — Summary of a Development Plan for a National Educational Information System.

develops. In view of this requirement, the initial steps of implementation must be designed to provide, within the constraints of the basic strategy, as broad an application as possible to assure sound development.

STRATEGY OF IMPLEMENTATION

The implementation strategy for a national educational system should be developed in the context of the following major considerations:

1. Interaction between the information system proper and the organizational EDP implementation in the various states.
2. Relative phasing of the participation of the U. S. Office of Education, regional centers, local districts, and state departments of education in the total network.
3. Desirability of an early, small-scale demonstration of the capabilities of the system by a suitable pilot program, which would also identify potential problems during an early phase of the project.

THE PILOT PROGRAM

A valued concept in the development of a large project involving a sizable expenditure of funds is the pilot operation. The pilot is a smaller-scale version of the total program which can be implemented on a shorter time scale (often in parallel with the design of the larger program) and which can be used to test and verify the precepts and concepts (technical, economic, and operational) of the overall project. The pilot program often results in modifications of the total program, based on experiences derived from the pilot operation.

Examination of the applicability of the pilot concept to the National Information System leads to the conclusion that this concept is generally applicable and would give tangible demonstration at an early phase of the total development plan, with concurrent proof of technical and operational feasibility as well as design to feed back into the main program.

As envisioned, the pilot program would be built around a particular subfunction. For example, this could be the establishment and upkeep of a family-oriented file for a small segment of population such as a school district. The need for such a file—to assemble a complete history of the family interaction (school district, with other school districts throughout the state as well as possible contacts with other state and federal offices)—has often been expressed by educators.

The general characteristics of the subsystem selected as a pilot program would be as follows:

1. The application should be a good candidate for EDP, with potential subsequent benefits.
2. The application should be capable of automation without detrimental effect on the major tasks of the parent organization.
3. The application should require some inputs from other organizations in order to demonstrate multi-organization tie-in. These inputs should preferably be available in machine format.
4. Local school district tie-in is desirable to demonstrate vertical interschool communications.
5. The application should be significant as a demonstration, yet be small enough to be accomplished in two or three years.
6. Funding for the conversion of the application to EDP (at least on a small demonstration basis) must be available.

INFORMATION SYSTEM MANAGEMENT

The implementation of a National Information System would be an activity potentially involved in the expenditure of sizable sums and a high degree of interaction with many organizations of state and federal governments. Success of the program would be strongly determined by the substance and staffing of its management organization. It is recommended that, following the example of the aerospace industries, the management technique of the program office be utilized to implement the nationwide information system.

Interest on the part of many states in integrated information systems is already high and is increasing rapidly. Certainly the federal government would have strong motivation to encourage the development of such systems. The success in attracting potential federal funding will be strongly increased by the identification of a senior official representing this National Information System. It would be natural for this individual to be the director of the program office.

The program office should be charged with complete responsibility for the implementation of the National Information System. As envisioned, the program office would consist of a program director and a small, tightly knit staff of senior personnel. The group would manage the program and operate through other state and federal personnel, contractors, and consultants. Because of the size of the program, the program office would likely employ the services of a prime contractor.

The major functions of the program office should be as follows:

- Program control, including schedules and budget

- Technical direction
- Coordination and negotiation with other governmental jurisdiction—local, federal, and state
- Contracting

The program office would also be the nucleus of the operational organization, assisting and guiding when the developmental effort translates into an operating phase.

INFORMATION SYSTEM POLICY

A national group should be brought together at the earliest possible date to formulate, on a continuing basis, the broad management and administrative policies needed to guide development of the total program. This phase should begin with an initial study to produce a basic policy document within the first six months. The document should enunciate policy on the following subjects:

1. *Capital equipment*
   This item will establish lease-or-buy policy for computers and and communication equipment as well as facilities.
2. *Organizational EDP review*
   This item will determine the policy under which existing organizational EDP will tie into the national network.
3. *State department of education relations*
   This item is concerned with relationships of the system with state departments of education. In particular, the document should consider the conditions under which state departments may be assisted in their EDP efforts by means of grants, loans, or technical assistance.
4. *Information access*
   This item will establish the access policy for information on the part of the public schools and the various elements in the private sector.
5. *Personnel*
   This item will establish appropriate personnel acquisition rates, recommend a wage structure policy, and formulate a training policy.
6. *Financing*
   This item will determine policy with respect to methods of financing the capital requirements of the National Information System.
7. *Developmental contracting*
   This item will develop the policy governing the work areas for the various personnel assigned to the project and contractor personnel, and the types of contractual arrangements to be used during the various phases of the program.

8. *Activation priority*
   This item will state priority policy for organizational (state and and local) tie-in to the network.
9. *Operation*
   This item will develop policy for operation of the various parts of the National Information System. Consideration should be given to conditions under which the system will lease a total service, grant or franchise, or operate purchased or leased equipment with operating personnel.

Information-system policy should be a continuing function during the entire life of the program. After publication of the initial policy document, it should be concerned with administration of the policy as well as updating of the policy document as required.

CAPABILITY AND INTERFACE STUDY

The objective of a *capability and interface study* would be to define the significant parameters that determine compatibility at the interface between the emerging national system and the EDP equipment of the various organizations which would be participating in the information system. A further objective would be to establish standards (1) for use by organizations that have not yet begun EDP activities; or (2) for more sufficient use of the system. The study should involve the following work elements:

1. Study the requirements associated with the interconnection of different organizational EDP systems including hardware and software. Develop criteria applicable to both hardware and software to enable compatible operation with the information system.
2. Review existing and planned hardware and software of the various states that will participate and selected local school district organizations so as to determine use, capability, limitations, and interfaces with the total national effort.
3. Develop an interface manual containing hardware and software compatibility criteria essential to interconnection with the National Information System and standards to be recommended to organizations instituting or planning EDP facilities.

This study should yield compatibility policy statements at the end of a six-month effort and, hopefully, an interface manual at the end of one year.

ORGANIZATIONAL ACTIVATION PLAN DEVELOPMENT

The objective in developing an "organizational activation plan" would be to establish a comprehensive organizational activation blueprint defining methods of scheduling and controlling the planning, design, development, testing, and activation of the information system in consonance with the organizational EDP systems' activation and subsequent integration into the National Information System. The plan could serve as a basic management tool for timely identification and correction of schedule inconsistencies and incompatibilities during the development and activation of organizational EDP systems. Work required encompasses the following items:

1. Study the nature of existing state organizational EDP systems in conjunction with local school district systems and initiate plans for developing the National Information System requirements.
2. Develop a preliminary master tie-in schedule of organizational EDP systems, considering the status of organizational development; the desirability of functional—or regional—common EDP systems; and a possibility of early culmination of some data files on a regional or functional basis.
3. Make a preliminary identification of organizational data systems tie-ins which would yield an early operational national system.
4. Make a preliminary identification of data needed for management planning and for a management reporting and control system.
5. Develop a control and scheduling model based on the pertinent parameters.
6. Develop detailed critical path scheduling network for the information system.
7. Develop a training plan, including levels of training, to prepare personnel to operate the National Information System.

The first phase of this activity should be able to deliver a complete organizational activation plan in a period of two years. Coordination management would be a continuing activity which would last for the duration of the project to ensure proper continued coordination and development of the National Information System vis-a-vis organizational EDP activations.

A massive effort on a broad front is needed to accomplish the goals of a National Information System. One would hope that the U. S. Office of Education, seeing the various states acting in concert, could mobilize the necessary funds so that the large-scale funding necessary could be secured. The further organization and placement of the program office and the elements of management and control would be left for determination to the advisory group in cooperation with the U. S. Office of Education.

REFERENCES

Bittel, Lester R. *Management by Exception.* New York: McGraw-Hill, 1964.

Grossman, Alvin, and Robert L. Howe. *Data Processing for Educators.* Chicago: Educational Methods, Inc., 1965.

Head, Robert V. *Real-Time Business Systems.* New York: Holt, Rinehart, and Winston, Inc., 1964.

Van Ness, Robert G. *Principles of Data Processing With Computers.* Elmhurst, Illinois: The Business Press, 1966.

Application of Electronic Data Processing Methods in Education. Project No. F-026. Washington: Cooperative Research Program, U. S. Office of Education, January 1965.

The California Statewide Information System Study. Lockheed Corporation, California, 1965.

6 an automated statewide information system

LORNE H. WOOLLATT

DR. LORNE H. WOOLLATT is a graduate of the University of Saskatchewan and Columbia University, where he received his PhD in Educational Research. He has experience in teaching, administration, and research in rural and city schools and at the university level.

Dr. Woollatt has served as director of research in the Baltimore Public Schools; he was previously assistant professor of educational administration assigned to the Institute of Administrative Research, working with the Metropolitan School Study Council, with the Association of Public School Systems, and with the Central Schools of New York State.

He is a member of AEDS; the American Educational Research Association; the American Association of School Administrators; a fellow of the American Association for the Advancement of Science; a member of the Study Commission, Council of Chief State School Officers; the Committee on Educational Data Systems of the latter organization; and a member of the Educational Research Association of New York State.

THE NEED

There is general recognition that education plays a critical role in the achievement of local, state, and national objectives. It is becoming increasingly clear that a strong relationship exists between education and factors such as economic growth, poverty, civil rights, and foreign affairs. It is natural, therefore, for the demands for information about vital educational activity to be abundant and ever increasing. The public wants to know what is going on in the schools; the legislator and the administrator must make accurate and judicious decisions based on the past and the projected future; the researcher must have valid and reliable data in order to assess and update educational programs. At the present time, educators do a less than adequate job of reporting to the public about schools; in addition, legislators, administrators, and researchers are hampered by a lack of related, reliable, and timely data. Duplication of effort, late and inaccurate reporting, and slow data processing too often characterize educational information systems today.

Concurrent with the demand for more accurate and timely educational information is the need to have a broader data base. The impact of new state and federal legislation, the appearance of new school organizational and staffing patterns, the proliferation of curricula and programs to meet a broad range of needs in a variety of ways, plus a multitude of other emerging factors, have given the educational information problem a character of exponential growth.

Within the past few years a national effort to deal with this rapidly intensifying problem has developed. The U. S. Office of Education (USOE) and the Council of Chief State School Officers (CCSSO), through the Committee on Educational Data Systems (CEDS)—organized in 1962, made up of members named by the chief school officers of each of the states and territories—are cooperating to initiate a nationwide coordinated system for collecting information on school professional staff, pupils, curricula, facilities, and finance. The system, called the Basic Educational Data System (BEDS), has concentrated initially on professional staff data. Since 1963 more than half of the states and territories have annually forwarded to the USOE selected items of information on professional personnel in elementary and secondary schools. Plans are being developed for the collection and transmittal of data in the other aforementioned categories as well. Up to the present, this effort has produced a very small quantity of information in relation to what is needed, but it is a beginning.

The realization of a completely operational national Basic Educational Data System depends in large measure upon the prior establishment of basic data systems in each of the states. The overall direction of education is, after all, a state function. It is the responsibility of the states to lead the effort in solving the information problem. It is a task that must be given highest priority by state education agencies, in accordance with the guidelines set forth by the USOE and CEDS.

THE SYSTEMS APPROACH TO INFORMATION COLLECTION, PROCESSING, AND DISSEMINATION

Stated simply, an information system is an organized arrangement for making the right information available to those who need it, when they need it, in the desired format, all at the least possible cost. The key to a systems approach in dealing with information is organization; the procedures for collecting, processing, and disseminating information must be *coordinated* and routinized.

A statewide educational data system will require that a central body within a state education agency be given responsibility and authority for *coordinating* all information handling. This central body would be a committee made up of executive level representatives of all major operating units in the agency or a separately organized administrative unit. Requests for information, from both within and outside the department, would be channeled through this committee or office. In turn, the requests would be evaluated in terms of: (1) whether the information requested is already available (either internally or externally); (2) the desirability of collecting the information, considering the overall objectives and responsibilities of the state education agency; and (3) the feasibility of collecting the information, i.e., the relative value of having the information, compared with the time and effort required of school and department personnel to get it. Such coordination would eliminate, at point of origin, data collection that is unnecessary, undesirable, infeasible, or redundant.

While the systems approach to information handling demands routinization, the data collected need not and should not be routine. A substantial portion of the information in a statewide system would necessarily be routine in the sense that it would be collected and processed periodically. However, the information—or at least some of it—would be changed from time to time to keep pace with changing needs. Indeed, a continuing department-wide evaluation of information needs should be an important part of any system.

One of the most salient characteristics of an information system is that it exists independently of the data that may be treated by it at any given moment in time. When effective data handling procedures are established they can easily be adapted to new data. An information system that must be changed whenever data are added or deleted is no system at all.

Implementation of a statewide educational data system will require the establishment of an information network leading from the working records maintained at the smallest operating unit of the educational enterprise to the largest organizational level and back again. It is of critical importance that this information network be founded on the proposition that with movement upward through the organizational levels, less and less detailed information is required.

The smallest operating unit in the network is a class—a teacher and a group of students in a classroom. The teacher needs a great deal of information about his students. He needs to know, for example, the students' names, ages, previous school records, standardized test scores, and special personal or learning difficulties, as well as what they did in class last month or last week and what they are going to do next week.

At the next level in the information network, the principal's office, there is generally more concern about how many pupils are taking a given course and how many are likely to take it next term than there is about individual, personal student data. Occasionally, of course, the principal does require detailed information about individual students, but not generally. In the day-to-day performance of his job, the principal needs summary information about what is going on in his school. At the school district level, the superintendent and board of education need, for the most part, summary information on all the schools that constitute the district in order to make policy and administrative decisions. In turn, a state education agency needs trend data derived from summary information on all of the school districts in the state. Finally, the U. S. Office of Education requires trend data derived from summary information on all of the states.

There will necessarily be occasions when upper levels in the information network need detailed reports about some specific activities at the lower levels; provisions in a data system must be built in to accommodate this. It is most important, however, that such details be transmitted upward *only* when there is a valid reason for doing so. To do otherwise would make a statewide educational data system unmanageable and fruitless.

In these days of automated factories and moon shots, a parallel is frequently drawn between sophisticated electronic computers and the concept of a total information system. This is not necessarily true. Any group of coordinated and routinized procedures for collecting, processing, storing, and disseminating information constitutes an information system. Even in the smallest states where the handling of large quantities of information is not the rule, a comprehensive data system can be developed using the simplest forms of data processing equipment. In general, however, the handling, tabulation, and manipulation of very large data banks is not easily accomplished without the use of high speed electronic computers. Modern technology has made available tools which are particularly suited to repetitive and complex data handling, thereby making possible the application of a true systems approach to the collection, processing, and dissemination of statewide educational information.

A SUGGESTED PATTERN

In keeping with the concept of diminishing detail in an educational information network, a statewide data system will necessarily focus on "basic data." The question arises, of course, regarding what is meant by the term "basic." The school principal's basic data would be grossly excessive detail to a state education agency. With few exceptions, basic educational data at the state level constitutes that information which will provide a broad overview of education in the state. In planning a statewide educational data system, it is critically important that ample attention be given to the matter of selecting the basic items to be included in the system. It has already been noted that USOE and CEDS have defined most of the data to be included in the national Basic Educational Data System. These data have been selected primarily for use at the federal level. They represent "basic" data for the USOE; state education agencies need more information (about their own states) than is called for in the USOE-CEDS recommendations.

Procedures and criteria for selecting items for the basic data system will vary according to the size, organization, and responsibilities of state education agencies. It is clear, however, and exceedingly important, that a detailed and intensive study be undertaken when an information system is contemplated. The following suggestions may be helpful:

1. *Conduct an inventory of all educational information presently collected by the state education agency.* Gathering and analyzing all forms and reports utilized by the department will probably be a good place to start.
2. *Ascertain how the information is processed and used.* Scrutinize each category of data in terms of the following questions:
   a. Is the information tabulated and summarized?
   b. Is the summary published and distributed?
   c. How often is the information collected?
   d. How often is it used?
   e. Who uses the information? Is its use limited or broadly applicable to department activities?
   f. How is the information used? Does its use relate directly to department responsibilities?
   g. Is the same information collected by more than one unit in the department?
   h. Is the information available through some other branch of state government or any other agency (e.g., a professional association)?
3. *Have each unit in the department prepare suggestions regarding information not presently available which should be collected.* Be sure each suggestion details why the information is needed and how it will be used.
4. *Analyze and synthesize the findings in (1), (2), and (3); prepare recommendations outlining information that should be available through the basic data system.* Recommendations will have to be

considered and acted upon by the top management of the department. An information coordinating committee (described earlier) would be an effective mechanism for making these decisions.

It should be recognized that a basic educational data system will not supplant all other data collection by a state education agency. The detailed reporting required for some programs, especially those utilizing federal funds, is so specialized that it cannot be included in a statewide basic data system. Other reports, sporadic in timing or individual in some particular way, will be in the same category. It is important, at the outset, to include only basic information in the data system. There is little doubt that at least two-thirds of the information needed by a state education agency can be extracted or calculated from carefully selected basic data.

Whatever procedures are employed, the selection process must be completed before the design of the basic educational data system can begin in earnest.

Since professional personnel are involved in almost every phase of the educational enterprise, a large proportion of the educational information needed by a state education agency can be *derived* from *basic* unit record data on professional staff. Those items of information placed in storage directly from source documents and which do not involve calculation are basic data. Derived information is a product of data manipulation. Basic data on a professional staff member might include age, degree status, and salary. The number of teachers 25 to 30 years of age, the number holding master's degrees and the percent earning more than $7,000 per year are examples of derived data.

Of the five major information categories outlined in the USOE-CEDS plans, much of the necessary data for three of the categories (staff, pupils, and curriculum) could be extracted from unit record data on professional personnel. Further, by analysis of information on teachers' assignments, some broad assumptions could be made about school facilities. (Detailed facilities information will have to be supplied at the school or school district level.) Likewise, reliable school financial data cannot be accessed through professional staff but will have to be separately supplied at the school district level. Perhaps it will be helpful to list here some items of "basic" information for each of the five broad categories of educational data. The list is illustrative and by no means exhaustive.

1. *Staff*
   a. Name
   b. Date of birth

c. Degree status
d. Certification status
e. Educational experience

2. *Pupils*
   a. Enrollments (by course, grade, school, etc.)
   b. Incidence and type of physical, mental, emotional and behavioral exceptionality
   c. Number in decelerated, regular, and accelerated classes
   d. Location and occupation of graduates
   e. Ethnic distribution (by grade, school, etc.)
3. *Curriculum*
   a. Regular course offerings
   b. Special education
   c. Experimental and innovative programs
   d. Pupil personnel services
   e. Non-course curricular activities
4. *Facilities*
   a. Location of building
   b. Type of construction
   c. Pupil capacity
   d. Number and type of instructional areas
   e. Number and type of service areas
5. *Finance*
   a. Revenue receipts
   b. Non-revenue receipts
   c. Capital outlay
   d. Debt service
   e. Federal and state participation

One of the biggest problems in assembling educational data has been late reporting—a major factor contributing to the untimeliness of educational information. This problem is generally not one of negligence or carelessness on the part of teachers and administrators who bear the reporting responsibility. Instead, the need for more and better educational information has imposed a terrible "paper burden" on school teachers and administrators who must necessarily concentrate their attention and effort on the task of educating young people. It is just not possible to respond, on time, to every request for information.

At the same time, there is a real need for timely information and the problem of late reporting must be solved. Once a state education agency has designed a basic data system that eliminates unnecessary and multiple requests for information, provision must be made to assure that respondents have time to complete required source documents. One effective way to accomplish this end would be to have the state commissioner or superintendent designate a specific day, early in the fall of the year, as "Basic Data System Day." On that day, teachers and administrators would be required to complete the basic data system forms. The majority of the information called for in the data system would then be recorded, simultaneously, in every school in the state and sent to the state education agency on time. It should be made clear to all involved that the new data system will satisfy, in a "one-day one-shot effort," a major proportion of the state department's information requirements for the year.

After the first year of operation, the time required to complete source documents for the new data system will diminish significantly. Since well-designed forms will not change drastically from one year to the next, teachers and administrators would be somewhat familiar with them. Further, not all data will have to be collected every year. Some can be derived by annual updating; e.g., a teacher with five years of experience last year could be assumed to have six this year. Other data might not be needed every year; information on school facilities, for example, will retain reliability for a considerable period of time and can be collected at intervals of several years. Finally, unchanging information will be collected the first year only. Once in the file, items such as a teacher's name, sex, date of birth, school name, etc., will be automatically carried forward from year to year.

Ultimately, an automated statewide information system could include regional data processing centers. Such centers might be essential, particularly in larger states, to assure the orderly development of efficient data processing capability. A regional center's prime function would be to provide data processing services to the elementary and secondary schools in its area and, in addition, augment the capability of the state education agency in the collection, processing, and dissemination of statewide educational information. These centers will not necessarily need to be operated by the state education department, but certainly their development will require coordination at the state level to eliminate duplication and ensure maximum utilization of personnel and equipment.

SOME MECHANICAL CONSIDERATIONS

It is clear that the *timely* conversion of a massive quantity of basic educational information into useful summary reports will require the employment of data processing equipment. Furthermore, considering the many kinds of data manipulation and wide variety of reports that would need to be generated, it is probable, at least in the larger states, that no less sophisticated equipment than a computer and associated peripherals would suffice. The precise configuration of equipment would, of course, vary with the scope of the data system, the size of the population, the legal responsibilities of the state department and so forth. There are, however, some broadly pertinent considerations in the selection of equipment.

First, all of the available "hardware" is basically good machinery and generally comparable in capability within given price ranges. Machine A may have a slightly faster internal speed than machine B, but the input-output devices on B may be slightly faster than those on A; machine C may be able to perform operation X more quickly then machine D, but it may not be quite as fast as D on operation Y. When the general size and capabilities required in a computer have been determined, and the particular machines offering the desired features have been identified, final selection must be based upon factors other than brand name. These factors may be broadly categorized as (1) software and (2) maintenance. The software features of a computer system, which are of critical importance, include such considerations as the availability of "canned" production programs as well as input-output routines and the ability of the equipment to work with one or more of the so-called standard machine languages (Cobol, Algol, Fortran, etc.). Programs for standard statistical processing and other data handling, supplied by the computer manufacturer along with tried and tested routines for moving data into and out of the system, can save the user long and expensive hours of programing and program debugging. Similarly, the ability of a computer system to execute programs written in one or more of the standard languages broadens the opportunity to borrow from other computer users who may have already written and tested programs capable of doing some of the required processing.

The importance of maintenance service provided by computer manufacturers cannot be overemphasized. Excessive downtime is expensive but perhaps more importantly, it is destructive of processing schedules. There is no quicker way to cultivate critics of a new information system than by demonstrating inability to deliver promised reports on time. Maintenance services must be fast—calls for maintenance must bring immediate responses—and they must be preventive as well as corrective. Regularly scheduled downtime for preventive maintenance can eliminate much unscheduled downtime for emergency maintenance.

No one has yet devised an information system that is completely automated. In a basic educational data system, the desired basic information first exists in the minds of human beings and in assorted files and records located in a variety of places. Before automated processing can begin, this information must be changed, by hand processes, into a form that machines can use. Such hand processes commonly involve punching cards or paper tape, or recording machine-sensible marks on coded sheets of paper. Up to the present, most educational data have been converted into machine-usable form via keypunching, resulting in a longstanding input bottleneck. Even the largest education agencies in the wealthiest states are limited in the number of keypunch machines they can purchase or rent, and in the number of keypunch operators they can employ. A keypunch operator can typically punch 500 to 600 cards a day; this varies, of course, depending upon factors such as the amount of information being recorded and whether the information is alphabetic or numeric. Furthermore, cards must be verified after punching, an operation which commonly requires about 80 percent of the time required for punching. Since the information system considered here is based upon unit record data for school professional staff, it is likely that four to six punch cards would be required to record the information contained in one record. The quantity of keypunch time required to enter into the system and annually update fifty, seventy-five or a hundred thousand unit records would prohibit, at the outset, the production of truly timely educational data. Clearly, the keypunch problem must be overcome.

The input vehicles which seem to hold the most promise for automated statewide information systems are mark-sense sheets and optical scanners. The outstanding advantage of these vehicles is speed. Optical scanners can typically read from 1,000 to 2,000 mark-sense sheets per hour; as a scanner reads, it automatically records the information on punch cards or magnetic tape. To illustrate the speed of this operation, assume that one mark-sense sheet contains one unit record, and that a scanner is punching four cards per record. At the rate of 1,000 sheets per hour, 7,500 records, or 30,000 punch cards, are processed in 7½ hours of operating time (a working day). Without considering verification, approximately 50 keypunch operators would be required to match this volume.

In addition to speed, mark-sense source documents offer other advantages:

- The completion of mark-sense sheets requires no special equipment or training, and consequently
- the task of converting data into machine-usable form can be accomplished by the suppliers of the data rather than by the processors, and thus distributed among tens of thousands of individuals rather than a few.

While the advantages in mark-sensing are significant, the procedure does present certain problems:

- Since the answer area for each question must allow for every possible response, there is a very real limitation on the amount of information that can be recorded on a single sheet.
- Mark-sense sheets are not as simple to complete as some of the more traditional types of forms and as a result;
- they are prone to human error and require extensive quality control procedures to yield valid data.

In short, mark-sense documents must be filled out in controlled situations. In addition, carefully designed edit checks must be built into the scanning operation so that questionable responses can be investigated and corrected, if necessary, before they are entered into the permanent file.

In any information system the design of source documents is of paramount importance. Design is particularly critical when the source documents are mark-sense forms which, as indicated earlier, are not as simple to complete as traditional forms. Whatever type of documents are employed, forms design embodies two prime objectives which, in a sense, are destructive of each other. Ideally, information collection instruments should be simple and concise to facilitate accuracy and speed in completion and processing. At the same time, the instruments need to be complicated to the extent that they must yield that information identified as necessary for sound decision making—without doubt involving some detail. The problem is not easily resolved.

While there are no hard and fast rules for the design of mark-sense sheets, some loose guidelines have emerged from the experiences of users.

1. *Clarity of instructions*
   A great deal of attention must be given to the refinement of instructions accompanying a mark-sense sheet. Whenever space permits, general instructions (i.e., method of marking spaces, care in erasing, sequence of completion, etc.) should be printed on the form itself. Moreover, it is absolutely necessary to provide detailed instructions for each item on the sheet that can be read to respondents as they are completing the form. Item instructions should include definitions of terms where appropriate. For example, asking for a teacher's salary seems a simple enough question. However, the teacher will not know exactly how to answer this question unless he knows whether "salary" should include the $300 additional he receives during the school year for supervising the dramatics club, or the $800 additional he receives for teaching summer classes, etc. Clearly, the term "salary" needs

to be defined as does every other term about which questions could arise.

2. *Mechanical simplicity*

   Since mark-sense forms are by nature more difficult to complete than traditional forms, every effort should be made to simplify, as much as possible, the format and appearance of the form. Questions should be logically grouped and coherently sequenced within groups. Alternate shading of code columns makes filling out the form easier, and thereby reduces errors.

3. *Error control*

   In each item on the sheet, provision should be made for every possible response, but care must be taken to assure that *only* possible responses are provided for. For example, in a question on teachers' total years of educational experience, it would be unwise to allow for more than a two digit response since it is inconceivable that a teacher could have more than 99 years of experience. An additional column or columns would tend to confuse people and raise the error count.

4. *Precision in wording*

   The wording of item titles should be as precise as possible to eliminate misinterpretation of items. An item entitled "months employed" with a two column numerical response area could be interpreted as meaning total number of months employed to date, or number of months employed per year, perhaps including summer employment at some other job. A few extra words in the title will make absolutely clear what is being asked (e.g., "Number of months employed per year by this district"). While such descriptive titles consume space, the benefits to be gained in "clean" information make the investment in space worthwhile.

5. *Objectivity*

   In order to obtain reliable information, questions on the form must be objective not only in format but in content. Simply providing for a "yes-no" response does not guarantee objectivity. The question, "Does your school provide opportunities to students for cultural enrichment?" could be answered positively or negatively depending upon one's judgment regarding what constitutes "opportunities" or "cultural enrichment." A tabulation of the responses to such a question would be virtually meaningless. A more meaningful question might ask whether certain specific procedures were employed to provide students with opportunities for cultural enrichment.

There is no doubt that a statewide information system would require continuous communication among all participants—the schools supplying the data, the processors, and the users. Questions about the meaning and pertinence of information and the validity of requests are bound to occur. When the system is initially implemented, and whenever a substantial change is made in the requested data or its formating, regional training programs will probably need to be conducted for the school superintendents and principals who have responsibility for administering the system in the field. Such training programs will help assure accurate responses and proper handling.

ADVANTAGES

A number of significant advantages will accrue to any state implementing an automated statewide information system. The full implications of such a system will probably not be realized until some years after the system is placed in operation. However, several are immediately apparent.

1. An automated statewide information system will simultaneously meet the basic data needs of the state education agency, the U. S. Office of Education, and other state and federal agencies, as well as local, state, and national professional associations. In addition, since such a system involves the establishment of a statewide bank of basic items of educational data, the implications for research are exciting and far-reaching. The data bank will constitute a universe of elements having clearly identified characteristics. In research problems, the computer will quickly and easily sort out those elements having particular characteristics and draw from them a sample. The sample elements will than be manipulated and studied as desired. In instances where more detailed information is needed than is available in the data bank, special forms will be used to gather those details from the persons and schools in the sample drawn by the computer.

2. In an automated statewide information system, data will be received by the state education department and converted into usable form early in the school year. At the present time, state education agencies are often unable to process and summarize reports received in September or October until the end of the school year; in some instances, summaries are not available until a year or two after data collection. Sadly, some of the information collected by state education agencies is used for specific purposes but never processed in full because the departments simply are not capable of processing it all by hand or by limited machine methods.

3. Computer manipulation will enable the extraction of more information from source data than has ever been possible in the past. Data have not been processed to the fullest benefit of all, again because hand or limited machine methods prohibit really comprehensive treatment. The outstanding value in using computers for information handling is that the speed with which they operate

makes feasible the examination of data from all points of view—turning data about again and again until they have been studied in almost every conceivable way.

It is clear that automated statewide information systems will relieve a large part of the clerical burden of processing information in state education agencies; earlier, it was mentioned that the same benefit would accrue to schools. But why is this so? As indicated in the section entitled "A Suggested Pattern," some two-thirds of the information needs of a state education agency could be satisfied by a well conceived and well operated data system. This is probably a conservative estimate; the full potential of such a system cannot now be realized. An automated statewide information system will yield the maximum of information on a minimum of contacts with the suppliers of the data. This will reduce substantially the number of separate requests for data, not only by the state agency but by other agencies as well. Once it became known that a comprehensive file of educational data existed, it is likely that these users (governmental, professional, etc.) would go to the department first with their information requests. Moreover, schools can be told to refer such requests to the department (if they so desire) on the grounds that even if the information were not available in a summarized form, the department might be able to derive it from its file of basic data. At the very least, the department's computer will draw a sample for the requesting agency so that the whole universe will not have to be surveyed again and again.

4. One other factor is worthy of mention. As an automated statewide information system is implemented, school districts will no doubt gradually begin to modify local records to make them compatible with the statewide system. In time, some degree of compatibility in record keeping among schools will result, thus helping to simplify what is now a difficult problem—data preparation for exchange.

A FINAL WORD

Education consumes an estimated $40 billion of the nation's wealth each year. It is no longer defensible to guide the operation and direction of so vast an enterprise on the basis of inadequate and outdated information. In the last 20 years technology has so developed as to make possible a sweeping assault on the information problem. With a not unreasonable investment of money and effort, streamlined information systems can be developed which will improve the quality of educational leadership and ultimately provide better education for young people. Educators bear primary responsibility for taking the necessary action to give new vigor to the education process; by default, they can allow a condition now barely manageable to deteriorate into chaos.

7 the concept of regional educational data processing centers

ROBERT L. HOWE

ROBERT L. HOWE *received his MA in 1960 from San Jose State College, and his BA in 1952 from the same institution. Mr. Howe's several years of experience include work as a coordinator of distributive education, as a counselor-teacher, and as an assistant in guidance and research.*

His recent activities have included service as chairman of the California State Advisory Committee on Integrated Data Processing, as an information systems consultant to educators on all levels, as executive secretary of the California Curriculum Compatibility and Course Coding Committee, as associate editor of the Educational Data Processing Monograph Series, as an editorial board member of the AEDS Monitor, *as chairman of the Information Systems and Data Processing Committee, of the American School Counselors Association, as state membership chairman for the Association for Measurement and Evaluation in Guidance, and as chairman of the California Educational Data Processing Association's Publications Committee.*

Mr. Howe has written extensively and is the co-author of a text on educational data processing.

Information systems using computers and other data processing equipment are playing an increasingly important role in the operation of educational institutions. These systems may be similar to the old manual methods of data handling, or they may be startlingly different, in that they focus on the means to collect and process data that can be used to generate reports for staff members to use in the decision-making process.

Mechanizing manual methods often is justified on the basis that "you must learn to crawl before you learn to walk." In practice, this is a self-defeating approach and results in doing faster many things that need not be done at all.

A more enlightened approach is to consider *systems* first and then investigate the technological means needed to implement these systems. Much already has been written about systems, but it is important to consider the total system approach to educational data processing. Fig. 8 shows the total integrated system approach.

This system includes data from each segment of the educational program. As part of the ongoing activities of each segment, data will

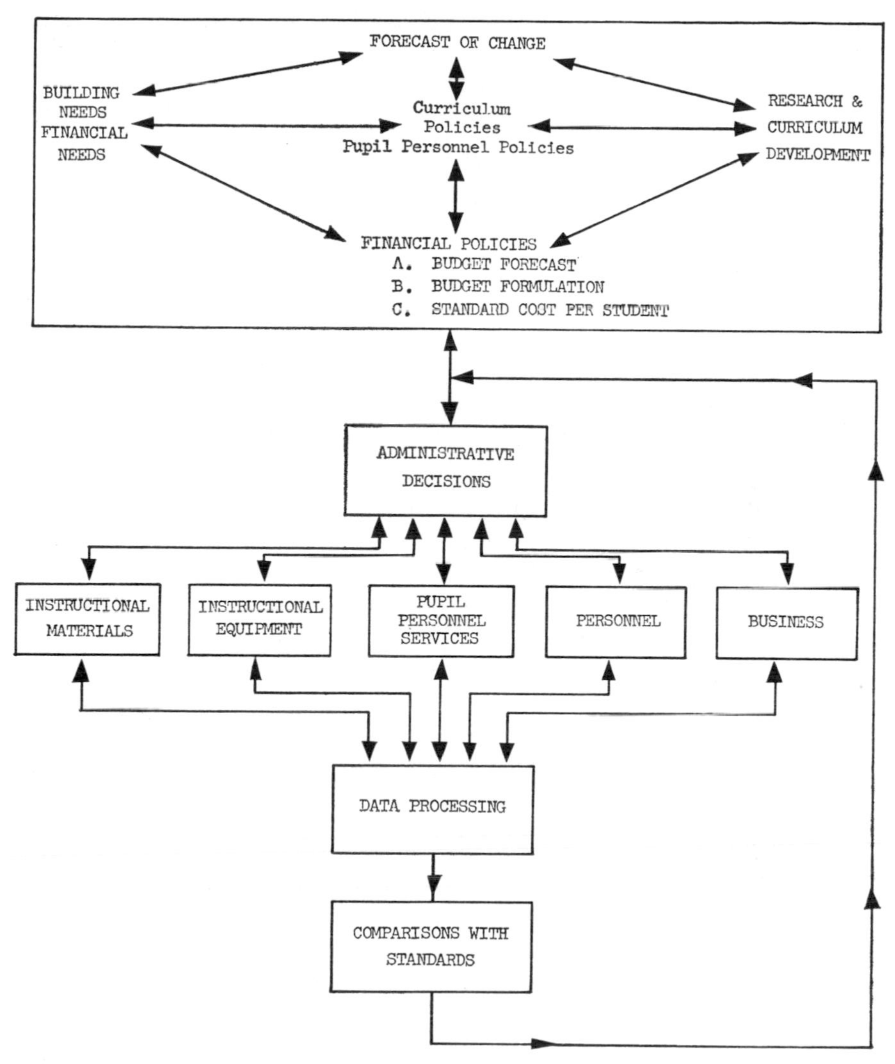

Fig. 8 – A Total Integrated System Approach.

flow into the information system. This information will be integrated so that it need not be collected by anyone else, but is available to those who appropriately can use it. This type of system will provide more effective use of information at each level of teaching, counseling, and administering, will require less clerical work at each level, and, ultimately, will result in a better educational program.

This systems approach to the information needs of an educational institution calls for a specification and definition of the data and reports needed for operating the school. It calls for the establishment of procedures for collecting, processing, and integrating these data so that a smooth flow results. The system will specify the reports to be generated either on a regular or exception basis, when they are to be prepared, and to whom they are to be directed. Once the system has been defined, technology can be called upon to speed the processing.

In defining the system, the basic data elements of the system also have been specified. Frequently, these data elements are common to similar educational institutions and can be used to establish a "common data base." The total system approach then becomes more and more reasonable as the information problem is viewed in a global sense.

Having data and data systems that are comparable between and among institutions will, for example, provide the bases for establishing some uniformity in transcript information and format. Additionally, this data base will provide the means of developing a better picture of the status of education at the local, state, and national levels. By providing this information to educational administrators and to the legislators who shape educational policy, it is likely that decisions affecting the educational program will be more realistic and favorable.

But, problems arise when an attempt is made to implement this total integrated system in a school or school district. These problems center on money, personnel, and facilities. Local districts, regional groupings, and state departments of education in several areas of the United States have initiated activities to resolve some of these problems. California has been involved in both systems development and systems implementation since 1958, and this chapter is based on the experience derived during that time.

DEVELOPMENTAL SYSTEMS WORK IN CALIFORNIA

In California a great deal of ferment has taken place during the past eight years. Under the leadership of the State Department of Education (CSDE) a successful state pilot project in data processing has been carried out. This further led the CSDE to set in motion a research and development undertaking that prepared the way for a statewide system of data processing and communication systems in education.

At the heart of this enterprise was a concept that looks to the establishment and demonstration of a series of regional centers in which each center ultimately will be linked by high-speed communication devices to each school under its operational jurisdiction. In turn, each center is to be linked to the other centers by additional communication devices. Summary data in precise reports can then be developed which are comprehensive, accurate, and timely. These are the tools that can and must build firm foundations for decision making. It is equally important that these tools be put into the hands of the counselors and the students at the time they are needed—when judgments are to be weighed and decisions are to be reached.

A team of skilled specialists working with the EDP (Educational Data Processing) Project of the CSDE developed the concept of an effective educational information system. The team, working with departmental personnel, to date has accomplished the following:

Phase 1: In 1958, the CSDE, recognizing the problem involved in meeting the challenge of the technology of our times, appointed an advisory committee to investigate the status of data processing systems in the schools of the state. Responsibilities of the committee were:

1. Investigating current operations involved in the processing of pupil information in an attempt to define effectiveness, efficiency, and cost of such operations.
2. Determining if data processing equipment and procedures could improve the efficiency and/or reduce the cost of processing pupil data.
3. Establishing a pilot data processing center to test procedures and theories in operational settings.
4. Determining the feasibility of establishing a statewide integrated data processing system for data in California schools.
5. Determining if a research and development center should be established for the purpose of continuing research and appraisal of data processing for education.

Phase 2: As a result of this study, a pilot center, supported by Title V of the NDEA (National Defense Education Act), was established in the Richmond, California, School District. This punched card equipment center was launched to determine if the committee's goals were realistic and to provide an operational view of the problems which might be encountered in developing machine programs with the flexibility and compatibility needed for educational record keeping, as well as to prepare the reports of desirable practice and illustrations of machine programs and procedures. This pilot project also provided an on-site inservice orientation for educators to familiarize them with data processing on a conceptual level.

The pilot center was in operation from July 1960 to June 1963 and served 35,000 pupils in 25 schools in five school districts located in five separate counties.

In the original documents reporting the work, views, and plans of the advisory committee, the possibility of extending or facilitating the local development of the types of services provided by the Richmond Pilot Project throughout the state was discussed. The committee recommended that as major support for such local centers and as a stimulus for improving the effectiveness of all such systems, a common center for research and development in data processing as applied to educational data be established. It was recommended that this center be established within the CSDE so that the organization and control of such a unit could be under state direction.

Phase 3: As a result of this recommendation a research and development project in educational data processing was established in the CSDE on July 1, 1962. This three-year project was jointly sponsored by the CSDE and the Cooperative Research Branch of the USOE. Responsibility for guiding the project to a successful conclusion rested with a team of professional educators and a competent technical staff, both of whom have had considerable experience in the areas of pupil personnel and curricular services as well as educational data processing.

The project was designed to serve the following major purposes:

1. Design and development of model systems of collecting and handling data to meet the requirements of educational functions, including the analysis of existing systems and a planned transition to more effective systems.
2. Conduct and support simulation studies in such areas as data processing (pre-trial of new systems), and in specific applications such as student scheduling, guidance, validation of counseling procedures, and curriculum changes.
3. Development of proposals for a cooperative establishment of compatible systems for the mutual benefit of local school systems.
4. Provision for consultation to local school systems.

Phase 4: The EDP Project staff completed the three-year project with the development of a comprehensive information system for pupil personnel services. From January to June of 1965 the system was demonstrated to groups of educators from throughout the country, using live data in actual settings supplied by the Sacramento and Ventura (California) Regional Centers. Results of this three years of work represented a dramatic breakthrough in systems creativity and a dynamic attempt to correlate the heretofore random data collected in an educational information system. This work illustrated the desirability of relating all aspects of pupil data into an integrated and meaningful system. In addition, it was felt that the time had come to enlarge the scope of the project and develop a complete educational information system. This meant broadening the concept to include not only pupil personnel services but all remaining areas of education including:

- Instructional materials and equipment.
- Professional and clerical personnel.
- Business services.

The USOE, through the Cooperative Research Branch, concurred in this appraisal and granted additional funds to extend the work of the ongoing EDP Project. In addition, the demonstration of an exemplary information system on a statewide basis, and the opportunity to train educators in the use of both information systems *and* information led to an Elementary and Secondary Education Act (ESEA) Title III operational grant to fund regional centers on a short-term basis.

PREPARING THE WAY FOR REGIONAL CENTERS

The work of the Richmond Pilot Project, and the continuing efforts of the EDP Project in Sacramento have proved that a regional cooperative venture in educational data processing is not only possible but workable. Until recently, data processing systems had been confined primarily to separate school districts. After three years of experimentation, however, the Richmond Pilot Project concluded that (1) large districts, those with 30,000 or more average daily attendance, and (2) organized regional groups, embracing several districts within each region, could operate data processing systems with foreseeably good results. It was further concluded that a regional type of system would offer more advantages than would a separate or local type, regardless of district size, and that the comparison is particularly pertinent to systems used by small and medium-size districts.

ADVANTAGES OF A REGIONAL SYSTEM

Among the advantages of a regional type of educational data processing operation are the following:

1. It is less expensive to furnish and operate one central installation for a region consisting of a number of school districts than to furnish and operate a separate installation for each of the same number of districts.

2. The benefits derived from the learnings, developments, and improvements that take place at the processing center in a regional system can be applied to a large number of schools, not just to a few schools.
3. A higher degree of central staff competency is more likely to be realized in a regional system than in a multitude of local district systems.
4. There is greater uniformity of procedures and products in a regional venture than can be found among separate district systems.
5. The various districts cooperating in a regional system can contribute valuable suggestions to the total effort. This is true because of the large number of schools participating and the unique differences existing among the districts in the system.

Data processing systems in scattered school districts have been developed rather haphazardly during recent years to meet the pressing needs of each local situation. Despite the hard work of the systems personnel in these districts, certain problems have been known to generate trouble—for example: inefficiencies due to inadequate equipment and/or lack of sufficiently trained personnel, failure to integrate properly the data processing applications with the district's educational program, and excessive involvement with needs of the moment at the expense of well-planned procedures that would take care of many needs over a reasonably long period of time.

In a regional type of venture, however, these problems are minimized or removed altogether. Much more thought, for example, is given to integrating data processing operations with the educational programs everywhere in the region served.

Any educational data processing system, whether district or regional, can run into serious difficulties if (1) the developmental phases of the processing program are not consigned to competent, well-trained personnel; and (2) quick and effective methods of communication between the center's staff and the schools are not established from the outset.

Moreover, the willingness of system participants to work out mutual problems, to cooperate, to compromise if necessary, to consider the progress of all users rather than the gain of a few—this is indispensable to the healthy functioning of a regional data processing system.

CLIENTS FOR REGIONAL CENTERS

The regional center should be considered a service organization. Its primary function should be that of providing data processing services which cannot be efficiently maintained or operated in local districts. On the basis of practical administration, regional centers can successfully handle the processing of data originating in three major types of districts.

Small School Districts

Small districts of less than 10,000 average daily attendance may wish to send original source documents (business office, payroll, and inventory records, teacher certification information, instructional and pupil data such as machine-scorable test answer sheets, registration materials, attendance-accounting records, mark-reporting rosters, etc.) directly to the regional center for processing. These districts typically do not have sufficient volume to warrant the purchase and use of their own data processing equipment for handling these materials; they could obtain data processing services for less financial cost and with greater speed than by manual methods. For such districts a regional center could offer tangible ways of meeting their needs.

School Districts of Medium Size

Medium-sized districts of from 10,000 to 30,000 average daily attendance typically find justification for minimal data processing equipment. The term "minimal" refers to that equipment which is necessary to convert information on source documents into punched card or tape form. In the field of testing, the typical example is a district having a scoring machine, a keypunch, and perhaps a sorter, a reproducer, a tabulator, and an interpreter. This equipment allows for punching the data onto cards, sorting information for desired groups, and printing rosters of results. Such a district could then submit punched card data to the regional center for specialized compilation, tabulation, and distribution, and for special reports and analyses.

Large School Districts

Large districts maintaining a fairly complete line of data processing equipment that allows for a number of operations, including the conversion of basic source material into data processing form, would frequently find it desirable to utilize a regional center for student scheduling, special computational analyses, and complex statistical analyses of data.

PROCESSING PROCEDURES AND REPORTING METHODS

A planned structure of regional processing procedures and reporting methods should, desirably, be developed by consensus of the school districts participating in the regional system. Uniformity of processing design will invariably result in economy, greater speed, and reliability. One of the major responsibilities of the regional center would be to offer coordination and leadership in effective and reliable methods of handling (1) pupil personnel data and (2) information in other important areas. Local reports for cumulative records could be made compatible with the data processing system to be utilized in the regional operation, and this would facilitate inter- and intra-district exchange of pupil information.

SUGGESTED CRITERIA FOR THE ESTABLISHMENT OF REGIONAL CENTERS

The following criteria and/or determinants are suggested for the serious consideration of county offices of education and school districts that wish to establish a regional center for processing educational data. These criteria have been derived almost entirely from practical field experience.

1. *Adequate student population*
   Estimates by the staff of the EDP Project, based on field observations, the Richmond Pilot Project, and projections from the Sacramento and Ventura (California) Regional Centers, indicate that a desirable student population serviced by a center will vary between a minimum of 100,000 and a maximum of 300,000.
2. *Administrative commitment*
   It is anticipated that no center will be able to function efficiently and effectively without the support of the top administrators (superintendent, board of education, and when appropriate the board of supervisors) in each of the user school districts. This support should be active rather than passive, because an indifferent approach by the administration may encourage the development of less than the full potential of the system.
3. *Demonstrated interest*
   Local districts and county offices of education should initiate activities in school information systems, rather than have their interest probed by others.
4. *Desire to develop compatibility systems*
   An added and greatly needed feature in school information systems is that of compatibility with other educational systems. The data must be in basic units that make it possible to exchange comparable information with other school districts, counties, the CSDE, and other agencies. The interchange of data is desirable within subsystems on an integrated basis (e.g., test data and achieved marks) at the local level, and it also is desirable to exchange appropriate data with other school districts and the county and CSDE. Compatible systems will relieve educators

of many of the clerical aspects of data preparation for exchange by shifting this burden to machines.

5. *Geographic location*
   The site of a regional center should be such that it is accessible for necessary meetings, inservice training, data delivery and/or pickup, etc. Cooperative efforts can be enhanced by a proper selection of the center site.
6. *Availability and/or cost of conversion of physical facilities*
   The facilities needed for housing a center should be located within existing educational structures. The cost of converting these to meet hardware (wiring, temperature, humidity, floor capacity, etc.) and other operating specifications (storage, classroom availability, etc.) must be considered.
7. *Operation by an intermediate unit*
   Most local districts are neither equipped nor staffed to service other districts. Intermediate units—the county office of education—have primary responsibility for this function. Areas considering regional efforts should be organized under the unit that best can develop, organize, and administer a regional operation.
8. *Willingness to share total costs*
   The support of a regional center entails more than the cost of direct services to the pupil. Site preparation, maintenance, and all other overhead expenses must be considered.
9. *Leadership personnel available*
   Each center also needs a top administrator (e.g., assistant superintendent) to assume overall responsibility for the success of the center. This person needs an understanding of electronic data processing concepts so that he will appreciate the problems and possibilities as they are presented by the user and the staff.
10. *Direct top administrative support by the intermediate unit*
    The administration of the unit housing a center must be totally committed to regional cooperation and educational data processing. Without this, the superintendent and/or the boards of education may find it necessary and/or more convenient to let regional problems slide, much to the detriment of the program.
11. *Ability to finance the program*
    A regional center requires a minimum yearly budget of $225,000. These funds may be from any legitimate source—county government, state, local district, etc.
12. *Willingness to promote uniform practices to improve efficiency in educational data systems*
    Local districts served by a center must be willing to use certain proven basic data systems, such as those developed by the EDP Project staff, or be willing to finance the development of their own system so that the data will be compatible with the EDP

Project format. This will obviate the need for a great deal of costly research and systems development, and will permit a more rapid extension of services to schools within the region. These basic systems will provide the means for better data exchange and report simplification. Local programs above and beyond the basic system would be developed by the center at the expense of its users.

BY-PRODUCT SERVICES

The regional type of processing center can offer substantial by-product services—for example, the compilation of common types of pupil personnel records for research and analysis. The center can provide unbiased and confidential analyses of data pertaining to educational functions in many districts. Being the depository for regional information, the center is in a position to conduct various significant studies of broad regional scope, such as salary surveys, certification analyses, etc.

REGIONAL STEERING COMMITTEES

It has been found that a realistic, practical method of maintaining uniformity and workability of operations in a regional EDP center is the guidance rendered by a regional steering committee. Such a committee (1) is typically composed of district and county personnel with well-defined leadership qualifications, and (2) gives active assistance to the regional center in terms of policy, operation, and guidance. Of basic importance, of course, is a policy statement which should be drawn up before the committee goes into action. The following statement by an existing steering committee can be considered a typical example. There will be variations as new regional centers are established, but all policy statements should strive for uniformity and compatibility of services rendered.

Policy Statement: Sacramento Regional Educational Data Processing Steering Committee

The Sacramento Regional Data Processing Center is established through the cooperative efforts of participating school districts and county offices of education in several counties, the California State Department of Education, and assistance from the U. S. Office of Education.

The purpose of the Center is to provide educational data processing services to the school districts of the region.

The Center is under the direct administration of the Sacramento County Superintendent of Schools and the Sacramento County Board of Education. The Office of the Sacramento County Superintendent of Schools and the Sacramento County Board of Education recognize that the cooperative nature of this service demands that the policies governing the administration of the Center must reflect the wishes and needs of the districts being served.

Therefore, a committee that is representative of the school districts being served by the Center has been established to develop and recommend, to the Sacramento County Board of Education and the Office of the Sacramento County Superintendent of Schools, policies that will govern the administration of this regional educational data processing center. Listed below is an outline of the organization and functions of the Committee that will determine the policies recommended for the operation of the Sacramento Regional Data Processing Center.

I. Name of Committee:

The name of the policy-determining committee shall be "The Sacramento Regional Educational Data Processing Steering Committee."

II. Committee Membership:

A. Voting members:

1. There shall be seven members.
2. Each member shall be elected at large by all the representatives of participating school districts that are contracting for services from the Regional Data Processing Center.
3. Candidates for election shall be district or county office of education personnel who have administrative responsibility for data processing in their respective school districts or county offices of education.

B. Non-voting members:

1. The Assistant Superintendent of the Office of the Sacramento County Superintendent of Schools: Chairman of the Committee
2. The Director and the Manager of the Regional Data Processing Center
3. Representatives from the Research and Development Center in Educational Data Processing, California State Department of Education
4. Selected advisory committees that may be organized for special data processing programs in areas such as business, curriculum, audio-visual aids, the school library

C. Term of membership:

The membership elected to the Committee will serve a term of three years, with two members being elected each year and three members being elected every third year. (Note:

Prior to the present revised policy statement, there were five elected representatives to the Steering Committee.)

Starting January, 1965, two active Committee members will continue their terms until January, 1966, and one active member will continue his term until 1967. Of the four new members elected in December, 1964, two will serve terms expiring in January, 1967, and two will serve terms expiring in January, 1968. Lots will be drawn to determine which members will serve terms expiring in 1967. Newly elected members shall become active members on the first day of January subsequent to their election in December of the immediately preceding year.

D. Officers:

The Assistant Superintendent from the Office of the Sacramento County Superintendent of Schools will serve as Chairman of the Committee and shall be responsible for keeping accurate minutes of the meetings and sending out notices of regular and special meetings.

E. Regular meetings:

The committee shall meet regularly on the morning of the first Tuesday of each month. Special meetings may be called at the discretion of the Chairman.

F. Annual meetings of participating school districts:

On the second Tuesday in December, the administrative heads of all participating school districts shall meet for the purpose of hearing reports on data processing services by the Center and to hear of proposed new services for the succeeding years.

This group shall have the responsibility for electing members to the Steering Committee and to review and approve the charges to be made to school districts for the succeeding year. Each administrative head among all participating school districts and participating county offices of education present at the meeting shall be entitled to one vote.

III. Functions of the Steering Committee:

A. To develop rules and regulations governing the operation of the Steering Committee

B. To develop policies for recommendations—to be made to the Board of Education and to the administrative staff of the Sacramento County Superintendent of Schools—concerning the operation of the Regional Data Processing Center. These policies shall be concerned with the following:

1. Determination of the extent of the services to the users of the system
   a. Addition of new services

b. Deletion of existing services
c. Quantity of services
d. Addition of new school districts or new county offices of education to the service region

2. Determination of the annual budget for EDP services
3. Determination of EDP procedures to be followed by contracting school districts and by operators of the Center's machine room and equipment—such procedures to be drawn up in written form
4. Determination of staffing for the Regional Data Pro cessing Center
5. Determination of plans for the improvement of data processing facilities, including the addition or deletion of hardware capabilities of the Regional Center

IV. Organization of the Service:

A. The Assistant Superintendent of the Sacramento County Office of Education, subject to administrative direction from the Sacramento County Superintendent of Schools, shall:

1. Provide administrative direction to the staff of the Regional Center and make recommendations to the Sacramento County Superintendent of Schools and the Sacramento County Board of Education regarding the staffing and operation of the Center
2. Develop and administer the budget for the data processing services
3. Develop and initiate service contracts between the Center and the contracting school districts, between the Center and county offices contracting on behalf of school districts, and between the Center and other agencies

B. County coordination:

Each participating county office of education shall appoint a staff member as an educational data processing coordinator whose responsibilities shall be:

1. To represent his respective county on a regional committee of county educational data processing coordinators
2. To organize and provide leadership as necessary, with the school districts in his respective county, regarding the use of educational data processing
3. To expedite the movement of EDP materials in and out of the schools of the county
4. To discuss possible new EDP applications with school district personnel and make recommendations to the Coordination Committee
5. In cooperation with the Director of the Center, to plan and conduct inservice meetings with district personnel in his respective county

SPECIAL CONSIDERATIONS FOR REGIONAL CENTERS

The following special considerations are proposed for the benefit of regional educational data processing systems:

1. *Charges for Services*
   The charges for services rendered by cooperatively shared data processing facilities are best based upon the actual costs of operation. Processing centers that are administered, planned, and maintained by public education funds need not operate at the profit that is necessary to private enterprise. Considerable financial savings are possible if appropriate educational groups or agencies are formed to secure maximum and efficient use of the processing equipment. Educational data processing units are not established to do contract work for private individuals, nor are they in competition with private enterprise. They represent an efficient service organization, the purpose of which is to provide with greater speed and accuracy and at lower cost the machine processing of heretofore manually processed data.
2. *Channels of Communication*
   Continuous communication must be maintained between individuals utilizing pupil personnel records and the data processing center. Questions concerning the accuracy or meaning of data may recur despite the fact that the same forms and procedures may have been used over a period of years. With any change in form or in methods of reporting data, thorough inservice activities must be conducted if the data are to be accurately reported on source documents and appropriately utilized.
3. *Administration of the Regional Center*
   The administration of any regional data processing center must be under the direct supervision of a central administrative officer. Without sufficient authority and proper judicial powers on the part of the administrative head of the regional system, data processing operations may be subjected to "pressure politics" in which favoritism, calamity, or expediency could destroy established procedure, nullify priority, and throw time schedules into confusion.
4. *Ownership of Materials*
   Materials handled by the data processing unit may not become the property of the data processing center. As a service unit within an educational system, the data processing group should provide assurance that data will be accurately and efficiently processed and that the results will be returned to the submitting school or agency as its own property for distribution and interpretation. The processing center can well be the custodian of the source information, documents, cards, and tapes but never the "owner."

With the exception of certain types of attendance accounting for financial reimbursement, as well as state testing program data, school data should not become public information and should not be available for general distribution or interpretation without the consent of the school or administrative officer responsible for the data.

5. *Periodic Conferences*
   Periodic meetings of data processors and cooperating school personnel for the purpose of compiling suggestions and evaluations should be a necessary function of any regional processing unit. While data processing centers should not dictate what records will be maintained, it is also true that school workers may not be able to visualize the most advantageous form or analysis of data through which the processing center can economically and quickly produce the desired end results. Such conferences will help the processors and the school personnel to achieve mutual benefits.

HOW TO ORGANIZE A REGIONAL EDUCATIONAL DATA PROCESSING CENTER

Experience has taught that a regional center for educational data processing cannot be brought into being by action of county administration alone. When decisions involving a regional system are made at top administrative level and are then filtered down through the ranks, local school districts often react negatively by resisting the program and showing an unwillingness to cooperate in the system. A project of this value and magnitude cannot be organized simply for the sake of organizing it. Its sights must be set on the schools—their staffs and their students. Its goal must be that of helping education.

It follows, then, that cooperation must be the keynote. Although spearheaded by the originating county office of education, a regional system needs to be based on the clear-headed understanding, mutual planning, and enthusiastic efforts of *all* the prospective users.

Suggested Plan of Organization

Over a period of years the staff of the EDP Project of the CSDE has worked cooperatively with county offices of education and local school districts throughout California in evolving a workable scheme of organizational planning and action for regional centers. This plan consists of the following practical steps, which may serve as guidelines for those who are interested in the regional concept:

1. The first step is usually that of holding an initial meeting for the purpose of discussing the regional center concept. To lay the groundwork, representatives of a county office of education

typically contact the director of the EDP Project, Sacramento, and request that such a meeting be arranged. The county superintendent then invites all the top personnel of his staff and, if possible, one or more members of the county board of education to attend. When the conference takes place, every effort is made by the CSDE personnel to impart whatever information is needed for basic planning.

2. If, as a result of this meeting, the members of the county superintendent's staff feel they wish to move ahead, the next step is to contact adjoining and nearby county offices of education and arrange a joint meeting of those staffs wishing to participate in a regional venture. A representative of the EDP Project would help to coordinate this second conference.
3. If agreements are reached among the counties to work cooperatively in the proposed project, the next task—a highly important one—is to conduct an overall informational meeting to which all local school district superintendents and other administrators in each interested county are invited. The need for district cooperation and the benefits that would accrue to the schools in a regional enterprise of this kind would be keynotes of the meeting.
4. With the assistance of the EDP Project staff, local meetings in each county would then be held to clarify the regional center concept, to encourage school district participation, to discuss details of services and costs, and to supply any other information that might be needed.
5. When sufficient interest is shown throughout the region to warrant moving ahead, the parent county, which is usually the one to house and administer the center, should then introduce the topic of a regional data processing system at the next meeting of the county board of education, this would be done to secure the authorization needed for drawing up plans for the center and preparing a tentative budget.
6. Final plans and a budget for the proposed center are presented to the county board. Approval is secured.
7. Next in the process is the hiring of a director for the regional center and allowing him, in turn, to hire his data processing manager at least six months prior to the center's opening.
8. Contracts for services with local school districts should be prepared and signed.
9. A document detailing the scope and extent of cooperation and assistance to be received from other county offices of education in the region should be drawn up. The document must be approved by all parties concerned.
10. With the guidance and cooperation of the EDP Project, decisions should be reached as to the equipment that will be necessary and appropriate to carry out the new center's objectives.

11. The parent county and the cooperating counties should then select and design the data processing site.
12. With the help of the manufacturers chosen to supply the needed equipment,
    (a) a timetable for delivery of the computer and related equipment should be planned; and
    (b) the timetable for site preparation should be completed.
13. A policy, or steering, committee should be established along the lines previously suggested.
14. Local school districts participating in the system should be asked to appoint district coordinators.
15. Cooperating county offices of education should be asked to appoint county coordinators.
16. A professional educator with background in counseling and guidance *and* educational data processing should then be hired to serve as assistant to the director of the regional center. This person would have primary responsibility for the testing program and also would be responsible for inservice training.
17. All plans should now be completed in cooperation with the elected steering committee and the staff of the EDP Project.
18. A volunteer school district should be selected, and pilot operations in cooperation with an already established data processing center should be launched. This phase is intended to test the plans, systems, and procedures that have been devised for the new center. The location for this phase, moreover, serves as an in-service training site.
19. Actual operations at the new center should commence with a limited population for the full range of proposed services.

It should take approximately 18 months to proceed from Step 1 to the time the new center is "on the air."

Suggested Staffing Pattern

The following is a suggested staffing pattern for a typical beginning regional data processing center:

- The director (professional educator with experience in data processing)
- Assistant director or consultant (professional educator who may have limited experience in educational data processing)
- Manager of educational data processing services (a technician)
- Two console operator/programers
- Two document reader and/or keypunch operators
- A secretary
- A control clerk

This pattern will vary with the size of the center and the extent of the services offered. However, it is vital that staff be adequate—

in both competency and numbers—to assure the success of the operation.

BASIC QUESTIONS AND ANSWERS ABOUT REGIONAL DATA PROCESSING CENTERS

In the relatively new field of educational data processing, many questions are apt to arise about its purposes, its functions, its operations, the kinds of equipment it requires, the personnel involved, budgetary costs, the benefits that can be realized from it, and so on. As the need for cooperative effort becomes greater, questions from school people about the regional center concept are being asked with increasing frequency. The following section attempts to answer some of the most basic questions in this field of inquiry.

Why should data processing centers be operated on a regional basis?

Data processing is a big business. It is also costly. While it is true that in the past few years the cost of automated equipment has gone down and, on the other hand, the power and sophistication of the equipment have increased, the fact remains that most school districts will never be able to attack the total problem of information without access to a computer. Keysort, punched card, and other piecemeal approaches will not solve the problem. Speeding up the handling of information that does not need to be handled at all is not the solution either.

Local districts, therefore, are increasingly faced with the choice of developing an information system within their own boundaries (or adopting an existing system); or taking the opportunity of participating in a regional EDP enterprise. Larger, more sophisticated equipment can process data on a lower per-unit cost than a multiplicity of smaller installations. It has been shown that a single, sophisticated, well-staffed regional center can better serve the schools within a geographic area than could a number of isolated centers in the same area, each serving one district.

What is a regional center for processing educational data?

A regional center for processing educational data is a central physical plant—equipped with appropriate facilities and personnel—which conducts data processing operations for the benefit of a number of school districts in one or more counties located in a convenient geographic area. This regional center is the core of a cooperative system that is typically the result of real needs of school districts which may not be able to afford the purchase and operation of their own equipment, and/or which subscribe to the proposition that a regional system is nearly always more practical and more efficient than a local one.

A regional system of this kind is a joint effort on the part of educators at the local and intermediate level to resolve the ever growing problem of how to collect, process, and report pupil personnel data and other school information in such a way that intelligence reports on the status of education can be assured on the basis of *reliability* and *efficiency*.

What does the regional center do?

The regional center processes school data by means of efficient, high-speed automation—in sharp contrast to the slow, tedious manual methods traditionally used by teachers, counselors, administrators, and clerks. Areas of information for machine processing at the center include testing of various kinds, mark reporting, preparation of data for cumulative folders and permanent records, attendance accounting, student registration, and scheduling of student courses and classes. In addition to these, district payroll operations can be run. While regional services now mainly involve pupil personnel services, the program soon will be expanded to involve all business functions, instructional materials and equipment, and both classified and professional personnel.

Automated processing at a regional center can relate items of information from any sub-unit so that the data can be correlated for useful purposes—for example, between test scores and marks achieved in class. The development of a total information system in education will allow a great many things to be accomplished, including the first true cost analysis of each aspect of various school programs.

What happens to local district data processing installations when regional centers come into being?

School districts that are large enough to justify current installations of data processing equipment can select their own future patterns. First, they may decide to continue using their equipment to do whatever things they can do best. In peakload periods they may choose to shunt certain overloads to the regional center for processing. They may also decide that they can better serve their schools by maintaining their district installations for the preparation of data for regional center processing. In this way, collection, correction, and coordination could be handled by district personnel while the ultimate processing would be handled at the regional level.

A second choice might be that the local district could dispense with most or all of its equipment but retain key personnel in its staff of data processors. The major role of the district staff would be the channeling of data processing forms and documents through the data processing staff, handling the district's inservice orientation, and coordinating district efforts with the regional center. The actual machine processing of all data would be accomplished at the regional center.

The region served by the center would include local school districts and county offices of education. Participants in the regional system would be those who would wish to utilize the center's services. Since the center would be run and managed by its customers, the system would be truly a cooperative endeavor. Areas of cooperation would include the development of information systems above the system developed by the EDP Project as a data base for all centers; the types, qualities, and volumes of data to be processed; input and output forms; and all other essential aspects of operations at the center.

What is the role of the State Department of Education?

California and the federal government are currently cooperating in the development of an efficient system for processing school data. The EDP Project, with headquarters in Sacramento, is acting as the developmental arm of this joint effort between the CSDE at the state level and the USOE at the national level.

The role of the CSDE, then, may be considered as twofold: that of development and coordination. The CSDE is assuming leadership in the development of educational intelligence systems. It is developing the systems from the standpoint of the local school district rather than from the departmental level. The EDP Project staff has worked with more than 100 educators throughout the state in developing the current pupil personnel subsystem and has expanded its work through the various associations and field workers to include business, curriculum, personnel, and all other essential areas. The ultimate goal is the development of a total system for processing educational data.

What is the cost of operating a regional center?

Several studies made in the past few years indicate that the yearly per-pupil cost for processing student information at the secondary level ranges from $2.50 to $3.50. Much depends on the type of equipment, the competency of the staff, and other related factors, including the volume of data being processed. The cost at the elementary level might range from $1.25 to $1.75 per pupil. On the basis of experience derived from a three-year pilot study, it is anticipated that all data processing applications, including all the elements in a total system, could be handled at a per-pupil cost of approximately $3. This is assuming that the regional center serves a minimum of 100,000 students. A simple projection would show that 100,000 multiplied by $3 would total $300,000. A maximum enrollment probably would be in the neighborhood of 300,000 students.

When do the regional centers begin operations?

The first regional centers working in conjunction with the EDP Project began operations in July of 1965. The Sacramento Regional Center serves 15 counties in northern California; The Central Valley Regional Center serves 7 counties in central California; the Ventura Regional Center serves 3 counties in southern California. Because considerable interest has been shown in the regional center concept, 9 additional centers have been designated, and it is believed that by 1970 there will be 15–20 regional centers operating in California. The twofold key to success in these regional centers is thorough planning and in-depth orientation of the participants.

Where should the equipment be located?

Location of regional data processing equipment is actually of little concern. This point must be emphasized because many feel that possession and/or location of the hardware is of prime consideration for successful information processing. This is not true. Today—and this would be even more applicable tomorrow—the fixed location of the processing equipment need not be a prime factor in the development of an educational processing system. Educators must be concerned with *access* to technological facilities but do not need to have the equipment located in any designated spot.

The really important factor is that the educator must devote his time and effort to the development of an *efficient information system*. Any technological problem in implementing this system should be left to the technical staff. If a computer or any other piece of hardware is needed, it can be as near or as far as practical considerations dictate.

Within the foreseeable future, computer techniques and facilities providing even the smallest school district with access to needed machines will be developed. Computing centers in Massachusetts are already processing data from sources halfway around the world. In southern California data are stored and retrieved on machines for the benefit of users thousands of miles away. These systems are classified as real-time or on-line systems. A more understandable term is "immediate information systems."

What kinds of reports can be generated by the regional center?

Once a data base has been established, the preparation of needed reports and statistics will be greatly facilitated. For example, an irregular attendance report (Fig. 9) is generated from the data collected as part of the attendance accounting system. This irregular attendance report can be used for administrative or counseling needs. It contains the names of those students who have been classified by a given district as irregular in attendance. This is an exception-type report and contains only the names of those students who qualify for this irregular classification. In addition to the student name, the number of days absent during the month and the cumulative number of days during the school year are listed. The cumulative absence by days of the week is listed so that patterns can be identified. Relevant aptitude and achievement test scores and the most recent mark-point average are included. Space is also allocated for computer generated remarks.

This type of management-by-exception report can easily be pre-

IRREGULAR ATTENDANCE ANALYSIS — ALTA MADRE (SCHOOL NAME) — 1212 VALLEYROAD (SCHOOL ADDRESS) — 4 2 — 65 5 5 65 (DATE OF ATTENDANCE PER) — JUAREZ (COUNSELOR)

STUDENT IDENTIFICATION	ABSENCES THIS		PATTERN					RELATED FACTORS					NOTES
	MONTH	YEAR	M	T	W	T	F	APT	READ	ARITH	LANG	CURRENT GPA	
BERLIN, GLORIA J.	3	14	7	1	1	1	4	7	8	8	7	3.15	
MOORE, THOMAS A.	5	26	5	3	4	3	9	5	3	5	3	1.99	
NOYES, TANIA R.	3	4	1	2	1	-	-	8	7	7	6	3.57	
OLSON, ROGER ---	6	6	2	1	1	1	1	6	5	5	6	3.13	
PIMENTAL, JESSE N.	4	12	6	-	-	-	6	4	4	4	4	2.65	
WASHINGTON, CARVER B.	14	15	3	3	3	3	3	6	6	5	6	3.35	

Fig. 9 — Irregular Attendance Analysis.

pared to spotlight those students who are not meeting the minimum attendance requirements established by the district. This report can be prepared for the counselor as a tool in working with his counselees or for the administrator assigned to the attendance area.

An example of a 100 percent report that is based on the integrated system concept is the California Guidance Record (CGR) This new secondary school guidance form (Fig. 10), which can be used as a college transcript, was developed by the EDP Project. The form contains information derived from the various segments of the pupil information system. A uniform statewide course code is an important aspect of this form's usefulness.

CALIFORNIA GUIDANCE RECORD

STUDENT NO.	STUDENT IDENTIFICATION	YEAR IN SCHOOL	SCHOOL NAME	SCHOOL ADDRESS	CURRENT DATE	COUNSELOR NAME
A266233145	THOMPSON JAMES	SOPHOMORE	BRUNSWICK H S	50 SPRING ST.	10/27/64	TONAN

BIRTHDATE	SEX	PARENT - GUARDIAN NAME	PARENT - GUARDIAN ADDRESS	PREVIOUS SCHOOL NAME	ENTRY DATE	DATE LEFT
4/17/49	M	THOMPSON ROBERT	2315 PLEASANT ST.	R P COFFIN JR. HIGH	9 - 64	

HOME TELEPHONE: 916 235 7450

FOR SCHOOL USE ONLY → MOTHER SEP. DEAD OCCUP. 14077 / FATHER SEP. DEAD OCCUP. 89711

COURSE NO.	COURSE TITLE	MARK	CR.	DATE COMPLETED
A06055	ENGLISH 2-A	C	5	2/65
G06055	U.S. HIST.	C	5	2/65
I06065	AUTO SHOP 12	C	5	2/65
N06055	GEN. MATH	D	5	2/65
P06055	P.E.	B	5	2/65
P06065	CADET CORPS	C	5	2/65

MARKING PERIOD

SPECIAL REPORTS

POLIO O.K.
JUVENILE COURT
SUMMARY 2/63

CURRENT SUMMARY

APTITUDE TOTAL SCORE:	83
ACHIEVEMENT TOTAL SCORE:	
GRADE POINT AVERAGE:	1.83
RANK IN CLASS:	479
NO. IN CLASS:	500
ABSENCES THIS YEAR:	28

MOST RECENT TEST PROFILE

TEST NAME CTMM-SEC DATE OF TEST 10/64

SUB TEST	RESULT
LANG	80
NON-L	85
TOTAL	83

DIFFERENTIAL APTITUDE TESTS

SUB TEST	RESULT
UR	21
NA	15
AR	20
SR	30
MR	33
CSA	40
SPELL	10
SENT.	17

NORM: NATION 1 2 3 4 5 6 7 8 9

COURSE NO.	COURSE TITLE	MK	CR	DATE
A02955	ENGLISH 1-A	C	5	2/64
A15955	ENGLISH 1-B	C	5	6/64
	G.P.A. 2.00			
B05955	GEN. BUSINESS	D	5	2/64
	G.P.A. 1.00			
G05955	WORLD HIST. 1	D	5	2/64
G15955	WORLD HIST. 2	D	5	6/64
	G.P.A. 1.00			
U05955	INDUSTRIAL ART	C	5	2/64
I15955	WOODSHOP 1	C	5	6/64
U05055	AUTO SHOP 10	C	5	2/64
I15055	AUTO SHOP 11	C	5	6/64
	G.P.A. 2.00			
L15955	FRENCH 1	F	0	6/64
	G.P.A. 0.00			
P05955	P.E.	B	5	2/64
P15955	P.E.	B	5	6/64
	G.P.A. 3.00			

STUDENT CURRENT REQUIREMENT EVALUATION

PREVIOUS CREDITS	CURRENT YEAR CR.	TOTAL CREDITS	REQUIRED AT CURRENT LEVEL	CREDIT DEFICIENCY	CREDITS REQD. FOR GRADUATION	PERIODS PER WEEK	MINUTES PER PERIOD	MINIMUM PASSING	A =	B =	C =	D =	ABILITY TRACK PLACEMENT
55	30	85	90	5	240				%	%	%	%	Z

REMARKS: PRINCIPAL'S SIGNATURE: DATE OF GRADUATION:

Fig. 10 — California Guidance Record.

The CGR is prepared on one side of a sheet in 8½" x 11" format and contains most of the vital data needed by both secondary schools and college admissions offices. A companion form is being developed for use at the elementary level.

The CGR is a comprehensive compilation of data on the pupil. In addition to the student and school identification, it contains much of the current information needed by various school personnel. Space has been allocated for the marks earned during the current semester plus a historical representation of marks.

The *special reports* area is reserved for indications of the availability of reports, such as attendance or child welfare reports, psychological studies, etc. The *current summary* area includes a concise overview of the test scores, the mark-point average, rank in class, college eligibility index, etc.

The items along the bottom line give the student's credit status as he progresses toward graduation and also give information regarding the minutes per period and the periods per week in a traditional schedule. It also has room for a date of graduation and a school official's signature.

The CGR replaces the typical semester report card by incorporating it as a part of the form itself. The record also deviates from most transcripts in that it provides for the listing of marks by subject area rather than by semester. The subject area mark-point average is automatically computed and placed just beneath each specific area. The completion date of each course is provided. This will permit a reconstruction of each semester's courses and marks, if this should ever be necessary.

A special section is provided for reporting the pupil's most recent test scores. As will be noted by inspection, the test score area provides a multiple interpretation of test data. In the section provided for subtest results, the publisher's method of reporting is listed. Across the top of the test section are arranged the various percentiles, 0 through 99. Corresponding to the percentiles is the stanine range recorded across the bottom of the test area. By placing a series of asterisks across this area, the score can be interpreted in the fashion provided by the test publisher, in percentiles, percentile bands, or in stanines. This format is used to indicate a unit score to the teacher and the counselor. It does not require the user to be an expert in test interpretation, but at one glance he has available a variety and a combination of scores that will assist in establishing a relationship between the various scores.

This form is prepared at the end of each semester and can be used as a transcript for both interschool movement and college admission. It is prepared on a multipart form, with copies distributed to the counselor, administration, teacher's room, etc. Maintaining current data will pose no problem since a new, completely updated form is prepared at the conclusion of each semester. Old copies may be discarded or filed in the pupil's cumulative folder.

One copy is prepared with some of the data masked so that it can be sent home with the pupil for review with his parents. In this way the student and his parents have a twice-yearly opportunity to examine the progress and to become aware of any problems that the

1ST SEMESTER 1965 (TIME PERIOD)						ADMINISTRATIVE PLANNING SERIES					SAN MARCOS UNIFIED SCHOOL DISTRICT
CALIFORNIA ACHIEVEMENT BATTERY (TEST NAME)						DIAGNOSTIC REPORT: STUDENTS HANDICAPPED IN READING					PREPARED FOR: DISTRICT SUPERINTENDENT
	STATUS INDEXES					PERCENTAGES BY GRADE					
GRADE LEVEL	05-09	1.0-1.9	2.0-2.9	3.0-3.9	4.0+	05-09	1.0-1.9	2.0-2.9	3.0-3.9	4.0+	TOTAL ENROLLMENT BY GRADE
GRADE 1	NOT TESTED										
GRADE 2	NOT TESTED										
GRADE 3	46	23	3	1	0	9.2	4.6	.6	.2	0	500
GRADE 4	NOT TESTED										
GRADE 5	34	30	21	10	0	5.8	5.1	3.5	1.7	0	585
GRADE 6	NOT TESTED										
GRADE 7	NOT TESTED										
GRADE 8	15	17	26	12	3	3.6	4.1	6.2	2.9	.7	415
GRADE 9	NOT TESTED										
GRADE 10	NOT TESTED										
GRADE 11	10	12	5	5	0	2.7	3.3	1.6	1.3	0	365
GRADE 12											
TOTAL NO. OF HANDICAPPED STUDENTS					274	PERCENTAGE OF HANDICAPPED STUDENTS					14.6%
TOTAL BY CATEGORY	105	82	56	28	3						1865

Fig. 11 – Superintendent's Copy, Diagnostic Report.

student might have been encountering in reaching his stated goal.

Information from the regular testing program can be compiled for use by each level of district and school organization. Figures 11–15 illustrate an administrative planning series of reports, and indicate various ways data can be tailored to meet the needs of

1ST SEMESTER 1965 — ADMINISTRATIVE PLANNING SERIES — SAN MARCOS UNIFIED SCHOOL DISTRICT

TIME PERIOD: CALIFORNIA ACHIEVEMENT BATTERY — DIAGNOSTIC REPORT — PREPARED FOR DIRECTOR OF INSTRUCTION

TEST NAME: STUDENTS HANDICAPPED IN READING

SCHOOL	STATUS INDEXES GRADE PLACEMENT 05-09	1.0-1.9	2.0-2.9	3.0-3.9	4.0+	PERCENTAGES BY GRADE 05-09	1.0-1.9	2.0-2.9	3.0-3.9	4.0+	TOTAL ENROLLMENT BY GRADE
ABRAHAM LINCOLN											
GRADE 3	3	1	0	0	0	10.3	3.4	0	0	0	29
GRADE 5	2	2	1	0	0	6.5	6.5	3.2	0	0	31
WOODROW WILSON											
GRADE 3	2	0	1	1	0	6.5	0	3.2	3.2	0	31
GRADE 5	1	1	1	0	0	3.3	3.3	3.3	0	0	30
JAMES MADISON											
GRADE 3	1	2	0	0	0	2.8	5.7	0	0	0	35
GRADE 5	1	2	0	1	0	3.3	6.6	0	3.3	0	30
RIO BRAVO J.H.											
GRADE 8	6	3	5	3	1	2.6	1.3	2.1	1.3	.4	230
LOS CONCHOS H.S.											
GRADE 11	6	7	2	2	0	2.3	2.7	.7	.7	0	260
TOTAL BY CATEGORY	22	18	10	7	1						676

Fig. 12 — Director of Instruction's Copy, Diagnostic Report.

specific staff members. The superintendent's report (Fig. 11) is concise and to the point. It provides information about the performance—by grade level—of his district. The report illustrated shows the results of students classified by the district as handicapped in reading, showing the index—grade placement in this example—by

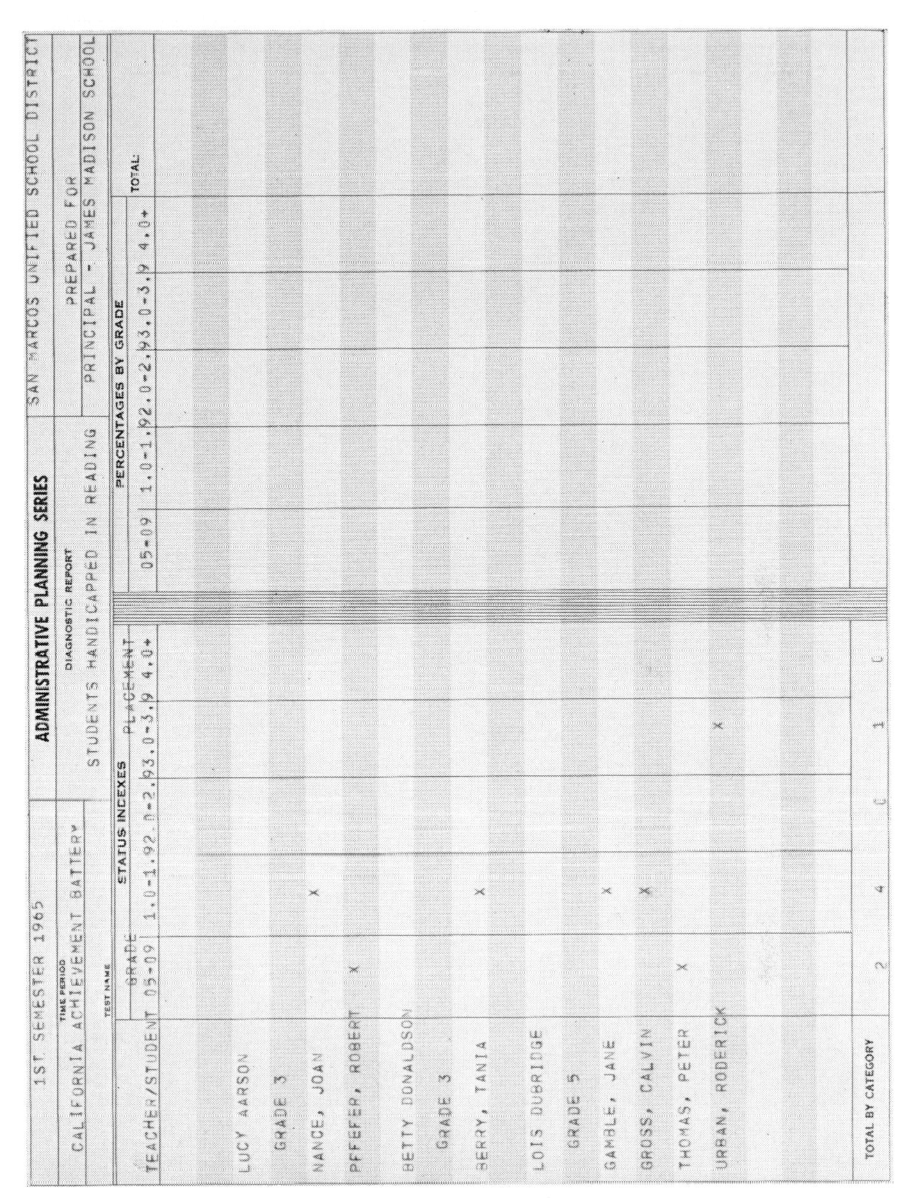

1ST SEMESTER 1965	ADMINISTRATIVE PLANNING SERIES									SAN MARCOS UNIFIED SCHOOL DISTRICT
TIME PERIOD: CALIFORNIA ACHIEVEMENT BATTERY	DIAGNOSTIC REPORT: STUDENTS HANDICAPPED IN READING									PREPARED FOR: PRINCIPAL - JAMES MADISON SCHOOL
TEST NAME	STATUS INDEXES GRADE PLACEMENT					PERCENTAGES BY GRADE				TOTAL:
TEACHER/STUDENT	05-09	1.0-1.9	2.0-2.9	3.0-3.9	4.0+	05-09	1.0-1.9	2.0-2.9	3.0-3.9	4.0+
LUCY AARSON										
GRADE 3										
NANCE, JOAN		X								
PFEFER, ROBERT	X									
BETTY DONALDSON										
GRADE 3										
BERRY, TANIA		X								
LOIS DUBRIDGE										
GRADE 5										
GAMBLE, JANE		X								
GROSS, CALVIN		X								
THOMAS, PETER	X									
URBAN, RODERICK				X						
TOTAL BY CATEGORY	2	4	0	1	0					

Fig. 13 – Principal's Copy, Diagnostic Report.

six months, one to two years, and so on. Percentages by grade and totals by grade and index also are included.

More detailed reports of the same basic data for other staff members are shown in Figures 12–15. Similar reports can be generated from the data base that would identify students accelerated in

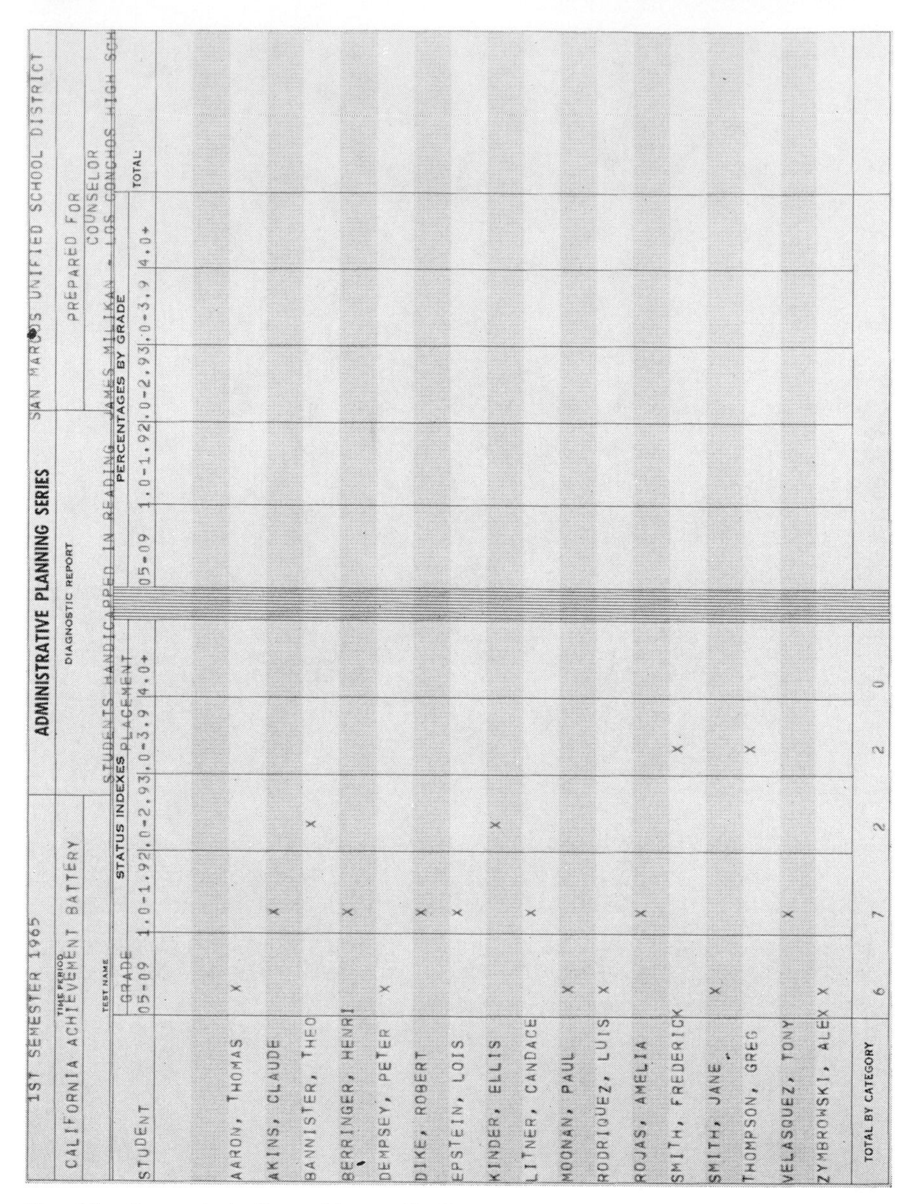

1ST SEMESTER 1965 — ADMINISTRATIVE PLANNING SERIES — SAN MARCOS UNIFIED SCHOOL DISTRICT

TIME PERIOD: CALIFORNIA ACHIEVEMENT BATTERY — DIAGNOSTIC REPORT — PREPARED FOR COUNSELOR

TEST NAME: STUDENTS HANDICAPPED IN READING — JAMES MILIKAN - LOS CONCHOS HIGH SCH

STUDENT	GRADE PLACEMENT 05-09	STATUS INDEXES 1.0-1.9	2.0-2.9	3.0-3.9	4.0+	PERCENTAGES BY GRADE 05-09	1.0-1.9	2.0-2.9	3.0-3.9	4.0+	TOTAL
AARON, THOMAS	X										
AKINS, CLAUDE		X									
BANNISTER, THEO			X								
BERRINGER, HENRI		X									
DEMPSEY, PETER	X										
DIKE, ROBERT		X									
EPSTEIN, LOIS		X									
KINDER, ELLIS			X								
LITNER, CANDACE		X									
MOONAN, PAUL	X										
RODRIQUEZ, LUIS	X										
ROJAS, AMELIA		X									
SMITH, FREDERICK				X							
SMITH, JANE	X										
THOMPSON, GREG				X							
VELASQUEZ, TONY		X									
ZYMBROWSKI, ALEX	X										
TOTAL BY CATEGORY	6	7	2	2	0						

Fig. 14 – Counselor's Copy, Diagnostic Report.

reading, mathematics, or any other combination of test content and reporting format.

Similarly, it is possible to produce reports from the data base that will assist in educational planning.

Illustrated in Figures 16–19 are reports that again have been

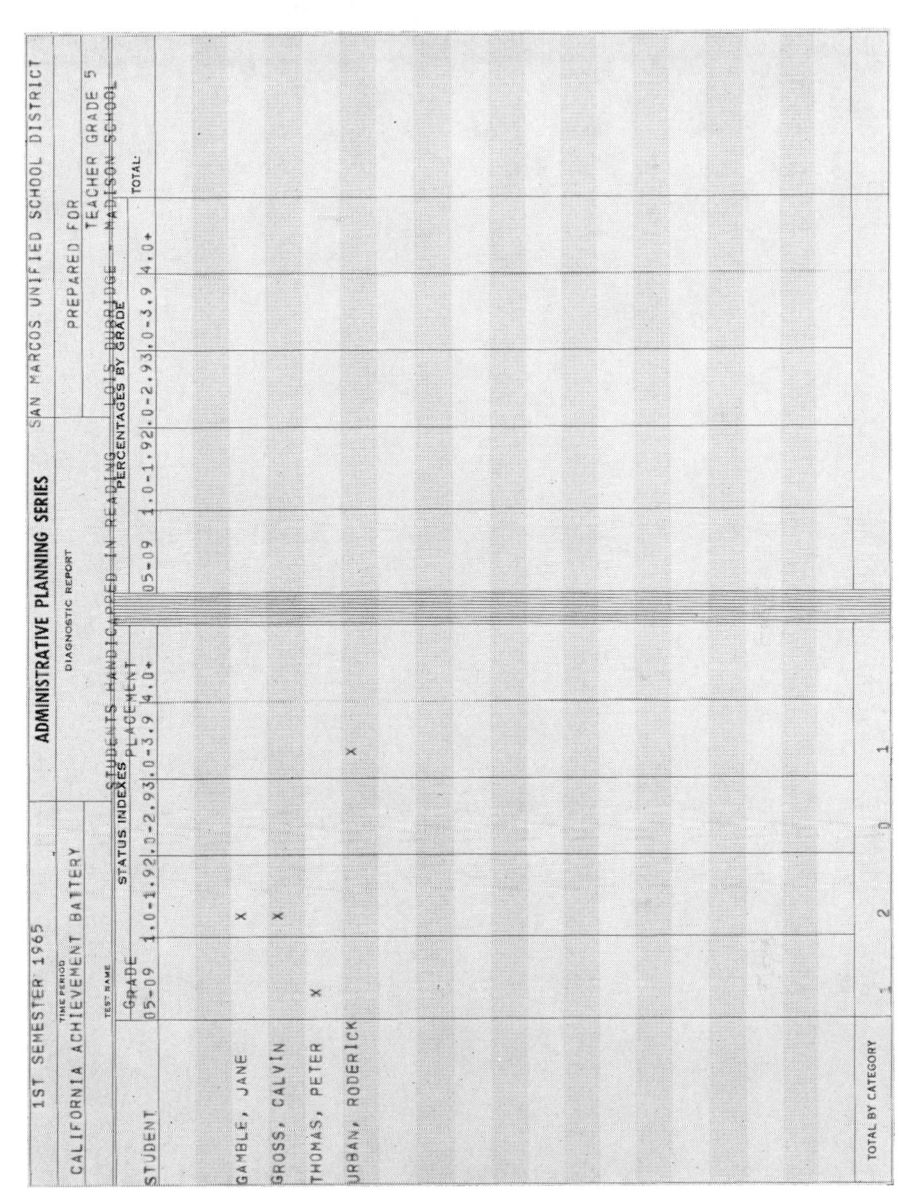

1ST SEMESTER 1965 — ADMINISTRATIVE PLANNING SERIES — SAN MARCOS UNIFIED SCHOOL DISTRICT

TIME PERIOD

CALIFORNIA ACHIEVEMENT BATTERY — DIAGNOSTIC REPORT — PREPARED FOR

TEST NAME

STUDENTS HANDICAPPED IN READING — LOIS BURRIDGE - MADISON SCHOOL — TEACHER GRADE 5

STUDENT	GRADE 05-09	STATUS INDEXES PLACEMENT 1.0-1.92	2.0-2.93	3.0-3.9	4.0+	PERCENTAGES BY GRADE 05-09	1.0-1.92	2.0-2.93	3.0-3.9	4.0+	TOTAL:
GAMBLE, JANE		X									
GROSS, CALVIN		X									
THOMAS, PETER	X										
URBAN, RODERICK				X							
TOTAL BY CATEGORY	1	2	0	1							

Fig. 15 – Teacher's Copy, Diagnostic Report.

prepared for specific staff members. These reports contain data that have been extracted from the standardized test program and the marks achieved in classes: test scores stanines, but percentiles or any other score could be used. Remarks are English language statements of analyses based on multiple regression equations, and are

SUPERINTENDENT'S **EDUCATIONAL PLANNING REPORT**

DATE 6/65.
DISTRICT ALTA MADRE UNION H. S
APTITUDE TEST SCH.& COLL. ABILITY
ACHIEVEMENT TEST SEQ.TESTS OF ED PR

SCHOOL	APTITUDE			ACHIEVEMENT				MARK AVERAGE BY AREA				REMARKS
	LANG	NON LANG	TOTAL	LANG	READ	ARITH	TOTAL	LANG ARTS	MATH	SOC SCI	TOTAL GPA	
HIGH SCHOOLS												
EL CAMINO	SATISFACTORY PROGRESS											
EL MIRADA	5	5	5	5	4	5	-	2.83	3.15	3.04	3.02	RECORDED GRADES ABOVE POTE
LOS RIOS	7	7	7	7	8	7	-	2.76	1.83	2.55	2.45	MATH GRADES BELOW POTENTIA
RIO GRANDE	4	6	5	4	3	5	-	1.53	1.94	2.00	1.76	READING/LANGUAGE BARRIER M BE SUPPRESSING GRADES
RIO PLUMAS	SATISFACTORY PROGRESS											
JUNIOR HIGHS												
GEORGE GOETHE	8	7	8	8	8	8	-	3.57	2.44	3.46	3.34	MATH GRADES BELOW POTENTIA
THOMAS MANN	SATISFACTORY PROGRESS											
ALBERT SCHWEITZER	SATISFACTORY PROGRESS											
LELAND STANFORD	SATISFACTORY PROGRESS											
THOMAS WATSON	SATISFACTORY PROGRESS											

EXPLANATION OF STANINE SCORES	
1	LOW
2-3	BELOW AVERAGE
4-5-6	AVERAGE
7-8	ABOVE AVERAGE
9	HIGH

Fig. 16 — Superintendent's Copy, Educational Planning Report.

CURRICULUM DIRECTOR'S **EDUCATIONAL PLANNING REPORT**

DATE 6/65
DISTRICT ALTA MADRE UNION H.S.
APTITUDE TEST SCH.&COLL. ABILITY T
ACHIEVEMENT TEST SEQ.TESTS OF ED PR

SCHOOL BY GRADE	APTITUDE			ACHIEVEMENT				MARK AVERAGE BY AREA				REMARKS
	LANG	NON LANG	TOTAL	LANG	READ	ARITH	TOTAL	LANG ARTS	MATH	SOC SCI	TOTAL GPA	
HIGH SCHOOLS												
EL MIRADA												
GRADE 12	5	6	5	5	5	5	-	2.97	3.44	3.55	3.37	RECORDED GRADES ABOVE POTE
LOS RIOS												
GRADE 9	7	6	7	7	7	7	-	2.83	1.32	2.77	2.65	MATH GRADES BELOW POTENTIA
RIO GRANDE												
GRADE 9	5	6	5	5	3	5	-	1.75	2.05	2.00		L. A. GRADES BELOW POTENTI READING/LANGUAGE HANDICAPS
GRADE 10	4	5	5	3	3	5	-	1.35	1.85	1.88		MAY SUPPRESS GRADES
GRADE 11	4	5	5	3	3	5	-	1.39	1.80	1.93		" " " " "
GRADE 12	5	6	5	6	4	5	-	1.88	2.13	2.23		L. A. GRADES BELOW POTENTI
JUNIOR HIGH SCHOOLS												
GEORGE GOETHE												
GRADE 7	8	7	8	8	7	8	-	3.52	2.02	3.50	3.30	MATH GRADES BELOW POTENTIA

EXPLANATION OF STANINE SCORES	
1	LOW
2-3	BELOW AVERAGE
4-5-6	AVERAGE
7-8	ABOVE AVERAGE
9	HIGH

Fig. 17 – Curriculum Director's Copy, Educational Planning Report.

PRINCIPAL'S **EDUCATIONAL PLANNING REPORT**

DATE 6/65
DISTRICT ALTA MADRE UNION H.S.
APTITUDE TEST SCH.&COLL. ABILITY T
ACHIEVEMENT TEST SEQ.TESTS OF ED PR

SCHOOL BY DEPARTMENT	APTITUDE			ACHIEVEMENT				MARK AVERAGE BY AREA				REMARKS
	LANG	NON LANG	TOTAL	LANG	READ	ARITH	TOTAL	LANG ARTS	MATH	SOC SCI	TOTAL GPA	
RIO GRANDE HIGH SCHOOL												
SOCIAL SCIENCES DEPARTMENT												
GRADE 9 COURSES	5	6	5	5	3	5				2.00		
GRADE 10 COURSES	4	5	5	3	3	5				1.88		READING/L. A. HANDICAPS MA SUPPRESS GRADES.
GRADE 11 COURSES	4	5	5	3	3	5				1.93		" " " "
GRADE 12 COURSES	5	6	5	6	4	5				2.23		
ENGLISH DEPARTMENT												
GRADE 9 COURSES	5	6	5	5	3	5		1.75				L. A. GRADES BELOW POTENTI
GRADE 10 COURSES	4	5	5	3	3	5		1.35				
GRADE 11 COURSES	4	5	5	3	3	5		1.39				
GRADE 12 COURSES	5	6	5	6	4	5		1.88				L. A. GRADES BELOW POTENTI

EXPLANATION OF STANINE SCORES	
1	LOW
2-3	BELOW AVERAGE
4-5-6	AVERAGE
7-8	ABOVE AVERAGE
9	HIGH

Fig. 18 – Principal's Copy, Educational Planning Report.

COUNSELOR - JAMES LOGAN'S
LOS RIOS HIGH SCHOOL

EDUCATIONAL PLANNING REPORT

DATE 6/65
DISTRICT ALTA MADRE
APTITUDE TEST SCH. & COLL. ABILITY T
ACHIEVEMENT TEST SEQ. TESTS OF ED PR

STUDENT NAME	APTITUDE			ACHIEVEMENT				MARK AVERAGE BY AREA				REMARKS
	LANG	NON LANG	TOTAL	LANG	READ	ARITH	TOTAL	LANG ARTS	MATH	SOC SCI	TOTAL GPA	
ANDREWS, JAMES A.	5	6	5	6	6	5	6	3.32	3.63	3.51	3.42	GRADES EXCEED RECORDED POT
BERLIN, GLORIA J.	7	7	7	7	8	8	8	2.8	3.75	2.95	3.15	L.A. AND S.S. GRADES BELOW POTENTIAL
CASTRO, RICARDO J.	5	5	5	3	3	7	4	1.74	2.55	1.85	2.25	LANG-READING DIFFICULTY SUPPRESS GRADES
HAVEN, EMIL P.	9	9	9	8	8	9	8	2.75	3.15	3.00	2.95	RECORDED GRADES BELOW POTE
MOORE, THOMAS A.	3	7	5	3	3	5	4	1.65	2.75	1.70	1.99	FLAG FOR INDIVIDUAL TESTIN AND REMEDIAL ACTION
PRYZNEWSKI, IGNATIUS R.	6	6	6	5	6	5	6	1.85	1.90	1.75	1.85	L.A.-MATH-S.S. GRADES BELO POTENTIAL

EXPLANATION OF STANINE SCORES	
1	LOW
2-3	BELOW AVERAGE
4-5-6	AVERAGE
7-8	ABOVE AVERAGE
9	HIGH

Fig. 19 – Counselor's Copy, Educational Planning Report.

established by the regional advisory committee or district research and curriculum specialists. The reports for the superintendent and principal (Figs. 16 and 18) are comprehensive, or 100 percent reports, while the others in the series are exception reports. The superintendent's report shows how each school is progressing, while the principal's report shows the status of each department by grade level. The other reports in the series show only the grade levels or pupils who have performed above or below the standards established by the district.

Who is in charge of regional centers?

In every case the answer to this question must be that the *user* determines how a certain operation will take place. It is anticipated that in each center there will be formed an advisory committee (or steering committee) composed of representatives from the various school districts being served. The advisory committee would function along the lines previously described in this chapter. (See pages 90 to 93.)

Administratively, of course, certain key personnel supervise the operations of the regional center. But these persons do not "run" the system in the sense of telling the schools what to do. The cardinal purpose of the center is always that of serving education.

Figures 20 and 21 show how one regional educational data processing center is organized. The finest equipment and the best housing would be worth nothing without good staffing; a regional staff would not progress far, if anywhere at all, without well planned pre-operational organization according to the abilities and roles of the personnel involved.

Note that special attention is paid to the placement and functions of the steering committee—the "policy determination" advisory group—and its relationships to the other components of the system.

Policy determination (Fig. 20) is initiated at the school level and transmitted to the county coordinator and coordinator's committee by the *one* person authorized to represent that school. This person usually is the principal, vice principal or head counselor. The county coordinator generally meets regularly with his school coordinators and the county coordinator's committee.

The director of the regional center is chairman of the county coordinator's committee and therefore is in direct communication with those who speak for the users of the center's services.

Feedback is directed to the elected steering committee as well, and all policy matters are resolved by that group at its monthly meeting. When policies are established, they are transmitted through

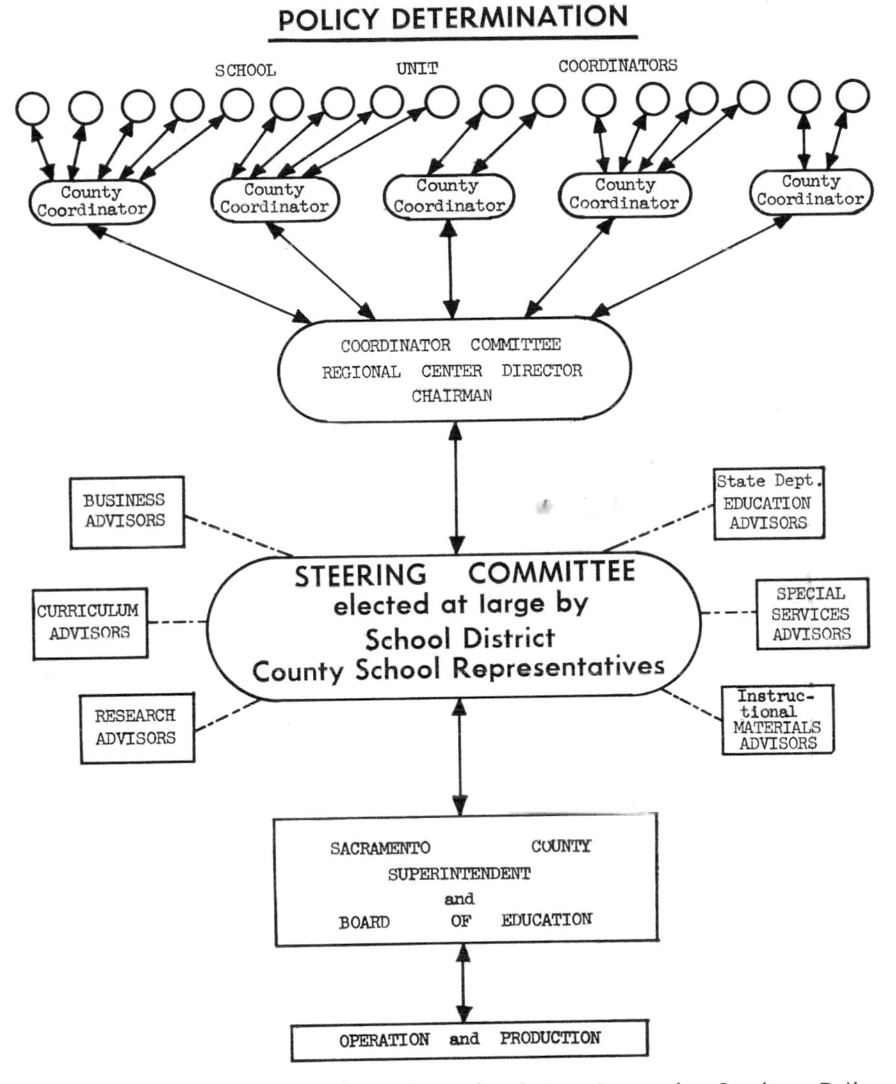

Fig. 20 – Organization for Regional Educational Data Processing Services, Policy Making Levels.

the county superintendent and board that provides the administrative umbrella, and these policies are transmitted to the operational side of the organization (Fig. 21).

Once the regional director has received these policy statements, he sets out to implement them in the most efficient and effective manner possible. Systems are designed or redesigned, programs are written, tested, and placed in operation.

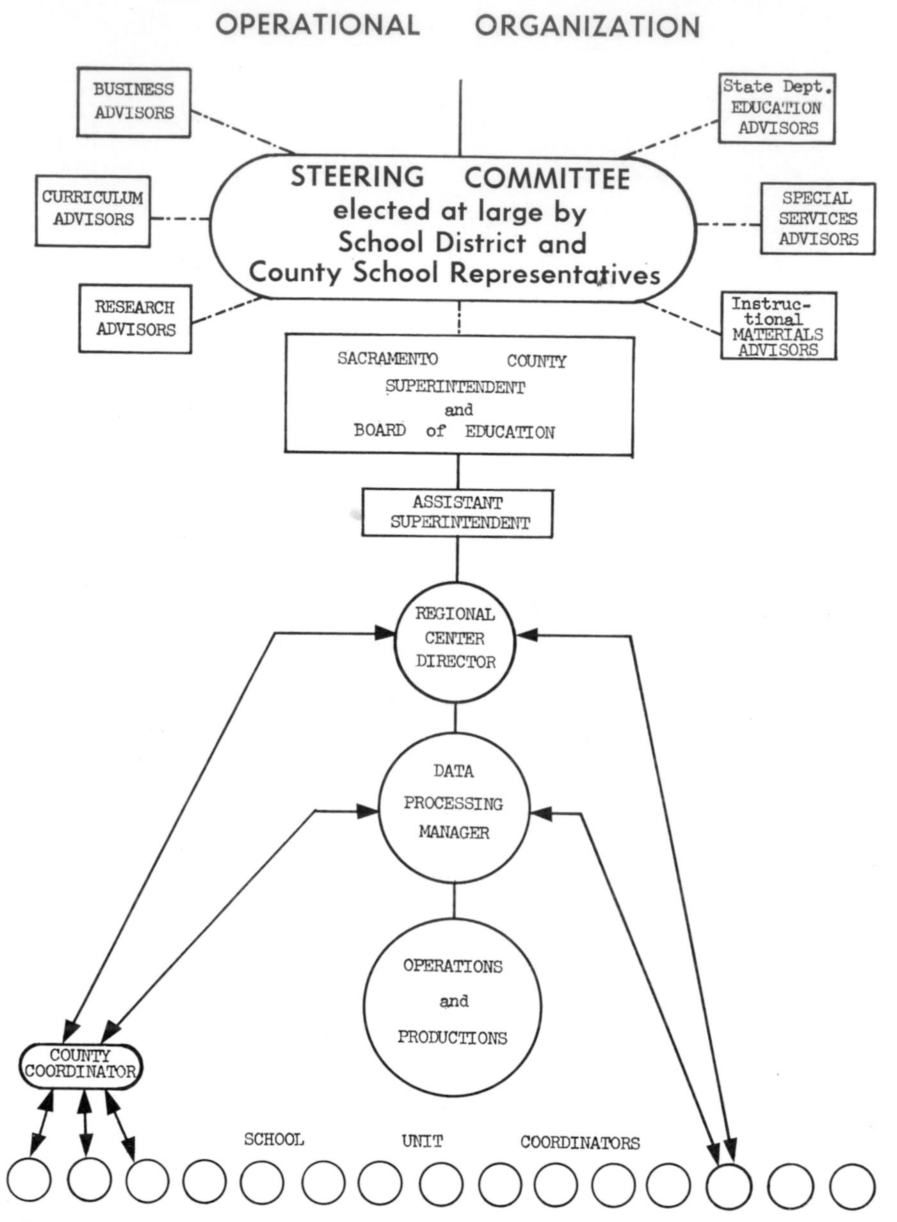

Fig. 21 — Organization for Regional Educational Data Processing Services, Operating Levels.

Communications from the schools then come into the picture. Questions, comments, or complaints do not have to proceed through the policy determination system, but can be directed to the most appropriate operational person. This provides a direct line and immediate response to any problem that might arise.

CONCLUSION

The growing importance of educational programs has brought increased attention to the goals and processes in use. To provide information about the educational system, educators are being forced to use modern technology to assist them in finding answers. Information systems are as complex as the technological devices needed to operate these systems. Educators are finding that a cooperative approach to systems development and use of regional data processing centers generally is the most efficient and economical direction to proceed.

Field experience has shown that this approach is workable, and has benefits that extend directly to the classroom. A prime question that educators must consider, however is whether they can function in a situation where the glamour and status of possessing machines is eliminated.

REFERENCES

Grossman, Alvin, and Robert L. Howe. *Data Processing for Educators.* Chicago: Educational Methods, Inc., 1965.

Grossman, Alvin, and Robert L. Howe. "Regional Centers in the State of California," *Journal of Educational Data Processing,* Spring 1965.

Howe, Robert L. "Solution to Report Preparation: The Common Data Base," *Automated Education Handbook.* Detroit: Automated Education Center, 1965.

8 a case for regional educational data centers

ROY A. SEDREL

ROY A. SEDREL *holds a BS in Accounting from Drake University, and he has done graduate work in Educational Administration at the University of Iowa.*

He has served as a systems analyst for the Iowa State Department of Public Instruction and for the IBM Corporation, and as statewide systems coordinator for the Iowa Educational Information Center. His articles have appeared in Midland School *and in* Automated Education Handbook.

The history of educational data processing, while relatively short, has been dynamic and stimulating. In our efforts to apply the technology of information and computer science to the functions of mass education, we have encountered a variety of problems which, in turn, have given rise to a variety of theoretical and practical solutions. The concept of regional data processing centers was, at one time, a theoretical solution. Today, regional centers are proving their merits as a practical solution to the problem of providing public education the facilities of modern technology.

A BASIS FOR DISCUSSION

The case for regional data centers can be built on a number of factors. However, common to many of these factors is the element of economics. I will construct my case for regional data processing centers by discussing some of the economic and related advantages of regional vs. local operation.

A basis for this discussion will be predicated on the following hypothetical situation: A geographical area in state X contains 2500 square miles. This area has 20 school districts with enrollments in grades K-12 ranging from 600 to 20,000 with 12 districts having enrollments of 2000 or less. Total enrollment in the area is 75,000 pupils in grades K-12. Total property valuation for tax purposes in the area is $500 million dollars with six of the wealthiest districts having a combined tax base of $300 million dollars. All of the school districts in this area desire the services of educational data processing for administrative functions. The alternatives for providing these services are a) establish 20 small installations, one in each district, or b) establish a regional data center with one medium- to large-scale computer system serving the 20 local districts. Society is continually placing greater and greater demands upon the already strained resources of education. Administrators at all levels must assess operational alternatives, such as those available in our hypothetical situation, in terms of producing the most efficient use of the various resources to be employed. What then, are the advantages in the second alternative which are not present in the first alternative?

ECONOMIES IN PERSONNEL UTILIZATION

It is estimated that the total need for personnel to manage and operate our nation's computer installations is over 600,000 persons. Reliable estimates indicate that only 150,000 persons are employed in the field.[1] This obviously means we must make the most efficient use of the limited personnel resources available. The regional center offers the maximum advantages of economic use of personnel. Considering our hypothetical situation, the regional center would require a staff of approximately 20 operational and administrative personnel. If each local district had its own installation, the total personnel requirement would be approximately 150. Therefore, the regional center offers a net savings in personnel resources of 130.

Not only is the regional center able to more efficiently use the personnel resources available, but it is also able to secure more competent and highly skilled individuals, which tends to increase the efficiency factor. In addition, the time and talents of technical specialists available from the various equipment manufacturers can be more efficiently used by concentrating their efforts in one large installation, as opposed to dividing their time over several small installations.

ECONOMIES IN EQUIPMENT UTILIZATION

I need not remind you that computers and related equipment are expensive devices. *A minimum computer system configuration is needed* in order to perform the basic administrative functions of student scheduling, grade and attendance reporting, financial accounting, personnel services and facilities accounting.

Even in light of substantial educational discounts allowed by various equipment manufacturers, a minimum computer and related

---

[1] Hamblen, John W. "Computer Personnel Needs," *AEDS* (Association for Educational Data Systems) *Monitor,* February 1966.

equipment configuration will rent from $3,000 to $5,000 per month. The total equipment costs for the 20 districts of our hypothetical situation would be about $80,000 per month. A regional computer system with sufficient capacity to handle the basic administrative functions of all 20 districts would rent from $10,000 to $12,000 per month, realizing a net savings, therefore, of approximately $70,000 a month.

The regional center offers other advantages of economies in equipment utilization. One cannot measure the cost of providing data processing services by simply determining the monthly equipment rental charges. For example, let us assume that we wish to prepare grade reports for 500 students. The hourly rental rate for computer X is $20, and the rate for computer Y is $45. Computer X will require 14 hours to complete the task; computer Y will require only 5½ hours. The total cost to prepare grade reports on computer X will be $280 and on computer Y it will be $252.

It is quite obvious that cost of equipment must be determined on the basis of total throughput per dollar invested. The regional data center can support a much larger and more efficient computer system than can the small individual school districts. The larger system will generally provide greater throughput capabilities per dollar invested and thus reduce the unit cost for data processing services.

ECONOMIES IN PHYSICAL FACILITIES AND INSTALLATIONS

In addition to the cost of hardware, one must also consider the cost of physical facilities to house equipment and personnel. Computer installations require special air-conditioning, raised floors, adequate electrical service, and other special physical considerations. Obviously, the regional center offers costs savings of several thousands of dollars through the elimination of the need for many duplicate physical facilities.

Establishing an operational data processing center is more than simply ordering a computer. Many man-months of time must be devoted to such activities as deciding what equipment is needed, preparing specifications for bidding purposes, planning physical facilities, supervising construction on remodeling of these facilities, hiring and training personnel, acquiring office furniture and fixtures, and ordering supplies, just to name a few administrative activities. The systems and programing efforts will require many more man-years of time to complete. Data specifications must be defined, forms must be designed, machine systems developed and programed, and operating instructions and procedures written. All of these initial installation efforts are expensive, yet necessary elements in the establishment of a data processing center. Again, the regional data center offers an economic advantage by eliminating the duplication of installation and developmental costs.

OTHER ADVANTAGES

Up to this point, we have discussed the advantages of regional data centers which are derived from economic utilization of personnel, equipment, and facilities. Perhaps a more basic factor which should be considered is the financial base required to support a data processing installation. Many school districts across the nation lack an adequate tax base to support even the most elementary data processing installation. The regional data center, through its economies of operation, is able to provide administrative data processing services at a cost the schools can afford. The cost to the local school depends upon the method used to administer and finance the regional center. One method is to establish the regional center as a "service bureau" administered by a governing body either independent of, or in conjunction with, a presently existing educational agency. This type of center operates as a nonprofit educational service facility, receiving its basic revenue from charges for service provided to the local districts. The regional centers being operated in California exemplify the service bureau approach.

Another method is for an intermediate unit to supply data processing services at no direct cost to the local school districts. The intermediate unit may be composed of one or more county boards of education or an area board of education. In either case, this intermediate board must have taxing powers from which to derive a source of revenue to support operations. The BOCES operations in New York exemplifies the "self-financed" type of center.

I feel that the intermediate unit approach has some distinct advantages over the service bureau approach. First, it would have an equalizing effect, i.e., economically wealthy districts would pay a larger proportion of the total operating costs than would the economically deprived district. For example, in our original hypothetical situation six districts would bear 3/5's of the total operating cost of the center with the remaining 14 districts bearing only 2/5's of the operating costs. Education in total has been concerned for many decades with the problem of equalizing the educational opportunities for our nation's youth. Evidence of this concern can be found in the writings of Cubberley, Strayer, Haig, and others, beginning as early as 1906. Another distinct advantage in the intermediate unit approach is that it tends to hasten the implementation of data processing in the local schools. Since there are no direct costs to the local school, no local board action is involved in the administrator's decision to utilize the services of the regional center.

Regardless of the method used to establish the regional center, inherent within its structure is the advantage of overcoming the financial handicap of economically deprived school districts.

The regional center offers another advantage in its ability to provide a wider range of services. The large-scale computer capabilities of the regional center permit a more sophisticated approach to the problem of fulfilling administrative data needs. Bus route scheduling, flexible student scheduling, integrated total information systems accessible through teleprocessing terminals, computer-assisted instruction, and simulation are but a few examples of the wider range of functions which are not always possible on the very small computer system.

There are obviously many other advantages in the regional approach to educational data processing. On the other hand, there are certain disadvantages inherent in the operations of a regional center. I strongly believe that under present technology the economic advantages of regional data centers far outweigh the disadvantages and that the regional approach will continue to gain wide acceptance from school administrators, boards of education, and the taxpaying public.

part II

APPLICATIONS AND TECHNIQUES

9 administrative organization for educational data processing services

MARTIN DeRODEFF

DR. MARTIN DERODEFF *obtained his EdD from Stanford University and his MA from Columbia University. His experience includes several years in data processing systems work in education, administrative work in instructional services and in administrative services, and several years as a secondary school teacher.*

Dr. DeRodeff has served as president of the California Educational Data Processing Association; as chairman, California Educational Data Processing Association, Bay Section; and as co-chairman, Data Processing Advisory Committee, Southern Alameda County.

It is logical to conclude from the content of the preceding chapters that electronic data processing will continue to accelerate as a technological tool and as an applied computer science. Industry and commerce are leading the way at a rate that projects the 40,000 computers now in use to a total of 85,000 operating computers by 1975. BEMA – Business Equipment Manufacturers Association – provided "the prediction that 1966 should see EDP Systems installed at the rate of three dozen per day."[1] Education, now the largest industry in the United States, will eventually find itself dependent upon automated data processing services to maintain an equilibrium between the forces of individualized educational objectives for burgeoning masses of people and the unprecedented surge of new knowledge and technology impinging upon teacher and student.

Paradoxically, education, as the epitome of information activity, is lagging behind all other sectors of our society in the use of electronic data processing—a technology described as "the most powerful information processing tool of the ages." The reason for this lag is not inherent in the traditional explanation of a "budget deficiency," and appears to exist in the lack of high level administrative commit-

[1] Richard D. Kornblum, "Scan '66—A Panorama of the Data Processing Field in the New Year," *Business Automation Magazine*, January 1966, p. 31.

ment. EDP, by virture of its centralized and pervasive services, cannot be subsumed under the traditional line and staff organization as it now exists in many instances. The problem lies within the rigid structure of the traditional organizational system.

Like many innovative concepts in education, the utilization of EDP manifested itself in diverse forms. In one institution it appeared as a payroll application under the administration of the comptroller or the division of business services. In another institution it materialized as an automated student report card system under the direction of the registrar or the pupil personnel office. New technology has typically been absorbed within an existing administrative unit. Projectors and tape recorders are the domain of the audio-visual department; electronic bookkeeping machines are the province of the business services division; publication equipment is managed by adminstrative services or business services. The electronic accounting equipment of the early 1950s (tab equipment) followed the same route and was administered by adding a duty to a line function.

In education, as in business, data processing applications first developed as single-purpose, one-area services produced with electronic accounting machines. As these applications increased in variety, the integrated phase of development appeared along with the first commercial use of the computer around 1955. Two or more inter-office applications were planned to complement each other by eliminating the repetition of similar source data. For example, the certificated "notice of employment" and the "personnel directory" are produced from the same personnel master file. The advanced phase of integrated data processing called the "total information system" approach has appeared in the past few years. There are many descriptions of "systems." For purposes of simplification a definition advanced by Leonard Silvern, educational consultant, describes the system as ". . .the structure or organization of an orderly whole clearly showing the inter-relationship of the parts to each other and to the whole itself."[2]

In the total information system concept, the confluence of all information flow is the electronic data processing center which provides an active communication network for the entire educational organization. A definitive analysis of the total information system appears in an earlier chapter. The development of an automated information system is a natural outgrowth of the utilization of computer capability and is an emerging trend in business and industry.

The utilization of a modern computer-based information system

[2] Leonard C. Silvern, "Reply to Questions About Systems," *Audio Visual Instruction*, May 1965, p. 2.

requires the creation of a managerial position under the superintendent or president of the institution separate from all other divisions. An illustration of electronic data processing potential supports this organizational need in education.

It is possible under the "total information system" or "integrated information system" concept, for one medium-size computer installation to fulfill any combination of the following objectives:

1. Relieving instructors of clerical tasks related to the preparation of student records and the scoring of objective tests so that more time can be alloted to giving individual student assistance.
2. Assisting counselors to program students through the use of grouping techniques and automatic scheduling, thereby permitting more time for student counseling.
3. Providing instructors and students with access to EDP equipment as part of the curriculum devoted to vocational training and the demonstration of a new body of knowledge—applied computer science—related to math, physical science, social science, and business administration. Computer-assisted instruction (programed learning) may someday exceed record production as a function of automated data processing.
4. Preparing personnel records and accounting applications for the business office.
5. Completing a statistical analysis of student census data and budget projections for the superintendent or president and the board of education.
6. Maintaining permanent student record information for the district pupil personnel office or registrar.
7. Providing statistical data used for curriculum research and evaluation.
8. Preparing reports for the documentation of myriad federally funded projects.

To date most of the educational applications tend to duplicate manual systems and do not reflect the potential of computer science for such total information system services as permanent storage information retrieval, computer-assisted instruction, and administrative decision making—new applications which are being demonstrated successfully in experimental projects.

The technology of EDP is complex due to the tremendous range of capability of the computer and its implication for the science of management in the administrative organizational system. EDP is providing management with new techniques to find answers to administrative problems. Trial and error judgments are being supplemented by mathematical models whereby the computer is fed sets of equations representing certain factors and alternatives in a problem; then, through a series of iterative steps, the solution closest to a specified objective is produced.

The traditional organizational structure as a series of compartmentalized functions interrelated to the whole organization through line and staff connections tends to duplicate manually much of the source data that feeds communication exchange documents and information files. An EDP service used by all offices and departments can capture source data once and quickly disseminate it to any user in any combination desired. This automated information process has many desirable side effects:

1. *Administrators will have more time available to assist with inservice education training programs, research and development projects and evaluations, when much of their "paper work" is completed by EDP.* For example, the school principal who has to fill out attendance reports, enrollment reports, and a grading pattern analysis by teacher, subject, and grade, will find that the computer can do these jobs automatically using the student master file maintained in cards, magnetic tapes, or disks. The assumption that this job is done by the school secretary is misleading, because the principal needs secretarial assistance for curriculum-related documentation and typically one or more types of desirable communications are sacrificed to the pressure of clerical reports.
2. *Symbols of communication and their meaning become more uniform and duplications of terminology are discarded.* Any data processing director or coordinator who has worked with several high schools in formulating common course titles, abbreviations, and special symbols will recall the disparity of terminology that exists among schools even when a district course guide is in use. Ability grouping techniques, prerequisites, semester versus full-year course designations, are typical of non-uniform descriptions and symbols. A greater unity of effort is achieved through a more uniform policy and procedure performance imposed by the exacting specifications needed for EDP programs. The organization becomes more cohesive and articulate when information flow has one central pumping station—the EDP center—and line and staff positions are all fueled by the same data mixture unadulterated by reinterpretation, omission, or a different vocabulary.
3. *EDP services combine basic data information for any variety of custom reports enabling offices and departments to receive data in a more usable form.* Examples are reconciliation of warehouse orders by department, budget reports, physical fitness test results, follow-up study tabulations, and any other data which is usually

prepared manually in one sequence and from which an abstract in a different order has to be made for separate offices or departments.

All of this sophisticated data manipulation is possible if the institution is "tooled up" with modern data processing equipment and has provided administrative leadership for its implementation. For the first time in history, education has access to equipment capability (hardware) which can answer most of its information processing needs. *Providing managerial skill (software) constitutes the single most pressing need in education today for the implementation of data processing services.*

What kind of a managerial system is needed for EDP if administration is to effect the most efficient use of personnel and material to provide individuals (the learners) optimum growth experiences? There are several implicit guidelines for organization:

1. EDP management must provide services to all divisions, departments, and offices under the direct authority of the superintendent or president and board. Any position of responsibility below this central level jeopardizes the optimum utilization of EDP services. Computer applications have advanced so fast that a priority list of services will have to be established. The list will be received with less disruption if it emanates from a neutral "nonpartisan" source. A single budget classification for EDP expenditures, one source of production, a total information system concept, are other justifications for a centralized administrative staff level for EDP management.
2. EDP management must be extensive enough to maintain service for all levels of the organizational structure. The size of the institution and kinds of EDP equipment available will also be determinants for personnel needs. The minimum requirement is one full time person with the responsibility for directing all EDP services. As the institution increases in size, one or two assistants will be needed. Figure 22 illustrates a basic organizational structure incorporating EDP management.
3. Management must be able to utilize the capability of modern EDP equipment. Capability in the broad sense can be the resources of a full computer installation on site, a satellite (small computer) hookup to a large computer off site, a commerical service bureau, an educational regional data processing center, a county EDP center, or sharing an installation with one or more surrounding institutions. The selection of hardware should be a determination of management predicated on current processing needs. It is important to establish an EDP management position before acquiring hardware or even contracting for limited services. Consultants in the EDP field, such as the Data Process-

ing Management Association, the Association for Computing Machinery, or a local educational data processing association, are available at little or no cost to counsel the superintendent's or president's office in establishing a projection of potential EDP services and recommending specifications for management organization.

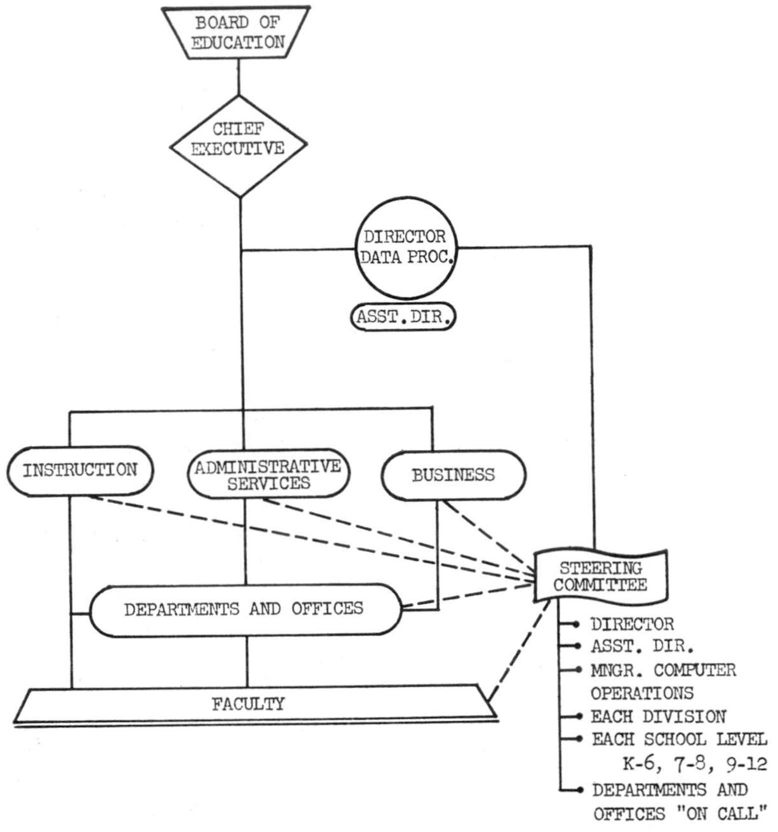

Fig. 22 – Basic Organizational Structure for EDP Services.

4. The growth and diversity of EDP applications are expanding rapidly and the EDP management structure must be flexible enough to permit an increase in personnel to assist the EDP director. The term "director" has been used as a typical management title for a staff position close to the superintendent or president. The title can vary as long as it connotes a level of administration directly under the direction of the superintendent or president, such as assistant superintendent, administrative assistant to the superintendent, or vice president or provost of EDP.

The field of EDP services is relatively new and it is important that the creation of an EDP administrative position include a complete and disseminated documentation of responsibilities. A basic list of duties may include:

1. Preparation of a list of data processing needs based on a minimum three-year projection.
2. Submittal of a recommendation for a priority list of applications with a tentative chronological schedule. (Made from list of data processing needs.)
3. A recommendation for equipment and personnel needs to support EDP services.
4. A budget proposal for EDP services covering a minimum of three years of operation.
5. Management of the EDP installation. Technical supervision for equipment programing and operation should be delegated to EDP specialists who were familiarized with educational specifications by the director or his assistants.
6. Submittal of periodic progress reports to the superintendent or president, including operational applications, costs, research, evaluation, and projections.
7. Acting as resource person to other staff members in the development of curriculum and inservice education for EDP instructional programs.
8. Acting as representative of the institution at professional and community meetings concerned with data processing.

In addition to creation of an EDP directorship at a high administrative level, an organizational system should include scheduled blocks of time for representatives of each divison and department to participate in an orientation of the EDP field and a joint study of desirable EDP services. This can be achieved by establishing a steering committee representing major divisions with additional representatives of departments and offices available "on call." Such committees have been called "information systems committees," "data processing steering committees," "record study advisory committees," or "computer science committees."

The major EDP activities can be classified under *specifications, machine programing* and *machine production.* Specifications constitute the detailed needs to be served by EDP services and include items of source data or input and kinds of output, such as forms, lists, cards, etc. The EDP study committee has the important and critical responsibility to formulate exact specifications pinpointing every item of data that will be required for processing. The documenting of explicit specifications forces an evaluation of manual processing and a uniformity of procedure that may not have existed under the manual process.

An EDP application study includes an additional complex determination. Should the automated application duplicate the manual system? or can the automated application be modified so as to integrate with other automated applications and actually change some of the input specifications? For example, enrollment tallies can be a by-product of an attendance report application, or a report card system application. It is at this point in a study that a dual competency of the EDP director becomes necessary. The director has to understand the needs of all users and the technological capability of his EDP hardware. Within the context of the EDP study committee function, the director can present a variety of EDP possibilities as alternatives for a committee decision on the final application format. The director does not have to know how to write the machine instructions (programing) but he should understand the input and output capabilities of the equipment. The director is also responsible for contributing to the study committee, as resource information, a description (with available samples) of similar applications being produced elsewhere. Figure 23 illustrates the personnel and the major functions needed in developing an EDP service program within an institution using the concept of a total information system.

Machine programing is usually completed by a specialist under the direction of the EDP manager. The EDP manager assists the director in systems study and individual applications development by providing flow charts with block diagrams of job steps and suggesting alternative data processing techniques. The computer programer uses the flowchart and application specifications to write machine instructions in a programing language. He is usually assisted by the EDP manager.

Machine production applies to the operation of the various EDP machines used to manipulate the input, processing, and output of data. Both the programer and machine operator jobs are centralized functions, whereas the director's job, and part of the EDP center manager's job, is a decentralized function requiring direct interaction with the users of EDP services who can best describe the specifications needed to eventually create an automated application. The total information system, sometimes erroneously considered a centralized operation, requires communication lines to each user for development and evaluation and is therefore partly decentralized. Successful applications in education depend as much upon faculty, student, and parent acceptance as they do upon tech-

A SYSTEM OF DATA PROCESSING SERVICES

	DEVELOPMENTAL STEPS--CYCLE OF ACTIVITIES	PARTICIPATION IN DEVELOPMENT						
		EDP DIRECTOR	ASST. EDP DIRECTOR	STEERING* COMMITTEE	MANAGER COMPUTER OPERATIONS	PROGRAMER	EQUIP-MENT OPERATOR	CHIEF EXECUTIVE
1	Identify information needs--all areas	✓	✓	✓				
2	EDP Steering Committee establishes a priority list	✓	✓	✓	✓			
3	Obtain chief executive and Board approval	✓						✓
4	Analyse the first system	✓	✓	✓	✓			
5	Create research file - study comparative applications	✓	✓	✓	✓			
6	Complete system specification & prepare flow chart	✓	✓		✓			
7	Present final system proposal to chief executive	✓						✓
8	Develop computer program				✓	✓		
9	Prepare forms operational schedules and detailed procedures	✓	✓		✓			
10	Conduct user orientation for new application	✓	✓					
11	Obtain input and process the data	✓	✓				✓	
12	Run parallel manual processing first time	✓			✓	✓		
13	Evaluate results with steering committee	✓	✓	✓	✓			
14	Report progress and evaluation							

*Steering Committee is augmented with representatives of departments and offices as needed

Fig. 23 – Chart Showing Participants in Development of Data Processing Services nical efficiency and productivity of EDP equipment. Personnel have to understand the relationship of the automated system to the manual system and why the change was made. It is the responsibility of the EDP director to meet this need by communicating in face-to-face relationships where feasible and by issuing periodic progress reports which document phases of development in lay terms. A director is in the unique position of "selling" desirable services to top administration as well as to prime users.

The EDP director can be assisted in fulfilling his multifaceted responsibilities by one or more assistants, depending upon the size of the institution and the scope of EDP services. The addition of an assistant is warranted when it is determined that schedules and services can be expanded to produce tangible results. It should be the responsibility of the EDP director to submit documented justification for assistance to the superintendent or president of the institution. An EDP director can be assisted in phases of systems development encompassing the preparation for group meetings, presentations of automated technique, and documentation of specifications. It is possible for example, to develop applications for the business office while also studying pupil personnel systems. An assistant can coordinate a study in one area under the guidance of the director. Data processing technology, as an instrument of innovation, demands many hours of group study and planning before myriad details fashion a new application—a transition requiring personnel role and responsibility adjustments as well as efficient equipment performance.

In larger colleges and universities, the managerial organization for EDP services is more complex, due to the extensive utilization of computer science for instruction and research. The recent advent of the high-speed computer, with large random access memory files and multiline data transmission capability, has made it possible for one central computer installation to serve the many branches of the university. In managing the complex schedule of EDP services, the director will spend much of his time coordinating the activities of several assistants who can each specialize in one area, such as instruction, research, pupil personnel records, or business services. At the university level, the EDP director should be management science oriented with a proficiency in hiring and motivating a large staff of specialists to whom he can delegate a specified realm of decision-making responsibility. His organization of EDP services must be flexible to allow for growth and modification. The rapid invention and production of computer-related equipment, such as visual display screens, graphic line plotters and voice communication devices, all part of computer output, are precursors of change that will inevitably affect the future of the equipment configuration and services provided by the data processing center. All of these factors of technological utilization, including the demand for precise communication and the comprehensive tie-in with all branches of the institution, create a managerial responsibility of the highest executive level.

The office of the director should include a full-time executive secretary who will school herself in the technical terminology of data processing. The director should depend on his secretary to interpret procedural and schedule bulletins to users. The secretary may accomplish this service by utilizing the resources of the EDP manager for information and clarification when the director is away from the office.

The basic objective of computer-based systems development is to improve the efficiency of doing things with information. Key activities are speed, simplification, combination, and elimination. Unlike the automated control of a manufactured product or a process, education has the problem of communication with people about people. Behavioral scientists have not advanced a singular theory of learning applicable to all individuals that can be readily adapted by teachers to produce a measurable outcome. The unique demands upon the data processing director are to produce tangible results, specified outcomes, and a financial justification. He has to be able to innovate, with an apparent degree of customer satisfaction, using the technology of a new science which enjoys its own rapid internal change. The paramount attribute of a successful director is his administrative ability to discover and utilize the skills of teachers, administrators, technicians, and consultants in providing for EDP services.

A complete training program for the preparation of a director of data processing probably does not exist and positions are generally filled by the most qualified person available for the job. There are several desirable attributes that can serve as guidelines in the screening process:

1. An interest and belief in the potential of EDP for education—a believer in planned innovation for the total educational system (not partial to any one division).
2. Three or more years each of teaching and administrative experience, with emphasis on grades 7 through 12 in K-12 systems, and college level for higher institutions of learning.
3. Knowledgeable in data processing concepts and principles. Does not have to know how to operate equipment or program a

computer, but should be able to identify qualified personnel in these areas and know where to obtain information and assistance. An understanding of punched card principles and computer capabilities is mandatory and can be learned in courses offered by computer manufacturers and colleges.

4. An understanding of basic accounting systems used in education.
5. Ability to write reports and demonstrate ideas and plans.
6. Experience in developing forms and procedures employing the "systems development" approach.
7. Ability to communicate with small and large groups of people at varying levels of interest and need.
8. Able to delegate responsibility, motivate individuals, and participate in team effort.
9. Able to accept criticism with the calmness of a stoic.
10. An orderly mind with a penchant for detail.

SUMMARY

In this era of educational "implosion," the schools are struggling to absorb the many changes inherent in:

- New scientific knowledge in the curriculum—to double in ten years.
- Staff utilization programs involving flexible scheduling and team teaching—many of which have been sponsored by private foundations such as Ford and Kellogg.
- Architectural redesign of buildings, multifunction classrooms, and special activity areas for greater diversity of activity.
- Federally funded projects and programs for almost every facet of the instructional program.
- New behavioral science and biochemical science learning concepts, such as the readiness to learn at ages three and four.
- Supplemental instruction from non-teacher sources, ranging from programed texts to computer-assisted instruction.
- A wide range of audio-visual materials, including language laboratories and television.

This caving in (implosion) of traditional education caused by the many external pressures is also fermenting an information explosion as educators attempt to communicate changes in policy, programs, and procedures.

In order to make sense of the information glut, educational institutions are utilizing technological tools, foremost of which is the modern high-speed, large-memory electronic computer. The information processing capability of the computer is limitless and present utilization comprises only a fraction of future potential.

In the preface of his book, *Management Standards for Data Processing,* Dick Brandon states, "There is no question that the installation of ADP (automated data processing) equipment is in many industries the most technical task that management has ever faced. The complexity of this technology is such that few management men have the time, inclination, or training to obtain sufficient knowledge to direct its use."[3]

It is encouraging that some institutions are using or are planning a total automated information processing system with apparent success. However, too many school people are still using computers or electronic accounting machines to duplicate manual information processing on a segregated application basis. The differences in the extremes of operation are reflected in the managerial structure established for EDP services. Institutions that have created a high level administrative responsibility for EDP services serving the entire district or university, are utilizing the computer more widely and efficiently. There are more services to more people with less duplication of information. Where this responsibility has been relegated to an existing line function, results are less favorable and the development of integrated information systems is practically nonexistent.

Direction and coordination of the pervasive and emergent automated information processing services requires a staff of highly skilled specialists led by an educator with curriculum experience and knowledge of computer science. The director of data processing services should be at one level below the chief executive and conversant with administrators and instructors at all levels. This recommendation is reiterated by Grossman and Howe in *Data Processing for Educators:* "The first steps for a district moving toward a truly effective educational intelligence system, is to appoint a Director of Information Systems. . . .The Director reports to the Superintendent. His rank tops that of line director or supervisor and is on a par with that of an associate superintendent."[4]

The directorship of EDP services should be established before a total information system is automated. Almost every institution of any size can benefit from EDP services available from outside the institution or through an installation on site.

Educational institutions can receive professional EDP guidance

[3] Dick H. Brandon, *Management Standards for Data Processing.* Princeton, New Jersey: D. Van Nostrand Company, Inc., 1963, p. 18.

[4] Alvin Grossman and Robert L. Howe. *Data Processing for Educators.* Chicago: Educational Methods, Inc., 1965, p. 19.

from data processing associations and computer manufacturers in setting up an EDP services program. Training programs for directors of data processing consist chiefly of educational experience and selected data processing courses offered by colleges, universities, and computer manufacturers.

An innovative educator interested in harnessing the technology of computer science for education can find the EDP director's job a challenging and rewarding task.

10 the Iowa educational information center and the CardPac system of educational accounting

RALPH A. VAN DUSSELDORP

DR. RALPH A. VAN DUSSELDORP received his PhD and MA degrees from The University of Iowa, and his BS from Central College of Pella, Iowa.

He taught mathematics for five years in junior high schools; served for four years as director of data processing for the Iowa State Department of Public Instruction; and joined the faculty of The University of Iowa's College of Education in 1963, where he now teaches graduate-level courses in educational data processing. In January 1964 he was named associate director of the newly formed Iowa Educational Information Center.

As a data processing specialist, Dr. Van Dusseldorp coordinated the Iowa State Department of Public Instruction's statistical processing with the U.S. Office of Education (USOE) and was a member of the board of directors of the Council on Educational Data Systems, which works closely with the USOE in developing data-collection procedures. He was instrumental in the formation of the 13-state Midwestern Educational Information Project funded in 1965 by the USOE. He serves as a consultant in educational data processing to other state departments and to local school districts; he helped develop and operate computer systems for the statewide Iowa CardPac System of Educational Accounting, and for scheduling, census, and pupil accounting services offered by the Information Center. Dr. Van Dusseldorp has edited a monograph and written numerous articles. In 1966 he was elected a director of AEDS.

To those in the educational data processing field, this is the information age. I'm obviously not being original in calling this the information age, but this rather ambiguous phrase does seem to be the best way of beginning a description of the Iowa Educational Information Center and the statewide information system initiated by the Center in May 1965.

For it was the alarming growth of school information—both available and potential—plus the development of the necessary technical tools to process this information, that led to the establishment of the Iowa Educational Information Center (IEIC).

> The schools and the various educational agencies in every state are now routinely collecting great masses of information of many types and in many ways. However, the methods of data collection and of data processing now being employed, in view of modern technological advances, are in general antiquated, cumbersome, inefficient, and repetitious. Not only are the techniques outmoded, but there is serious lack of coordination among the many different data-collecting agencies; there is much overlap and duplication involved, and there is very frequent repetition of tasks required of the person supplying the information. Teachers and administrators, in filling out report forms for different agencies and for different purposes, are supplying exactly the same detailed information over and over again from agency to agency and from year to year. . .[1]

Therefore, it is not surprising that school personnel are becoming more and more concerned about the growing burden being placed upon them by the data-collecting activities of various agencies. This burden certainly does not bring about any improvement in the willingness of school people to comply with all requests for information. As a result, a small percentage of replies and a disturbing incidence of error characterizes many of the data-collecting activities, thereby often defeating basic purposes.

INADEQUATE FEEDBACK

One of the reasons for the increasingly negative attitude of school personnel to requests for information is that adequate provision for feedback to the persons or schools supplying the information frequently has not been made.

The local schools likewise are concerned with their own internal data-collecting activities. Many schools have systems of pupil, personnel, and financial accounting with which they are not completely satisfied. In many instances the records kept locally are incomplete, or inadequate, and in even more instances the data that have been collected are not used to full advantage.

> During the last few years, particularly, the schools have noted the amazing progress made in the development of high-speed automatic data processing equipment, especially of electronic computers, and have recognized that these machines must have great potential for public education, as well as for science, business, and industry. Many of the more progressive school systems have made determined efforts to try to utilize modern technology in their own data-collecting, recording, processing, and reporting activities. In gener-

[1] E. F. Lindquist, "Implications and Potential of Information Systems in Public Schools," *Computer Concepts and Educational Administration.* Iowa City, Iowa. Iowa Educational Information Center, The University of Iowa, 1966, pp. 41-53.

al, they have found that the problems of equipping and staffing a local data processing center, and developing the necessary systems, computer programs, forms, and procedures, are very complex, oftentimes confusing and frustrating. Furthermore, because of the very rapid changes taking place in this field, the equipment installed or systems developed often seem obsolete or outdated almost before they can be put into operation. Only the largest school systems have thus far been able to make any use of electronic equipment, and even they find that many of the things they would like to do are beyond their capabilities.[2]

Although it is impossible for the schools and agencies to be too well informed about the many facets of their operations, it is possible to collect and have available more detailed information than can be assimilated or interpreted and used effectively. The needs of school administrators for better methods of data collection and for more information are surpassed only by their need for help in organizing, integrating, interpreting, and using the information that is being and may be collected.

Closely related is the need for improved research facilities in education and for more effective utilization in research of the great masses of data that are being and can be collected by the schools and other educational agencies. Large-scale electronic computers and improved mathematic and statistical techniques for data analysis are now available, but it has been impossible to utilize these facilities to full advantage because the data have not been brought together and stored in a central location in a form accessible to electronic processing.

There exists, then, a very real need for more efficient data-collection procedures, for better ways of analyzing and interpreting data and for reporting 'digested' information to the schools, for means of making the data collected centrally available for research, and for more effective utilization in research of the masses of data that can now be collected. The Iowa Educational Information Center represents a major effort to meet these needs in Iowa and to serve as a pilot operation for the benefit of other states.[3]

SERVICES BEGUN IN 1963

Although IEIC has been in existence only since December of 1963, some of its services were made available to Iowa schools in March of 1963 through the Iowa Center for Research in School Administration, also based at The University of Iowa. At that time the Center for Research, with the cooperation of the State

---

[2] E. F. Lindquist ,"A Proposal for the Establishment of a Central 'Information Center' for Iowa Educational Institutions and Agencies." Unpublished.

[3] Iowa Educational Information Center. A brochure of the Iowa State Department of Public Instruction and the College of Education, The University of Iowa, 1965.

Department of Public Instruction and the Measurement Research Center of Iowa City, launched a program of cooperative data processing for Iowa public schools called Update (Unlimited Potential Data through Automation Technology in Education).

Funds to support this pioneering effort in Iowa were provided initially by Measurement Research Center (MRC). MRC's role in the operation will be described in detail later. Different types and sizes of schools were selected as pilot schools to ensure that services would be fitted to the needs of schools with varied resources and problems. Various data processing procedures were studied to see which ones could be adapted.

As a beginning effort, 12 schools were chosen for a pilot computer scheduling project using a revised IBM Class (Class Load And Student Scheduling) Program.[4] Planned and coordinated by Professor Robert W. Marker, the scheduling project proved that such services are feasible.

Success of the pilot program strengthened plans for a complete educational information center which would bring the benefits of electronic data processing to Iowa schools and establish The University of Iowa as a leading source of information needed by educational psychologists and others engaged in behavioral study.

In addition to MRC, beginning financial support included a $248,227 grant from the U. S. Office of Education over an 18-month period and another of $750,000 from the Ford Foundation over a five-year period.

JOINT ENTERPRISE

On December 20, 1963, IEIC was formally organized as a joint enterprise of the State Department of Public Instruction and the College of Education of The University of Iowa. A three-man Coordinating Board was named to guide policy procedures and this Board remains intact today. Paul F. Johnston, State Superintendent of Public Instruction, serves as Chairman. Other members are Dean Howard R. Jones of the College of Education and Professor E. F. Lindquist, President of MRC. Professor Marker was appointed Director, and the author, who is now Director, Associate Director.

Bringing the three key agencies together—the State Department of Public Instruction, College of Education, and MRC—served to fuse an organization with all the necessary tools for the ambitious undertaking of a statewide educational information cen-

[4] *Class,* an IBM Computer System for Using the 7070 (7074) and 1401 in Class Loading and Student Scheduling, Version "C," July 15, 1962.

ter. The State Department with its forward looking Superintendent provides personnel (the author is an Associate Superintendent of Systems) and access to its facilities, and perhaps most important, the legal force needed to install an effective statewide information system. The College of Education provides experienced educational administrators, teachers, and facilities, and also makes available statewide test data for grades 3–12 through its Iowa Testing Programs. The systems and machine aspects are the responsibility of the Measurement Research Center, which has available some of the newest and most sophisticated data processing equipment in the nation.

MEASUREMENT RESEARCH CENTER

MRC is a not-for-profit, professional organization governed by a Board of Trustees who are key administrative officials of The University of Iowa. Under its charter any excess of income over operating expenses and reserve requirements must be spent only on educational research at The University of Iowa.

> The corporation serves test users everywhere, through the medium of the major test publishers and the sponsors of state, regional, and national testing programs such as American College Testing Program. . . .
>
> Most of the documents processed by MRC are unique forms, designed for the MRC electronic scanners. They are mainly test answer sheets or cards, but an increasing proportion are questionnaires, application blanks, and a wide variety of other data-collection forms. Answers or other data are recorded on the forms by marking circles or ovals with ordinary soft lead pencil. Almost any information that can be expressed by an alphabetic, numeric, or position code can be recorded on an MRC sheet. The MRC scanners 'read' the information on these documents (up to a rate of 30,000 sheets per hour) and transcribe it directly to magnetic tape. The tapes are then run through computers, which convert the raw scores to derived scores and perform a great variety of computational operations. Various types of reports to schools and agencies are produced as output of the operation.[5]

MRC has five computers—an IBM 1401, an IBM 1460, two CDC 160's, and one CDC 160A—and has access to an IBM 7044 and System 360/30 in the University's Computer Center.

Although MRC has its own large service center and a separate engineering research and development building, several systems analysts and programers have offices at IEIC to facilitate communica-

[5] "The Measurement Research Center Way." Measurement Research Center, Inc., 1964.

tion and produce the close coordination necessary among the education and systems personnel.

IEIC'S INTERNAL STRUCTURE

What sort of an internal structure is necessary to keep an information center working at peak efficiency? IEIC found this to be one of its most difficult problems and experimented with several structures, including one in which all project administrators were responsible only to the Directors. This system proved particularly vulnerable because of duplication of effort and often a lack of consistency among projects using similar procedures. To correct this weakness, individual coordinators were named in the following areas: (1) educational specifications, (2) systems development, and (3) field operations.

An individual with a strong background in education and a knowledge of data processing was placed in charge of educational specifications, i.e., deciding what information would be most valuable to the schools and the state and federal agencies who need school information for decision making. All projects must begin in this area.

Once the educational specifications have been written, the systems coordinator enters the picture (although not necessarily for the first time since his advice might be needed by the "ed specs" people in the beginning stages of the project). The systems coordinator must design data-collection forms and procedures to enable the computers to digest the educational specifications and print out meaningful data.

The problems involved in a statewide information system are bared when uniformity must be achieved and at the same time enable schools to keep individual identities. An example is the development of a uniform coding structure for course offerings, many of which are given under different titles and for different lengths of time and to different levels of pupils. Another thorny issue still being grappled with by the systems people involves file maintenance, i.e., keeping pupil files up-to-date as the pupil changes courses and schools or perhaps drops out.

Once the systems have been designed, the field operations personnel have the highly sensitive job of interpreting them to the school administrators. This area encountered some problems. In some cases it was IEIC's lack of communicating effectively. In other instances it was simply a long-time administrator fighting change. And in the most populous area of the state, cries of "invasion of privacy" were heard from a small segment of the public.

The Center is constantly working to improve and simplify its statewide information system known as the CardPac System of Educational Accounting—the target of the above-described forces. Better communication is sought with the administrators through periodic letters and more effective instructions. IEIC has tried to expose the shallowness of the "invasion of privacy" move through news releases and appearances of key personnel on radio phone forums. Each newspaper, radio, and television station in the state was mailed a copy of the spring 1966 pupil inventory questionnaire.

This should give some indication of the public relations problems involved in the implementation of the CardPac information system.

The CardPac System

The term "CardPac" comes from the packs of cards used to collect data. Although the system became operational in May 1965, many months of preparation were necessary before the actual data-collection process began. This included a review of related research and available data-collection materials. The handbooks developed by the U. S. Office of Education in the areas of pupil accounting, financial accounting, property accounting, and instructional program accounting were used as basic guides in determining the specific items of information to be collected. Considerable use was made of highly qualified consultants on a national level. Previous efforts, such as Project Talent of the University of Pittsburgh, were also reviewed in designing large-scale data-collection instruments. Research leaders in various major areas participated in selecting specific information items they felt would most likely be needed in the various longitudinal research studies presumably to be carried out on the basis of the information collected.

Also necessary in the beginning stages of the project was development of a schedule of events for conferences, experimental tryouts, and full-fledged administration of the system.

STATEWIDE PROGRAM

The proposal under which U. S. Office of Education funds were granted contemplated only the field testing of procedures in a large representative sample of schools. As the work progressed, it became evident that a crucial part of the problem of large-scale systems development would be the actual implementation of the system on a statewide basis. It was decided, therefore, to install the system in all public secondary schools in the state in order that all of these problems could be studied.

The reasons for the decision to go statewide are many. IEIC found that orientation of local district personnel was a major part of any significant change in procedures. Much more care must go into instructional material and written procedures. Many different procedures are used in local districts for collecting and handling information, and many different organizational patterns exist in the secondary schools. If a system was to be usable on a statewide basis, it must take all of these various patterns and procedures into account; otherwise, it would not serve the needs of all.

Certain objectives of a statewide system could not be tested with a sample. The preparation of state summaries of data normally collected manually could not be compared with older methods. Stratified samples for research purposes cannot be useful unless the entire population of pupils is included in the system. The transfer of records from one school to another for longitudinal studies cannot be done unless all schools are included in the data bank.

Pilot Tests

Pilot tests were made of the stencil card method of preparing input. The tests were very successful in grades 3 through 12. Primary children exhibited some difficulty in keeping the cards aligned for stenciling. This created no problem since primary schools were not to be included in the initial administration of CardPac and plans were made for other approaches for future primary use.

A field test of a proposed 73-item pupil questionnaire was administered to 408 pupils in grades 7–12 in one school, approximately three months before the questionnaire was administered statewide. The purpose of the trial administration was to test the appropriateness of individual items (were they understandable, answerable, confusing, etc.?), the time for administering the questionnaire, and to test the clarity of instructions. Other objectives were to obtain photographic records of pupils completing questionnaires and proctors administering them, and impressions of the pupils concerning their feelings about completing the questionnaire (prying, use of items, items which need improvement, etc.).

During the entire time pupils were taking the questionnaire, two or more proctors (IEIC personnel) circulated, giving aid where requested. The specific type of aid given was noted on a comment page; in this manner items of greatest difficulty were identified.

Questionnaires were administered to entire grades, the order of administration being 12, 11, 10, 9, 8, and 7. Three different persons administered the directions, the first taking two grades, the next taking two grades, etc.

A tabulation was made of the data collected for each item and each response by grade level and the percentage of pupils making each response computed. These results were used to make recommendations concerning adaptation or change or deletion of items and responses.

Overall evaluation of the directions showed them adequate to get pupils started on the questionnaire. After the administration, senior high pupils suggested that pupils should have been given more details concerning how the questionnaire is to be used and what benefit it will be to the pupil. It was also indicated that emphasis was needed on the point that pupils were to select the one best answer, even though several answers may have been possible.

The time needed for reading the directions to the questionnaire remained constant for each group (four minutes). The six grade levels averaged 36 minutes in completing the questionnaire, ranging from 32 minutes in the 11th grade to 42 minutes in the 7th grade.

Bringing in Course Data

To bring course data into the information system, principals were asked to fill out a master course list, which included a list of courses compiled by the State Department of Public Instruction. For coding purposes, course numbers were furnished by the State Department. Principals were asked to supply the number of sections of each course and, in addition, the name of the school district, school name, school address, name of principal, county number, district number, school number, area number, and organization (7–8, 7–9, 9–12). As the system became more sophisticated, principals had to supply more specific course data—local course title, number of sections, minutes meeting per week, weeks meeting per year, units, credit or noncredit, required or elective, vocational or nonvocational, and weights or percents given to letter grades (if used).

Orientation Meetings for Administrators

Plans for introduction of the information system statewide began with a one-hour briefing on the overall program for all superintendents having a secondary school in their district. Nineteen area meetings were conducted. Presentations began with a flipchart introduction showing the need for an information system and what it is; a slide narration probed the system in further detail; then the flipcharts were used again for review. A question-and-answer session followed.

The principals were given a day-long orientation at 12 sites and were informed ahead of time to bring lists of teachers and courses. Audio-visual materials for the principals' presentation were prepared with great care. A thorough analysis of the elements of the CardPac information system indicated that the success of the system would rest largely in the hands of individual school principals, and that each of them must thoroughly understand certain basic principles and procedures if the effort were to be genuinely successful.

The principals' meetings began with a flipchart presentation of the relationship between the Information Center, The University of Iowa, the State Department of Public Instruction, and the principal. The presentation also included the organization and functions of the Information Center. A slide presentation introduced some principles of data processing, with emphasis on the fact that data in machine-readable form can be read, printed, sorted, reproduced, correlated, and treated arithmetically, and with particular emphasis on the principle of interspersed gang punching or gang reading. Flipcharts stressing the need for a CardPac information system were shown, followed by a slide presentation of what the actual administration would entail.

Then the principals were divided into small groups for a simulated run of CardPac in the classroom with the principals assuming the role of pupils. The "pupils" filled out the materials as it would be done in the classroom. Through this procedure the principals were able to anticipate questions they would get in their own schools.

Later, in these same small groups, the principals assumed their normal administrative role. First, they were given a step-by-step review of the entire procedure for updating course and teacher lists, and then they actually updated these lists.

The CardPac consultant then took the principals through the administration manual step by step, answering questions. The consultants impressed upon the principals the necessity of distributing the materials correctly, putting cards in the proper sequence, and packing them correctly.

So that concentrated efforts could be made on areas of immediate concern prior to and during the delivery of CardPac materials to the schools, several task forces were set up in the Center, with one staff member designated as a leader of each task force. The leader was given the responsibility for the progress and completion of work in this area.

All manuals, cards, instructional material, and publicity releases were completed, a processing and delivery system established, and the materials delivered to the schools in May 1965. Measurement Research Center handled the processing and packing, and a parcel delivery service was chosen to distribute the materials.

10 MILLION PAGES OF MATERIAL

As an example of this massive undertaking, 10 million pages of printed material were delivered to the principals. These included five data cards to be distributed to the pupils (stencil card, student information card, student address card, questionnaire answer card, and student course card), two card forms for the teachers (course header, teacher header), a 32-page Principal's Manual, two-page Teacher's Instructions, eight-page Proctor's Instructions,

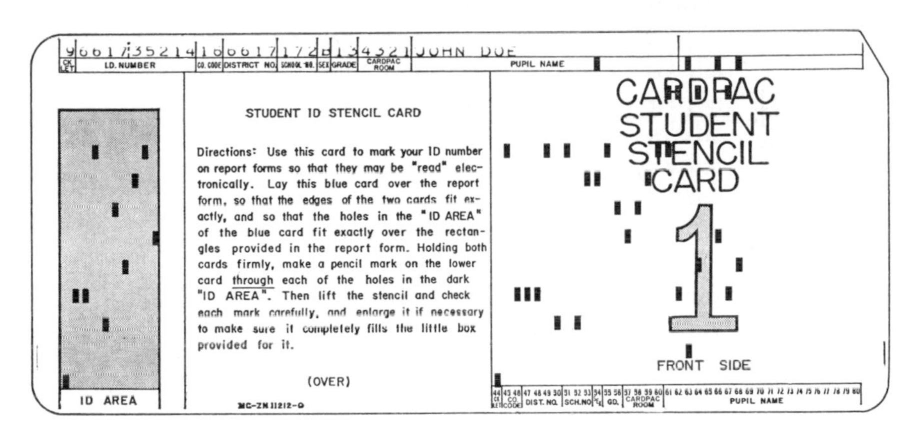

JOHN DOE

I.D. NUMBER | CO. CODE | DISTRICT NO. | SCHOOL NO. | SEX | GRADE | CARDPAC ROOM | PUPIL NAME

STUDENT ID STENCIL CARD

Directions: Use this card to mark your ID number on report forms so that they may be "read" electronically. Lay this blue card over the report form, so that the edges of the two cards fit exactly, and so that the holes in the "ID AREA" of the blue card fit exactly over the rectangles provided in the report form. Holding both cards firmly, make a pencil mark on the lower card through each of the holes in the dark "ID AREA". Then lift the stencil and check each mark carefully, and enlarge it if necessary to make sure it completely fills the little box provided for it.

(OVER)

ID AREA

CARDPAC STUDENT STENCIL CARD

1

FRONT SIDE

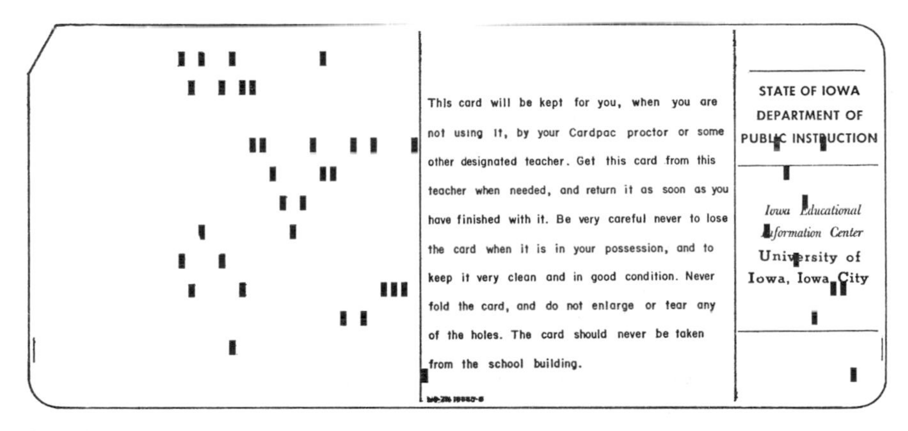

This card will be kept for you, when you are not using it, by your Cardpac proctor or some other designated teacher. Get this card from this teacher when needed, and return it as soon as you have finished with it. Be very careful never to lose the card when it is in your possession, and to keep it very clean and in good condition. Never fold the card, and do not enlarge or tear any of the holes. The card should never be taken from the school building.

STATE OF IOWA DEPARTMENT OF PUBLIC INSTRUCTION

Iowa Educational Information Center

University of Iowa, Iowa City

Fig. 24 – Student Stencil Card, Front and Back.

two-page Teacher's Brochures, four-page CardPac Newspaper, and a 16-page Pupil Questionnaire.

Since the data cards are the heart of the CardPac System, a description of each is necessary.

1. The student stencil card (Fig. 24) contains a prepunched student identification number. The pupils use these cards to stencil their ID numbers on the other card forms and therefore do not have to know their ID number. There are two types of stencil cards:
   a. Assigned student stencil cards are supplied for pupils who have participated in the Iowa Tests of Basic Skills and Iowa

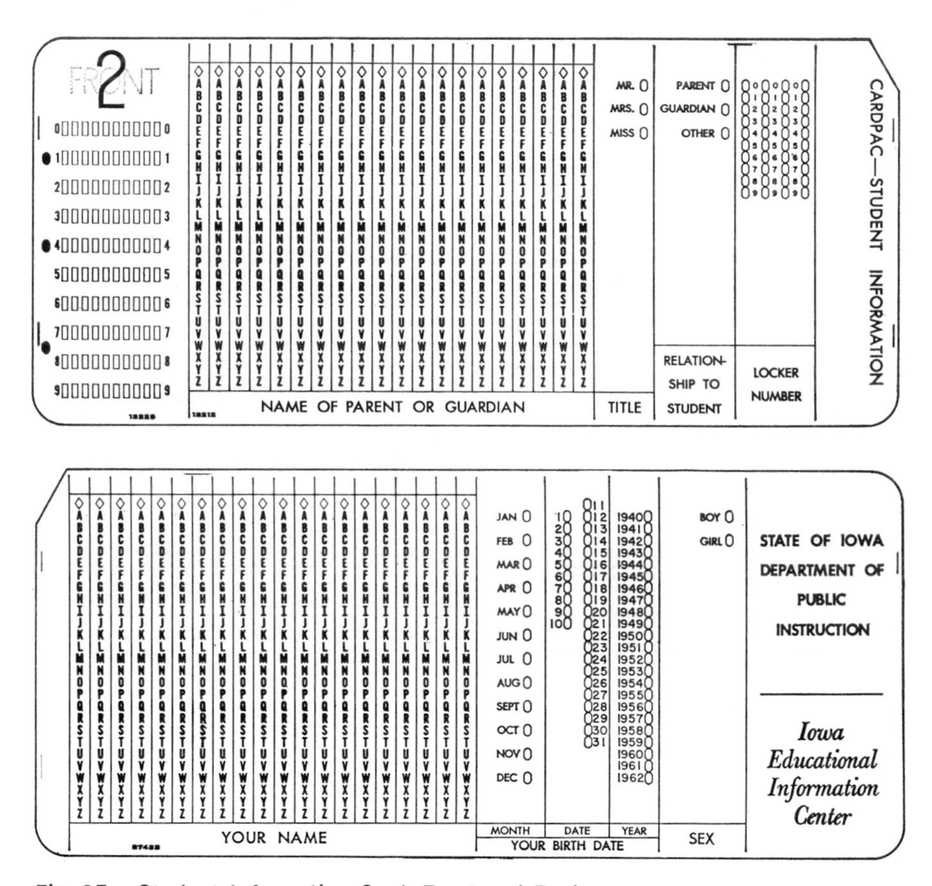

Fig. 25 — Student Information Card, Front and Back.

Tests of Educational Development and for whom the Information Center already has on file the name and ID number, grade level, county, district, and school number. This information is both preprinted and prepunched in the assigned stencil cards.

b. Unassigned student stencil cards are supplied for all other pupils. These cards are prepunched with a pupil ID number and county and district numbers, but carry no name or grade level. They are for pupils who have not been assigned an ID number from the Iowa Tests of Basic Skills or Iowa Tests of Educational Development.

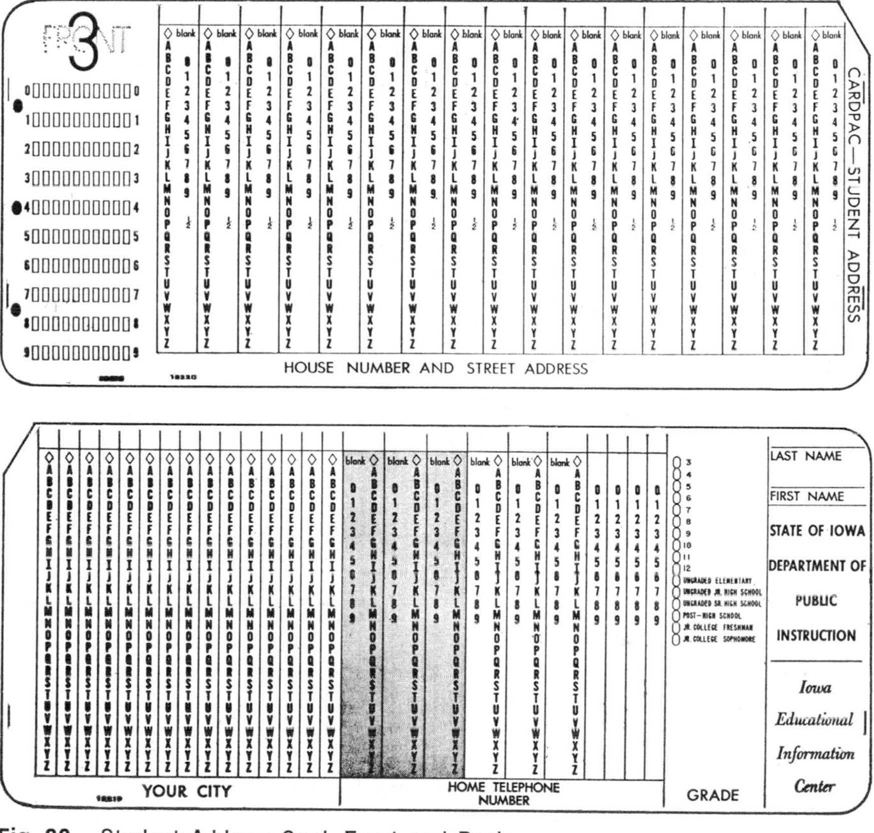

Fig. 26 – Student Address Card, Front and Back.

2. Student information card (Fig. 25). On this card the pupil records biographical facts such as his name, date of birth, sex, name of parent, etc.
3. Student address card (Fig. 26). On this card the pupil records his mailing address, phone number, and grade level.
4. Student questionnaire answer card (Fig. 27). On this card the pupil records his answers to the questionnaire.
5. Student course card (Fig. 28). There were eight of these cards in each CardPac envelope. The pupil enters his name, ID number, and course name on one of these cards for each subject he is

taking and distributes the cards to his teachers, who mark the semester academic marks on the cards at the end of the year.

6. Teacher header cards. These are assembled with the pupil course cards for purposes of identification and machine control. Each teacher needs one such card for each section of each course taught. There are two types of these cards:

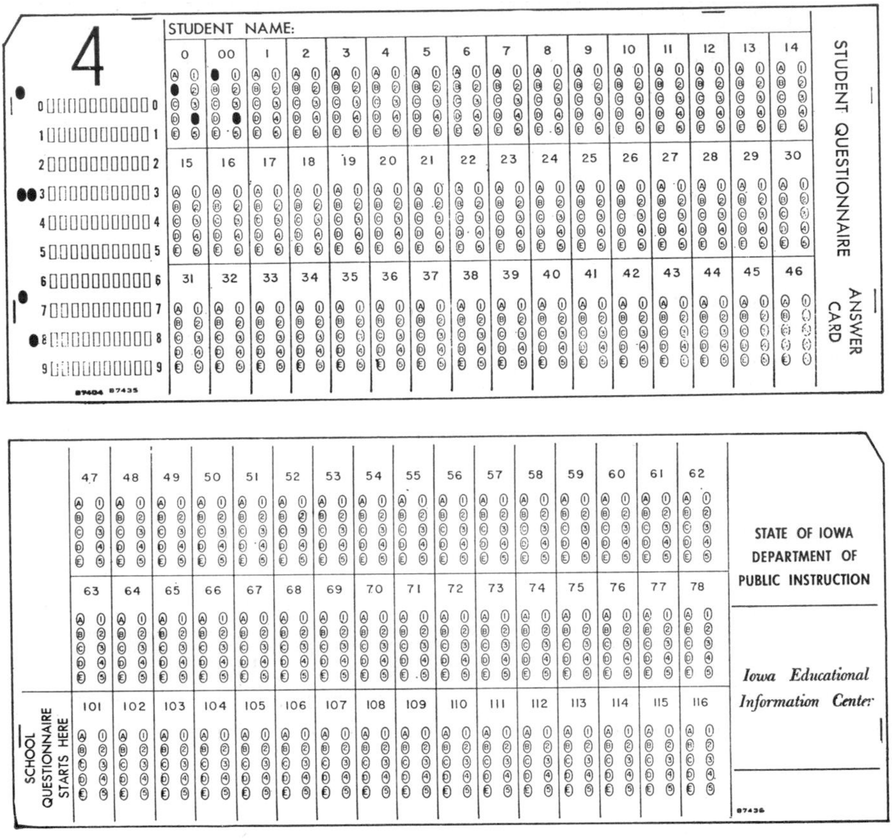

4

STUDENT NAME:

STUDENT QUESTIONNAIRE ANSWER CARD

87404 87435

SCHOOL QUESTIONNAIRE STARTS HERE

STATE OF IOWA
DEPARTMENT OF
PUBLIC INSTRUCTION

Iowa Educational Information Center

87436

Fig. 27 — Student Questionnaire Answer Card, Front and Back.

a. Assigned teacher header cards. These cards are provided for each teacher who completed an Iowa professional school employees data sheet. The teacher's name and number are punched in the card and printed across the top.

b. Unassigned teacher header cards. These contain no teacher number or name. They are to be used by teachers who do not receive assigned header cards, or to replace lost or damaged cards.

7. Course header cards. These will be used to identify packs of

pupil course cards. One is needed for each section of each course taught. Again, there are two types:

a. Assigned course header cards are produced from the master course list described previously. The course name and the course and section number are preprinted and prepunched. The first three digits are the course number and the last two the section number. The section numbers are assigned sequentially. For example, if a teacher indicated that she is teaching three sections of English, numbered 105, the numbers 105–01, 105–02, and 105–03 are assigned.
b. Unassigned course header cards. These are blank cards for use whenever an assigned card is not available.

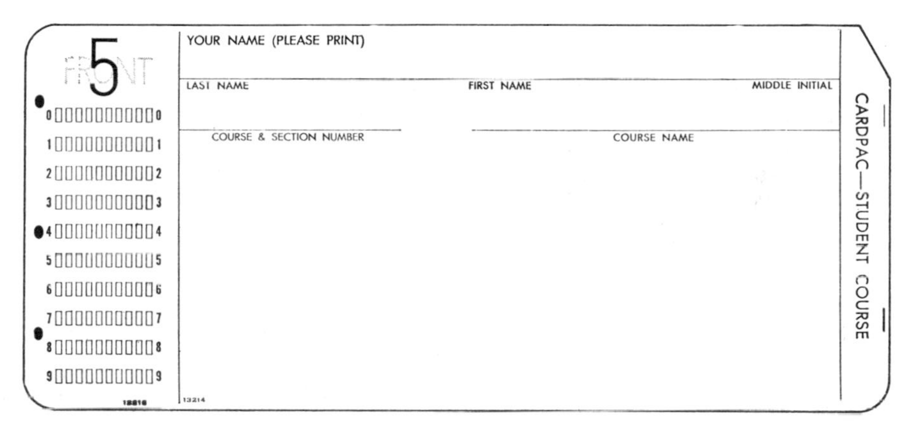
5 FRONT

YOUR NAME (PLEASE PRINT)

LAST NAME FIRST NAME MIDDLE INITIAL

COURSE & SECTION NUMBER COURSE NAME

CARDPAC—STUDENT COURSE

13214

Fig. 28 – Student Course Card.

Prior to the actual administration of CardPac, the principal is asked to check the contents of his CardPac shipment and to report any shortages or mistakes in packing so that corrections can be made.

CARDPAC GROUPS

The CardPac System requires that the pupils be organized into groups, with each group under the supervision of a staff member. For this purpose the principal may use whatever groups are most convenient. Previously organized groups such as homerooms, first period classes, or classes in a particular subject in which all pupils are enrolled, such as English, may be used, or special groups may be set up in designated rooms. Whatever grouping method is used, each such group is referred to as a "CardPac group." The teachers who supervise the administration of the material to each group are called "CardPac proctors."

The major part of the materials are administered to all groups in one day. The initial administration—completed in May 1965—was expected to take about one hour and fifteen minutes in senior high schools and about one hour and thirty minutes in junior high schools, based on the pilot tests. The principals were to select any convenient day about two or three weeks before the end of the school year.

The general questionnaire included 71 items, and the principal was given the option of adding as many as 10 local items.

Proctor's Materials

It was emphasized that materials should be distributed early enough so that the proctors have time to familiarize themselves with the materials and instructions prior to CardPac Day. Each proctor received the following materials:

1. Assigned student stencil cards for the pupils for whom such cards are furnished. The principal's list of student numbers is used as a checklist for dividing and distributing the cards. The cards are in alphabetic sequence by grade level to facilitate distribution.
2. Unassigned student stencil cards for the pupils for whom assigned stencil cards are furnished.
3. Student CardPacs, one for each pupil. These are the same for all pupils and are not identified by pupil.
4. Extra course cards, one for each junior high pupil. Extra cards were not considered necessary for senior high pupils.
5. General questionnaires, one per pupil. These are the same for all pupils.
6. Local questionnaires (if used) for each pupil.
7. Proctor's instructions.
8. Local supplement to proctor's instructions (if used). This would be developed by principals who wished to localize some of the instructions.

Teacher's Materials

Each classroom teacher receives:

1. Teacher header cards with the teacher's name and number printed on them. The teacher needs one for each section of each subject he teaches. If there are not enough preprinted cards for a particular teacher, blank header cards are used and the teacher's Social Security number and name added in the spaces at the top of the card.
2. Course header cards. One of these is furnished to the teacher for each section of each class he teaches. If there are not enough of

these cards with the course name and course section number printed on them, blank cards are filled out and used.

3. Classroom teacher's instructions.
4. Local supplement to classroom teacher's instructions (if used).

A few days before CardPac Administration Day, the principal ordinarily holds a briefing session with the faculty. At this time he also may distribute the CardPac materials to proctors and classroom teachers.

CardPac Administration Day

A typical CardPac Administration Day follows this pattern:

1. The proctor passes out assigned student stencil cards to the pupils for whom he has assigned cards.
2. Unassigned student stencil cards are distributed to pupils who do not receive assigned cards.
3. Pupils who receive unassigned cards write their names on these cards.
4. CardPac envelopes are distrbuted to all pupils.
5. There are eight course cards in the envelope. Pupils fill in one course card for each subject they are taking. The proctor distributes extra course cards where they are needed and picks up surplus cards.
6. Pupils stencil their numbers on all pupil cards.
7. The proctor collects the stencil cards.
8. Pupils return the course cards to the envelope and save them for later use.
9. Pupils fill out basic data about themselves on the student information card (#2) and the student address card (#3).
10. The proctor passes out the general questionnaires and the local questionnaires, if the latter are used.
11. Pupils mark their responses to the questionnaires on the questionnaire answer card (#4).
12. The proctor collects cards #2, #3, and #4.
13. The proctor collects the sample cards and questionnaires.
14. Pupils are instructed to carry their course cards to their classes and give the appropriate course card to teachers the first time they meet each class.
15. Proctors return the following groups of material to the principal's office:
    a. Student stencil cards for pupils present and participating in CardPac.
    b. Assigned student stencil cards for absent pupils.
    c. Cards #2, #3, and #4 grouped together for each pupil.

d. Sample address cards.
e. General and local questionnaires.
f. All unused unassigned student stencil cards.
g. All unused student course cards.
h. Extra CardPac envelopes.

Course Identification

As mentioned, the pupils take their course cards to teachers, who perform the following steps:

1. The first time the teacher meets each of his classes after CardPac Administration Day, the teacher takes the appropriate course header card from his deck of header cards.
2. The teacher writes on the board the course number from that course header card.
3. The pupils copy the course number on their course cards for this class.
4. The teacher collects the course cards from the pupils.
5. The teacher takes a teacher header card from his desk and places it in front of the student course cards for this class.
6. The teacher writes the room number of the course header card and places it in front of the teacher header card.
7. The teacher will put a rubber band around these cards and save them, along with the cards for his other classes, until the end of the semester.
8. At the end of the semester, the teacher puts pupil grades on the course cards.
9. The teacher then turns the packs of course cards in to the office.

The principal's responsibilities do not end once he has briefed the faculty and distributed materials. After CardPac Administration Day, the principal must take care of pupils who were absent that day. The CardPac proctor turns in the stencil cards for these pupils separately, and the principal saves these cards along with the other CardPac materials needed by the pupil. When the pupils return to school, the principal has them fill in the CardPac materials by (1) stenciling ID number on all cards, (2) completing course cards, (3) filling in student information and student address cards, (4) and responding to the questionnaire on card #4. These pupils give their course cards to their teachers as they go to classes.

Two alternative plans are possible:

1. The proctors keep the stencil cards and envelopes of the absentees. Then when the absent pupils return, the proctors have them complete the CardPac materials.

2. A few days after CardPac Day, a makeup session might be held for all pupils who were absent.

If a pupil is present on CardPac Day, but absent afterwards, he keeps his course cards and distributes them to his teachers after he returns to school.

Once the principal has taken care of the absentees, his next important task is to make sure the proctors turn in all completed cards and other materials promptly after administration on CardPac Day. At the end of the semester he makes sure the classroom teachers return a pack of course cards, preceded by the proper teacher header card and course header card, for each section of each course taught.

Careful Packing of Materials

The principal is told to follow directions carefully for packing the materials to be returned to IEIC. The original shipping containers are used. All rubber bands and other such devices are removed from the cards, and the cards are packed so that all of them face the same direction and none is upside down. A card divider is inserted between each of the different types of cards. The cards should be firmly packed in each container with any vacant space stuffed with paper so that the container is completely filled. The principals were then told to package the materials in the following order:

1. Student information card, student address card, and questionnaire answer card for all pupils. These cards should be kept together by pupil.
2. Course cards. The deck of cards for each course section should be kept intact, with the course header card first, the teacher header card second, then the student course cards for that section.
3. Used student stencil cards. In senior high schools these are packaged together in any order. In junior high schools the stencil cards for the highest grade are grouped according to the probable school to be attended by the pupil the next year. A stencil divider card is filled out and inserted in front of each group of stencil cards.
4. All unused cards.
5. School header cards identifying the school. One of these cards, properly completed, is placed in the front of each box of cards.
6. A copy of the local questionnaire. This is needed in tabulating responses to the local questionnaire.

The container is bound or taped securely, marked "1 of 3," "2 of 3," etc., and returned to IEIC. The method of sending the materials is left to the discretion of the principal.

The schools were told the materials should be returned to IEIC by June 15. However, a portion of the schools were unable to meet this deadline, complicating the processing procedures involved.

Of course, the big question at this stage is how successful was the initial administration of the statewide information system.

227,079 Pupils Identified

The answer is that 227,079 pupils in 695 schools were identified and tied to the proper school, course, and teacher. An additional 6,110 pupils could not be entered into the system because their schools closed too early to administer CardPac or returned materials too late for processing.

The frequency of errors on cards returned by the schools and processed at the Measurement Research Center was small in a sampling of 12,000 basic data, questionnaire, and course cards for 1,200 pupils. Only 348 identification number errors—slightly under three percent—were recorded. Of these errors, 192 involved marks in the wrong column, 87 were marked too light to be read by the optical scanner, 9 had more than one marking in a column, 31 had blank columns, and 29 were properly marked but were bent or for some other reason were misread by the machine. Many of these errors were corrected by clerical help, so the actual number of cards rejected totaled less than 50.

As for problems encountered, the most significant one involved tardiness on the part of the schools in meeting the June 15 deadline for return of materials to IEIC. Five percent of the schools had not returned their cards two weeks after the deadline, creating a production problem for the Measurement Research Center, which had to hire additional clerical personnel to handle cards as they arrived.

Some of the schools had packaging problems—cards were packed upside down, backward, or for various other reasons were not in the proper sequence. In some isolated cases, cards on different rows in the box had filtered together because of improper packing. This required extra clerical work to put them in order. Some of the schools separated cards they had been asked to group together.

Some of the public relations problems involved already have been mentioned. Another problem in this regard—or perhaps a better word for it would be oversight—was that some communities were not sent four-page CardPac Newspapers. Each pupil participating in CardPac was to take this tabloid-size newspaper home to his parents to acquaint them with this new computerized system. The newspaper included illustrations of the data cards involved, cartoons involving computers, Charles Schulz "Peanuts" comic strips on teacher problems, a picture taken during the trial questionnaire administration and an accompanying story, and other articles designed to introduce the parents and pupils to CardPac. The communities which did not receive the CardPac Newspaper subscribed to other IEIC computerized services and had previously supplied much of the information needed in the CardPac system. Therefore, no effort was made to get the newspapers to them. In at least one of these communities, CardPac was criticized by the school board, and an ensuing editorial in the local paper placed much of the blame on a lack of communication. Thus, distribution of the newspapers might have headed off this criticism.

Mentioned previously was the fact that a "sin of omission" committed by data-collection agencies was improper feedback to the school personnel who had provided the original information. For this reason IEIC makes every effort to feed back to superintendents, principals, teachers, and counselors, digested, meaningful data to improve individualized instruction and the educational program in general.

THREE TYPES OF FEEDBACK

IEIC provides three major types of feedback:

- Student data summary sheet
- An item analysis of questionnaire responses, and
- Frequency distributions of relationships between selected items.

Student Data Summary

The student data summary, delivered to schools prior to the opening of the fall term, was produced for each pupil in nine copies so that the principals, teachers, and guidance counselors could have copies for their own files.

The summary includes the following information: name, address, city, telephone number, county, district, and school numbers, birth date, composite Iowa Testing Program score, courses and academic marks, mark-point average, health, hours of work outside of school for pay, hours of work outside of school for no pay, hours of study outside of school, participation in various extracurricular activities, person living with, father's and mother's occupations, and the number of hours the mother works.

Principals are asked to distribute the data summaries to the teachers at the beginning of the school year so that each teacher has, early in the year, cumulative information about each pupil in his class. Teachers may then be better prepared to offer individualized aid and instruction, especially to pupils they are working with for the first time. The student data summary represents progress in reducing teacher time spent in searching through cumulative folders for pertinent information.

Item Analysis of Responses

The second feedback item mailed to principals and superintendents was a computer printout "item analysis of responses" to the 71 items in the CardPac student questionnaire, listing total responses by grades within the respective schools and comparable statewide totals. The questionnaire items consisted of such topics as parents' occupation and education, the child's educational and occupational goals, the amount of work the pupil does outside of school and the amount of home study, participation in extracurricular activities, pupil feelings about school, teachers, and subjects, and the ownership and/or use of cars.

A four-page "Administrator's Supplement to CardPac Feedback, Spring, 1965," accompanied the item analysis of responses. As explained in the supplement, each of the 71 items in the questionnaire was designed to gather pupil information that might conceivably contribute to a better understanding of some educational problem. The item analysis presented responses of the pupils in a particular school by grade, giving the number and percent of pupils selecting each of the suggested answers to each question. The report also showed the percent of the entire Iowa public secondary school population in the same grade who selected the same response.

Administrators were told that a study of this report might prove useful to local school authorities in finding solutions to known problems or in identifying new ones. They also were told the analysis may stimulate some fresh thinking about possible general improvements in the local educational offering.

For example, if there were local concern over a possible imbalance in the curriculum between vocational and so-called college preparatory courses, it would be helpful to have an objective description of the student body in terms of: (1) the amount of schooling beyond high school the pupils hope to obtain, (2) the kinds of colleges they hope to attend, (3) the vocations or professions they expect to enter, (4) the extent to which they are prepared to finance their own higher education, and (5) the influence of parental desires. The information obtained from the questionnaire could shed considerable light on such factors in the local situation. It would also reveal, in concrete figures, whether the local student body differs significantly from the general school population in respect to these factors. Hitherto, few, if any, Iowa school systems have had really precise information of this kind. Administrators have had to rely on subjective impressions, which may not be at all consistent with the real facts.

The value of an analysis of this kind clearly depends upon the nature and quality of the items in the questionnaire administered. A great deal has yet to be learned about what questions need most to be asked, how they may best be phrased, and how the data collected may best be presented. Each time a questionnaire of this kind is administered, more will be learned about how the next one can be improved. Much also will be learned about how to make the next more useful and more readily interpretable.

Frequency Distribution Study

Thirteen of the 71 items in the questionnaire were chosen for the frequency distribution study comprising the third major feedback report. The criteria for this selection were: (1) is the content of the item of strong interest to school personnel, and (2) does the content reveal pupil behavior in specific school and home situations? Statistical results did not influence the selection.

The report shows how pupils classified at various levels of achievement responded to each of nine selected items. Two academic measures were used in this classification. One is the mark-point average (MPA), also commonly called grade-point average. This is the unweighted average of the pupil's academic marks assigned by teachers during the second semester of the 1964–65 school year. The other measure is the percentile rank of the pupil composite score on either the Iowa Tests of Educational Development in the fall of 1964 or the Iowa Tests of Basic Skills in January of 1965. Questionnaire data, MPA, and percentile rank on the Iowa Tests were available for 172,789 public school pupils in grades 7–12. The statewide data reported for these nine items are based on these 172,789 cases.

The analyses not only show relationships between variables, but also indicate the distribution of each variable in the Iowa secondary school population and also in the local school situation. With these twin descriptions, school officials can make state and local comparisons and assess the possible interaction of certain demographic and scholastic aspects in either school population.

In addition to the three major feedback reports, participating schools receive different lists of data as output of the information system: course headers, roster of professional staff, pupil directory, room list, class list, master course list, mark report form, attendance card monitor, error suspect list for computing mark-point average, attendance list, error list of marks, and an attendance error list. These provide valuable aids in day-to-day administrative activities.

CHANGES IN THE SYSTEM

What has been described up to this point are procedures, materials, and output involved in the May 1965 administration of the statewide information system. There were changes, additions, and logical extensions of the system for the second administration in the fall of 1965. That is another story entirely, but some of these changes are listed to show the metamorphosis involved.

1. The word "front" was printed on all data cards to facilitate packing and deter errors in this procedure.
2. The name of the CardPac student questionnaire was changed to CardPac pupil inventory, the number of questions reduced from 71 to 37, some questions were changed, and the administration time shortened from the 45–60 minute range to the 20–30 minute range.
3. The student data summary feedback was discontinued because of disuse and an unfavorable response from school people. This was the only feedback linked directly to individual pupils. Other feedback involved only school and state totals.
4. The 10-question "local option" section of the pupil questionnaire was discontinued for two reasons: (a) because of costs, and (b) because of lack of control over items added by local schools.
5. Responsibility for initial editing of all incoming CardPac materials shifted from Measurement Research Center to Information Center personnel, the goal being correction of more errors before materials are processed. The schools, of course, have the primary responsibility of sending in accurate materials that will necessitate only a minimum number of corrections.
6. As a logical followup to the initial administration, "old" pupil information was verified and updated. The preprinted data were fed back to the pupil on a student information printout. Any corrections or additions were made by the pupil on the student information and student address cards.
7. Another logical extension was the development of a file maintenance system to give schools an up-to-date accurate file of pupil, course, and teacher information. Careful maintenance of the file would enable IEIC to (a) provide average daily attendance figures for the secondary schools, (b) provide feedback to the schools in the form of class lists, summary reports of

attendance, and academic mark labels, and (c) provide data on the number of original entries, re-entries, transfers, completions, and dropouts to state and federal agencies.

PROJECTS RELATED TO IEIC

The CardPac System of Educational Accounting is only one of many Iowa Education Information Center projects dedicated to a total information system. Following is a description of related projects:

School Facilities Accounting

Facilities data collection procedures and instruments are being developed and identification has been made of types of data to be collected and methods to be used.

The system will begin with the identification of school plants (sites and buildings on those sites where instruction takes place). Later, floor location of the classroom, its area, and the number of pupil stations in the room will be added and a space utilization study made.

Additional information also will be collected on all sites, including non-instruction areas (e.g., square footage in the corridors), and adjunct instructional spaces (e.g., preparation rooms next door to biology rooms).

Integrated Personnel-Payroll System

IEIC is working with a local school district in preparing an integrated personnel-payroll system that can be adapted statewide. As the finance track is implemented, efforts will center on areas identified by the Financial Accounting Committee of the State of Iowa: (a) budget, (b) procedures for recording receipts, (c) procedures for recording expenditures, (d) procedures for recording payroll expenditures, (e) maintaining clearing account records, and (f) prorating for unit costs.

Elementary Pupil Accounting

A statewide elementary pupil accounting system has been initiated. Only the name, grade, sex, and birth data for public elementary pupils are being collected at the start, along with certain staff data. Some of the information already is on file as a result of the pupils' participation in the Iowa Tests of Basic Skills. This latter information is preprinted for school use during administration of the program.

COMPUTER SCHEDULING

IEIC's computer scheduling program exemplifies the growth of the Center's activity in general. Twelve secondary schools were scheduled initially in 1963 and that total has grown to 79, including several non-Iowa schools for the 1966–67 school year.

The scheduling program adapted from the IBM Class program does not build the master schedule—it provides aid for the principal in building the master schedule and loads pupils into classes defined by the principal in this master schedule.

Among other things, the IEIC scheduling system makes possible the separation of a single large group of pupils into smaller groups of various sizes for different kinds of activities and classes. It also enables the school to combine small groups which were originally members of different larger groups. Thus two groups of 60 boys and 60 girls could be assigned to different physical education classes on two days of the week, regrouped to assign 30 boys and 30 girls together for music on two other days, and bring the whole group together into a single large study hall on the fifth day of the week. This type of procedure will accommodate nearly unlimited combinations of schedules, classes, and activities.[6]

The service includes pupil directory information, conflict matrix, master section list, error list, class loading report, homeroom, grade, and school rosters, schedule cards, list of sections taught each period of the day, list of pupils requesting each course, preliminary schedules, class lists, homeroom lists and class rosters, study hall lists, a continuous form listing of all pupil schedules, and identification cards.

The system offers four distinct advantages not generally available:

1. Educational data processing consultants with experience as school administrators to assist principals in scheduling
2. A commitment to provide the best possible schedules without specified limitations on the number of individual course request changes needed
3. Capability to hold pupils in groups and/or subgroups for a series of classes or activities, and
4. An on-going research program to improve the educational services to local schools.

The Center also is offering Stanford's Flexible Scheduling Program through an agreement with that California university. Schools are given an opportunity to remain in the regular scheduling program or enter the flexible program.

ATTENDANCE AND MARK REPORTING

IEIC's attendance and mark reporting service, now being used

[6] *UPDATE Principal's Manual for Pupil Scheduling by Computer.* Iowa City, Iowa: Iowa Educational Information Center, The University of Iowa, January 1966.

by 51 schools and 24,000 pupils, is compatible with computer scheduling and CardPac. It offers nonreturnable pupil report forms for the parents plus two copies for school use, class lists with cumulative pupil marks for teachers, counselors, and principals, anecdotal remarks from teachers to parents, computed mark-point averages and rank-order lists, frequency distributions of pupil marks by teacher, course, and schools, attendance summaries for pupil report forms, office use, and state reports, and self-adhesive pupil attendance and mark labels.

As part of the attendance and mark reporting service research, a survey was made of academic mark procedures and mark-point averages in Iowa's secondary schools. The results were published in booklet form and fed back to administrators.[7] The summary was forwarded to administrators without interpretation as a status study of practices that now exist in Iowa secondary schools. It may serve as a guide to each principal as he evaluates practices in his own schools. After analyzing the data, principals were asked to make suggestions for other information needed in planning future studies.

In developing the attendance and mark reporting service, the systems planners provided considerable flexibility so that schools may select a procedure most applicable to the individual district. The system was modified to conform to the practices found to be most widely used among the schools in the above-mentioned survey.

STUDENT RANKING SERVICE

IEIC's student ranking service (SRS) evaluates pupils according to selected attributes for differential grouping into sections so that instruction can be more closely tailored to the majority of pupils and course marks can be assigned more objectively within the sections.

SRS employs the modern digital computer to do the routine computational tasks involved in evaluating pupils on multiple variables and assigning each pupil a respective rank. STS also produces, as a by-product, summary statistics useful to school personnel engaged in other pupil evaluation or guidance procedures.

The service is designed to utilize data already available through the CardPac information system, the Iowa Testing Programs, computer scheduling, and attendance and mark reporting. This enables

[7] "Summary of Survey of Marking Procedures and Mark-Point Averages for Iowa Secondary Schools," State of Iowa Department of Public Instruction and the Iowa Educational Information Center, November 1965.

the school to take advantage of the SRS program with a minimum of additional data collection.

The service enables the principal or guidance counselor to evaluate pupils for placement in various course sections according to measures established on the basis of past experience, or as a result of a statistical analysis, such as multiple regression. Some of the more frequent measures used are:

- Sub-tests or composite scores of the Iowa Tests of Educational Development.
- Prior course marks.
- Intelligence test scores.
- Differential aptitude test scores.
- Teacher recommendations.
- Special area tests such as the Coop English Test and the Iowa Algebra Aptitude Test.
- Interest measures such as Kuder Preference Schedule, Strong Vocational Interest Blank, etc.[8]

The goal of the student ranking service is to provide the means for determining a pupil's relative rank within a group based on measures which are definable on a numeric scale. SRS ranks pupils in appropriate groups according to specifications set forth by the local school system. SRS does not establish the criteria on which to base this ranking. Schools utilizing the ranking service must answer the following questions:

- Which pupils are to be ranked?
- What measures or variables are to be used in evaluating rankings in each group?
- How much weight is to be given each measure used?
- Which pupils are to be evaluated for which groups?

The counselor or principal specifies data to be prepunched into group SRS identification cards and student SRS data cards, and then completes the cards by filling in additional information.

The group SRS identification card provides space for identifying a course in which pupils are to be grouped, and space for variable weights or multipliers to be used in ranking pupils in the course. One card is completed for each group in which pupils are to be ranked.

The student SRS data card provides space for identifying up to six groups in which the pupil is to be ranked, and scores made by the pupil on variables to be used in ranking. One card is completed for each pupil to be ranked.

---

[8] William G. Miller, *UPDATE Student Ranking Service Manual.* Iowa City, Iowa: Iowa Educational Information Center, The University of Iowa, June 1965.

TOUCH-TONE DATA TRANSMISSION

A successful experiment in transmitting pupil attendance data by Touch-Tone telephone from an Iowa City elementary school to IEIC showed the advantages and economic feasibility of such a system.[9]

The only equipment required at the elementary school was an ordinary telephone line, a Touch-Tone telephone, and a box of perforated plastic cards. Punched holes in the cards are used to dial the receiving location and transmit the data. The cards have a capacity of 14 characters or signals and are easily prepared with a stylus or ordinary pencil point.

The Touch-Tone telephone employs pushbuttons instead of a dial. These pushbuttons transmit tones in various combinations that are translated at the receiving end into electrical impulses by a data set. The data set interprets the signals received over commercial telephone lines for the data processing equipment, which in this case was an IBM Model 6 Card Punch.

The impulses fed to the card punch activate numeric keys as well as other functional switches. Two extra keys on the Touch-Tone telephone send signals to talk and to indicate the end of the record. The resulting punched cards can be fed directly into a computer.

The school's attendance procedures, which remained unchanged during the month-long data transmission test, involved teachers submitting lists of absent and tardy pupils to the principal's office each morning and afternoon. In turn, the school secretary used the Touch-Tone telephone to transmit the data to the receiving set at the Center.

She used two decks of plastic cards—a set of pupil cards arranged by homeroom and a set of header cards for each type of transaction, such as, absent a.m., absent p.m., absent all day, and tardy.

One of the objectives of the project was to develop a system simple enough to explain to a new clerk or secretary by phone, and this was accomplished.

An advantage of Touch-Tone transmission is that the data are accumulated in a central location for preparation of attendance reports needed by local schools, the State Department of Public Instruction, and federal agencies. In addition, this procedure eliminates many time-consuming steps now used by schools and provides school people with an up-to-date file.

---

[9] "Touch-Tone Transmission," *AEDS Monitor,* April 1966, pp. 15-16.

SCHOOL CENSUS

The Information Center has helped three Iowa communities automate their school census procedures—Council Bluffs, Des Moines, and Cedar Rapids. IEIC personnel serve as consultants in the development of data-collection forms. Measurement Research Center processes the collected data.

Cedar Rapids has the most sophisticated program, identifying all persons under 21 in individual city blocks, and, in turn, tying them to appropriate schools.

EDUCATIONAL DATA BANK

The Information Center's data bank duplicates some of the information in State Department of Public Instruction and Iowa Testing Program files to give the data bank as broad a base as is possible at this time. Much of the information has been integrated, making it possible to relate any item of information concerning any phase to any other item in the file.

The information collected by the Center consists chiefly of pupil, staff, and curriculum data. The Center also stores data on school censuses, North Central Association membership, attendance and mark reporting, student ranking, and computer scheduling. The State Department data to which the Center has access includes such items as the Secretary's Annual Report, General Annual Report, teacher certification, program accounting, graduate followup material, and private and parochial school reports.

A Data Bank User's Manual to assist the researcher in determining the availability of data and procedures for their retrieval has been prepared.[10]

HEAD START IDENTIFICATION

The first statewide study in the United States of the educational record of Operation Head Start boys and girls through their first two years of elementary schooling is being made by IEIC under a $31,498 grant from the U. S. Office of Economic Opportunity (OEO)

The 4,300 four- and five-year-olds who were in the eight-week Iowa project in the summer of 1965 were identified in the spring of 1966 at their respective schools.

In planning procedures to identify the children, IEIC used OEO tapes which included information in nine categories: (a) parent evaluation, (b) worker evaluation (nonprofessional), (c)

[10] *Educational Data Bank User's Manual.* Iowa City, Iowa: Iowa Educational Information Center, The University of Iowa, December 1965.

worker attitudes toward Head Start, (d) preschool inventory on children, (e) psychological screening, (f) behavior inventory, (g) professional staff information, (h) parent participation, and (i) medical-dental records.

IOWA PROFESSIONAL SCHOOL EMPLOYEES DATA SHEET

The Center, working with personnel of the State Department of Public Instruction, has developed a form used to collect professional staff data known as the Iowa professional school employees data sheet.

The following data are collected: county number, district number, home school number, Social Security number, folder number, name, total hours of credit earned, undergraduate major, graduate major, highest degree held, year the highest degree was received, institution from which the individual graduated, salary, subject and grade level assignment, title and previous titles held, contract period, marital status, sex, previous occupation, semester hours of credit in the area being taught, different schools in which the individual may work, grade or area in which the person may be teaching.

Information is collected on all public, private, and parochial professional staff through the 12th grade and also junior college and vocational personnel.

Although they are not part of this total school information system, two other IEIC activities are worthy of mention. The Center provides the computer programing and systems design for the interagency case information service, a computerized data processing system aimed at improving care given the mentally retarded in Iowa. The service was organized under a $107,633 grant from the U. S. Public Health Service, Division of Chronic Diseases.

The service would make pertinent information on the retardate, as his needs change, available on a confidential basis to the participating agencies who are providing patients with direct-care services.

The Center also has established its own library of educational data processing literature, which utilizes the mechanized KWIC (Keyword-In-Context) indexing system. The KWIC process is applied to the titles and abstracts of the documents for retrieval purposes.

REFERENCES

Dunn, Francis R. "A Comparison of Selected Educational, Socio-Economic, and Attitudinal Characteristics of Seniors in Two Groups of Iowa School Districts," *Research Digest*. No. 20. Iowa City, Iowa: Iowa Center for Research in School Administration, The University of Iowa.

Feldt, Leonard S., and Robert A. Forsyth. "The Relationship of ITED Composite Score to the Expectations, Aspirations, Activities and Sociological Characteristics of Iowa High School Students," *Iowa Testing Programs Research Report*. No. 1, Iowa Testing Programs. Iowa City, Iowa: The University of Iowa, March 1966.

Marker, Robert W. "Computer-Based Educational Information Systems, The Iowa Case," *Computer Concepts and Educational Administration*. Iowa Educational Information Center, The University of Iowa, Iowa City, 1966, pp. 77-99.

McCaffrey, Kenneth J. "CardPac," *Iowa Output*. Iowa City, Iowa: Iowa Educational Information Center, The University of Iowa, September 1965.

——. "Iowa Educational Information Center," *AEDS Monitor*. October 1965. pp. 4-7.

——. "Iowa Educational Information Center Expands Its UPDATE Services," *Midland Schools* (Des Moines, Iowa), November-December 1965, pp. 29, 38.

——. "Iowa Educational Information Center," *Epsilon Bulletin*, Vol. 39 (Phi Delta Kappa, College of Education, The University of Iowa), 1965, pp. 14-17.

——. "Educational Data Bank," *Iowa Output*, January 1966.

——. "How Study and Teachers Rated by Iowa Students," *Midland Schools*, January-February 1966, p. 21.

——. "Iowa Study Explores Academic Marking Practices," *Midland Schools*, March-April 1966, p. 20.

Van Dusseldorp, Ralph A. "It's in the Cards," *Midland Schools*, May 1965, p. 26.

——. "CardPac . . . Controversy With a Future," *Iowa Educational Bulletin* (Des Moines, Iowa), October 1965.

11 automated pupil accounting procedures—disk and tape approach

ORLANDO F. FURNO and MICHAEL E. KARAS

DR. ORLANDO F. FURNO *received his PhD from Columbia University in 1956, having left his position as high school teacher of physics and chemistry to work for his doctorate at Teachers College. After being discharged from naval service in 1946, Dr. Furno attended the University of Washington, majoring in physics and mathematics and minoring in chemistry. He received his BS degree* magna cum laude *in 1949, and was elected to Phi Beta Kappa.*

Dr. Furno joined the staff of the U.S. Office of Education (USOE) in 1958 as a specialist in the analysis of school expenditures. While with USOE, and in collaboration with School Management *magazine, he developed* School Management's *Cost of Education Index. Dr. Furno left USOE in 1960 to assume his present position.*

Dr. Furno holds memberships in the American Association of School Administrators, American Education Research Association, Federal School Men's Club, and others. He is the author of numerous publications.

WHY AUTOMATE PUPIL ACCOUNTING?

Any pupil accounting system should provide statistical data such as the following: (1) day of attendance—i.e., whether a given pupil has been absent or present; and (2) original entry—i.e., a pupil who enters school for the first time in a given school year in a given school district.

From these two basic statistics, data on pupil aggregate days absence, aggregate days attendance, aggregate days membership, average daily attendance, average daily membership, enrollment, etc., may be obtained. This information is useful for such purposes as:

1. basis for state and federal aid,
2. basis for compliance with local, state, and federal legal regulations,
3. future school population projections,
4. basis for local, state, and federal reports,
5. publication of reports concerning enrollment and attendance,

6. apportionment of state aid for special education programs,
7. transportation needs of local school system, and
8. distribution of textbooks and other audio-visual, instructional materials.

Automating pupil attendance procedures is advantageous to teachers:

1. The homeroom teacher does not have to set up a roll book on the first day of school.
2. The homeroom teacher does not have to perform a tedious, time-consuming clerical chore—balancing the roll book each day to get year-to-date and end-of-month statistics.
3. Homeroom teacher does not have to waste time doing tedious, error-prone arithmetical tasks such as preparing a daily attendance report or a teacher's monthly and semester report.

Automating pupil attendance reduces tedious clerical chores for the classroom teacher and for the principal. Thus, the principal has more time for carrying out his most important task, supervision of instruction.

- The principal does not have to spend hours preparing a principal's monthly report.
- The principal does not consume days preparing the principal's semiannual and annual reports.

Automating pupil attendance is not only advantageous to teachers and principals, but is also beneficial to the school system as a whole.

1. Automation makes for increased accuracy in the reporting of pupil and faculty statistics. The repetitive, tedious arithmetical chores are done by the computer rather than by teachers and principals.
2. Automation almost eliminates the central office audit and tabulation function, saving many man-years of clerical time. Because of built-in checks and balances in the computer program, auditing reports are minimized.
3. Automation provides for development of a basic pupil card file (particularly a pupil numbering system) which permits later expansion into other areas of automated record keeping such as
   a. Pupil report cards. Teachers do not have to laboriously make out pupil report cards. Parents retain an IBM copy of their child's report card.
   b. Grade-point average automatically computed.
   c. Pupil cumulative folders automatically prepared.
   d. Census of child population registers automatically developed.

e. Location of each child by block number, tax block, enumeration district, and census tract available for population prediction studies, location of school facilities near pupil population centers, etc.
f. Development of central repository of pupil information, storage, and retrieval system.
g. Flexible pupil scheduling systems.

SYSTEM SPECIFICATIONS

The automated summary pupil attendance system described here requires disk and tape capability as well as a computer. The pupil attendance programs were written in Fortran IV. The user can utilize either the original Fortran source statement decks or the same programs translated into machine language decks. Several thousand pupils are presently being processed. Pupils at the elementary, junior high, and senior high school levels are involved. The equipment actually in use for this pupil attendance system is as follows:

- Two disk storage drives (IBM 1311)
- Four tape stations (IBM 7330)
- Card reader and punch (IBM 1402)
- High speed printer (IBM 1403)
- 16 K central processor (IBM 1401)
- Digitek optical scanner (Model "100")
- Keypunch (IBM 024 and IBM 026)
- Sorter (IBM 083)
- Reproducer (IBM 514)
- Tabulator (IBM 407)
- Numeric collator (IBM 085)
- Alphabetic collator (IBM 087)
- Interpreter (IBM 557)
- Card verifier (IBM 056 and IBM 059)

Getting Started — Over the Summer Procedures

Over the summer is the best time for a school district to implement this pupil attendance system. However, a school district could phase in schools during the school year, preferably in the fall. Implementation requires not only setting up efficient data center job procedures but also in school training procedures.

To facilitate understanding of the automated summary pupil attendance system, procedures are presented in terms of who does what and when, the action to be taken, and the date action is to be completed. This procedure is most highly recommended by leading systems and procedures personnel. (See Figs. 29 and 30.)

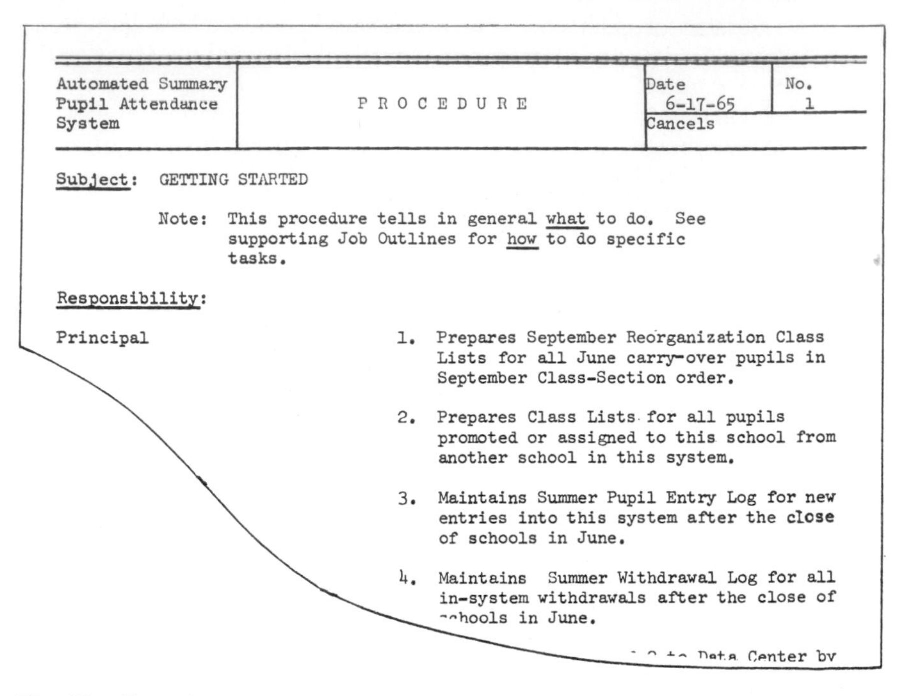

Automated Summary Pupil Attendance System	PROCEDURE	Date 6-17-65	No. 1
		Cancels	

Subject: GETTING STARTED

Note: This procedure tells in general what to do. See supporting Job Outlines for how to do specific tasks.

Responsibility:

Principal

1. Prepares September Reorganization Class Lists for all June carry-over pupils in September Class-Section order.
2. Prepares Class Lists for all pupils promoted or assigned to this school from another school in this system.
3. Maintains Summer Pupil Entry Log for new entries into this system after the close of schools in June.
4. Maintains Summer Withdrawal Log for all in-system withdrawals after the close of schools in June.

Fig. 29 — Procedure.

Preparing Class and Faculty September Lists

Responsibility for the preparation of a school's class lists lies with the school's principal. By the first week of July, the principal should prepare class lists of June carryover pupils. These lists should be arranged by September's class and section order. The principal should also prepare class lists for all pupils promoted or assigned to his school from other schools in the school system. Again class lists should be by September's class and section order. Copies of these September reorganization class lists are shown in Figure 31. The principal then forwards these class lists to the data center. This should be done by July 5. Of course, the dates referred to here are only suggested. They were based on work loads involving the processing of about 20,000 pupils. Smaller school systems would naturally have different cut-off dates than larger ones. What is important here is that cut-off dates for job procedures be determined and adhered to.

The data center has responsibility for keypunching the class lists. From the class lists, individual pupil cards are keypunched. Figure 32 shows the punched card layout. Also shown is the variable's name, code, format specification, card columns occupied, and

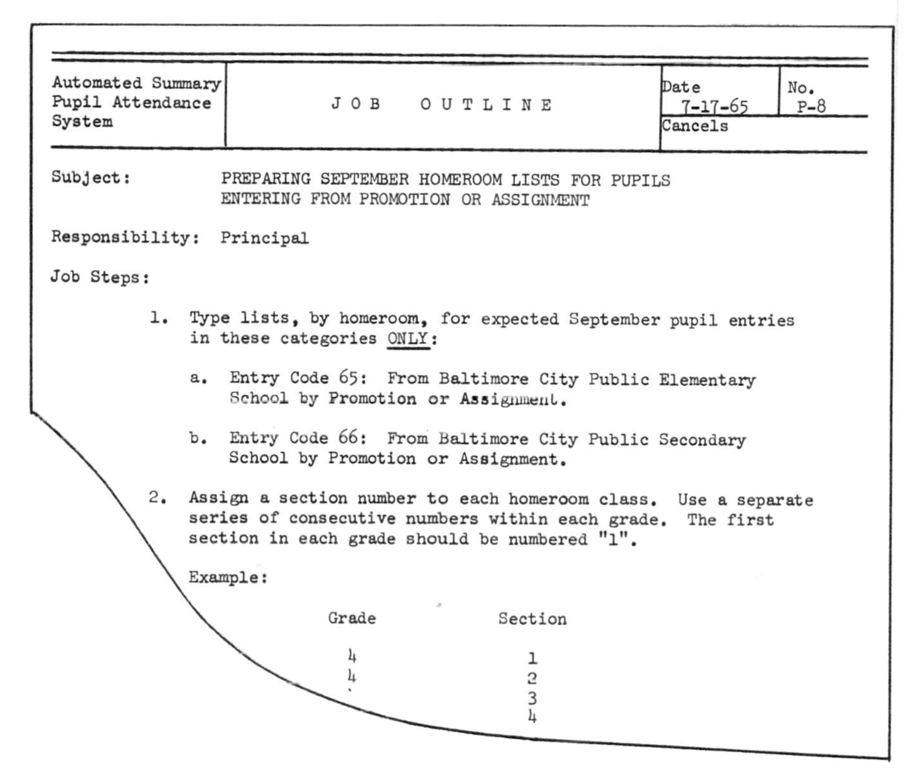

Automated Summary Pupil Attendance System	J O B O U T L I N E	Date 7-17-65	No. P-8
		Cancels	

Subject: PREPARING SEPTEMBER HOMEROOM LISTS FOR PUPILS ENTERING FROM PROMOTION OR ASSIGNMENT

Responsibility: Principal

Job Steps:

1. Type lists, by homeroom, for expected September pupil entries in these categories ONLY:

   a. Entry Code 65: From Baltimore City Public Elementary School by Promotion or Assignment.

   b. Entry Code 66: From Baltimore City Public Secondary School by Promotion or Assignment.

2. Assign a section number to each homeroom class. Use a separate series of consecutive numbers within each grade. The first section in each grade should be numbered "1".

   Example:

Grade	Section
4	1
4	2
.	3
	4

Fig. 30 – Job Outline.

field width. The data center completes the keypunching of the individual pupil cards by July 15. Utilizing the IBM 1401 computer system, the data center prints out temporary September reorganization class lists. The data center mails each school its own class lists. Each school should receive its lists by July 20.

Each principal reviews his school's temporary September reorganization class lists. He updates these class lists to reflect the following: (1) summer school promotion results; (2) school administrative needs, i.e., addition or deletion of classes, etc.; and (3) elimination of errors.

From the time school closed, each principal was to record each new pupil registrant in his summer pupil entry log, and each withdrawing pupil in his summer pupil withdrawal log. (See Figs. 33 and 34.) In school districts which have continuous pupil accounting procedures, entry and withdrawal logs are a must for over-the-summer pupil attendance procedures.

The principal is also responsible for the September faculty list. (See Fig. 35.) This list indicates the name of each educa-

SEPTEMBER REORGANIZATION CLASS LIST

School No.	Level	Grade	Section	Curricular - Program Code
60	1	4	1	--

Entry Code

65

BOYS (2)		GIRLS (1)	
Last Name	First Name	Last Name	First Name
BLAIR	JOE	BEASLEY	ARMINTA
BLUNT	WILLIAM	CARTER	LINDA
BOYD	EARL	JOHNSON	SANDRA
BROADWAY	RAYMOND	MURDOCK	INDIE
CORBIN	ERIC	PURNELL	SHERL
DAVIS	CALVIN	ROBINSON	ALICE
FINCH	THEODORE	TAYLOR	PAMELA
JOHNSON	DUANE	WILLIAMS	ELIZABETH
LIPSCOMB	MCKINLEY		
PIERCE	ANTHONY		
PRYOR	CHARLES		
SNYDER	JERRY		
YATES	MELVIN		

Fig. 31 – September Reorganization Class Lists.

tional employee in the school, as well as selected data such as homeroom class and section assignment, department classification, etc.

On or about August 15, the principal must send to the data center the following materials: (1) the updated temporary September reorganization class lists; (2) the pupil entry log; (3) the pupil withdrawal log; and (4) the September faculty list. In many instances, not all faculty members have been assigned or hired. The principal handles this by indicating for the name of that faculty assignment "Vacancy." Later, when the name of the person who will handle a specific "vacancy" is known, the faculty change program will routinely take care of this situation.

Upon receipt of the updated data from the individual school principals, the data center corrects keypunching errors in the mainline individual pupil attendance cards. Next, data from the summer pupil entry log are keypunched and the individual pupil attendance cards are interfiled with the mainline deck. Then data from the summer pupil withdrawal log are keypunched. The process is a simple one. A clerical employee pulls out each pupil's individual pupil attendance card (arranged by school number, class and section order, then alphabetized by sex). Keypunch operators then punch the appropriate pupil withdrawal data into the pupil cards. Pupils so withdrawn are given the grade and section code of 50-00, called the principal's office roll, and their pupil cards are interfiled with the mainline deck.

The data center also keypunches the individual faculty card using the September faculty lists as source documents. The faculty card is shown in Figure 36.

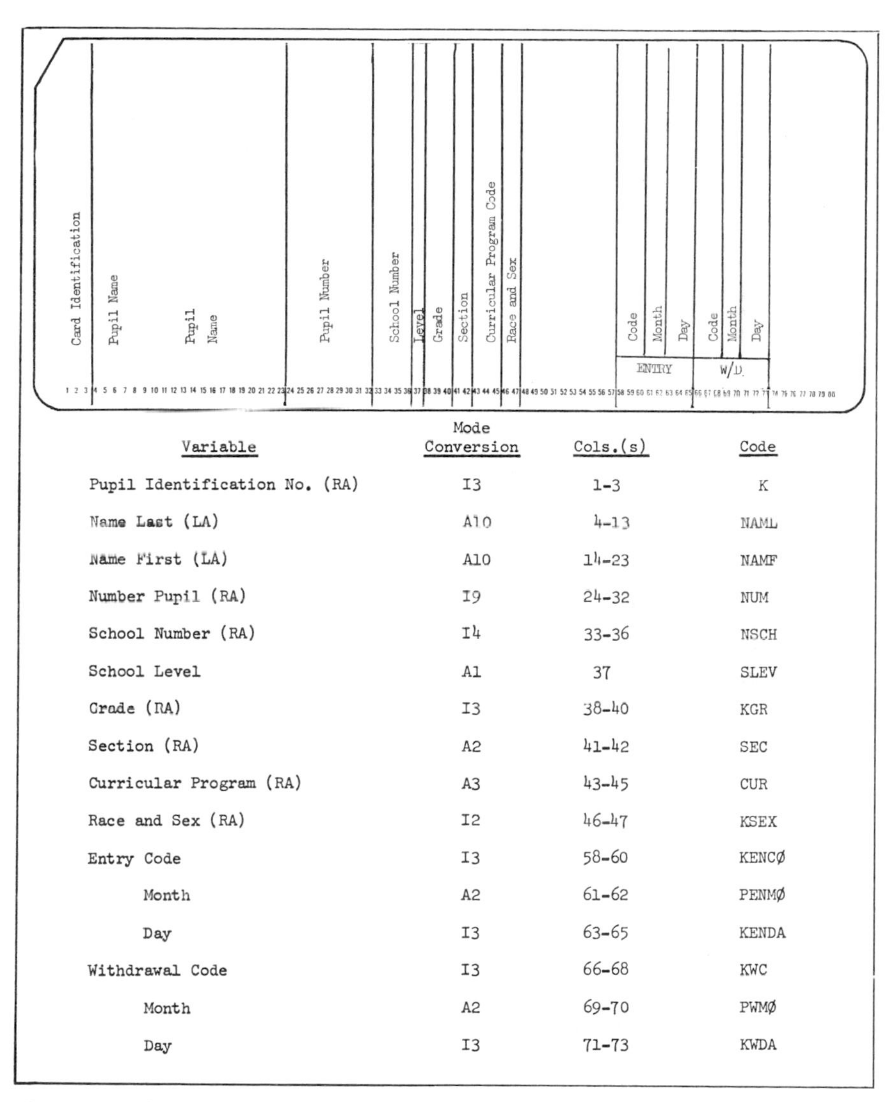

Variable	Mode Conversion	Cols.(s)	Code
Pupil Identification No. (RA)	I3	1-3	K
Name Last (LA)	A10	4-13	NAML
Name First (LA)	A10	14-23	NAMF
Number Pupil (RA)	I9	24-32	NUM
School Number (RA)	I4	33-36	NSCH
School Level	A1	37	SLEV
Grade (RA)	I3	38-40	KGR
Section (RA)	A2	41-42	SEC
Curricular Program (RA)	A3	43-45	CUR
Race and Sex (RA)	I2	46-47	KSEX
Entry Code	I3	58-60	KENCØ
Month	A2	61-62	PENMØ
Day	I3	63-65	KENDA
Withdrawal Code	I3	66-68	KWC
Month	A2	69-70	PWMØ
Day	I3	71-73	KWDA

Fig. 32 — Individual Pupil Card.

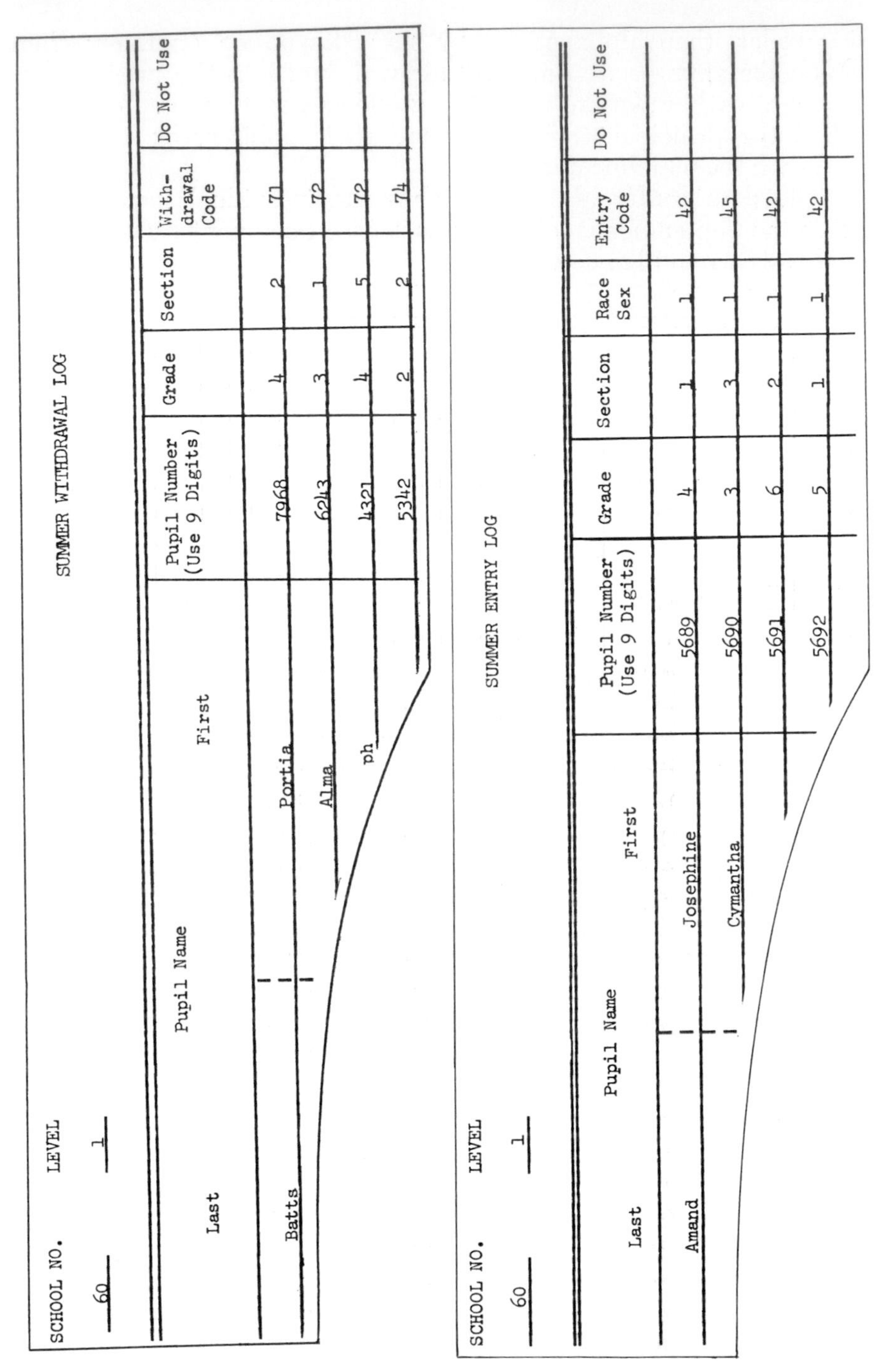

SUMMER WITHDRAWAL LOG

SCHOOL NO. 60 LEVEL 1

Pupil Name Last	First	Pupil Number (Use 9 Digits)	Grade	Section	With-drawal Code	Do Not Use
Batts	Portia	7968	4	2	71	
	Alma	6243	3	1	72	
	ph	4321	4	5	72	
		5342	2	2	74	

Fig. 33 – Summer Pupil Withdrawal Log.

SUMMER ENTRY LOG

SCHOOL NO. 60 LEVEL 1

Pupil Name Last	First	Pupil Number (Use 9 Digits)	Grade	Section	Race Sex	Entry Code	Do Not Use
Amand	Josephine	5689	4	1	1	42	
	Cymantha	5690	3	3	1	45	
		5691	6	2	1	42	
		5692	5	1	1	42	

Fig. 34 – Summer Pupil Entry Log.

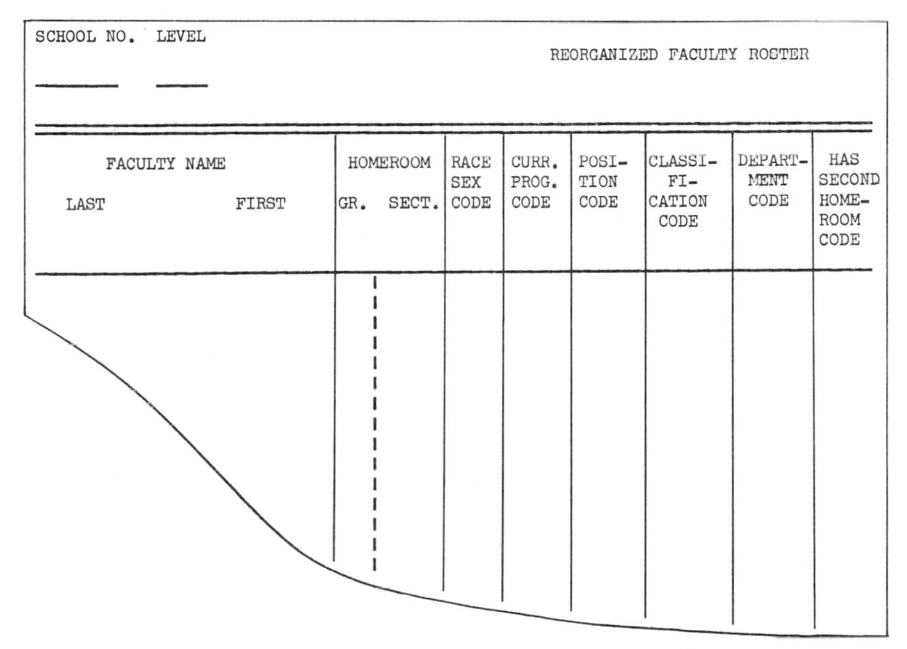

SCHOOL NO. LEVEL

REORGANIZED FACULTY ROSTER

FACULTY NAME LAST	FIRST	HOMEROOM GR.	SECT.	RACE SEX CODE	CURR. PROG. CODE	POSI-TION CODE	CLASSI-FI-CATION CODE	DEPART-MENT CODE	HAS SECOND HOME-ROOM CODE

Fig. 35 — September Faculty List.

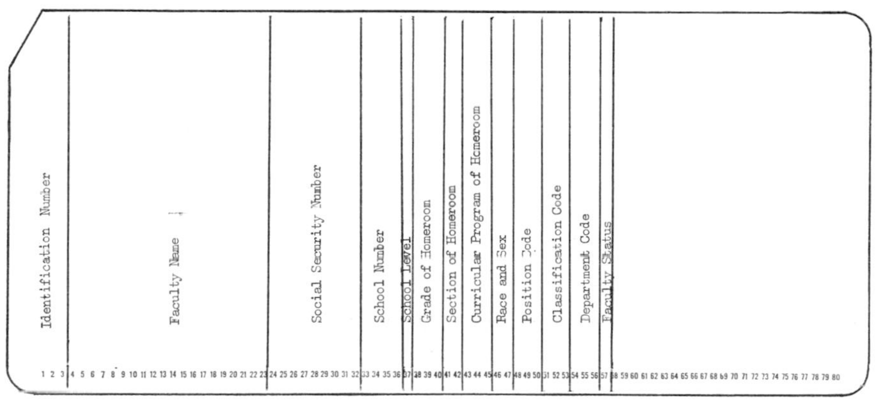

Identification Number | Faculty Name | Social Security Number | School Number | School Level | Grade of Homeroom | Section of Homeroom | Curricular Program of Homeroom | Race and Sex | Position Code | Classification Code | Department Code | Faculty Status

Fig. 36 — Faculty Card.

After the principal has sent his summer pupil entry log and summer pupil withdrawal log to the data center, all subsequent pupil entries and withdrawals are kept on individual optical scan sheets. (See Figs. 37–40.) Procedures with respect to filling out and handling the optical scan entry and withdrawal forms will be discussed later.

Usually school systems with many individual schools assign a

PUPIL ENTRY FORM

INSTRUCTIONS FOR COMPLETION:

GENERAL:

1. Use ordinary pencil - Not ball point pen.
2. Print appropriate data in boxes at top of each requested item.
3. Code each letter or digit of the printed entry data with a "score type" mark in the column below it by connecting the dots with a heavy, straight line.
4. Print and code leading zeros where necessary. Example: School No. 5 is printed and scored as 005. 8th Grade is printed and scored as 08.
5. Make clean and complete erasures to correct any errors in marking.

SCHOOL OFFICE:

6. Complete Items 1 through 10.
7. See reverse side of this form for ENTRY and CURRICULAR-PROGRAM codes.
8. Forward to appropriate Homeroom teacher along with Teacher's Summary Attendance Report.

HOMEROOM TEACHER:

9. Complete Item 11 ONLY for current month.
10. Return to School Office along with Teacher's Summary Attendance Report.

Baltimore City Public Schools
Automated Summary Pupil Attendance System
349 65 0115

1. For Month of__________, 196___.

2. PUPIL NAME (LAST NAME, SKIP 1 SPACE, FIRST NAME)

3. SCHOOL NUMBER — 4. GRADE — 5. SECTION — 6. ENTRY CODE (SEE REVERSE SIDE) — 7. DATE OF ENTRY — 8. CURRICULAR PROGRAM CODE (SEE REVERSE SIDE) — 9. RACE SEX — 10. PUPIL NUMBER (PRINT AND CODE LEADING ZEROS) — 11. FIRST MONTH ATTENDANCE: TIMES LATE, DAYS ABSENT

NEGRO FEMALE / NEGRO MALE / OTHER FEMALE / OTHER MALE / WHITE FEMALE / WHITE MALE

DC 1303A

Fig. 37 — Pupil Entry Form, Front.

school number to each school. For systems which have only names for their schools, an arbitrary number, not to exceed three digits, should be assigned to each school. Also, each school level should be assigned a one-digit level code, such as an elementary school, 1; a junior high school, 2; and a senior high school, 3. For combination schools these level codes still hold. Although the school is under the administrative jurisdiction of a single principal, separate reports are made for each level. For example, an elementary-junior high combination school would receive two reports: (1) one report for its elementary pupils and faculty; and (2) a separate one for its junior high pupils and faculty. Without such distinct separations, system-wide level reports could not be generated nor could meaningful breakdowns be obtained for state department and United States Office of Education use.

Figure 41 shows how the mainline pupil attendance deck must be organized. Schools are arranged by school number and school

ENTRY CODES

TRANSFERRED-IN:

40-From another CLASS this school
41-From another BALTIMORE City Public School

NEW:

42-BEGINNER first time at school
43-Maryland County public school
44-Maryland County non-public school
45-FOREIGN country-public or private school
46-FOREIGN country-not in school

47-Baltimore City non-public school
48-Public evening school
49-Other state-non-public school
50-Other state-public school (includes D.C., possessions and territories)
67-Institution

REENTERED WITHDRAWAL:

51-Withdrew from this Baltimore City Public School in current school year*--now returning

WITHDRAWAL PREVIOUS SCHOOL YEAR:

52-No school since withdrawal
53-Withdrawal for marriage
54-Withdrawal for physical disability
55-Withdrawal underage

PROMOTION OR ASSIGNMENT:

65-From Baltimore City Public Elementary School
66-From Baltimore City Public Secondary School

*Current school year starts the next day after close of school in June and ends with close of school in the following June.

For further clarification of Child Accounting procedures refer to Administrative Handbook-Section 148.30.

CURRICULAR-PROGRAM CODES

ELEMENTARY

KINDERGARTEN

Early Admissions. 201
Regular Kindergarten. 202
Physically Handicapped Nursery. 203

REGULAR

Grade
1. 211
2. 212
3. 213
4. 214
5. 215
8. 216

NON-GRADED. 220

SPECIAL EDUCATION

Opportunity (No Grade Assignment) 231

Trainable. 232

Physically and/or Mentally Handicapped (Excluding Opportunity and Trainable). 233

Day Camp. 234

SECONDARY-VOCATIONAL

JUNIOR HIGH

310--Trainable
311--Special Curriculum
312--Day Camp
321--Basic

322--Regular
323--Enrichment
324--Accelerated
330--General Vocational
333--Physically Handicapped

SENIOR HIGH

340--Special Curriculum
341--Basic
342--General Technical (Non-College)
343--General Business (Non-College)
344--Business Education, Regular

345--General Academic (Non-College)
346--Advanced College Preparatory
347--Special College Preparatory (Enriched)
348--Regular College Preparatory

355--Vocational-Technical
356--General Vocational

Fig. 38 – Pupil Entry Form, Back.

level order. Thus a junior high school numbered 42 and an elementary-junior high combination school numbered 80 would carry school-level codes of 422, 801, and 802 respectively, and would be so sequenced. Within each school, the mainline deck is color coded and arranged as in Figure 41.

Loading Mainline Pupil Attendance Cards on Disk

The mainline pupil attendance cards are loaded on disk. The entire file must be readied for the operation about the first day of school in September. Each IBM 1311 disk pack contains 20,000 sectors of 100 characters each. While the attendance file could be resident on tape, disk was selected because of its random access capability. Figure 42 shows pupil, homeroom faculty, nonhomeroom faculty, and divider disk sector files.

Loading the mainline pupil attendance card deck on disk is accomplished by utilizing the load disk program. See Figure 43

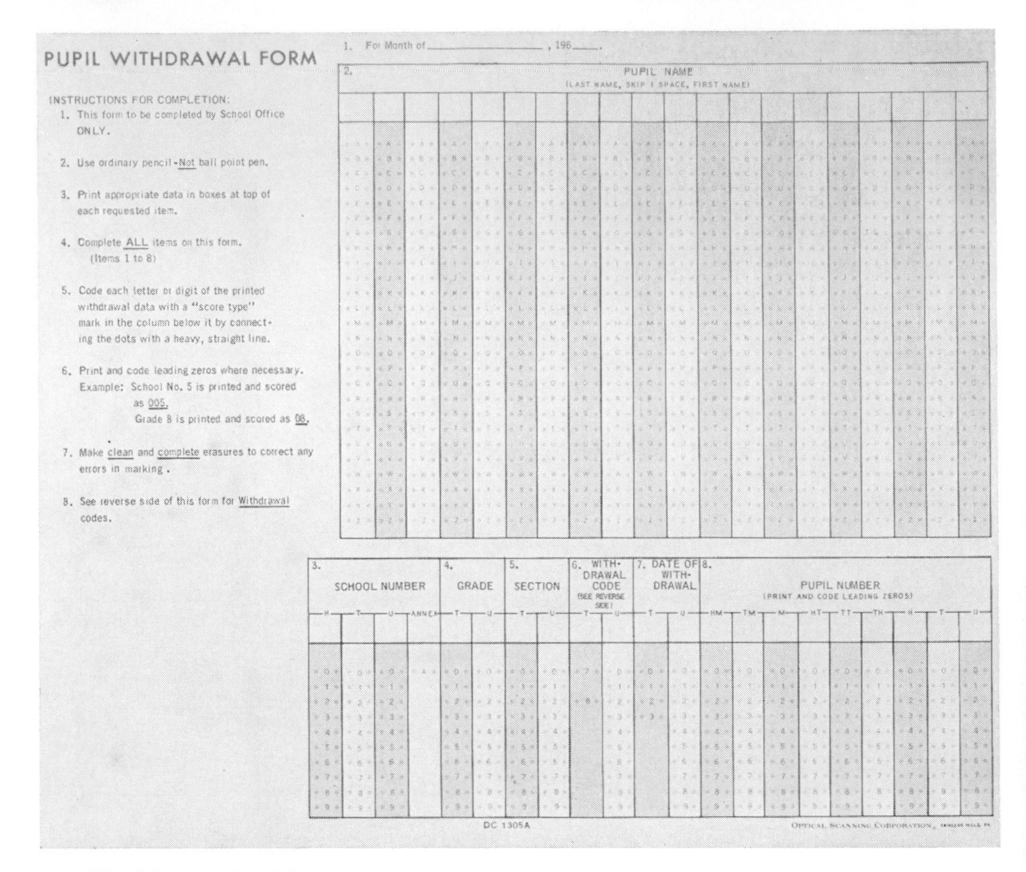

PUPIL WITHDRAWAL FORM

INSTRUCTIONS FOR COMPLETION:

1. This form to be completed by School Office ONLY.
2. Use ordinary pencil - Not ball point pen.
3. Print appropriate data in boxes at top of each requested item.
4. Complete ALL items on this form. (Items 1 to 8)
5. Code each letter or digit of the printed withdrawal data with a "score type" mark in the column below it by connecting the dots with a heavy, straight line.
6. Print and code leading zeros where necessary. Example: School No. 5 is printed and scored as 005. Grade 8 is printed and scored as 08.
7. Make clean and complete erasures to correct any errors in marking.
8. See reverse side of this form for Withdrawal codes.

1. For Month of ________________, 196___.

2. PUPIL NAME (LAST NAME, SKIP 1 SPACE, FIRST NAME)

3. SCHOOL NUMBER — H T U ANNEX
4. GRADE — T U
5. SECTION — T U
6. WITHDRAWAL CODE (SEE REVERSE SIDE) — T U
7. DATE OF WITHDRAWAL — T U
8. PUPIL NUMBER (PRINT AND CODE LEADING ZEROS) — HM TM M HT TT TH H T U

DC 1305A

OPTICAL SCANNING CORPORATION

Fig. 39 — Pupil Withdrawal Form, Front.

for the flow diagram schema for the load disk program. The Fortran IV computer is resident on disk drive 0. The mainline pupil attendance deck is loaded on disk drive 1. For some 20,000 pupils, the program takes about 7 hours.

After the mainline deck has been loaded on disk drive 1, the cards are saved. These cards are retained in card trays in the identical sequence that they were loaded. This is principally to provide backup protection in the event the disk was not loaded properly. Since the disk is not file protected, saving the mainline deck also provides for the possibility of the disk being "clobbered." However, proper labeling of the disk pack and proper data center handling and storage procedures should prevent this occurrence. Note that each disk sector record is 100 characters long.

After the mainline pupil attendance deck has been loaded on disk, the data center is responsible for printing, in triplicate, a

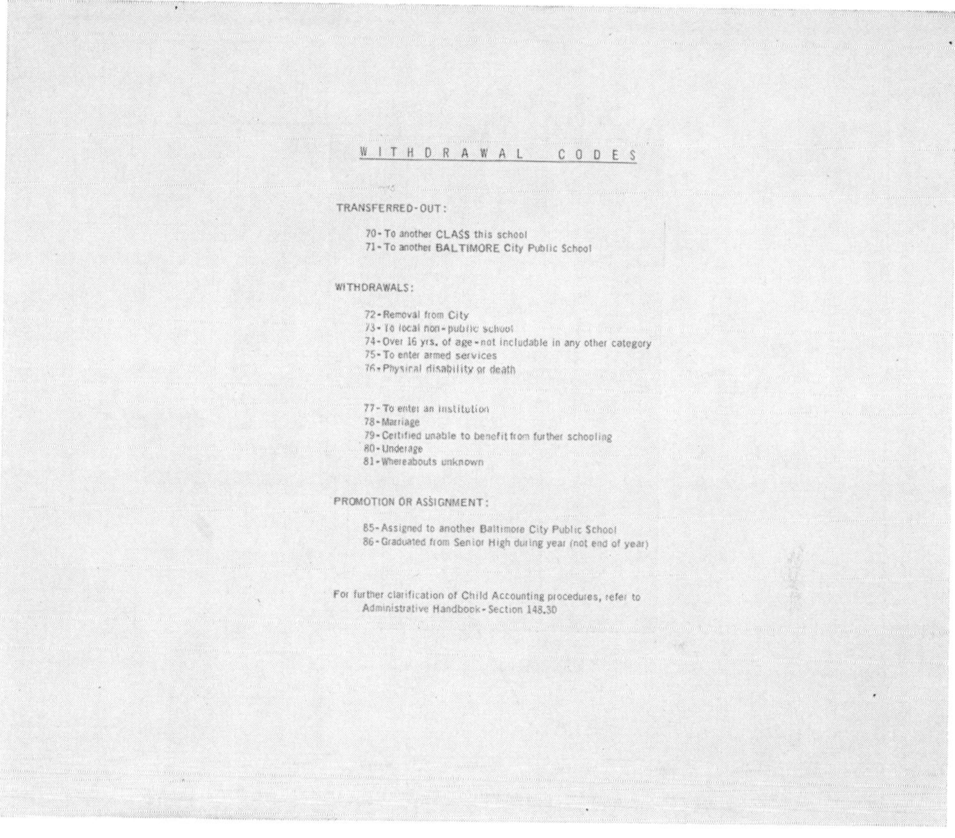

WITHDRAWAL CODES

TRANSFERRED-OUT:

70-To another CLASS this school
71-To another BALTIMORE City Public School

WITHDRAWALS:

72-Removal from City
73-To local non-public school
74-Over 16 yrs. of age-not includable in any other category
75-To enter armed services
76-Physical disability or death

77-To enter an institution
78-Marriage
79-Certified unable to benefit from further schooling
80-Underage
81-Whereabouts unknown

PROMOTION OR ASSIGNMENT:

85-Assigned to another Baltimore City Public School
86-Graduated from Senior High during year (not end of year)

For further clarification of Child Accounting procedures, refer to Administrative Handbook-Section 148.30

Fig. 40 — Pupil Withdrawal Form, Back.

September temporary roll sheet for each homeroom class. Figure 44 shows a September temporary roll sheet. The data center must print out these roll sheets and have them into the hands of each homeroom teacher prior to the opening of school.

Figure 45 depicts the September temporary roll sheet program flow diagram. The program is straightforward, reading data on disk, and printing it out on the roll sheet.

Using the September Temporary Roll Sheet for Attendance Reporting

The September temporary roll sheet routine was devised for several purposes. First, it permits the withdrawal of June carry-over pupils into the principal's office roll (class and section 50-00). Thus, only live net roll pupils will be retained on disk, uncluttered by pupils who have been withdrawn from the school's net roll but

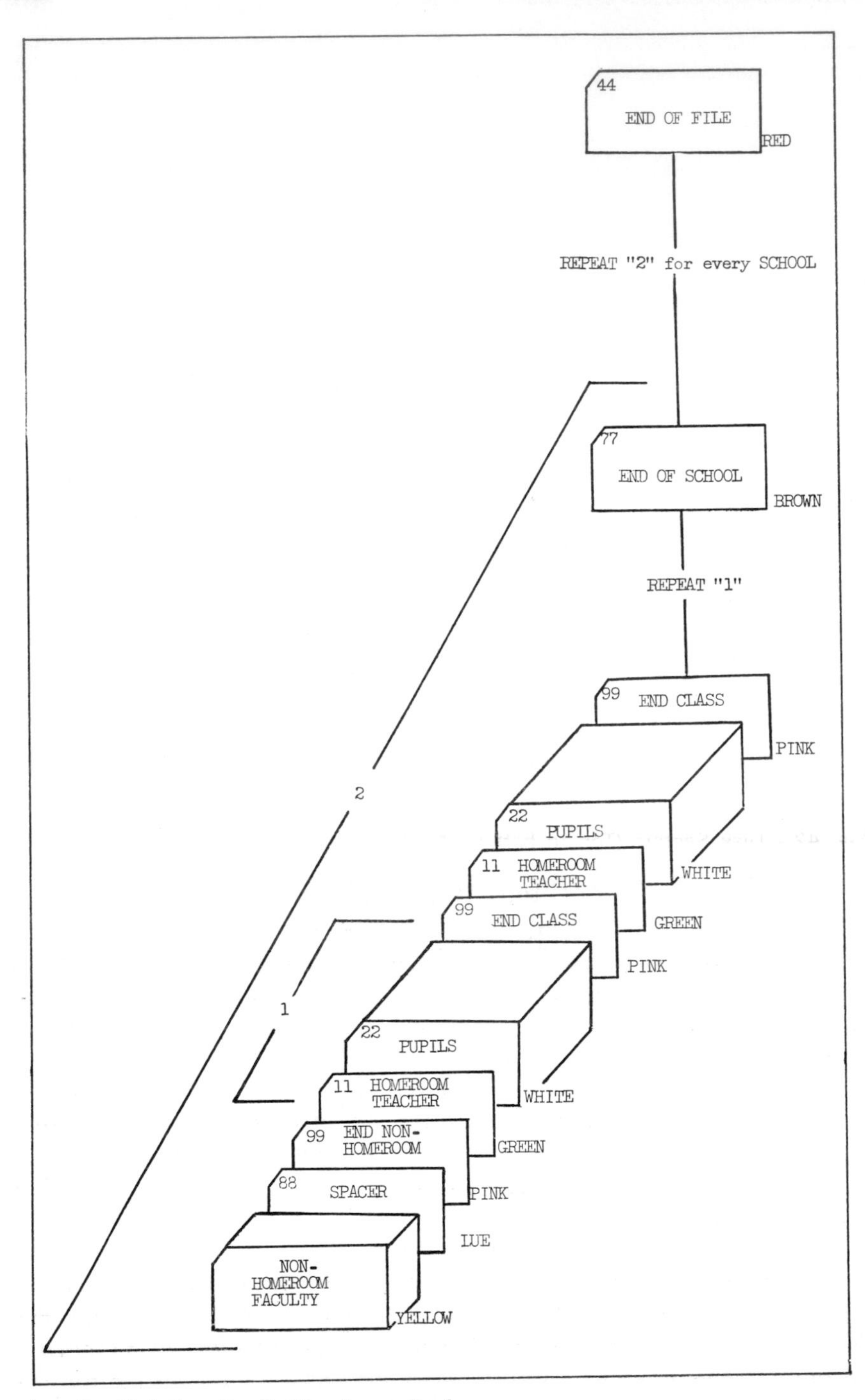

Fig. 41 – Mainline Pupil Attendance Deck.

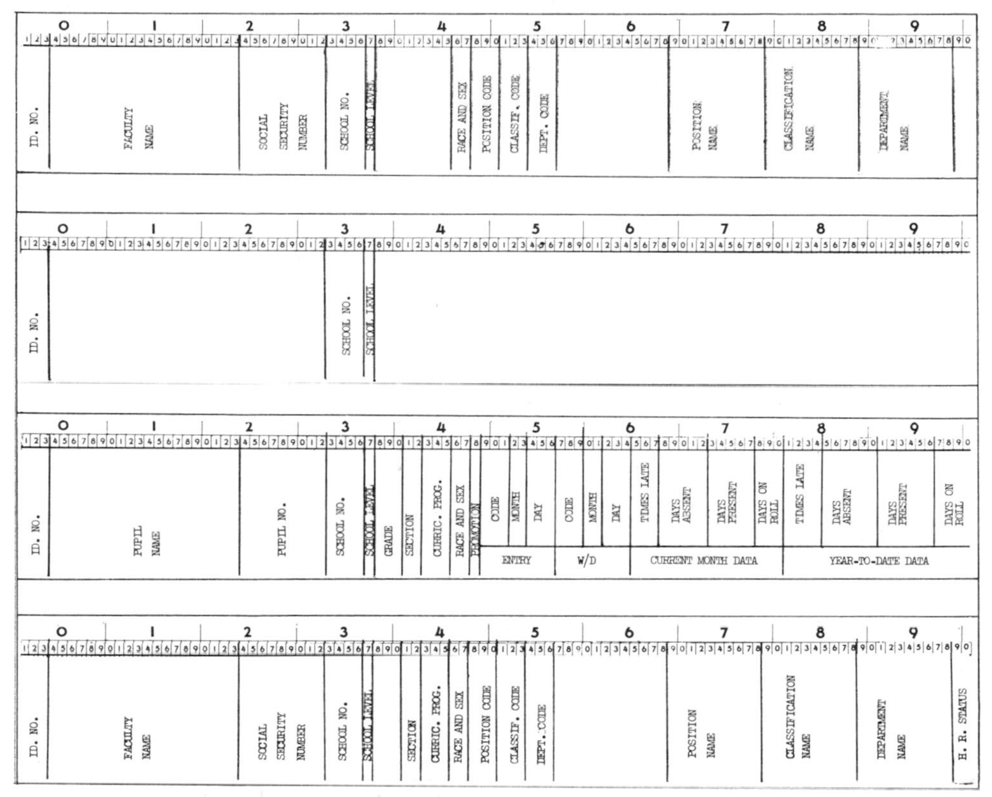

Fig. 42 — Disk Sectors (Top to bottom: Nonhomeroom, divider, pupil, homeroom).

who must be accounted for under a continuous pupil accounting system. Second, it permits the withdrawal of pupils who registered to enter a given school from outside the system but who didn't, and therefore (not being June carryovers) need not be accounted for at all. Third, it permits the homeroom teacher to mark attendance on these temporary roll sheets for the first five school days when classes are not yet stabilized. The teacher's class register, therefore, will have a minimum of crossed out pupil names (pupil withdrawals) and pupil insertions (new pupil entries).

Automated summary pupil attendance system, job outline, No. P-6, indicates the September temporary roll sheet for attendance reporting. Part of this job outline is shown in Figure 46.

After the homeroom teacher has taken roll on the fifth day of school, the principal collects the three-part carbon-sensitized roll sheets. He sees to it that these sheets are arranged in numerical order by page. He checks that all pupils who were absent for the first five consecutive days of school are indicated by an asterisk.

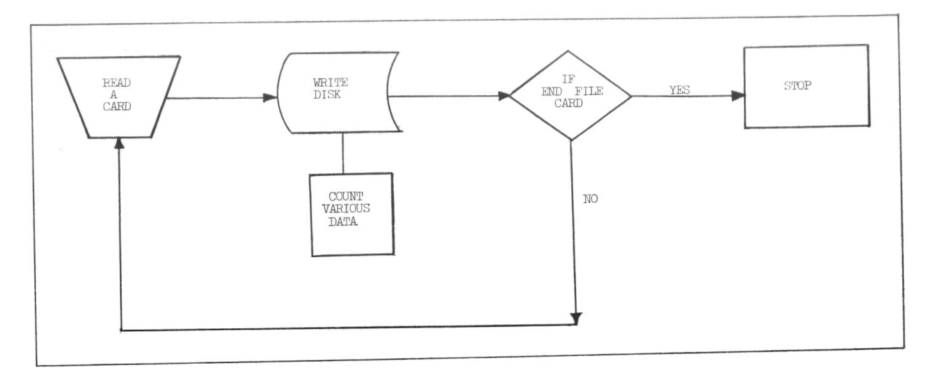

Fig. 43 – Load Disk Program Diagram.

SEPTEMBER TEMPORARY ROLL SHEET

PAGE NO.

HOMEROOM TEACHER	SCHOOL	GRADE	SECTION
CROWNER AVA	601	4	1

See Instructions on Reverse Side

STUDENT NAME	ENT CODE	M	T 7	W 8	T 9	F 10	* M 13	T	W	T	F			REMARKS
BEASLEY ARMINTA 11011	65													
CARTER LINDA 9734	65													
JOHNSON SANDRA 625	65													
MURDOCK INDIE 1567	65													
ELL SHERL 2378	65													
ALICE 11068	65													
1639	65													
H 1419	65													
	65													
	[illegible]													

Fig. 44 – September Temporary Roll Sheet.

Under the remarks column, and only for June carryover pupils, the principal may write, if desired, "Office Roll 50-00." He may also write "PIF," if desired, for those pupils who are new to the school system (i.e., not June carryover) and who were asterisked, indicating that such pupils must be removed from the live attendance rolls and placed on the principal's investigative file. When these tasks have been completed, the principal sees that the September temporary roll sheets are separated and that the original copies are sent to the data center by the seventh day of school in Septem-

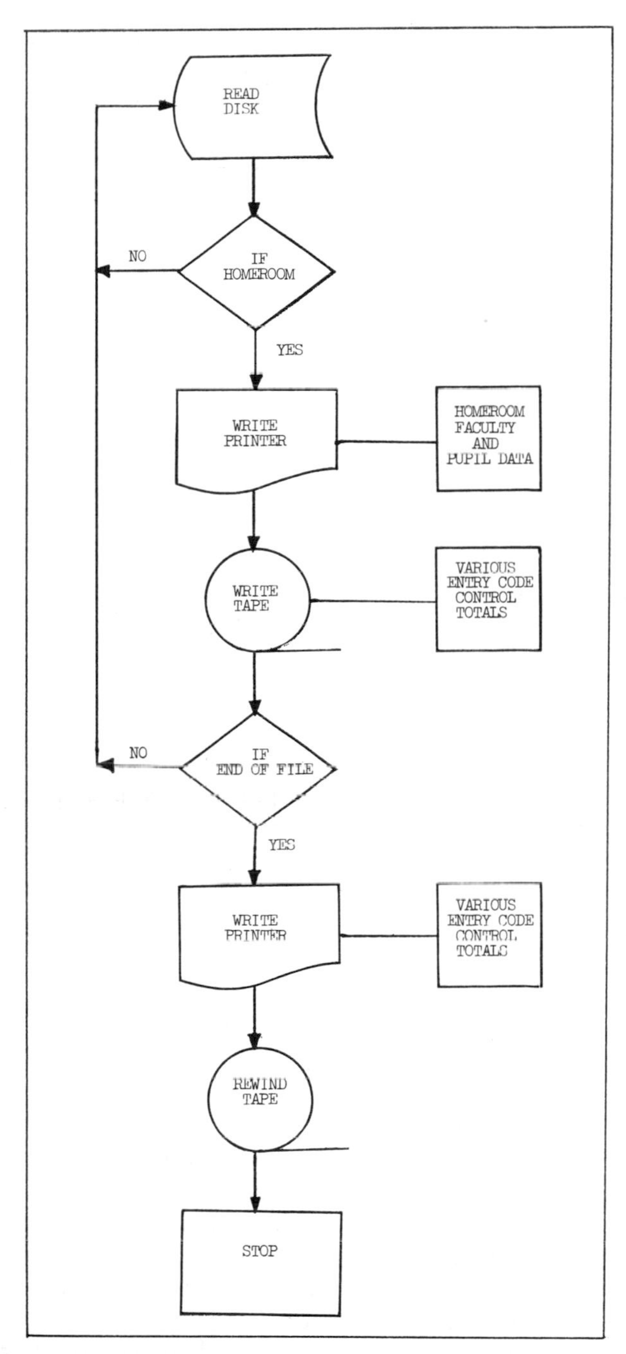

Fig. 45 – Print September Temporary Roll Sheets Program Diagram.

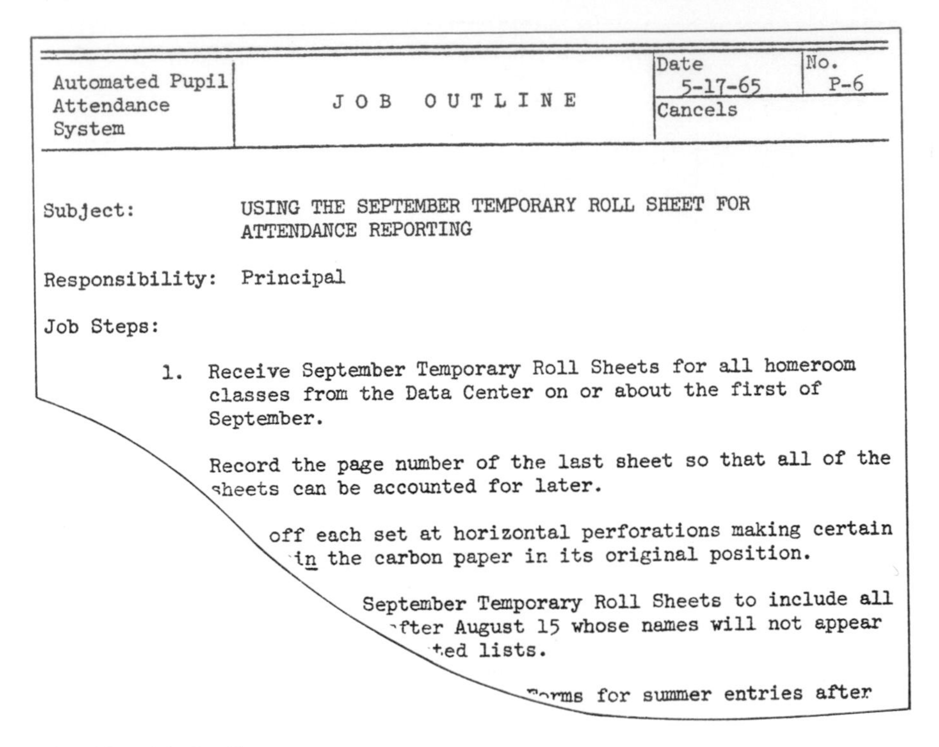

Automated Pupil Attendance System	J O B O U T L I N E	Date 5-17-65	No. P-6
		Cancels	

Subject: USING THE SEPTEMBER TEMPORARY ROLL SHEET FOR ATTENDANCE REPORTING

Responsibility: Principal

Job Steps:

1. Receive September Temporary Roll Sheets for all homeroom classes from the Data Center on or about the first of September.

   Record the page number of the last sheet so that all of the sheets can be accounted for later.

   off each set at horizontal perforations making certain in the carbon paper in its original position.

   September Temporary Roll Sheets to include all fter August 15 whose names will not appear ted lists.

   orms for summer entries after

Fig. 46 – Job Outline.

ber. The second carbon is returned to the homeroom teacher in time for her to take roll the following morning and transfer such attendance statistics to her rollbook. The first carbon copy is retained in the principal's office for future reference and backup.

Purging the Summary Pupil Attendance System of Nonattending Pupils

As soon as the September temporary roll sheets are received in the data center, records and statistics personnel check the forms for accuracy and verify any questionable items. The card of each pupil asterisked on the September temporary roll sheet is pulled from the mainline pupil attendance deck. These cards are retained in the same school level, class, and section order as they were loaded on disk. The reason for this is evident from Figure 47 which depicts the A* program flow diagram.

Tape 2 contains June carryover pupils for whom withdrawal data must be obtained. The data center prints out for each principal a list of those pupils in his school who are nonattending June carryovers. Why these pupils withdraw must be discovered

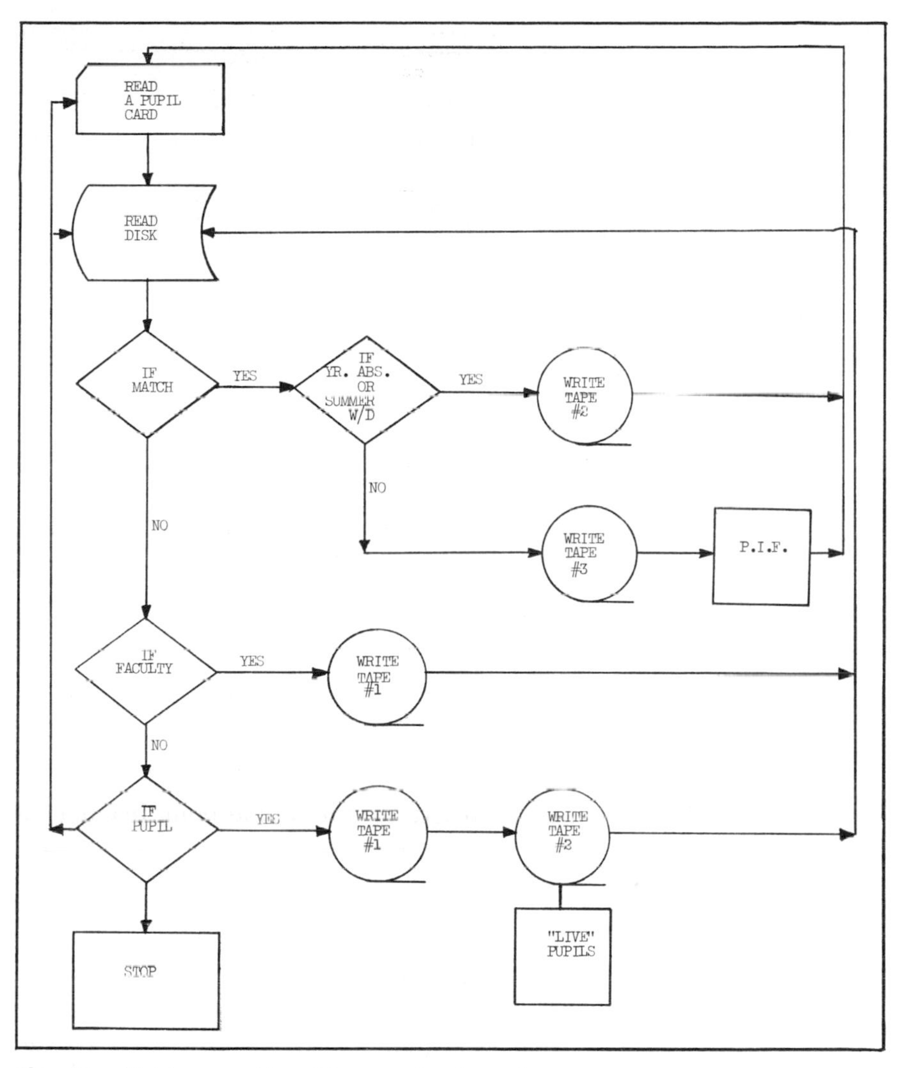

Fig. 47 – A* Program Flow Diagram for June Carryover Pupils Not Attending in September.

and recorded at a later date for such statistical purposes as dropout reports, etc.

Tape 3 contains nonattending pupils who are not June carry-overs but who did register to attend school. The data center also prints for each school a list of these pupils. In a continuous pupil accounting system, these pupils need not be investigated unless the principal desires to do so on his own.

Tape 1 and tape 2 are now merged to form September's pupil

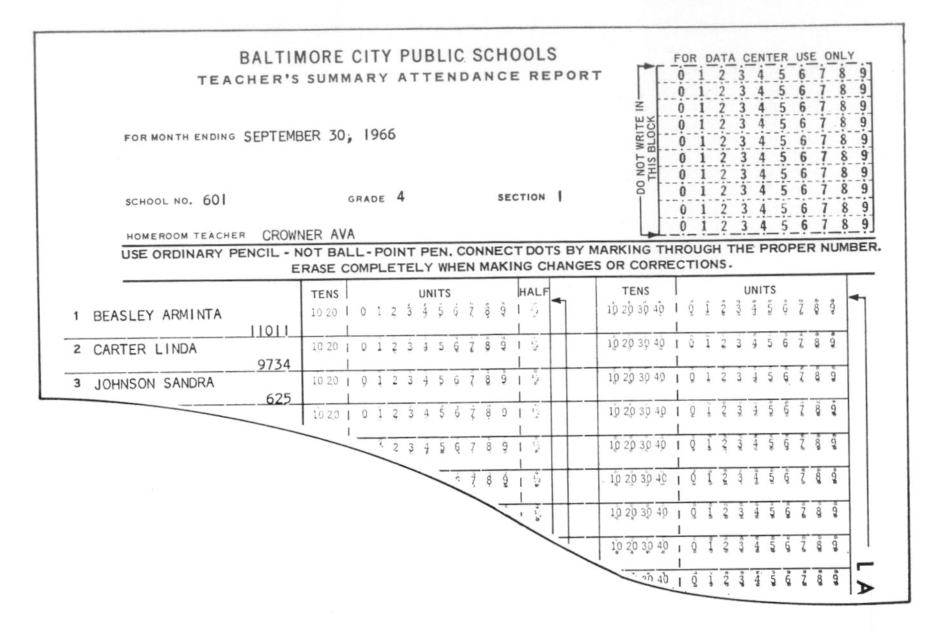
BALTIMORE CITY PUBLIC SCHOOLS
TEACHER'S SUMMARY ATTENDANCE REPORT

FOR DATA CENTER USE ONLY
DO NOT WRITE IN THIS BLOCK

FOR MONTH ENDING SEPTEMBER 30, 1966

SCHOOL NO. 601 GRADE 4 SECTION 1

HOMEROOM TEACHER CROWNER AVA

USE ORDINARY PENCIL - NOT BALL-POINT PEN. CONNECT DOTS BY MARKING THROUGH THE PROPER NUMBER.
ERASE COMPLETELY WHEN MAKING CHANGES OR CORRECTIONS.

	TENS	UNITS	HALF	TENS	UNITS
1 BEASLEY ARMINTA 11011	10 20	0 1 2 3 4 5 6 7 8 9	5	10 20 30 40	0 1 2 3 4 5 6 7 8 9
2 CARTER LINDA 9734	10 20	0 1 2 3 4 5 6 7 8 9	5	10 20 30 40	0 1 2 3 4 5 6 7 8 9
3 JOHNSON SANDRA 625	10 20	0 1 2 3 4 5 6 7 8 9	5	10 20 30 40	0 1 2 3 4 5 6 7 8 9

Fig. 48 — Teacher's Summary Attendance Report.

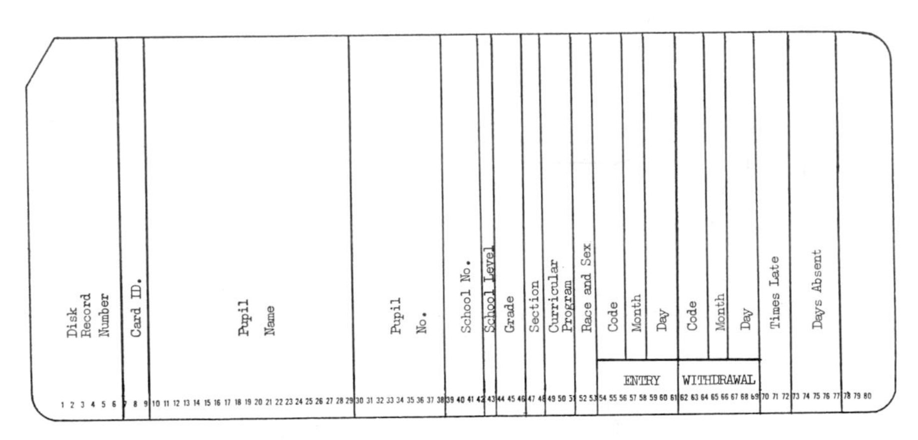

Fig. 49 — Pupil TSAR Card.

attendance disk. The program to do this is called the merge-tape-to-disk program. This program is used only this one time during the year. The merge takes about five hours for some 20,000 pupils.

Teachers' Summary Attendance Report Procedures

About September 20, the data center prints out teachers' summary attendance report and punches out pupil TSAR cards. Figure 48 depicts part of a teacher summary attendance report (TSAR

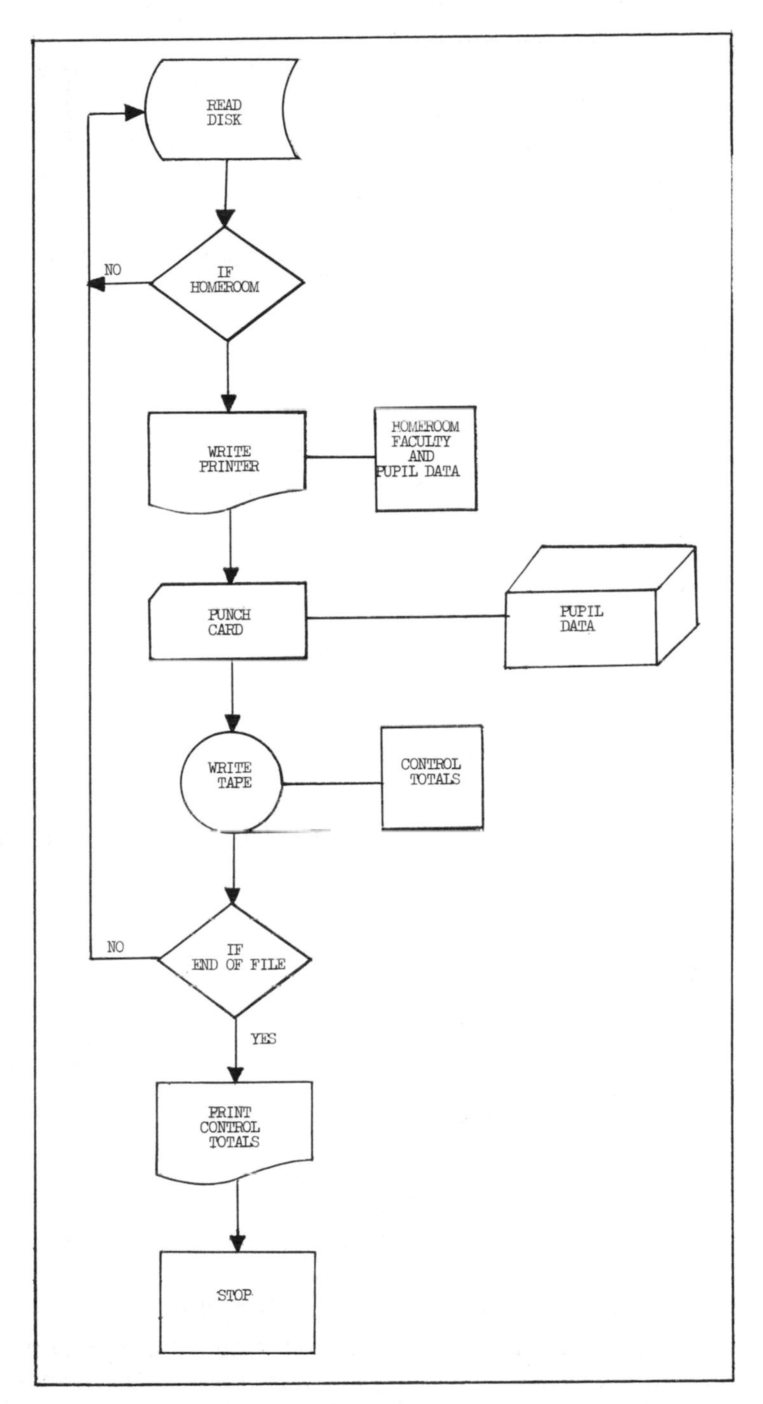

Fig. 50 — Print Teacher's Summary Attendance Report Program Diagram.

Automated Summary
Pupil Attendance
System

Month Ending_________, 196____

School . . . . ________

Last TSAR Sheet Page Number ____

CONTROL SHEET

Here is a record of the control number printed on the last sheet of the Teacher's Summary Attendance Report (TSAR sheets).

This record is needed so that all of your forms may be accounted for before they are returned to the Data Center after completion.

(Reference: Job Outline P-3, Item 2 and 6-b).

PLEASE ATTACH THIS RECORD SHEET TO YOUR TSAR SHEETS AND RETURN IN THE TRANSPORTATION FOLDER.

CHECK OFF:

1. TSAR SHEETS ________________

2. PUPIL ENTRY FORMS ___________

3. PUPIL WITHDRAWAL FORMS _______

4. FACULTY CHANCE FORMS ________

5. PUPIL CHANGE FORMS __________

6. FIRE DRILL INFORMATION _______

Fig. 51 — Control Sheet.

sheets) and Figure 49 shows the layout of the pupil TSAR card punch out. The Fortran IV program utilized to do this is called the TSAR sheet program. (See Fig. 50.) To print out these reports and punch out the cards utilizing the IBM 1401 computer takes about six hours for 20,000 pupils.

Utilizing the load-TSAR-cards-to-tape program, the data from the pupil TSAR cards are written onto tape 1. This program takes about 20 minutes on the computer. For systems not having an optical scanner (Digitek 100), the pupil attendance data (absences and latenesses), and withdrawal and entry data, must be manually keypunched into the pupil TSAR cards in the appropriate card columns. For large numbers of pupils, keypunching time would upset the tight time schedule that must be followed. For this reason, the optical scan procedure that we shall discuss later is recommended.

The data center distributes the teachers' summary attendance reports to the schools by about September 25, and certainly never later than three days prior to the end of the school month.

Inschool TSAR Report Procedures. On the last day of the month, the principal distributes to each homeroom teacher her TSAR sheets and pupil entry forms. The teacher merely counts the number of times each pupil in her class was absent and late for the month of September and records it on the TSAR sheet or on the pupil entry form, as appropriate, by use of a "score-type" mark. We recommend that a heavy black kindergarten pencil be used to mark the data on the optical scan sheets.

Before the end of the school day, all homeroom teachers must send the TSAR sheets and the pupil entry forms to the principal's office. The principal arranges the TSAR sheets in numerical order from page 1 to the last numbered page. On a control sheet, the principal records the number of the various forms he is sending to the data center. The control sheet enables records and statistics personnel in the data center to maintain tight control over the number of forms received from each school. (See Fig. 51 for a copy of the control sheet.)

Pupil Entry and Withdrawal Forms. Responsibility for entering and withdrawing pupils should reside not only in the principal's office, but should also be delegated to one person. While this person need not do the clerical work involved, only he should have the authority to authorize pupil entries or withdrawals from the school. To facilitate this, a pupil entry form and a pupil withdrawal form (differently color coded) have been designed. (Copies of these forms have been shown in Figs. 37–40.)

Faculty Change Forms and Pupil Change Forms. During the course of the year, faculty personnel get married, resign, die, get promoted, or receive different assignments. Pupils also have name changes, names incorrectly recorded, sex incorrectly recorded, etc. With respect to pertinent changes in pupil and faculty data, change forms were designed. (Copies of these forms are shown in Figs. 52–54.)

Data Center TSAR Sheet Procedures. When the data center receives a principal's attendance forms (see control sheet for various forms received), records and statistics personnel edit the forms for

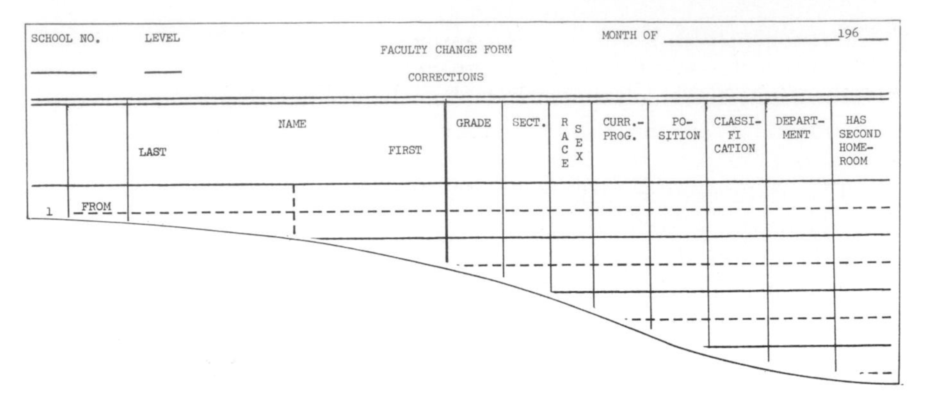

SCHOOL NO. LEVEL MONTH OF ____________ 196__

FACULTY CHANGE FORM

CORRECTIONS

	NAME LAST	FIRST	GRADE	SECT.	RACE	SEX	CURR.-PROG.	PO-SITION	CLASSI-FICATION	DEPART-MENT	HAS SECOND HOME-ROOM
1 FROM											

Fig. 52 — Faculty Change Form, Corrections.

SCHOOL NO. LEVEL MONTH OF ____________ 196__

FACULTY CHANGE FORM

ENTRIES AND WITHDRAWALS

ENT.	WITH.	NAME LAST	FIRST	GRADE	SECTION	RACE	SEX	CURR.-PROG.	PO-SITION	CLASSI-FI-CATION	DEPART-MENT	HAS SECOND HOME-ROOM

Fig. 53 — Faculty Change Form, Entries and Withdrawals.

count verification, accuracy of data, poor optical scan marks, missing TSAR sheets, and sequential order of returned TSAR sheets. When a given school's forms have been edited, the TSAR sheets are sent to the optical scan room. A school header optical scan sheet is placed before each school's TSAR sheets and the batch of forms are fed into the optical scanner (Digitek 100). Each TSAR sheet yields two punched cards. Identification data (school level, columns 1–5; grade, columns 6–7; and section, columns 8–9) are punched into the first nine columns of each card. A "J" in column 80 indicates that the card is the first of the two cards punched for each TSAR sheet, whereas a "K" in column 80 indicates that it is the second card punched.

Columns 13–79 are reserved for pupil attendance data. When the TSAR sheet is optically scanned, each pupil's attendance data is punched into a field five columns wide. The first three columns

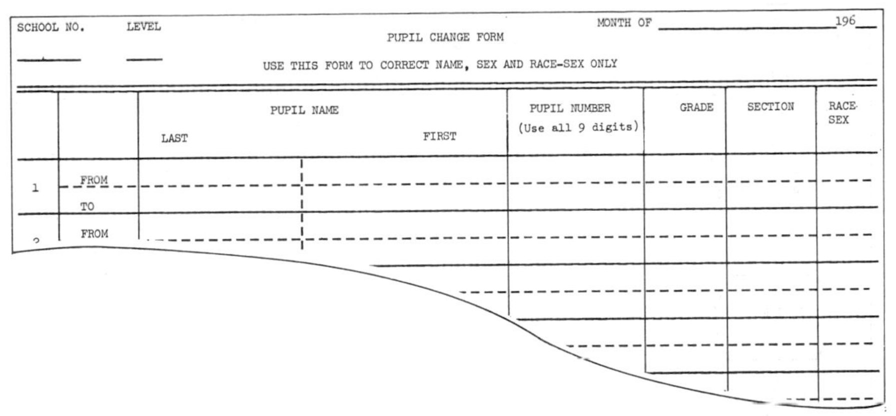

SCHOOL NO. LEVEL
PUPIL CHANGE FORM
MONTH OF ____ 196_
USE THIS FORM TO CORRECT NAME, SEX AND RACE-SEX ONLY

		PUPIL NAME LAST	FIRST	PUPIL NUMBER (Use all 9 digits)	GRADE	SECTION	RACE-SEX
1	FROM						
	TO						
2	FROM						

Fig. 54 – Pupil Change Form.

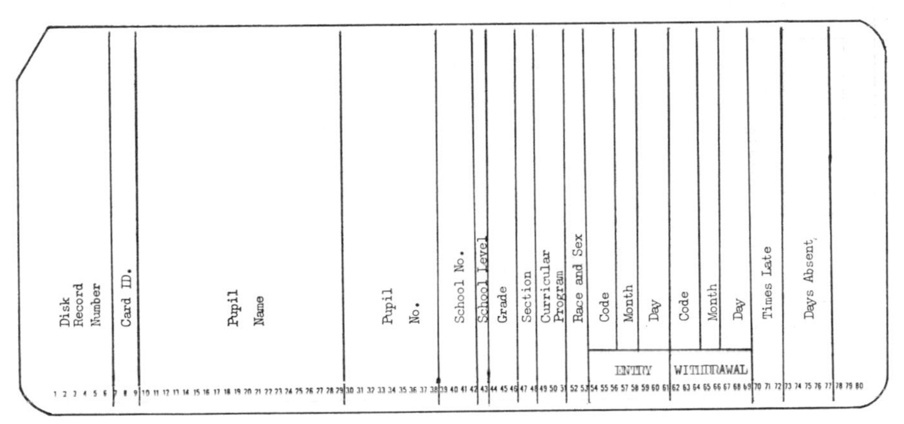

Fig. 55 – Post Attendance Pupil Card.

contain the number of times the pupil was absent, and the remaining two columns the number of times he was late. For example, the first pupil's attendance data on the TSAR sheet would be punched into columns 13–18; the second pupil's into columns 19–23, etc.

The optical-scan-punchout deck is edited for omissions of identification data (school level, grade, and section data) or identification data incorrectly scanned and punched. The deck is also checked for missing cards and then sequence checked. It is absolutely essential that the optical-scan-punchout deck be in the same school-level-grade-section order as the pupil TSAR cards were put on tape 1. The edit routine discussed takes about two hours. hours.

Utilizing the IBM 1401 computer, the optical-scan-punchout

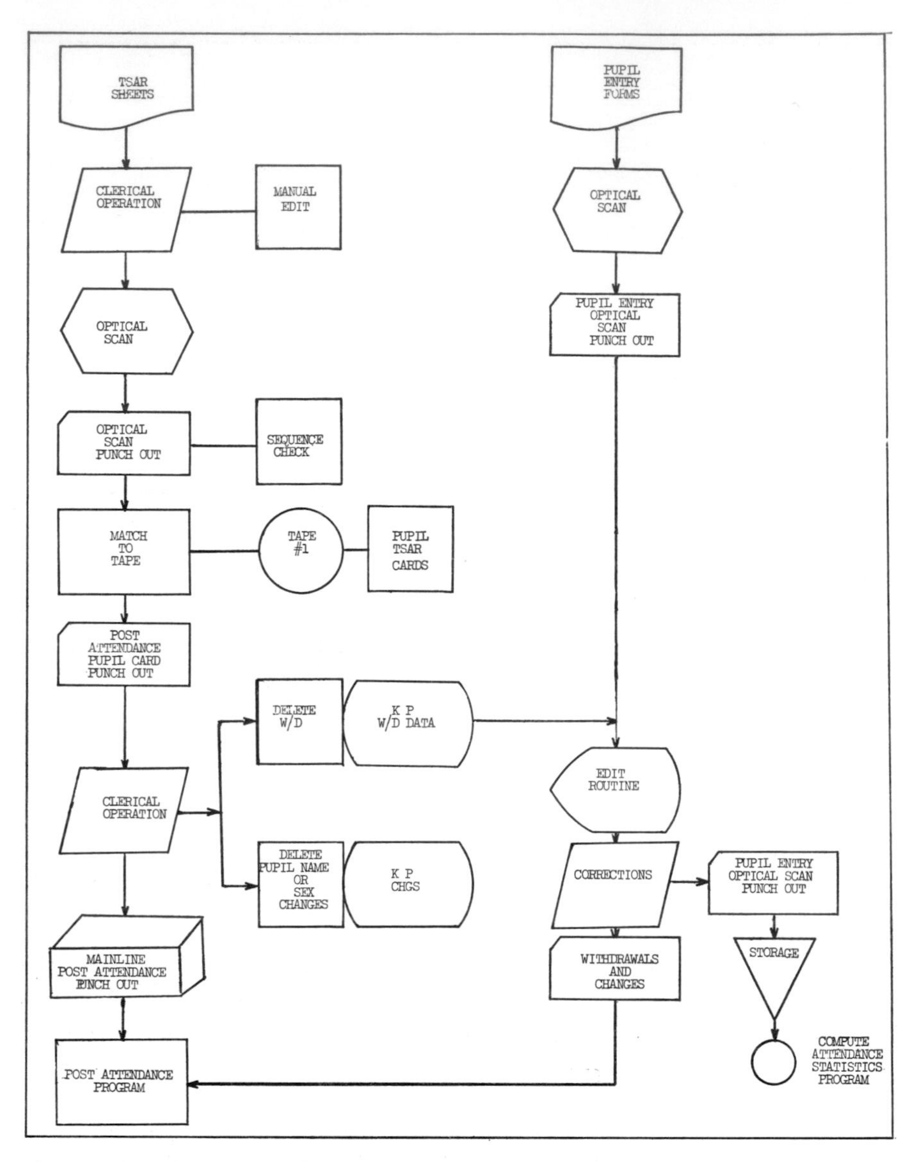

Fig. 56 — Teacher's Summary Attendance Report Routine.

deck is read and collated with the pupil TSAR cards put on tape 1, and a post attendance pupil card is punched out for each pupil. This program takes about one hour. Figure 55 shows what data each post attendance pupil card contains.

Next, records and statistics personnel extract from the post-attendance-pupil-card deck the cards of all pupils who have with-

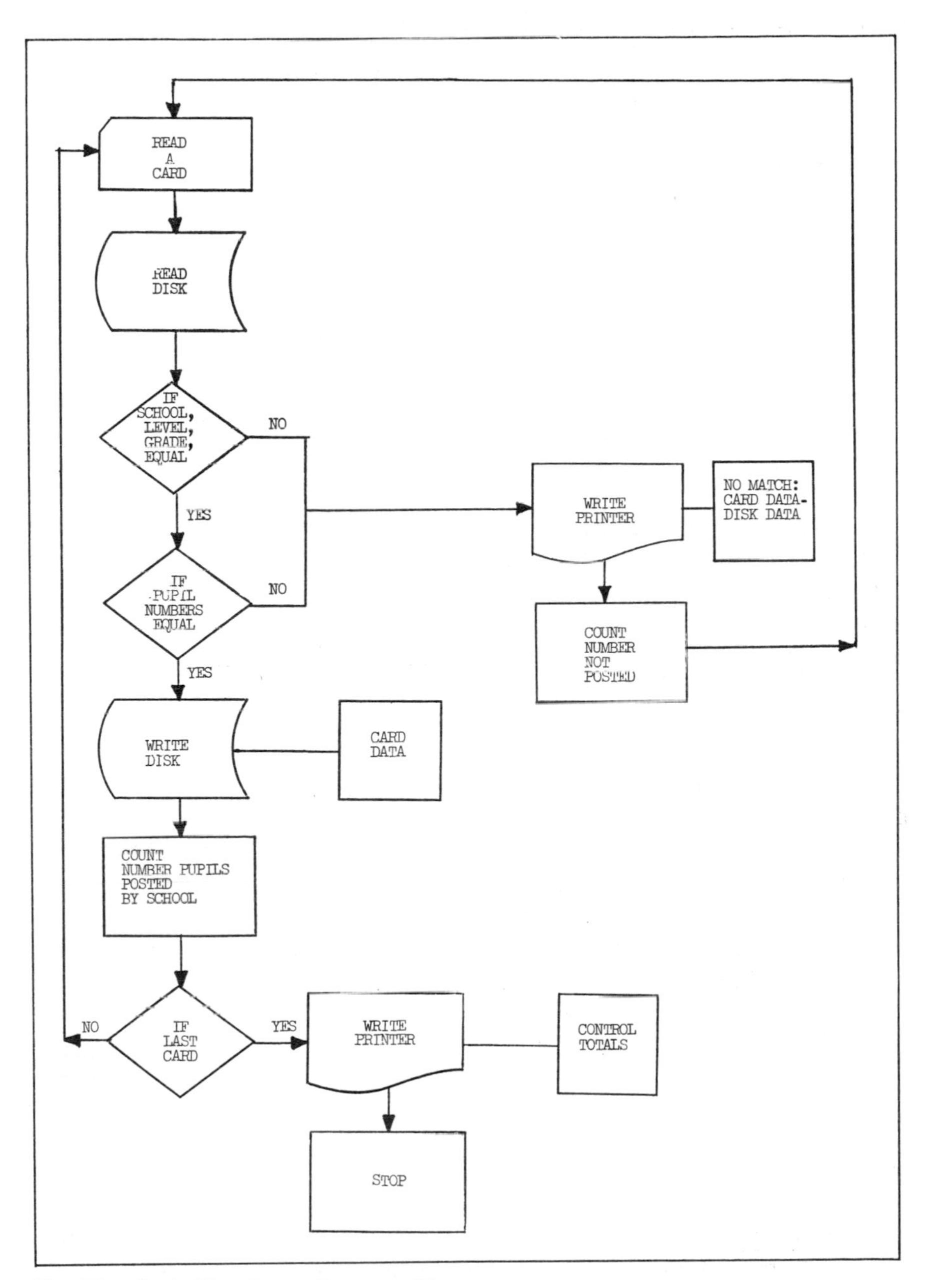

Fig. 57 – Post Attendance Program Diagram.

drawn from a given grade and section and for whom the principal has sent pupil withdrawal forms to the data center. Into the appropriate card are keypunched a withdrawal code, day of withdrawal, and month of withdrawal code. Before these cards are returned to the post-attendance-pupil-card deck, they are checked against the pupil-entry-card deck. This edit program checks for errors in grade and section data, and to assure that inschool pupil transfers balance exactly for each school.

The pupil-entry-card deck is created as follows: each school's pupil entry forms are optically scanned. For each pupil entry, a card is punched out. This punched out card agrees in both form and content with the layout of the post attendance pupil card (see Fig. 55), except that no disk sector number is punched out. Since pupils who entered school during the month of September are not on the September pupil attendance disk, no random access disk sector number can be given. How pupil entries get into the pupil attendance system will be discussed shortly with the compute statistics program routine.

Figure 56 shows the schema or procedures with respect to the teachers' summary attendance report routine in the data center. In practice, the routine is simple to follow. At some points, it takes longer to describe the procedure than to carry it out. Moreover, many of the operations described separately can be carried out concurrently in the data center.

Post Pupil Attendance Routine

Figure 57 depicts the flow diagram for the Fortran IV post pupil attendance program. Briefly, this program posts, randomly on the September pupil attendance disk, each pupil's days absent, times late, withdrawal data (code, day, month), and, if applicable, pupil name changes, curricula changes, etc.

In practice, most of the pupil attendance data are posted sequentially. Such a procedure, of course, speeds up the posting process. However, in order not to interrupt and delay this computer operation, pupil cards can be withdrawn from the main deck whenever withdrawal data must be keypunched into these cards, or whenever pupil changes need to be reflected in these cards as reported by the principal on the pupil change forms. These operations are carried out by the data center staff during the time the post pupil attendance program is in operation. The post pupil attendance cards in which changes have been made are filed behind the mainline deck. The data on these cards can be randomly posted to disk because of the disk sector number feature. When a pupil's card is read, the disk sector number tells the computer where the data on that card are to be posted. Moreover, no data are posted unless the school level, grade and section, and pupil number on the disk match with those read on the post pupil attendance card. This provides file protection and ensures that the correct attendance data for each pupil is posted. The post pupil attendance program takes about 6 hours and 40 minutes.

Faculty Change Routine

As indicated earlier, the principal sends to the data center at the end of the month, in this case September, faculty change forms. Records and statistics personnel in the data center edit these forms, manually recording the data on the faculty keypunch change sheet to facilitate keypunching operations. (See Fig. 58.) Faculty change card 1 is keypunched from the faculty keypunch change sheet as indicated. This card is color-coded (red). When the keypunchers have completed punching the faculty change card 1, records and statistics personnel write on card 1 the position name, columns 10–19; the classification name, columns 20–29; and the department name, columns 63–72. The keypuncher then reproduces from card 1, columns 1–9; manually keypunches position name and classification name in columns 10–29; reproduces columns 30–62 from card 1 into card 2; keypunches department name in columns 63–72; and reproduces columns 73–80 from card 1 into card 2. Card 2 is color-coded (blue).

The faculty change program is utilized to correct faculty data on the September pupil attendance disk. The disk sector number permits faculty changes to be posted randomly (See Fig. 59 for the Fortran IV faculty change program flow diagram.)

Compute Attendance Statistics Routine

When the September pupil attendance disk has been updated to reflect posting pupil attendance and withdrawal data, pupil changes, and faculty changes, the next procedural routine is to compute statistics. This is accomplished through the compute attendance statistics program. (Fig. 60 depicts the flow diagram for this program.)

Briefly, the routine operates as follows: each month the days-on-roll deck must be computed. This deck consists of 31 separate cards. It provides the basic data for a table lookup on days-on-roll. These data, plus those on pupil day-of-entry and pupil day-of-withdrawal, are used to compute the pupil's days on roll for that month and his average daily attendance.

The compute attendance statistics program, then, first reads the days-on-roll deck. Next, it reads each pupil's data card in the pupil-entry-card deck, computing that pupil's attendance statistics

FACULTY KEYPUNCH CHANGE SHEET

Field	Card Columns
Disk Record Number	1 2 3 4 5 6
Card Identification Number	7 8 9
Faculty Number	10 11 12 13 14 15 16 17 18 19 20 21 22 23 24 25 26 27 28 29
Social Security Number	30 31 32 33 34 35 36 37 38
School Number	39 40 41 42
School Level	43
Grade	44 45 46
Section	47 48
Curricular Program	49 50 51
Race and Sex	52 53
Position	54 55 56
Classification	57 58 59
Department	60 61 62
	63 64 65 66 67 68 69 70 71 72 73 74 75 76 77 78 79
Status	80

Fig. 58 – Faculty Keypunch Change Sheet.

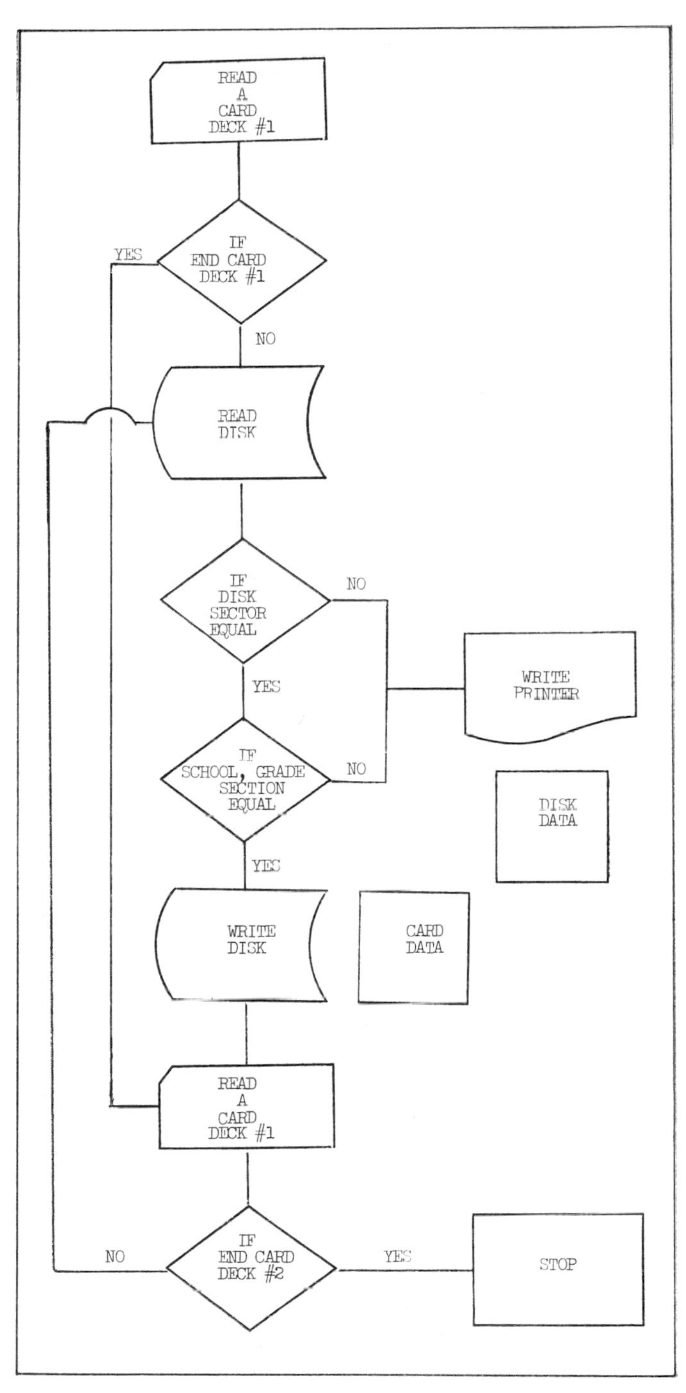

Fig. 59 Faculty Change Program Diagram.

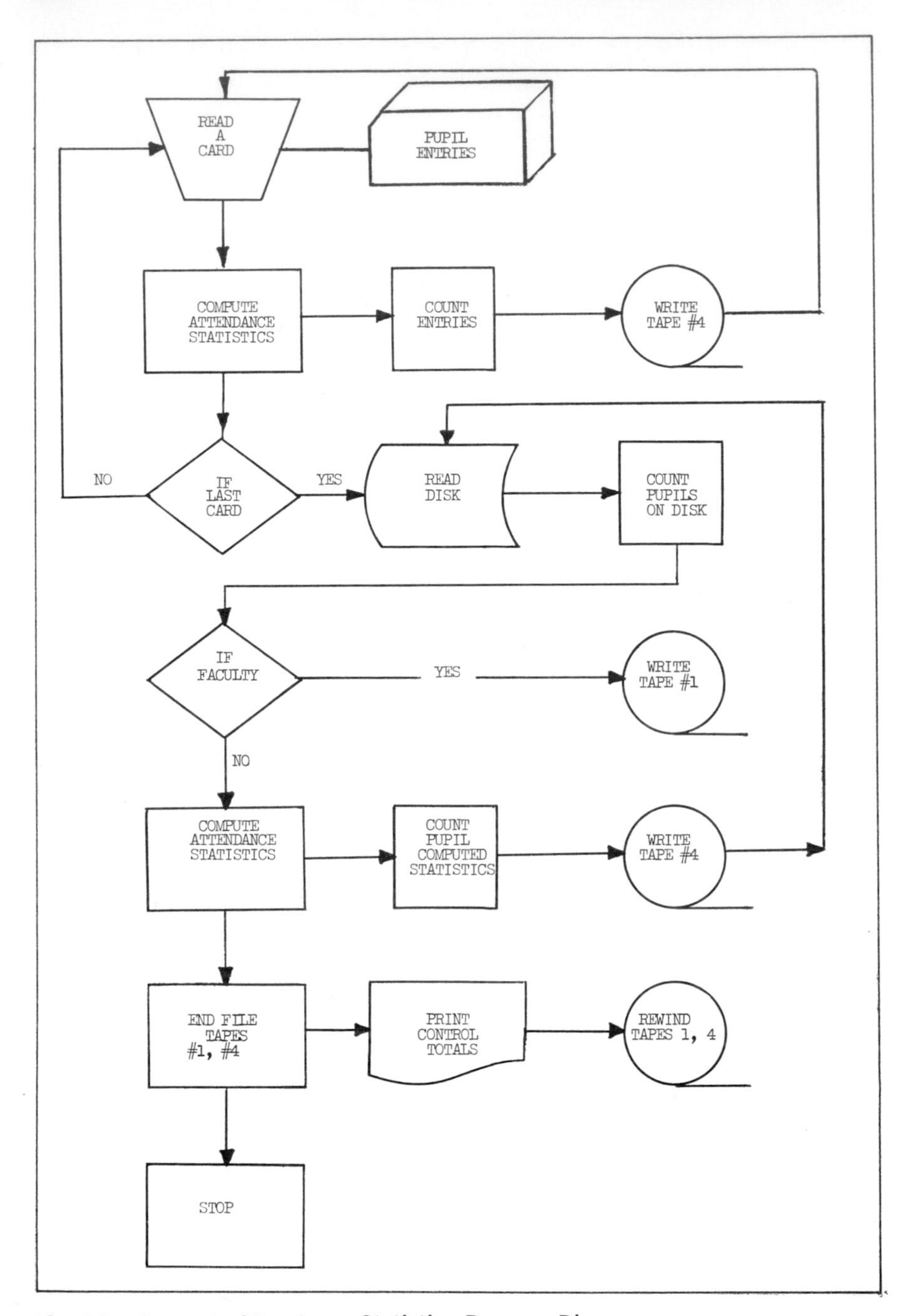

Fig. 60 – Compute Attendance Statistics Program Diagram.

and posting the results on tape 4. After all pupil entry cards have been processed, the program reads the September pupil attendance disk. All disk sector records are posted to tape 1, except pupil disk sector records. Whenever the program encounters a pupil disk sector record, it computes that pupil's attendance statistics and posts the entire record to tape 4. When the entire pupil attendance disk has been processed, the summary totals which the program has been accumulating are printed out for control purposes. Thus, the number of old pupils and the number of newly entered pupils, school by school, are indicated. This program takes about six hours.

Alphabetizing Pupil Records

The pupils who were resident on disk were already sequenced by school level, grade and section, sex, and then alphabetized by name. However, pupils newly entered during the month, in this instance September, are processed randomly. It is necessary then to utilize a standard sort program to sort tape 4 in the sequence indicated above. The standard utility program used is the IBM sort 7 program. The two control cards needed are shown in Figure 61. Because the majority of these records are already sorted, the sorting task takes only 40 minutes.

Print Teachers' Class Registers Routine

After the pupil tape records (tape 4) have been sorted, the print teachers' class register program routine follows. (See Fig. 62 for flow diagram.) Tapes 1 and 4 are merged to print the teachers' class register, as indicated in Figure 62. Class and school control totals are stored on tape 2. After all teachers' class registers have been printed, control totals on tape 2 are printed out and saved for reference and check out purposes. The teachers' class registers are printed in triplicate, bursted and decollated, and distributed as follows: the original copy to the principal's office for distribution to the homeroom teacher; the second copy to the principal for his files; and the third copy is retained in the data center for reference purposes. The print-teachers-class register program takes about 4 hours and 25 minutes to run. Usually, printed teachers' class registers are in the hands of the classroom teacher some 10 to 11 days after the end of the month. For example, September teachers' class registers would be in the hands of homeroom teachers about October 10–11. It must be remembered that the homeroom teacher always has her class rollbook available for reference purposes. But whereas she had to compute pupil days-on-roll, pupil days

CONTROL CARD 1			CONTROL CARD 2		
Punch	Col.	Indicates	Punch	Col.	Indicates
1	1	Input/output tape	0	1	Control-data
2	2	unit numbers	0	2	field-2
	3		4	3	location
3	4		7	4	
4	5		0	5	Control-data
	6		0	6	field-2
0	7	No. of input reels	1	7	length
1	8		0	8	Control-data
0	9	Input record length	0	9	field-3
2	10		0	10	location
0	11		4	11	
0	12		0	12	Control-data
0	13	Input blocking	2	13	field-3
0	14	factor	0	14	length
1	15			15	Control-data
0	16	Output blocking		16	field-4
0	17	factor		17	location
1	18			18	
P	19	Unreadable block option		19	Control-data
1	20	Phase 2 tape density ✓		20	field-4
	21	In-tape header-labels		21	length
	22	Out-tape header-labels		22	Control-data
	23	Output tape-mark option		23	field-5
	24	In-tape trailer-labels		24	location
	25	Out-tape trailer-labels		25	
	26	Padding indicator		26	Control-data
6	27	Core-storage size		27	field-5
0	28	Total number of		28	length
3	29	control-data fields		29	Control-data
0	30	Total number of		30	field-6
3	31	characters of		31	location
1	32	control-data		32	
0	33	Control-data		33	Control-data
0	34	field-1 location		34	field-6
3	35			35	length
3	36			36	Control-data
0	37	Control-data		37	field-7
1	38	field-1 length		38	location
0	39			39	
	40	Expected file size		40	Control-data
		[illegible] by		41	field-7
				42	length
				43	Control-data
				44	field-8

Fig. 61 – Control Card Formats for IBM Sort 7 Standard Utility Program.

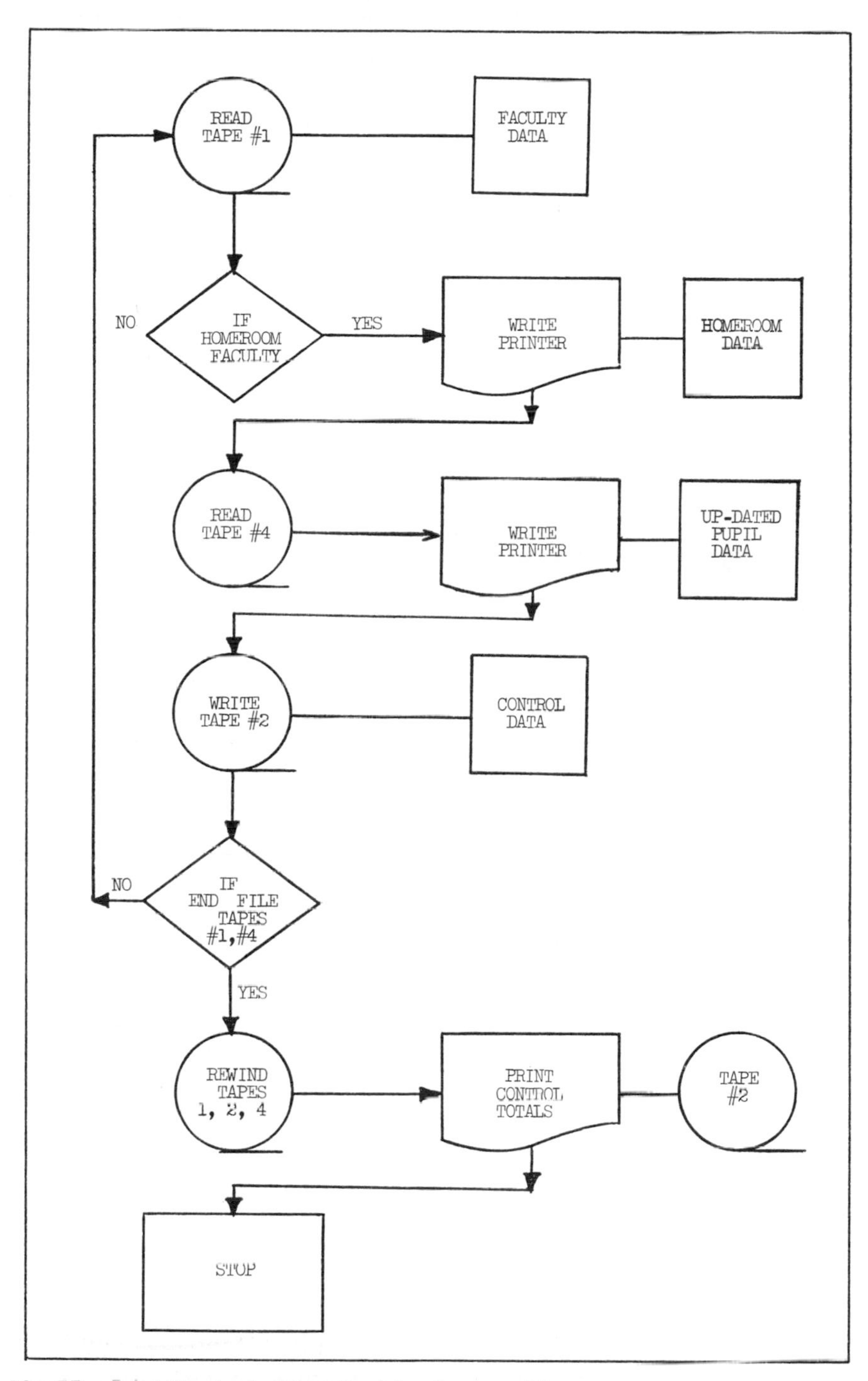

Fig. 62 – Print Teacher's Class Register Program Diagram.

SEPTEMBER 30,1965 TEACHER'S CLASS REGISTER

Teacher: CROWNER AVA | School: 601 | Grade: 4 | Section: 1

NAME OF PUPIL	PUPIL NUMBER	ENTRY DATA			WTHDRW. DATA			CURRENT MONTH: TIMES LATE	DAYS ABSENT	DAYS PRESENT	DAYS ON ROLL	YEAR TO DATE: TIMES LATE	DAYS ABSENT	DAYS PRESENT	DAYS ON ROLL	REMARKS
BATTS PORTIA	625	65	09	7	0		0	0	3.0	15.0	18	0	3.0	15.0	18	
BOYETTE DOTTICE	1212	0		0	0		0	0	0.0	18.0	18	0	0.0	18.0	18	
BROWN DENE	13942	41	09	7	0		0	0	0.0	18.0	18	0	0.0	18.0	18	
BROWN FRANCINE	13943	41	09	8	0		0	0	0.0	17.0	17	0	0.0	17.0	17	
BROWN PAMELA	1567	0		0	0		0	0	0.5	17.5	18	0	0.5	17.5	18	
CLAIBORNE SHARON	2282	0		0	0		0	1	1.5	16.5	18	1	[illegible]	16.5	18	
COBBS CLAUDETTE	2378	0		0	0		0	0	0.0	18.0	18	0	0.0	18.0	18	
FOSTER BETTY	4119	65	09	7	0		0	0	6.0	12.0	18	0	6.0	12.0	18	
HAYNIE VERNAE	5417	0		0	0		0	0	1.0	17.0	18	0	1.0	17.0	18	
MOORE DIANE	8700	0		0	0		0	0	3.0	15.0	18	0	3.0	15.0	18	
ORANGE DORA	9188	0		0	0		0	1	0.0	18.0	18	1	0.0	18.0	18	
POWELL CONSTANCE	9734	65	09	7	0		0	0	0.0	18.0	18	0	0.0	18.0	18	
SHAW LILLIE	11011	0		0	0		0	0	0.0	18.0	18	0	0.0	18.0	18	
SHIELDS KAREN	11068	0		0	0		0	0	1.0	17.0	18	0	1.0	17.0	18	
THOMPSON THERESA	12276	0		0	0		0	0	0.0	18.0	18	0	0.0	18.0	18	
WILLIAMS HATTIE	13380	0		0	0		0	0	0.0	18.0	18	0	0.0	18.0	18	
WINKEY ANNIE	13948	65	09	29	0		0	0	0.0	2.0	2	0	0.0	2.0	2	
NUMBER OF GIRLS	17															
BLANDING CHARLES	979	65	09	7	0		0	0	1.0	17.0	18	0	1.0	17.0	18	
BROOKS PAUL	1419	0		0	0		0	1	1.0	17.0	18	1	1.0	17.0	18	
BRUNSON CURTIS	1639	0		0	0		0	0	2.0	16.0	18	0	2.0	16.0	18	
BUTLER BRIAN	1830	0		0	0		0	0	1.0	17.0	18	0	1.0	17.0	18	
CASEY ARTHUR	2101	0		0	71	9	27	2	7.0	8.0	15	2	7.0	8.0	15	
CRUMP IRVIN	13944	41	09	8	71	9	10	0	0.0	3.0	3	0	0.0	3.0	3	
DAWKINS CHARLES	3023	0		0	0		0	1	1.0	17.0	18	1	1.0	17.0	18	
DOUGLAS SHELTON	13945	65	09	30	0		0	0	0.0	1.0	1	0	0.0	1.0	1	
FOSTER RANDOLPH	4128	0		0	0		0	0	0.0	18.0	18	0	0.0	18.0	18	
JOHNSON ANTHONY	13946	65	09	30	0		0	0	0.0	1.0	1	0	0.0	1.0	1	
JOHNSON GRAYLING	6395	0		0	71	9	7	0	0.0	0.0	0	0	0.0	0.0	0	
JOHNSON WILLIAM	6541	0		0	0		0	0	0.0	18.0	18	0	0.0	18.0	18	
MOANEY RICHARD	8610	0		0	0		0	0	1.0	17.0	18	0	1.0	17.0	18	
MOORE FREDERICK	8704	0		0	0		0	0	0.0	18.0	18	0	0.0	18.0	18	
MOORE MICHAEL	8721	0		0	0		0	1	4.5	13.5	18	1	4.5	13.5	18	
RICHARDSON GARY	13947	65	09	29	0		0	0	0.0	2.0	2	0	0.0	2.0	2	
ROBINSON MAURICE	10367	65	09	7	0		0	2	3.0	15.0	18	2	3.0	15.0	18	
STOKES LEON	11825	0		0	0		0	0	1.0	17.0	18	0	1.0	17.0	18	
TAYLOR JAMES	12052	0		0	0		0	0	0.0	18.0	18	0	0.0	18.0	18	
WINKEY DARNELL	13606	65	09	7	0		0	0	1.0	17.0	18	0	1.0	17.0	18	
WITHERSPOON ABRAM	13643	0		0	0		0	0	0.0	18.0	18	0	0.0	18.0	18	
NUMBER OF BOYS	21															
TOTAL CLASS ROLL	38															

HOLIDAYS

Fig. 63 – Teacher's Class Register.

absent, pupil times late, pupil average daily attendance, as well as class aggregate statistics, under the pupil summary attendance system, the teacher now does none of these tasks. (Fig. 63 shows the teacher's class register.)

Print Monthly Reports and Create Next Month's Pupil Attendance Disk Routine

Upon termination of the teachers' class register program routine, the data center begins the monthly report program routine. Tape 1 and tape 4 (the same two tapes used in the teachers' class register program) represent input for the monthly report program. (Figure 64 depicts the flow diagram for this routine.)

Briefly, the monthly report program operates as follows: tape 1 is read and the tape sector records are posted to October's pupil attendance disk. Nonhomeroom faculty records are posted to tape 3 as well as to disk. When a homeroom teacher tape sector record is encountered, the program posts this record to disk and to tape 3, and then begins to read tape 4, which contains the pupil sector records for that homeroom class. The program posts to tape 2 each pupil record that has either an entry or a withdrawal code, or both. No pupil record which contains a withdrawal code is posted to disk. Thus, pupils who have withdrawn from the school during the month (in this example September) are purged from next month's pupil attendance disk (i.e., October's pupil attendance disk).

When the school level and grade section on the pupil record do not match those of the homeroom teacher record on tape 1, class statistics (net roll girls, net roll boys, aggregate days on roll, average daily attendance, etc.) are posted to tape 3.

Tape 1 is now read again and the cycle is repeated until all the records on tape 1 and tape 4 have been merged and posted to disk, tape 2, or tape 3, as applicable. Then the monthly report program prints out each school's monthly report, using tape 3 as input data. (How this report looks and the statistics it contains are shown in Figure 65.) The monthly report program takes about six hours. The monthly report for each school is printed in triplicate. These reports are usually completed about 11–12 days from the end of the month (i.e., September's monthly reports are finished about October 12). The data center forwards the original to the bureau of research for archival purposes, the second copy is sent to the appropriate assistant superintendent, and the third copy to the principal.

Tape 2 contains data on each pupil who withdrew or enrolled in the school system during the month of September. Each month these tapes are saved. These tapes provide the data for an annual

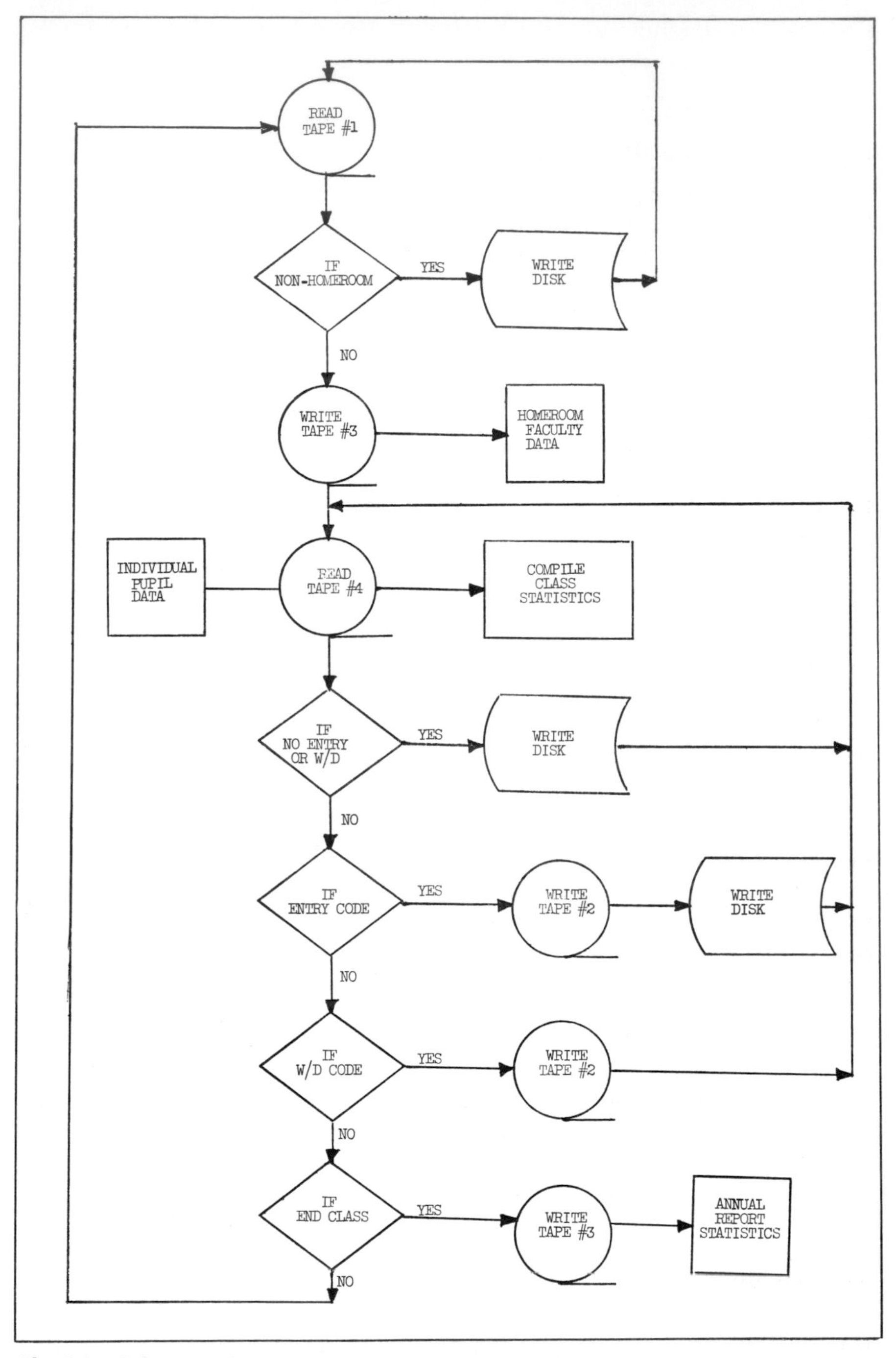

Fig. 64 – Print Monthly Report Statistics Program Diagram.

BALTIMORE CITY PUBLIC SCHOOLS — MONTHLY REPORT — SCHOOL NO. 60 1
FOR MONTH ENDING SEPTEMBER 30,1965

TABLE 1

NONHOMEROOM FACULTY DATA

FACULTY NAMES	POSITION	CLASSIFICATION	DEPARTMENT
WRIGHT VIOLA	PRINCIPAL	ELECTED	
TILDON LOUISE	VICE PRINC	ELECTED	
BUTLER MABEL	TEACHER	ELECTED	
LAWSON ELSIE	LIBRARIAN	ELECTED	

TABLE 2

HOMEROOM FACULTY DATA

FACULTY NAME	POSITION	CLASSIFICATION	DEPARTMENT	GR/SEC	CUR/PRG	AV. DAYS ATTENDED	AV. DAILY MEMBERSHIP	NET ROLL STATISTICS GIRLS	BOYS	TOTAL
CROWNER AVA	TCH IN CHG	ELECTED		4- 1	214	30.08	32.28	17	18	35
WILSON DELORES	TEACHER	ELECTED		4- 2	214	34.64	36.00	18	18	36
HENDERSON EVALENA	TEACHER	ELECTED		4- 3	214	35.89	37.00	18	19	37
JEFFERSON BEATRICE	TEACHER	ELECTED		4- 4	214	35.22	36.28	18	20	38
LUCAS MAIZIE	TEACHER	ELECTED		4- 5	214	36.14	30.00	20	18	38
WALDEN CELONIA	TEACHER	ELECTED		5- 1	215	35.67	37.00	19	18	37
PRESS VERNON	TEACHER	ELECTED		5- 2	215	36.11	37.72	13	24	37
CURRY JEANETTE	TEACHER	ELECTED		5- 3	215	32.19	34.00	18	17	35
FINNEY ISIS	TEACHER	ELECTED		5- 4	215	32.33	34.22	17	20	37
WESTCOTT BEULAH	TEACHER	ELECTED		5- 5	215	34.25	36.00	15	21	36
LYNCH SONIA	TEACHER	NOT ELEC		5- 6	215	35.47	36.22	22	14	36
HILL BARBARA	TEACHER	NOT ELECT		5- 7	215	39.17	40.00	23	17	40
GIBSON CORA	TEACHER	ELECTED		6- 1	216	35.06	36.56	17	21	38
TAYLOR SARA	TEACHER	ELECTED		6- 2	216	34.75	36.00	20	17	37
LEE LEILA	TEACHER	ELECTED		6- 3	216	36.19	36.89	16	22	38
WINNER JACOB	TEACHER	PROV		6- 4	216	36.17	37.11	24	14	38
CLEMMONS EDWARD	TEACHER	ELECTED		6- 5	216	34.81	36.00	22	16	38
HARRIS DEBORAH	TEACHER	ELECTED		40- 1	202	34.39	35.89	15	21	36
HARRIS DEBORAH	TEACHER	ELECTED		40- 2	202	30.00	31.00	16	14	30
BROOKS DOLORES	TEACHER	ELECTED		40- 3	202	30.89	31.78	14	17	31
BROOKS DOLORES	TEACHER	ELECTED		40- 4	202	29.00	30.11	12	19	31
JOHNSON FRANCES	TEACHER	ELECTED		71- 1	231	24.06	25.00	8	17	25
DUNAWAY ANNIE	TEACHER	PROV		71- 2	231	20.53	23.00	3	20	23
GAMBRILL JULIA	TEACHER	PROV		71- 3	231	22.39	23.72	10	13	23
MATTHEWS EUNICE	TEACHER	ELECTED		99- 1	220	29.72	31.06	15	16	31
RICE BARBARA	TEACHER	PROV		99- 2	220	29.78	31.33	14	16	30
SHERMAN GERTRUDE	TEACHER	NOT ELEC		99- 3	220	29.64	30.17	13	17	30
DANIELS MARION	TEACHER	ELECTED		99- 4	220	28.50	29.50	17	12	29
PARKER DOLORES	TEACHER	ELEC		99- 5	220	31.00	31.67	21	10	31
OWINGS CARLEAN	TEACHER	ELECTED		99- 6	220	31.94	33.14	14	19	33
URQUHART JULIA	TEACHER	NOT ELEC		99- 7	220	29.97	32.44	13	21	34
WALLACE HILDA	TEACHER	ELEC		99- 8	220	33.83	35.00	17	18	35
DUTTON ELLEN	TEACHER	NOT ELEC		99- 9	220	32.28	33.33	21	12	33
ARCHER YVONNE	TEACHER	ELECTED		99- 10	220	36.00	36.72	19	17	36
BEARD VICTORIA	TEACHER	ELECTED		99- 11	220	32.83	33.89	11	22	33
SENIOR PHOEBE	TEACHER	ELECTED		99- 12	220	33.89	34.33	9	25	34
PINKETT MAY	TEACHER	ELECTED		99- 13	220	33.78	34.78	12	23	35
SMITH MARGARET	TEACHER	NOT ELEC		99- 14	220	34.81	35.61	14	21	35
MITCHELL ELEANOR	TEACHER	ELECTED		99- 15	220	31.92	34.39	21	12	33
PARKER JOYCE	TEACHER	NOT ELEC		99- 16	220	34.33	35.00	22.	13	35
SCHOOL TOTALS						1299.61	1350.44	640	709	1357

LIVE NET ROLL EXCLUDES YEAR ABSENTEES

Fig. 65 — The Monthly Report.

pupil withdrawal table (for each school, for each level, and for the entire school system). These tapes also provide the data for an annual pupil entry table.

Pupil Attendance Disk Dump Routine

After the monthly report program has been run, the next month's pupil attendance disk has been created. While this file need not be dumped, experience has shown that to do so is extremely valuable. A standard disk dump utility program is utilized, except that the program was modified to achieve single- instead of double-spaced printing.

Printing the Teachers' Summary Attendance Reports

After the October pupil attendance disk has been dumped, the TSAR sheet program is run. (See the section previously described in detail, entitled "Teachers' Summary Attendance Report Procedures." The October TSAR sheets are printed out about October 20 and distributed to the schools about October 25. The October pupil TSAR cards punched out are saved. The cycle, as already indicated from the TSAR sheet routine to the pupil attendance disk dump routine, is repeated monthly until the close of school, when the over-the-summer procedures cycle is instituted.

CONCLUSION

The Fortran IV pupil summary attendance system described in this chapter works and is in actual operation. More complete details may be obtained by writing to the authors. Yet even now computer and optical scan advances have made it possible to revise certain programs so that they will operate with greater speed and efficiency.

12 pupil scheduling—a disk approach

ORLANDO F. FURNO and MARTIN H. RAILA

MARTIN H. RAILA *is a doctoral candidate at Teachers College, Columbia University. He received his bachelor's degree in Chemical Engineering from Johns Hopkins University. During World War II, he did research on chemical munitions at the University of Illinois; he was granted a patent on catalytic control of pyrotechnic fuel mixtures. After several years in industry, Mr. Raila left engineering to earn his MEd, and education has been his field since that time.*

Since 1957 Mr. Raila has been with the Baltimore City Public Schools, where he has worked primarily in population studies and in systems and procedures for pupil scheduling and for fiscal matters. Previously, he taught science and mathematics in junior and senior high schools, and in adult classes; he has taught mathematics, statistics, and tests and measurements in evening classes at Johns Hopkins and Loyola (Baltimore).

DR. ORLANDO F. FURNO *(see biography, Chapter 11.)*

WHY SCHEDULE PUPILS WITH A COMPUTER?

No one can question the fact that principals can schedule pupils manually, since they have been doing so for more than a century. But can principals in general schedule pupils as efficiently as computers? Should high-priced professional educators do the endless hours of clerical work required to schedule pupils manually? We think not. Computer scheduling of pupils offers a number of distinct advantages. For example, it:

1. Enables the schedule-maker to adjust, alter, or reconstruct the master schedule repeatedly, and up to the last minute, to an extent completely impossible in a manual operation.
2. Reduces conflicts to a minimum, thus giving more pupils the courses they desire.
3. Organizes and balances classes better.
4. Minimizes the disruption caused by pupil changes (entries and withdrawals, course or curriculum choices, summer school work), thus permitting changes to be made late in the summer but before the opening of school.
5. Produces a greater variety of useful records in more legible form, in any quantity desired.

6. Increases the accuracy of data, including that recorded in the pupil's permanent record.
7. Frees scheduling personnel from laborious and inefficient clerical tasks.
8. Reduces peak work loads for clerks, letting them devote more time to needs of the administrative staff and teachers.
9. Can form the basis for printing of report cards, permanent pupil records, and other automated pupil record processes.
10. Provides a better basis and method for carrying out research studies.

Numerous computer scheduling programs have been written, utilizing a variety of computers, and numerous commercial scheduling services are available. Regardless of the student scheduling program or procedure, regardless of the computer utilized, regardless of how many schools have successfully used a particular pupil scheduling program, the principal should make sure that he knows what that program can and cannot do. Before the principal and his staff buy a "pig in a poke," they should consider these questions about their school operating procedures:

1. How many instructional periods will there be in the school day?
2. Is a given subject always taught during the same period? Or might English be taught in the 3rd period on Monday, 6th period Tuesday, etc.?
3. Will it be necessary to schedule certain subjects into consecutive periods? (chemistry and chemistry laboratory, for example.)
4. Is it necessary to connect certain sections so that the same pupils who are scheduled into one are also scheduled into the other or others?
5. How many lunch periods will there be?
6. What is the maximum number of separate courses that an individual student can take?
7. What is the maximum total number of individual courses to be offered?
8. What is the maximum number of teaching sections which will be formed?
9. Will every course be offered for the full year or will some courses be offered for the first semester only and others for the second semester only?
10. Will study halls be scheduled for otherwise vacant periods?
11. Are there students (such as those in work-study programs) for whom classes must be scheduled only during certain specific parts of the day?

12. What documents does the school wish the scheduling operation to produce? (Documents include pupil schedule cards, class lists, homeroom lists, pupil roster, master schedule printouts, etc.)
13. How many copies of each document are required?
14. Are there specifications as to size and shape of the documents because of the filing methods to be used?
15. What items of information are to be included on the pupil's schedule card?
16. What will be the source of this information?
17. What are the various deadlines which must be met in sending and receiving information?

Is the computer scheduling program applicable to the school situation defined by answers to these questions? If so, there is no problem. If it is not applicable and cannot be modified to be applicable, the school has two choices. It can seek a different computer program which *is* applicable, or it can modify its school procedures to conform to the requirements of the first program. If the latter course is taken, the principal should weigh carefully what he is gaining against what he is giving up. The scheduling "tail" should not "wag" the educational "dog."

SOME STEPS TO BE FOLLOWED

Pupil scheduling is assigning pupils, teachers, classrooms, and time in such a way that students can take required courses as well as desired electives. The following list summarizes the procedure necessary to accomplish this when computer scheduling is used:

1. Appoint a scheduling coordinator.
2. Establish discrete instructional groups.
3. Prepare a course catalog (subject listing).
4. Finalize scheduling information.
5. Design appropriate data gathering forms.
6. Gather necessary pupil data.
7. Check accuracy of pupil request records.
8. Correct inaccurate pupil scheduling data.
9. Establish rigid control over school data sent to computer center.
10. Compute course request tally.
11. Modify course offerings.
12. Run potential conflict matrix.
13. Construct school master schedule.
14. Specify pupil scheduling sequence.
15. Schedule pupils.

16. Analyze scheduling results.
17. Repeat process of revising master schedule, pupil course requests, and analyzing results.
18. Make final scheduling run and print out all pertinent documents.

In the remainder of this chapter, we shall discuss each of these steps more fully.

Pupil Scheduling Coordinator

Each school should appoint a pupil scheduling coordinator. "Too many cooks spoil the broth" is apropos here. One person only should be responsible for the gathering, flow, and control of pupil scheduling data. Whether the principal assumes this role or delegates it to his vice principal or other staff member is immaterial. But it is essential, if confusion and chaos are to be avoided, that one person be in charge of pupil scheduling.

Such a requirement is not unreasonable. Data coming from the computer center is cast in unaccustomed forms. By working regularly with such material the scheduling coordinator develops a familiarity with the data. He gets to know what errors are serious and which are minor. In time, he acquires the knowledge necessary for efficient communication between the computer center and the school.

If the principal appoints someone other than himself to the job of pupil scheduling coordinator, he should also delegate to that person the authority to make decisions concerning pupil scheduling. Obviously, these decisions must fit the general design and scheduling policy established by the principal. Clearly, the scheduling coordinator should keep the principal informed of pupil scheduling progress. If time permits, he should discuss with the principal decisions concerning the master schedule and pupil course requests. However, time does not always permit the scheduling coordinator to consult with the principal on needed changes and corrections in master schedule data or pupil course requests. In these instances, the scheduling coordinator should have the authority to resolve the computer center's questions immediately. Otherwise, pupil scheduling progress will be inordinately delayed.

The pupil scheduling coordinator should be appointed as soon as possible after school has opened, certainly no later than October 15.

Establish Discrete Instructional Groups

Contrary to popular belief, computers do not make decisions nor exercise judgment. A computer can be programed to follow a given set of instructions if a given condition exists, but this is not decision making. Computers cannot *per se*, then, assign pupils to discrete instructional groups.

Accomplishing this task requires a change in attitudes and thinking on the part of school administrators, counselors, and teachers. For example, the principal, in manually assigning pupils to particular instructional groups, need not decide in advance which group a pupil will go into. He can make, and change, that decision at the moment of assignment. But making this assignment on a computer cannot be done so freely or loosely. Here's why: first, the instructional group must be identified by a code (usually numerical); second, all pupils who are to be assigned to that group must be so identified. Now the computer can be programed to make the appropriate assignment.

Undoubtedly, the phrase "discrete instructional groups" requires more explanation in practical terms. The content of a subject listing or course, say English 3, would not be the same for pupils pursuing an academic curriculum as it would be for pupils pursuing a vocational technical curriculum. Moreover, for instructional purposes, it may be considered desirable to group pupils according to ability levels—say high, average, or low.

Even where pupils pursue the same curriculum and have about the same ability, there may be good reason to want to put certain of them in a given class. For example, let's assume that all sections in course 110, English 3, will be taught the same material. However, the staff of the yearbook is drawn from this group and the advisor wishes this group scheduled for the last period in the school day. These pupils now must be identified as a discrete group and must have a different number, say 111.

Let's assume further that an experimental reading program is established in this school. Certain pupils taking academic English 3 are to take special reading, organized in the same class sections as those in which they take English 3. Assume that there are three such sections. Each of these English 3 sections is now a discrete group and must have a particular number, say numbers 115, 116, and 117. If these pupils are identified for assignment to special reading, but not to any particular section, there will be only one discrete group (those pupils taking both courses) rather than three (those pupils in each of the three identical sections for both courses), and only one new course number will be required, say 115, although there will still be three teaching sections, all having that same course number.

Thus we have one course, academic English 3, with the same

material being taught to all pupils taking that course. But while we have one course from the standpoint of content, we have several discrete groups whose pupils must be identified and kept separate for other purposes. As a result we have now English 3—110, English 3—111, English 3—115, English 3—116, and English 3—117, and the pupils whom we want in each group must have the appropriate number entered in their course request.

A frequent use of discrete groups within a given subject is that of assigning pupils according to ability. If the technical pupils are to be grouped in English 3 according to high, average, and low

FOREST PARK HIGH SCHOOL

DISCRETE GROUPINGS - - - - - - 1966-67

ENGLISH

CODE #	DESCRIPTION OF GROUP
001	10th Grade - Spec. Col. Prep. English
002	10th Grade - Acad. and Col. Bus. Eng. mark of 75 or better
003	10th Grade - Acad. and Col. Bus. Eng. mark of 74 or less
006	10th Grade - Gen. Bus. and Gen. Tech. English
007	10th Grade - Remedial Reading
008	11th Grade - Spec. Col. Prep. English
009	11th Grade - Academic and College Business
013	11th Grade - Reading-Speech - Gen. Tech. and Gen. Bus.
014	11th Grade and 12th Grade Journalism-Creative Writing, SCP & Acad.
017	12th Grade - English Regular Business
021	12th Grade - English Honors
022	10th Grade - Drama I
023	11th Grade - Drama I Acad., Reg. Bus., Gen. Bus., Gen. Acad.

Fig. 66 — Portion of Course Catalog Showing Listing of Courses With Three-Digit Code Numbers.

ability in English, then again three numbers are required, so that instead of English 3—120 we would have, say, English 3—120, English 3—121, and English 3—122.

Establishing the school's discrete instructional groups should be a cooperative school faculty responsibility. This task should be done

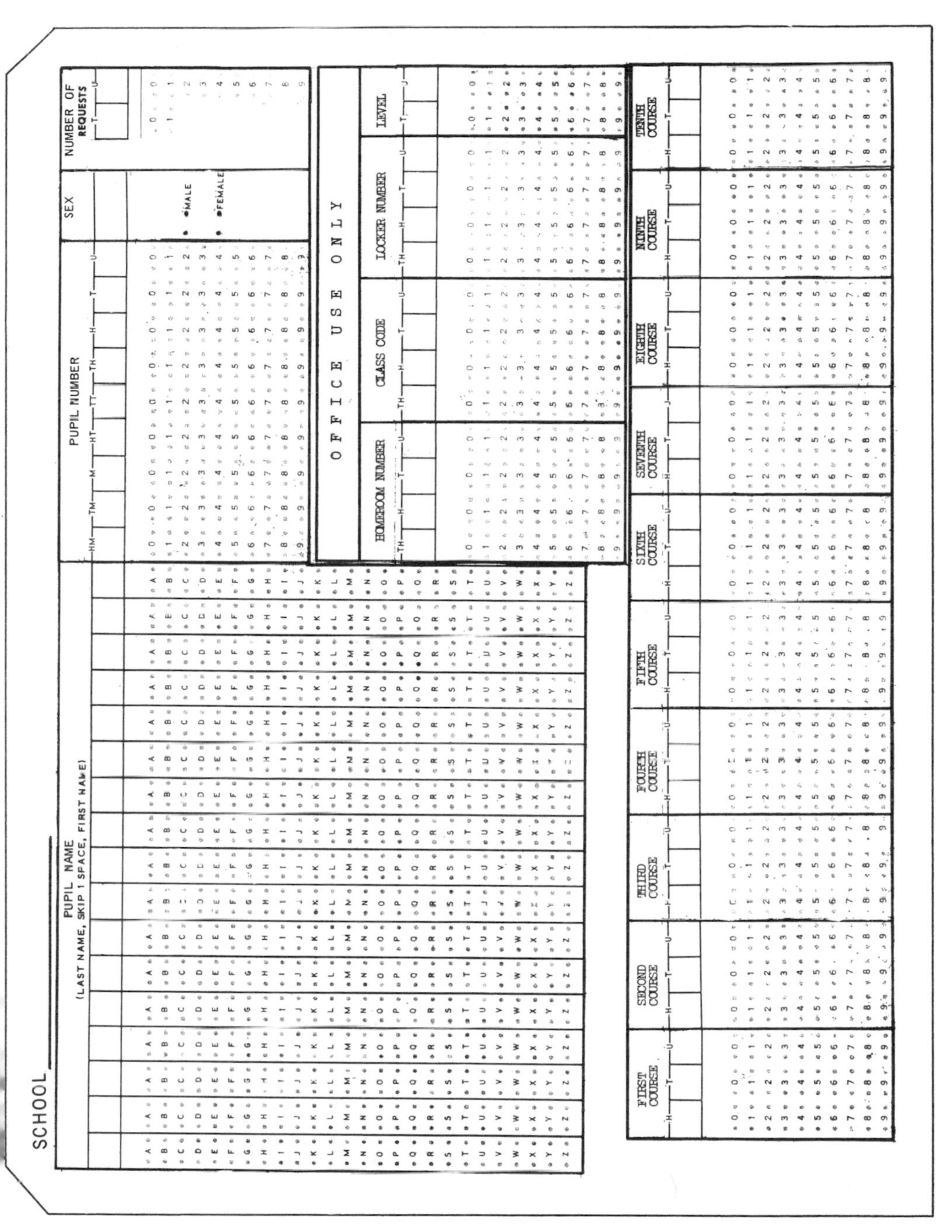

Fig. 67 – Design for an Optically Scanned Pupil Course Request Form.

during the fall term and be completed not later than January 30. Unless this is done, a course catalog (subject listing) cannot be prepared.

Prepare A Course Catalog

This task cannot be finished until all discrete instructional groups have been identified by the school faculty. Baltimore City's pupil scheduling program calls for a three-digit course code (subject listing). (See Fig. 66 for a course catalog listing.) Appropriate information about criteria used in placing pupils in discrete instructional groups should be included in the course catalog for counselor, teacher, pupil, and parent use.

Finalize Scheduling Information

School personnel, systems and procedures analysts, forms design specialists, and computer center personnel should all be consulted about the information to be included on each scheduling document. Preparation of each scheduling document should not be done unilaterally. The pupil scheduling process requires a total systems study.

For example, how will schedules be given to pupils? Will pupils returning to school in the fall report to their present homerooms and have schedules distributed there? If so, their present homeroom must be included as one item of information in the pupil record, and the computer center must be instructed to run off final schedules grouped by the present homeroom of pupils. Will schedules be mailed to pupils, with the addresses coming from an alphabetical file of all pupils? If so, the school will want schedules turned over to them in that same alphabetical sequence.

Counselors will need to relate school file information to information coming from the computer center. The two should follow the same sequence. How are the school files arranged? By grade? By curriculum? By sex? By homeroom class? Any such item which is used as a basis for sorting or arranging must appear in the computer's pupil record, and appropriate plans must be made for getting this information into that record. Obviously, the computer can neither print out nor act upon information which it does not have.

Whereas a pupil scheduling documents committee can meet off and on throughout the school year, its principal work should be done in the fall. What information to collect should be decided by the end of February. This timetable applies to both input and output scheduling documents.

Design Scheduling Documents

After the pupil scheduling documents committee finally agrees on the data to be amassed for scheduling purposes, the systems and procedures, forms design, and data processing personnel design the input and output scheduling documents. The data gathering forms must provide for the collection of all the information decided upon. The forms design must also facilitate manual recording as well as keypunching of data. Those school districts having optical scanners may design input documents accordingly.

Forms design embodies a number of basic principles. Several important ones are:

- Make the form easy to read.
- Make the form easy to follow.
- Reduce to an absolute minimum the writing the respondent has to do.
- Design the form for economical processing of data.

Figure 67 shows a possible design for an optically scanned pupil scheduling form that could be used by school districts having optical scanners. Figure 68 shows a pupil registration card designed to facilitate keypunching of pupil data needed for scheduling. Some school districts prefer a mark sensing approach to gather pupil scheduling data; others prefer a Port-A-Punch approach.

PRESENT HOMEROOM	STUDENT'S NAME (LAST NAME FIRST)		INFO. FOR SCHOOL YR. 19 -19
DATE OF BIRTH			IBM NUMBER:
ENTR. DATE TO FPHS	ADDRESS (INCLUDE ZIP CODE)		BOY ☐ GIRL ☐ CHECK ONE
CAME TO FPHS FROM:	NAME OF PARENT OR GUARDIAN (MALE)	RELATIONSHIP	GRADE / CURRICULUM
"W" DATE	NAME OF PARENT OR GUARDIAN (FEMALE)	RELATIONSHIP	NEW HR / ROOM
REASON FOR "W"	ADDRESS OF PARENT OR GUARDIAN	PHONE NO.	NEW LOCKER NO.

SUBJECT CHOICES	COURSE NUMBER

FOREST PARK HIGH SCHOOL CURRICULUM CHOICE CARD

Fig. 68 — Pupil Registration Card Designed to Facilitate Keypunching of Scheduling Data.

Gather Pupil Request Data

Pupils, in cooperation with their parents, teachers, and guidance counselors, select the courses they want to take for the next school year. At this point, reference to the course catalog is essential. Whether or not the pupil fills in course name and number, the counselor is responsible for seeing that the course number recorded is correct. The counselor is also responsible for seeing that graduation requirements are being met, and for assigning students to appropriate ability grouping. Student course selections should be completed by April 30.

Processing Student Course Requests

The scheduling coordinator is responsible for assembling the individual student course request cards, maintaining forms control, and distributing forms to the computer center, including a copy of the course catalog.

Generating Pupil Numbers. The computer stores, retrieves, and relates data for an individual pupil by means of a unique identification number assigned to each pupil. Rather than have the school identify each pupil by number and record that number on the student course request form, the computer center generates a deck of cards for each school, automatically punching into each student request card the pupil's school number, a pupil scheduling identification number, and any other generally applicable constant number, such as the school year. The program that does this is called the pupil number generator program. To run through about 2,000 pupils takes about five minutes.

In some school systems an identification number may have already been assigned for some other purpose, such as an automated attendance system. In such a case, the school should supply this same number instead of using randomly generated new and different numbers.

Keypunching Pupil Request Data. When the student request card deck has been generated, data on the student course request forms are keypunched into it. One card is generated per pupil. For about 2,000 pupils, the keypunching task takes about three man-days, including verification. Figure 69 shows the student request card layout.

Preparing Pupil Lists and School Tally Run. The computer center runs off a roster of pupil data, listing all the data about each pupil for whom the center received a student course request form. The data are printed out in the pupil sequence specified by the school. Figure 70 shows such a roster. The school examines this roster carefully. Any omissions, errors, or modifications to be made are noted by the school and made known to the computer center, using a standard procedure which has been agreed upon by the school and the center.

Any corrections necessary are made and the cards are then sorted into the file sequence which the school wishes to use during

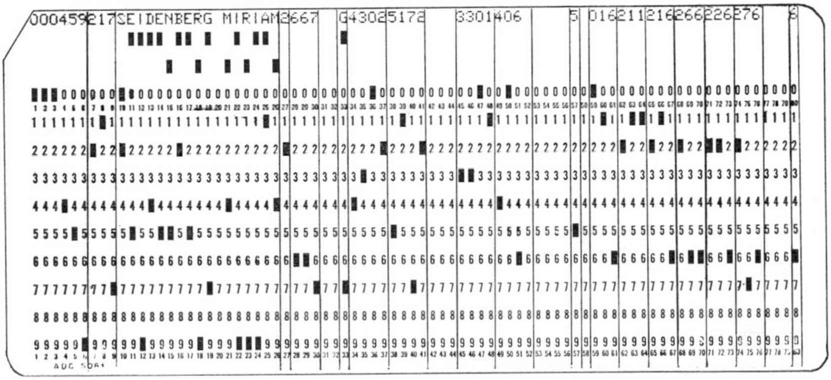

Field	Card Columns	Field Width
1. Pupil Number	1-6	6
2. New Homeroom Number	7-9	3
3. Pupil Name	10-26	17
4. Grade Level	27	1
5. School Year	28-30	3
6. Sex	33	1
7. Code for New Homeroom Class	34-37	4
8. Locker Number	38-41	4
9. Code for Previous Homeroom Class	45-48	4
10. School Code Number	49-52	4
11. Curriculum Code	57	1
12. Courses Requested, by 3 Digit Codes	59-79	21
13. Number of Courses Requested	80	1

Fig. 69 — Baltimore City Public Schools Student Request Punched Card Layout.

the subsequent scheduling operations. A sequence which has been found to be convenient in Baltimore is: by grades in descending order, by curriculum within grades, by sex for each curriculum, and alphabetically for each sex.

Next the computer center prepares the school tally run. (See Fig. 71 for sample output.) The school tally run lists each course or discrete group by its code number, its abbreviated name, the number of pupil requests, how many sections are needed (based on an arbitrary average class size), and the pupil overflow for each course. It is possible to make separate tallies for each grade or each curriculum, or to tally boys and girls separately, if this is useful to the school.

A new pupil roster is also run. This is in the new file sequence and incorporates all changes which have been made to date in pupil requests.

Pupil Number	Pupil Name	Grade	Sex	Home-room Class Code	Cur-ricu-lum Code	Code Numbers of Courses Requested					
392	THOMPSON RUFUS	2	B	1306	2	016	314	110	159	054	310
14	TRAYNHAM JOHN	2	B	1302	2	016	063	316	256	112	309
114	TURNER C MICHAEL	2	B	1304	2	016	266	063	202	073	309
44	TUTMAN DANARDA	2	B	1301	2	016	054	069	261	316	077
80	VALENTINE MICHAEL	2	B	1303	2	016	063	054	261	409	410
45	WEER GARY	2	B	1301	2	016	063	069	110	314	310
149	WHITE CLIFTON	2	B	1305	2	016	261	073	069	313	230
81	WHITE JOSEPH	2	B	1303	2	016	054	110	402	265	309
393	WHITSON ROBERT	2	B	1306	2	016	014	409	073	110	405
15	WILLIS CHARLES	2	B	1302	2	016	156	110	303	063	310
1068	WISE OTIS C	2	B	403	2	016	063	159	307	309	014
47	WOOD JAMES	2	B	1301	2	016	058	110	107	409	405
394	WOODLAND CHARLES	2	B	1306	2	016	069	261	202	054	455
150	ADELSON SHARON	2	G	1305	2	016	262	074	226	110	360
115	AMES DENISE	2	G	1304	2	016	063	113	074	252	077
82	AMIS BRENDA	2	G	1303	2	016	256	274	014	112	027
83	BALL NAOMI	2	G	1303	2	016	216	270	112	063	077
395	BAYLOR MICHELLE	2	G	1306	2	016	074	159	274	256	358

Fig. 70 – Portion of Pupil Roster.

Scheduling Coordinator Establishes Rigid Control Over Pupil Scheduling Data

The school will receive copies of the pupil roster and school tally run. This represents the starting situation for the scheduling process. *It is imperative that changes from this situation be channeled through the school coordinator.* He must maintain absolute control of this matter, and his copy of all documents should be dated and annotated to make clear what changes are reflected in *his copy* of each document.

COURSE NAME	COURSE NO	REQUESTS	SECTIONS	OVERFLOW
BOOKEEPG 1	219	029	01	
BOOKEEPG 2	220	011	01	
BUS PROC 1	221	107	03	17
BUS PROC 2	222	065	02	05
BUS ARITH1	223	131	04	11
BUS ARITH2	224	090	03	00
BUS ARITH3	225	029	01	
BUS LAW EC	226	085	02	25
BUS ARITH1	227	037	01	07
BUS ARITH1	228	066	02	06
OFF PRAC 1	229	038	01	08
PERS TYPE	230	039	01	09
BUS MATH1G	233	066	02	06
FRENCH 1	251	032	01	02
FRENCH 1	252	018	01	
FRENCH 1	253	024	01	
FRENCH 2	254	020	01	
FRENCH 2	255	152	05	02
FRENCH 2	256	028	01	
FRENCH 2	257	021	01	
FRENCH 3	258	046	01	16
FRENCH 4	259	021	01	
SPANISH 1	260	018	01	
SPANISH 1	261	047	01	17
SPANISH 1	262	024	01	
SPANISH 2	263	066	02	06
SPANISH 2	264	045	01	15
SPANISH 34	265	032	01	02
SPANISH 2	266	048	01	18
GERMAN 1	267	027	01	
GERMAN 1	268	006	01	
GERMAN 2	269	029	01	
GERMAN 2	270	020	01	
GERMAN 2	271	002	01	
GERMAN 34	272	016	01	
LATIN 2	273	009	01	
LATIN 34	274	013	01	
LAN LAB FR	275	016	01	
LAN LAB SP	276	023	01	
IND ARTS 1	301	210	07	00
IND ARTS 1	[illegible]	[illegible]	[illegible]	[illegible]

Fig. 71 — Portion of Printout Made from Course Tally Run.

Numerous changes will occur between spring, when original data gathering takes place, and fall, when school opens. Some pupils will leave the school, others will transfer to it, some may change their curricular path, some may have to attend summer school, etc.

It is the coordinator's responsibility to make certain that the computer center has one record, and no duplicates, for each pupil to be scheduled, and that this record is correct and up to date.

Modify, If Necessary, School Course Offerings

The tally run may show that it is necessary to modify the number and kind of courses to be offered. Suppose, for example, that only seven pupils request German 4, a course which is not required for graduation. The administration must decide among several alternatives. Should they set up a section for just seven pupils? Should they make a combined section of pupils taking German 3 and pupils taking German 4? Should they drop German 4 entirely, and have these seven pupils substitute some other course?

Such a decision is often needed when subject matter is essentially similar, but where imbalanced groups have resulted from attempts to achieve homogeneity with respect to class or curriculum or ability. For example, one group may contain 18 particular pupils, and another 42. Should the grouping criteria be dropped, making this one group of 60 pupils to be later assigned indiscriminately to smaller sections? Or should grouping criteria be altered to cause some shifting between groups to achieve a better balance? If the former decision is made, the computer center will have to be notified that two courses are to be combined into one, and be told which of the two original course numbers should be used for the combined course. If the latter decision is made, the computer center will have to be notified of the changes which are to be made in the course requests of individual pupils.

After careful scrutiny of the pupil course request lists and school tally run, the scheduling coordinator should notify the computer center of changes to be made in courses and in pupil requests. If the number of changes is extensive, the computer center will run new pupil course request lists and a new school tally run.

Run Potential Conflict Matrix

The potential conflict matrix, which the computer center produces next, is simply a two-way table which shows how many pupils have requested both of any two courses. This information is very useful in constructing the master schedule.

If, for example, 17 pupils have requested both course 110 and course 542 and there is only one section in each course (such a course is known as a "singleton"), it is clear that if these courses are offered during the same class period there will be an irreconcilable scheduling conflict for these 17 pupils.

Clearly, the individual school must indicate which course offerings are to be included in the potential conflict matrix run. All "singletons" would normally be included. "Doubletons" may or may not be. There is usually no advantage in including courses which have more than two sections. Indeed, it may be a disadvantage because it makes the matrix more difficult and time consuming to read, and the added information is of little or no use.

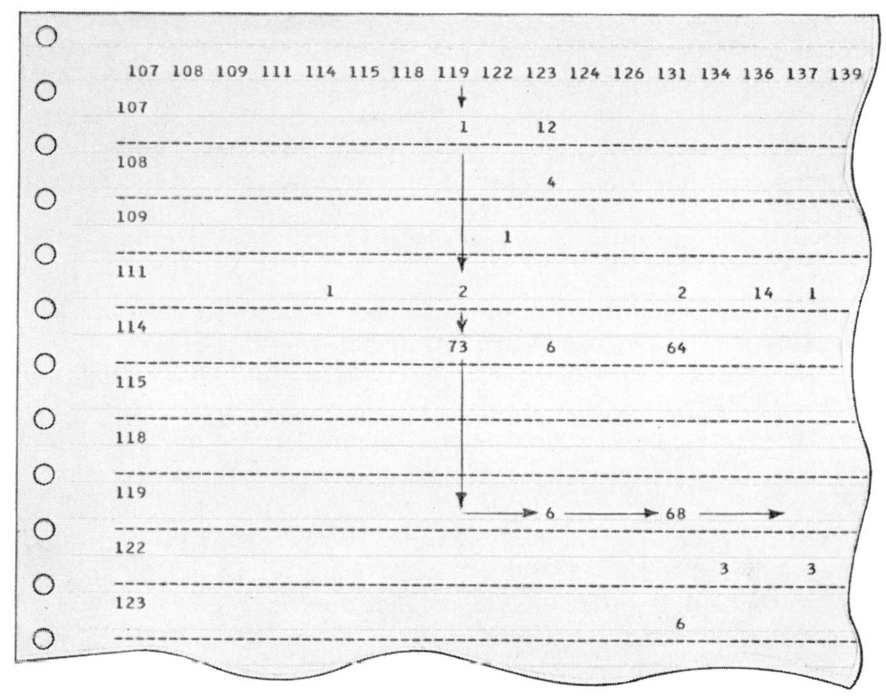

Fig. 72 — Cutout of Portion of a Potential Conflict Matrix.

Figure 72 shows a potential conflict matrix. The potential conflict matrix program takes about 25 minutes. The first run is usually completed by June 30.

Construct the School Master Schedule

Constructing the school master schedule is the most critical step in the entire scheduling process. The skill with which the master schedule is constructed and later adjusted determines the subsequent success and efficiency of the entire scheduling operation. The computer will assign pupils to the extent that the master schedule permits such assignment, and that is all it will do. (Efforts are being made to use computers to generate the master schedule. At this writing no completely successful, generally applicable program has been developed.)

Based on the tally, the number of teachers available, the class sizes considered appropriate, and other pertinent factors, the school decides how many teaching sections it will form in each course.

Based on the potential conflict matrix, availability of rooms, and numerous other relevant factors, the school establishes for each section where it will be taught, when, and by whom.

The individual school cannot always construct a meaningful master schedule at a desired time. In large school systems, the superintendent must balance secondary staffing needs against total budgetary needs. He then informs the person in charge of secondary education how many educational personnel he can employ. The assistant superintendent in charge of secondary education then allots each secondary school a quota of personnel. The principal then informs the director of personnel of his particular needs (so many English teachers, Latin teachers, physics teachers, math teachers, etc.). The director of personnel proceeds to recruit those teachers requested by each school principal.

Reorganization procedures should be completed by the first week in June. Not until the principal knows how many staff members he is authorized to employ can he develop his school's master schedule. The principal and his scheduling coordinator consider staff, facilities, time period patterns, curriculum needs, and amalgamate them into the master schedule. Whatever magic the principal and his scheduling coordinator make use of in developing the master schedule, the potential conflict matrix report provides a significant test of success or failure.

All the elements of the master schedule must be supplied to the computer center. These include, for each course:

- Title of course.
- Code number of course.
- Number of teaching sections available.
- Total number of seats available.
- Number of different periods during which the course is taught.
- The days on which the course is taught.
- For each teaching section:
  a. A one-digit code number.
  b. Class period in which that section meets.
  c. Days on which that section meets.
  d. Number of seats available.
  e. Number of room in which section meets.
  f. Code number of instructor.
- Number of teaching sections meeting during any period when course is offered.

When the computer center has keypunched the master schedule data, it prints out the school's master schedule. To keypunch the master schedule takes about one man-day. This schedule is sent to the scheduling coordinator. He checks over the printout, verifies its accuracy, and indicates any data that should be changed. He then returns the form to the computer center. The center keypunches all corrections indicated by the scheduling coordinator. A

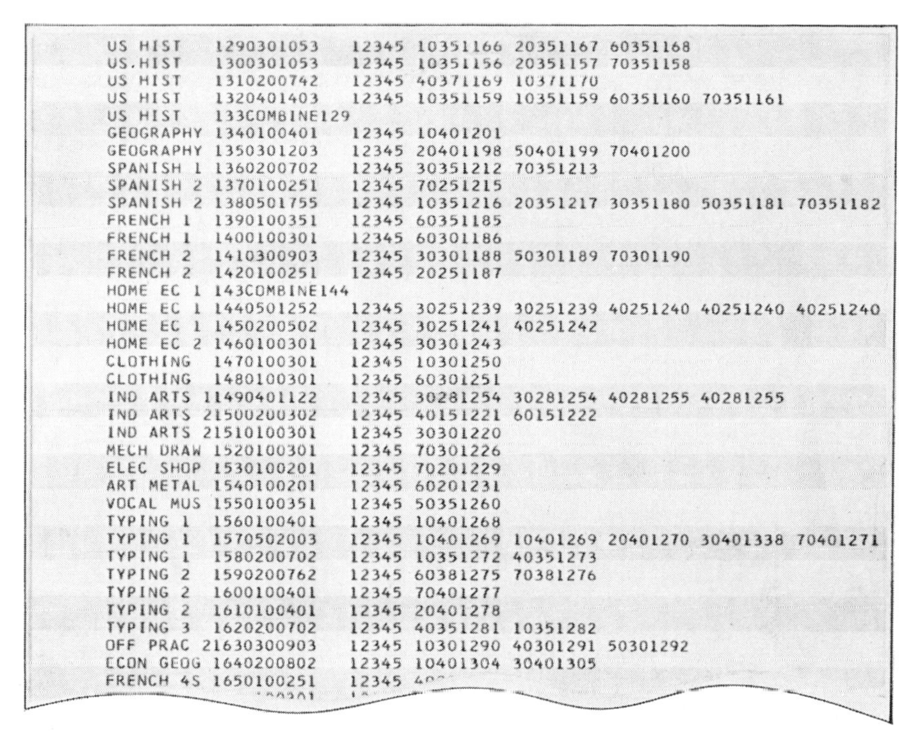

```
US HIST    1290301053   12345 10351166 20351167 60351168
US.HIST    1300301053   12345 10351156 20351157 70351158
US HIST    1310200742   12345 40371169 10371170
US HIST    1320401403   12345 10351159 10351159 60351160 70351161
US HIST    133COMBINE129
GEOGRAPHY 1340100401   12345 10401201
GEOGRAPHY 1350301203   12345 20401198 50401199 70401200
SPANISH 1 1360200702   12345 30351212 70351213
SPANISH 2 1370100251   12345 70251215
SPANISH 2 1380501755   12345 10351216 20351217 30351180 50351181 70351182
FRENCH 1  1390100351   12345 60351185
FRENCH 1  1400100301   12345 60301186
FRENCH 2  1410300903   12345 30301188 50301189 70301190
FRENCH 2  1420100251   12345 20251187
HOME EC 1 143COMBINE144
HOME EC 1 1440501252   12345 30251239 30251239 40251240 40251240 40251240
HOME EC 1 1450200502   12345 30251241 40251242
HOME EC 2 1460100301   12345 30301243
CLOTHING  1470100301   12345 10301250
CLOTHING  1480100301   12345 60301251
IND ARTS 11490401122   12345 30281254 30281254 40281255 40281255
IND ARTS 21500200302   12345 40151221 60151222
IND ARTS 21510100301   12345 30301220
MECH DRAW 1520100301   12345 70301226
ELEC SHOP 1530100201   12345 70201229
ART METAL 1540100201   12345 60201231
VOCAL MUS 1550100351   12345 50351260
TYPING 1  1560100401   12345 10401268
TYPING 1  1570502003   12345 10401269 10401269 20401270 30401338 70401271
TYPING 1  1580200702   12345 10351272 40351273
TYPING 2  1590200762   12345 60381275 70381276
TYPING 2  1600100401   12345 70401277
TYPING 2  1610100401   12345 20401278
TYPING 3  1620200702   12345 40351281 10351282
OFF PRAC 21630300903   12345 10301290 40301291 50301292
ECON GEOG 1640200802   12345 10401304 30401305
FRENCH 4S 1650100251   12345 4
```

Fig. 73— Portion of Master Schedule Printout.

new master schedule is printed out and returned to the scheduling coordinator for verification. The first master schedule should be keypunched and verified by June 30. Figure 73 shows a printout of a master schedule.

Schedule Pupils

The scheduling coordinator should indicate to the computer center the sequence in which pupils are to be scheduled. This is his responsibility. It is preferable to schedule first those pupils for whom a change in course selections is not possible or is least desirable. Typically, this would be the graduating class, but it could be pupils in some special program.

First Scheduling Run. When the student course request, master course, and the master schedule files have been created, the computer center is ready to make its first scheduling run. A scheduling run usually takes about two hours for 2,000 pupils. Basically, here's how the process works:

The computer attempts to schedule pupils by matching their course requests against the master schedule. It does this by trying

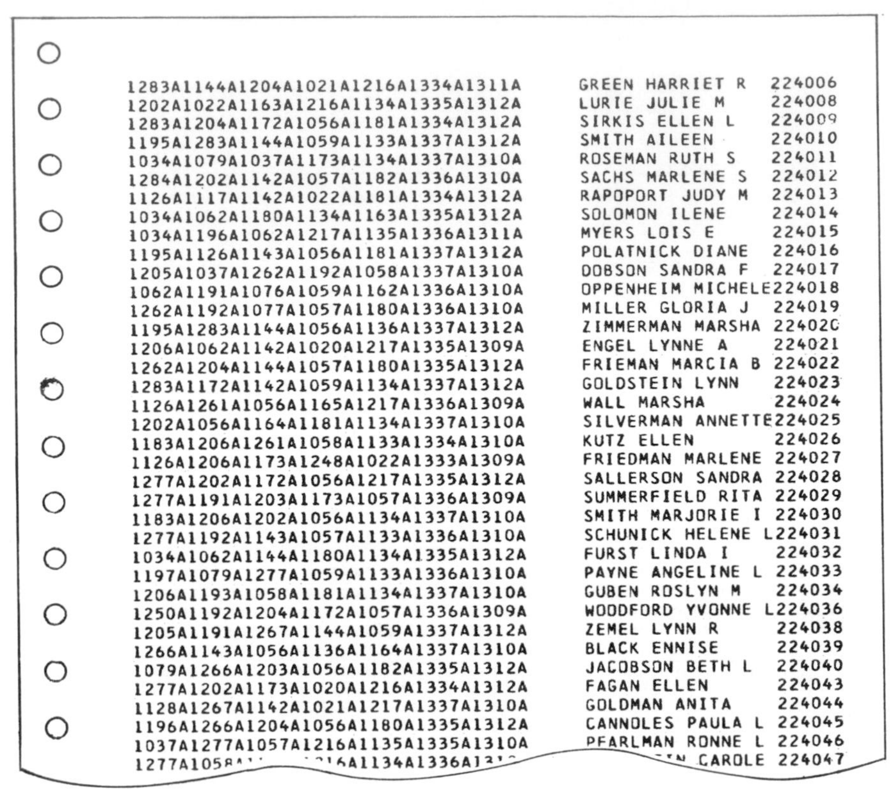

```
1283A1144A1204A1021A1216A1334A1311A    GREEN HARRIET R   224006
1202A1022A1163A1216A1134A1335A1312A    LURIE JULIE M     224008
1283A1204A1172A1056A1181A1334A1312A    SIRKIS ELLEN L    224009
1195A1283A1144A1059A1133A1337A1312A    SMITH AILEEN      224010
1034A1079A1037A1173A1134A1337A1310A    ROSEMAN RUTH S    224011
1284A1202A1142A1057A1182A1336A1310A    SACHS MARLENE S   224012
1126A1117A1142A1022A1181A1334A1312A    RAPOPORT JUDY M   224013
1034A1062A1180A1134A1163A1335A1312A    SOLOMON ILENE     224014
1034A1196A1062A1217A1135A1336A1311A    MYERS LOIS E      224015
1195A1126A1143A1056A1181A1337A1312A    POLATNICK DIANE   224016
1205A1037A1262A1192A1058A1337A1310A    DOBSON SANDRA F   224017
1062A1191A1076A1059A1162A1336A1310A    OPPENHEIM MICHELE224018
1262A1192A1077A1057A1180A1336A1310A    MILLER GLORIA J   224019
1195A1283A1144A1056A1136A1337A1312A    ZIMMERMAN MARSHA 224020
1206A1062A1142A1020A1217A1335A1309A    ENGEL LYNNE A     224021
1262A1204A1144A1057A1180A1335A1312A    FRIEMAN MARCIA B 224022
1283A1172A1142A1059A1134A1337A1312A    GOLDSTEIN LYNN    224023
1126A1261A1056A1165A1217A1336A1309A    WALL MARSHA       224024
1202A1056A1164A1181A1134A1337A1310A    SILVERMAN ANNETTE224025
1183A1206A1261A1058A1133A1334A1310A    KUTZ ELLEN        224026
1126A1206A1173A1248A1022A1333A1309A    FRIEDMAN MARLENE 224027
1277A1202A1172A1056A1217A1335A1312A    SALLERSON SANDRA 224028
1277A1191A1203A1173A1057A1336A1309A    SUMMERFIELD RITA 224029
1183A1206A1202A1056A1134A1337A1310A    SMITH MARJORIE I 224030
1277A1192A1143A1057A1133A1336A1310A    SCHUNICK HELENE L224031
1034A1062A1144A1180A1134A1335A1312A    FURST LINDA I     224032
1197A1079A1277A1059A1133A1336A1310A    PAYNE ANGELINE L 224033
1206A1193A1058A1181A1134A1337A1310A    GUBEN ROSLYN M    224034
1250A1192A1204A1172A1057A1336A1309A    WOODFORD YVONNE L224036
1205A1191A1267A1144A1059A1337A1312A    ZEMEL LYNN R      224038
1266A1143A1056A1136A1164A1337A1310A    BLACK ENNISE      224039
1079A1266A1203A1056A1182A1335A1312A    JACOBSON BETH L   224040
1277A1202A1173A1020A1216A1334A1312A    FAGAN ELLEN       224043
1128A1267A1142A1021A1217A1337A1310A    GOLDMAN ANITA     224044
1196A1266A1204A1056A1180A1335A1312A    CANNOLES PAULA L 224045
1037A1277A1057A1216A1135A1335A1310A    PEARLMAN RONNE L 224046
1277A1058[illegible]6A1134A1336A1[illegible]    [illegible]N CAROLE 224047
```

Fig. 74 — Portion of a List of Pupils Who Have Been Successfully Scheduled, Giving Each Pupil's Name, Identification Number, and the Disk Address of the Section Into Which the Pupil Has Been Scheduled for Each Course Requested.

various combinations of different sections of the courses which the pupil has requested until it finds a combination which results in a workable schedule. At that point, it assigns this pupil to each of the sections which made up this combination, decreases the number of seats available in each of those sections by one, and goes on to the next pupil.

The computer attempts to balance section loading—that is, where two or more sections of a course are equally available to a group of pupils, the computer assigns pupils to them alternately, so that the sections are filled in level fashion.

Some pupils will not be successfully scheduled, either because the master schedule structure is such that no workable combination of nonconflicting sections exists for their particular group of course requests, or because a section which would give them a workable combination has been completely filled during the scheduling of students who preceded them.

Typically, this first scheduling attempt will succeed to a limited extent, leaving an undesirably large number of pupils unscheduled and creating imbalanced sections (some too small, some filled to capacity) in certain courses.

The computer center sends to the school various documents which show:

1. The pupils who have been scheduled successfully, and the sections to which they have been assigned. (See Fig. 74.)
2. The pupils who could not be scheduled, the master schedule provisions for the courses requested by each of these pupils, and the number of seats available in each section of each requested course at the time the scheduling of each student was attempted. (See Fig. 75.)
3. The status of the master schedule at the end of this run, showing how many seats are still available in each section of each course, as well as for the course as a whole.

The first scheduling run should be made by early July.

Analyze Scheduling Run

The school examines these documents to locate any errors which may have occurred, such as specifying an insufficient number of seats to accommodate all requests for a given course, omitting a requested course from the master schedule entirely, or assigning an invalid course number to a pupil request.

The correction of such errors is essential, but a relatively minor task. A more time-consuming and difficult one is that of carefully analyzing these first-run results to discover what alterations should be made in the master schedule to facilitate the scheduling of pupils and to achieve a more balanced distribution of pupils among sections of the same course.

Reiterating a point made earlier, the ultimate success of the entire scheduling operation will depend more than anything else upon the skill and thoroughness with which this work is done. It is a step which will be repeated later, with the same need for careful, thoughtful work.

Depending upon the complexity of the situation, this analysis and adjustment may require anything from a few hours of work to several man-weeks.

Reiterate Scheduling Runs

The scheduling coordinator who can, on his first try, develop a master schedule which requires no changes is rare indeed. His degree of success is a function not only of his skill and effort but

```
     PERIOD CONFLICT

104029    SHIRKLEY PATRICK 0      B                FOREST PARK00101913603710117317 27

ART 1      037070054501812345 10111110 30081339 20151111 50001112 60001113 60071113 70131114

PHYS ED B 173010010100012345A30101313
SPANISH 1 136020029200912345 30281212A70011213
BIOLOGY B 101030022300912345A10041123A60071124 70111125
ENGLISH 2 001040035400012345A10131001 20001002A60071003 70151004
GEOMETRY  019050055500912345A20021066A20091066 50001068 30281069 70161070
ART 1      037070054501812345 10111110 30081339A20151111 50001112A60001113 60071113 70131114
LUNCH      172040701400912345 32501309A40631310A52181311A61701312



     PERIOD CONFLICT

114073    SHUB A DANIEL     1      B                FOREST PARK00505802103108117617 27

FRENCH 3   058020017200912345 10071193 40101194

BIOLOGY 2 031010009100012345A40091126
ORCHESTRA 081010016100012345A10161265
FRENCH 3   058020017200912345 10071193A40101194
MATH 3     021030033300012345A10081073 20101074 40151075
ENGLISH 3 005060062600912345 10031016A30121017 40141018 50051019 60211040 70071041
PHYS ED B 17604012040091 3 5 10491317A20171318 60261319 50281320
LUNCH      172040696400012345A32491309 40631310A52161311A61681312
```

Fig. 75 – Portion of a Conflict Listing, Giving Information About Pupils Who Could Not Be Scheduled Sucessfuly, and Showing the Status of the Master Schedule for Their Requested Courses at the Time of the Scheduling Attempt.

also of the relative complexity of the school's educational plan and curricular offerings. Presumably, upon analysis of the first scheduling run, the scheduling coordinator will submit master scheduling changes to the computer center. Another scheduling run, incorporating the changes, must then be made. Typically, the changes will result in the desirable objective of markedly improved scheduling.

Analysis of the first scheduling run eliminates gross scheduling errors. Adjustments in the master schedule improve certain problem situations revealed during analysis of the earlier run. However, it is unlikely that *all* problems will be identified and corrected. Furthermore, these same adjustments may create unforeseen problems for some pupils who were successfully scheduled earlier. Care in making the first adjustment will minimize this result, but is unlikely to prevent it entirely. Thus, the outcome of the second scheduling run must be carefully analyzed in the same fashion as the first, and necessary adjustments made.

In addition to making further master schedule changes, the school may find it necessary to make changes in the course requests of individual pupils, either arbitrarily or after consulting with the pupils involved. Some cases of "hard conflicts" will have been established—situations in which a pupil has requested two conflicting courses (usually "singletons") and the school is unable to reschedule the time of these courses. In such a case, the pupil obviously cannot be scheduled, regardless of how many scheduling runs are made, and one of these courses must be replaced by another which is compatible with the course in conflict.

The process of scheduling, analyzing, and adjusting is repeated until an acceptable degree of success has been achieved. Typically, about three scheduling runs are made.

Some school administrators criticize computer scheduling because they believe that computers take away the principal's decision-making responsibility. Nothing could be further from the truth. While the computer assigns pupils to teaching sections, the criteria for assignment and the structure of the master schedule are decided by the school administration and staff—not by the computer. Furthermore, it is at this point that the principal has to make his "go/no go" decision. He alone decides whether there are too many student conflicts or staff requests not sufficiently considered. He alone has the responsibility to decide whether or not the master schedule is a good one. If he's satisfied, he can tell the computer center to make the final scheduling run. If he isn't, then he should prepare a new master schedule.

STUDENT'S COPY

SCHERR JULES #	123003	1400	1	656	FOREST PARK
STUDENT NAME	STUDENT NO.	CLASS	SEM	SCHOOL YEAR	SCHOOL NAME

COURSE TITLE	COURSE NO.	SECT. NO.	ROOM NO.	PER.	DAY	TEACHER NAME
ENGLISH 4	009	01	101	1	MTWTF	BOBBITT
WORLD CULTURE	048	01	410	2	MTWTF	LEVINSON
MATH 4 AA&C	023	01	230	3	MTWTF	HARDMAN
LUNCH	172	02		4	MTWTF	
PHYSICS	032	02	333	5	MTWTF	DIPAULA
CHEMISTRY 2 LAB	171	01	437	6	W F	HASHAGEN
STUDY HALL	555	01	104	6	MT T	
CHEMISTRY 2	034	01	433	7	MTWTF	HASHAGEN

STUDENT NAME	CLASS	HOME ROOM	LOCKER NUMBER
SCHERR JULES #	1400	321	

Fig. 76 — Individual Student's Schedule in Final Form (Duplicates Provided for Principal, Counselor, and Others).

Make Final Scheduling Run

The best time to make the final run is determined by balancing two conflicting demands. The closer this run comes to the opening of school, the more late-entering pupils can be included in the run (and withdrawing ones omitted). The earlier the run is made, the more time is available to the school to distribute schedules and other documents. Also, there is more time to handle the cases, manually, of those pupils who remain unscheduled after the final run. A small residue of such pupils is to be expected. The demands of other jobs which require the use of the computer may also influence the time when the final run is made. A good compromise date for making the final scheduling run is approximately two weeks before school opens.

The school distributes pupil schedules and other documents as necessary, denoting one complete set of all documents to serve as the scheduling coordinator's control copies. Examples of an individual student schedule and a class list are shown in Figures 76 and 77.

Some manual scheduling of pupils, and changing of class lists and other documents, will almost certainly be required. This need arises when new pupils turn up at the opening of school and former pupils leave, as well as from the residue of unscheduled pupils mentioned above.

CLASS LIST

COURSE TITLE	COURSE NO.	SECT.	ROOM	PER.	INSTR.	YEAR
ENGLISH 4	011	01	121	4	121	65/6

BURGER

H/R	PUPIL NAME	PUPIL NO.
2403	DIXON THEODORE	125007
2403	DUNDEE BOBBY	125008
2402	HARRIDAY WILLIAM	125026
2404	HOLBROOK RUSSELL	125015
2402	REED JOSEPH W	125014
2403	ROBERTSON HOWARD	125030
2404	STOKES RAY E	125019
2402	ADDISON BARBARA #	225032
2402	CAPLAN RANDY B	225022
2402	CARPENTER PAMELA	225054
2403	COHEN ANN	225099
2403	COHEN SANDY	225023
2402	CRISWELL ANN	225047
2402	EISMAN LOIS A	225064
2403	FANT JANET	225118
2402	FEINTUCH HELEN	225090
2402	FEINTUCH SONIA	225091
2403	MEDLEY MARGARET B	225109
2404	ROBINSON ELLA M	225108
2401	ROE VICKI C	225103
2403	ROLL DIANE E	225001
2404	WEBSTER PEGGY A	225114
2403	ZIMMERMAN SHERRIE	225077

BOYS	GIRLS	TOTAL
7	16	23

PRINTED IN U.S.A.

Fig. 77 — A Class List of the Kind Provided to Each Teacher in Advance of the First Meeting With Each Teaching Station.

All such transactions and changes *must* be recorded directly in the coordinator's control copies, and changes in other copies made only *after* this has been done. This will provide a complete, up-to-date, and accurate reference for settling conflicts and confusions when they arise. Such problems are perhaps inevitable in any complex undertaking such as the opening of a reorganized school, but the computer's accuracy reduces these to a surprisingly small number when the details requiring manual human intervention are performed in a careful and orderly manner. Indeed, after school has been open for an hour or so, the typical reaction in the school office should be, "My, it's quiet around here!"

13 computer sectioning and class scheduling for a university

MARTIN A. FAULKNER

Martin A. Faulkner received an MBA from Washington State University in 1960, a year after taking his BA in Business Administration from the same institution.

Mr. Faulkner served at Washington State University for two years as an IBM research assistant, and four years as a junior computer analyst and instructor of business administration and of information science. He is advisor to the student chapter of the Association for Computing Machinery (ACM) at Washington State University.

University management, like the management of any organization, depends upon timely information for decision making in all areas. Historically, decisions in areas such as student records, schedules, space administration, and academic facilities planning have been based on rules of thumb rather than information. Until very recently, much potentially good information was obtained too late to be of value or was too expensive to capture.

The computer industry has provided the tools necessary to change this continuing problem. Unfortunately, school administrators have done very little creative thinking on how to use these tools to upgrade the quality of information. Initially, computers were installed in universities solely for the purpose of education and scientific research, with little thought given to their use as an administrative data processing tool.

Computers have been used very effectively by a small number of schools in assigning students to classes, experimenting with time schedules, and allocating space. As student class assignment is the easiest of these problems to handle, it has received the greatest amount of attention.

COMPUTER SECTIONING

The concept of computer sectioning has been formalized now for at least ten years. Most universities are interested, few have done more than give it lip service. The gains have been substantial for those few who have implemented an efficient computer sectioning system.

Computer sectioning can be defined as the process of using a stored program computer to assign students to courses of their choice from a fixed time schedule of class offerings. This is a rather narrow definition as it implies the use of a computer to do what was previously done by hand. This in itself supplies no new and useful information to management and may in fact be more expensive than the manual method it replaces. A good computer sectioning system will not only fit the definition given above but will also provide a variety of timely decision-making and planning information.

Under a manual system the demand for courses is almost impossible to know in advance of actual class assignment, but a well-conceived computer sectioning system will easily provide this information. The system will also aid in section balancing, room allocation, and time schedule definition problems. Accurate course reject statistics are also readily available.

Even though the definition of computer sectioning assumes that the time schedule is fixed, it is in no sense independent of the sectioning system. For current purposes we will define the time schedule as the schedule of courses to be taught in a given semester or quarter, along with the time and place the course is to meet. Many courses are further subdivided into sections and these will also show a meeting time and place. No sectioning system, manual or computer, will work if the time schedule is not properly defined. In other words, to give everyone a chance to enroll in courses of his choice, there must be an adequate number of sections of each course. Sections must be offered at a large variety of times to eliminate conflicts. Even though time schedule construction is dealt with as a separate topic, the points noted above must be borne in mind.

Purdue University opened the field in the art of computer sectioning in 1957. In December 1957, 1,804 freshmen agricultural and engineering students were sectioned by computer for the spring semester 1957–58. Computer sectioning was used the following academic year for all undergraduate students.[1] The original computer sectioning algorithm was developed at Purdue University by George Morgan and Gordon Sherman. The ensuing program was submitted to the SHARE organization library as a demonstration program. The program was then modified by IBM under the direction of Loren Bullock at the New England College Computing Center, for

[1] James F. Blakesley, "Registration is Now a Matter of Minutes," *College and University Business,* November 1959, pp. 38-44.

production use at the University of Massachusetts. Other universities have modified the basic Purdue algorithm to suit their own needs. (This information was kindly provided by Mr. James Blakesley, Coordinator of Schedules and Space, Purdue University, Lafayette, Indiana.) At present there are not more than a dozen large schools actually using the computer for sectioning, but numerous universities are investigating or are in the process of implementing a computer sectioning system.

A number of small schools in the United States and Canada have successfully used the IBM 1620 computer as the hardware for limited sectioning systems. This computer can be made to do a creditable job where the enrollment and number of courses offered are limited. However, due to storage size and input/output speeds, the magnitude of a problem this computer can handle is severely restricted.

The basic logic of most sectioning systems is much the same. The kinds of decisions made are inherently binary, so for our purposes we will assume a binary machine. A "vector" of meeting times is established with a bit position for each time a class can begin during the week. Each course in the time schedule of classes has its own time vector with a bit turned "on" (a one bit) for each time the class meets. Each student is also given a time vector which has initially been set to zero. The time bits for the first course assigned to the student are combined with the student's time vector with a logical OR. The time bits of the next request are ANDed to the student's time vector and a test is performed. If the result of the AND is a vector containing all zeros, there is no conflict and a logical OR is performed to add this request to the student's time vector. If, as a result of the AND, the vector contains any nonzero bits, a conflict is indicated and appropriate action must be taken. This may take the form of trying a different section of the same course, or it may require backing up and using a different section of a previously assigned course. If the conflict cannot be resolved, the request may be deleted, or the student's entire set of requests may be rejected, depending on the logic of the program.

Take an oversimplified example to illustrate the sectioning logic (see Fig. 78). Assume a very small school that offers only five courses. Classes meet one day a week and there are six one-hour time periods during the day. Each class and its associated time vector is indicated in Figure 78. Students are processed sequentially and we will follow a single student through the basic sectioning logic. Initially the student's time vector is set to zero. The student in question wishes to enroll in courses A, C, D, and E. From Figure

```
Assume a small school that offers only five courses and meets
but one day a week.  The day is broken into six one-hour periods.
Students initial time vector    (000000)
Time vector of each course in the time schedule

     Course A (100000) meets at 8 a.m.
     Course B (000100) meets at 11 a.m.
     Course C (010001) meets at 9 a.m. and 1 p.m.
     Course D (001100) meets at 10 a.m. and 11 a.m.
     Course E (010010) meets at 9 a.m. and 12 p.m.

Student requests course A, C, D, and E
Denote the student's time vector by S.   Initially S(000000)
The sectioning process is as follows:

                             S (000000)
     AND                     A (100000)
     Test for zero             (000000)   no conflict

     OR                      S (000000)
                             A (100000)
                         S (A) (100000)   first request sectioned

                         S (A) (100000)
     AND                     C (010001)
     Test for Zero             (000000)   no conflict

                         S (A) (100000)
     OR                      C (010001)
                       S (A,C) (110001)   second request sectioned

                       S (A,C) (110001)
     AND                     D (001100)
     Test for zero             (000000)   no conflict

                       S (A,C) (110001)
     OR                      D (001100)
                      S(A,C,D) (111101)   third request sectioned

                      S(A,C,D) (111101)
     AND                     E (010010)
     Test for zero             (010000)   conflicts

Student cannot be sectioned into Course E
```

Fig. 78 — Sectioning Logic Sequence in a Small School.

78 we can see that the student has no problems until course E is encountered. After performing the AND with course E there is a one bit at the nine o'clock hour. Course E is in conflict with another course. Inspection shows that this is course C. In this simple case, the computer enrolls the student in courses A, C, and D and would probably write a message indicating that course E was not sectioned because of a conflict.

In a more realistic situation a number of alternatives are usually available in a conflict situation. Generally a student's requests are sorted into ascending order of the number of sections in each request. Thus, single-section courses will be processed before multiple-section courses. If two single-section courses are in conflict, nothing can be done and the last request attempted will usually be rejected. This was the case in the example in Figure 78. If a section of a requested multiple-section course is in conflict with a course previously sectioned, a new section of the last requested course will be tried. Should all sections of this request still cause a conflict, we can either reject the course or back up and try a different section of a previously processed course, and then return to try the last course again. The latter is the preferable alternative. If the conflict still cannot be resolved, the last course in conflict is rejected.

OBJECTIVES OF A COMPUTER SECTIONING SYSTEM

As the needs of every school are slightly different, not all will have the same objectives. However, it is possible to enumerate some objectives that should be common to all schools. Most important among these is generation of the highest possible percentage of conflict-free schedules. This is not as easy as it might seem. Program logic exerts a strong influence. For example, consider a university which offers 1,500 courses and 3,000 sections in a given quarter or semester. The average student will make about eight requests. Thoughtful reflection will quickly indicate that the number of section combinations is very large. For many students it will turn out to be impractical or impossible to examine all possible combinations. What subset do you examine and how large should this subset be? The answer depends upon such things as computer size and speed and the logic of the sectioning algorithm.

More important than program logic in generating conflict-free schedules is time-schedule definition. If the time schedule is inherently full of conflicts, the best algorithm will not yield conflict-free schedules. Unfortunately, it is very difficult to isolate most conflicts under a manual system because of data collection and analysis problems. In more than one actual case, it has taken a computer sectioning system to focus attention on conflicts built into a time schedule. Closed sections also exert a strong influence on conflicts. Again, this is generally not apparent under a manual system. One good standard practice is to schedule multiple-section courses evenly throughout hours of the day and days of the week.

A second objective is to be able to accurately determine the demand for courses before sectioning takes place. Only in this way is it possible to assure that space is made available for all who wish to enroll. Failure to insure adequate space for enrollment creates two major problems. First, an increased number of conflicts is guaranteed. Second, a backlog of requests for a course builds up a demand which may require as much as two years to satisfy. In many curricula, postponement of an essential course may influence a student's entire academic program. The timing for accumulating exact information on the number of student requests for the various courses is quite important. The ideal time is just a few hours preceding sectioning. The longer the time between course request collection and sectioning, the greater likelihood of the student changing his mind. Many schools with pre-advisement or pre-registration experience a request change rate of between 30 and 40 percent.

The third objective is to be able to balance sections in some meaningful way. For example, in one university with a known freshman enrollment, 50 sections of English composition are offered. The English department wants each section to contain between 23 and 25 students. Using the computer, this is a simple objective to achieve; by hand it is time-consuming, confusing, and difficult to control. At the same university, the history department offers eight sections of American history. Three of these sections are taught by major professors who prefer to lecture to 150 to 200 students. The other five sections are taught by graduate students, and the section size is held to a maximum of 50 students. The computer successfully forces this type of balancing. Additional flexibility can be built into the system by establishing "blind" sections of key multiple-section courses. A "blind" section is a section in the time schedule which initially will allow no students to enroll. If the number of course requests warrants, the section can be opened to accommodate a specified number of students. This provides a mechanism for handling additional course requests not anticipated by the department. Other benefits of section balancing are consistent room utilization and better room scheduling.

A fourth objective is to acquire information in a readily digestible form for better time-schedule planning. This overlaps to some extent the other objectives but can still be considered on its own merits. For instance, exact course demand information is necessary for planning future course and facility needs. Accurate data are necessary to convince the conservative dean or department chairman that he must have more sections of a given course or that current sections should be offered at a wider variety of times and days.

A manual sectioning system does not provide this kind of information. For example, under a manual system, when a course closes the number of students denied a chance to enroll is next to impossible to record.

PLAN FOR IMPLEMENTING A SYSTEM

The first step in implementing a computer sectioning system should be some form of feasibility study. The breadth and formality of the study will depend on the needs of the individual university. However the study is carried out, at this point some basic questions must be answered. Is there enough computing power readily available to do the job? A "yes" is required or there is no advantage in proceeding. A key policy question centers on the issue of student choice of section, time, and instructor. There are valid arguments both for and against student choice, and each institution must make its own decision.

Once feasibility has been established, the objectives of the proposed system should be set out. With the objectives properly defined, it is possible to plan the flow of information through the system, outline the logic, and write the necessary programs and procedures. Problems too numerous to mention will occur during program development. One definite aid is to determine at the detail level what others have done to solve these problems. A visit to one or more institutions having practical experience, or procuring the services of a consultant from one of these institutions, will prove to be a most worthwhile investment.

Programs and procedures must be tested in an actual registration environment to ensure that ideas have practical application and that programs are working properly. Chances are that program logic and procedures will go through numerous levels of change. As much as two years may be necessary to fully test the system. The best plan is to parallel the manual process two or three times, using the data collection methods planned for production. Attempt to run the system within the time constraints imposed during an actual operation. Provide schedules for the students and generate all other reports that will be a part of the full operating system. There are a number of advantages to be gained by following this plan. First, you determine if you can do the job in the time allotted. Second, you make sure that every step proceeds according to plan and the programs are working properly. Third, you instill confidence in the system before it actually goes "on the air." This is a great aid in insuring that no one attempts to sabotage the system during the initial run.

EDUCATING THE UNIVERSITY COMMUNITY

It almost goes without saying that a machine sectioning system must be "sold." Most people distrust rapid technological change. Those who will be affected by the system must be made aware of how the changes will benefit them. This means that someone must do an active selling job.

Students can be the most vocal group on the campus, as we have seen in recent years. Yet they can be the most cooperative group if they have a thorough understanding of what is expected of them and how they stand to benefit by the change. There are numerous ways the student will gain by a computer sectioning sytem. One of the easiest points to sell, although not necessarily significant, is the time saved. In some cases this might be as much as a day. Of much greater significance is the ability of the computer sectioning system to generate better schedules with a decrease in the number of manual changes necessary. Under most manual systems, the student at the front of the line gets all of the breaks and the fellow at the end gets what is left. A well-conceived computer system will give everyone an equal opportunity. Washington State University found, on the basis of a questionnaire, that 65 percent of the students considered their machine schedules better than the ones they received under the manual system. Twenty-five percent of the students felt there was little difference in schedules, and 10 percent thought the machine-generated schedules were definitely inferior. Other benefits, such as section balance, fewer closed sections, and more conflict-free schedules can be used as selling points.

Numerous bitter experiences have indicated that a computer sectioning system must have a means of blocking out time for work and other approved activities. Students must be made aware of how this blocked-time operates and under what conditions it can be used. Lack of a system may cause free time scheduling rebellion.

The campus newspaper is one excellent means of educating the students. Picture stories are particularly effective. However, a better means of communication is through group discussions, panels, and special small group meetings where students have an opportunity to ask questions and express themselves.

University faculties are just as skeptical as the students when confronted with new and different procedures. Special effort is needed to properly sell deans, department chairmen, and faculty members, because only through their backing and efforts will a computer sectioning system have a chance to survive. There are a number of distinct advantages offered to the faculty, especially those involved in administration and advising. Section balance is a strong selling point. Lack of section balancing is one of the greatest criticisms of a manual system. When a department chairman knows the exact number of students requesting a particular course in advance of sectioning, and is able to act upon that demand with dispatch, a most distinct advantage of a computer sectioning system is apparent. This can be counted on to generate enthusiasm. Documented information about time schedule problems is also salable. In addition to providing help in cutting down conflicts and knowing when to offer sections of a course, special scheduling procedures can be implemented which would be most difficult to accomplish manually. The economics department of one university wanted certain help sections associated with specific lecture sections of an introductory course. The manual implementation of this proved very frustrating because it could not be controlled closely enough, but the computer successfully made the assignments.

The faculty must be brought into the discussions of a computer sectioning system at an early stage. One effective way of doing this is to assign a committee to study the feasibility of computer sectioning. The committee should be composed of an enthusiastic administrator, the director of the computing center, and one or two carefully selected faculty members. Once the "go-ahead" has been given to implement a system, faculty members on a departmental basis should be contacted. This can best be accomplished in departmental staff meetings where the case for machine sectioning is presented honestly, and where faculty members may ask questions and express their feelings about the project.

Selling the system to the university administration is not much different from selling it to the faculty and students. The advantages to be expected must be clearly shown. The question of cost is likely to arise, and is touchy at best. It is not clear that cost (within reason) is really a relevant question, although it is hard to convince administrators of this. It is not too difficult to measure out-of-pocket costs for the implementation and operation of a computer sectioning system. The problem comes in trying to measure the benefits to be derived from the system. It is nearly impossible to assign a dollar value to many of these, while others won't be discovered until the system has been in operation for awhile. If the system is established in a framework in which costs and values can be assigned, then the computer is probably not really being used creatively.

INPUT PREPARATION

The most troublesome problems in getting a system operating center around input preparation. The information must be coded correctly at the source. Once contact has been lost with the student, it is virtually impossible to make corrections. For this reason, it is essential to insure careful editing at the point of source document origin. To ease the burden, the source document must be simple and straightforward to code and should be acceptable as computer input as recorded, if possible. Hand transcription away from the source document, apart from being expensive, is actually an invitation for errors.

A variety of considerations are involved in deciding on the kind of source document to use. A wide assortment of recording media is available. One possibility is pulling prepunched class cards from a tub file. The student submits his course requests on an enrollment card or similar document and a class card is pulled from the tub file for each course requested. The enrollment card plus the class cards form the imput documents for the student. The method works well if time is not a limiting factor. Pulling cards is a slow and expensive operation. On the other hand, if tub files are available the job may be done over a four to six-week interval with existing help, and the need for additional part-time help may be avoided. This method has been used successfully where formal pre-advisement or pre-registration is practiced.

Keypunching of request cards should not be ignored as a means of recording course request information in a machine-acceptable form. Again adequate time and keypunch facilities must be available to do the job. Keypunching would probably be most acceptable where pre-registration is practiced.

Where time is a substantially limiting factor, the method of recording course request information must be compatible with the time constraints. Washington State University, which has a severe time limitation, has solved the input problem by using mark sense request cards. The entire registration and advising process is carried out in one and a half days, one day before the beginning of classes. Under the system, the student lists, with the approval of his adviser, the courses he plans to take. He then marks a request card for each course request on his enrollment card. These cards are turned in to the registrar's office after careful checking to insure that the student has made no mistakes. The marked cards are then punched and the information recorded on tape. The method has worked extremely well and the error rate from student marking has been very low (less than one-half of one percent).

Another method of recording requested information that will see much greater acceptance is the use of specially marked sheets which can be optically scanned at a high rate of speed. The scanned request data can be punched into cards, written directly on magnetic tape, or can be recorded on a relatively fast access storage device such as a disk. Through proper coding of requested information, all of the data related to a single student can be recorded on a single scanning sheet. As optical scanners become more reliable and recording formats more flexible, this method of data recording will certainly outmode the mark-sense card.

The method of student request recording of the future will be the remote keyboard terminal coupled directly to the computer. In a matter of a few minutes a student can key in, or have keyed in, all of his request information, have it edited, and receive a response from the computer indicating that his requests are correct and can be scheduled, or that he has an error or conflict and a change must be made This is a rapid, inexpensive means of data collection which provides almost instantaneous error feedback. (Terminals are inexpensive as long as they are already "in house" and being used for other purposes the rest of the year.) With the proposed installation of time-sharing systems on many of the larger campuses, terminals will be readily available in the next three to five years.

The University of Indiana has a computer sectioning system currently in operation which utilizes IBM 1050 terminals for input of student request information.

ANTICIPATED PROBLEMS

Many universities with pre-registration or pre-advisement programs will encounter special problems with a computer sectioning system. Assume that registration takes place six weeks to three months before the beginning of classes. The crux of the problem is that a high percentage of students will change their minds about the courses they want to take by the time classes begin. If sectioning is done concurrently or just after registration, data collection and sectioning generally will proceed in an orderly fashion. Major institutions report from 30 to 40 percent drops, adds, and change of sections the first few days of classes. The difficulty relative to the computer sectioning system is that much of the information generated by the system becomes invalid. Section balancing will be very difficult to maintain, demand figures will no longer hold, much conflict and time schedule information will be of doubtful value. Much can be salvaged (for a price) by essentially running all adds and drops through a "resectioning" process.

One way of partially circumventing the problem is to refrain from sectioning until just prior to the beginning of classes. Provide a "Swap Day" before sectioning to allow students to make changes in their requests. The problem of request change is still present but valuable information is not lost.

Schools who practice mass registration just before classes begin generally face only the problem of doing the data collection and processing job in a relatively short period of time. The machine system should operate just as fast as the manual system.

Many universities feel that a sectioning system must allow the student to exercise section preference. There are numerous arguments both for and against this practice. If the student is guaranteed preference there seems little value to a computer sectioning system. Students will almost always choose electives or multiple section classes that meet on Monday, Wednesday, and Friday mornings or early afternoons. Conflict-free schedules are virtually impossible, section balancing can only be a dream, and resources of the institution will be badly underutilized.

On the other hand, if a section preference scheme is implemented that does not take precedence over other necessary university goals, some reasonable compromise is possible. In fact it can be argued that if, say, 30 percent of the students requesting a preference get the preference without jeopardizing the position of other students, gain has been made. (It is not clear that the rest of the students can be protected.) With a partial section preference procedure, it would be possible to determine section demand before sectioning, which would have some advantage.

Three partial section preference schemes are worth mentioning. One way of handling the problem is to arbitrarily set an imbalance limit. As long as a requested section was not outside this limit, preference would be given. For example, as long as a requested section was not more than 10 percent out of balance with the rest of the sections of the course, the preference would be honored. The second method computes an "availability number" for each section based on the number of seats available and the known demand for a section. Then, at the time sections are assigned, they are ordered by the "availability number" rather than the number of seats remaining as a result of previous requests. The advantage of this method is that sections are assigned on the basis of known section demand rather than just previous sectioning experience. (These two methods are currently in the experimental stage at Washington State University. Student preference data was collected during the 1966 spring semester registration for use in the experiments.) The third method utilizes a random number scheme to determine if the preferred section will be assigned. Briefly, if the ratio of the number of seats available in a section to the number of requests for that section remaining is greater than a given random number between zero and one, the preferred section is assigned. Otherwise the conflict-free section of the course with the largest ratio is assigned.[2] Insufficient information is currently available to indicate which is the better scheme.

From the administrative viewpoint there is one significant factor which warrants greater elaboration. This is the problem of assigning "free time" or "block time" for work and approved activities. First, it must be decided which will take preference in the sectioning algorithm, free time or a requested course. This is a policy decision of extreme gravity. Irrespective of how this decision goes, it will be necessary to set up a procedure for assigning free time. It must be decided on what basis free time will be assigned, who will be responsible for assigning it, and how it will be recorded on the input media. Unwarranted time will most certainly be taken advantage of if it is not carefully controlled.

CONCLUSION

The most significant problems in designing and implementing a computer sectioning system are selling the system to the university community and preparing the student request information for processing. A computer sectioning system *must be sold.* This means that everyone must understand how the system will affect and benefit them and the university. Procedures must be established to ensure that data will be collected rapidly and accurately. Nothing will undermine the system faster than errors.

A well-conceived and efficient operating computer sectioning system should be a real boon to any university. It will rapidly and accurately provide previously unavailable information for planning and control. It will also point the way to other uses of the computer in the areas of student records, time schedule construction, and space utilization.

CLASS SCHEDULING

Class scheduling by computer is the process of assigning rooms, instructors, and times to classes in such a way that the number of sectioning conflicts will be a minimum. Sounds easy; unfortunately, except for the trivial case, it is quite difficult. The primary objective of a class scheduling system is to generate a time schedule of classes to be offered that will minimize the number of student schedule conflicts. In the broadest sense, this means that class-

[2] N. Macon and E. E. Walker. "A Monte Carlo Algorithm for Assigning Students to Classes," *Communications of the ACM,* May 1966, pp. 339-340

room space, class meeting time, and instructors are assigned by the computer in such a way as to meet the minimization criteria.

In the last few years there have been a number of attempts to generate class schedules by machine with varying degrees of success. Some theoretical papers have been written on the subject.[3] At least one program has been developed that will build a satisfactory time schedule at the high school level and seems to work reasonably well for very small colleges.[4] Purdue University has been developing a system which will construct a time schedule for large universities. This system is still in the experimental state.[5]

Generally, the approach has been to take student requests for courses, either on a sample basis or for the entire student body, as a point of departure. The time schedule is then constructed in such a way as to cover the greatest possible number of requests. This is done by manipulating space, meeting time, and instructors. There is a mathematically optimum solution. Unfortunately, from an applied point of view, it is not a practical solution. The biggest problem is lack of adequate high-speed storage in the current generation computers. The number of combinations of classes, rooms, times, and instructors precludes a truly optimum solution. For this reason current experimental programs have been written using heuristic techniques. It is not completely clear that an optimum solution is really required for most universities.

Apart from theoretical considerations, there are some practical problems worth considering regardless of the approach. In most universities the administration does not manipulate instructors at will. You simply do not tell a full professor with 40 years seniority, who is heavily involved in research, that he is going to teach an eight o'clock section on the other side of the campus. Many instructors do have fixed commitments and instructional assignment must remain somewhat flexible.

Assignment of classrooms also creates some ticklish problems. Many facilities are special purpose and are practical for only a

---

[3] Two such papers are the following: J. Csima and C. C. Gotlieb, "Tests on a Computer Method for Constructing School Timetables," *Communications of the ACM*, March 1964, pp. 160-163, and C. C. Gotlieb, "The Construction of Class-Teacher-Time-Tables," *Proceedings of IFIP Congress 62*. Amsterdam: North Holland Publishing Co., 1962, pp. 22-25.

[4] Robert E. Holz, "School Scheduling Using Computers; a Prospectus." Cambridge: Massachusetts Institute of Technology, February 1, 1963. Also Robert E. Holz, "State of the Art of Automatic Scheduling and Registration," *Proceedings, Ninth College and University Machine Records Conference*. April 1964, pp. 253-258.

[5] Victor A. Abell, "An Introduction to CUSS," and George Morgan, "Bookmaker: Version I of a Computer Program for Scheduling Construction," *Proceedings, Tenth College and University Machine Records Conference*. East Lansing: Michigan State University, May 1965, pp. 207-26 and pp. 227-38.

narrow range of classes. Academic departments prefer to do most of their teaching in the general vicinity of departmental offices. Some classes require special demonstrational or teaching aids which are difficult to move and set up in more than one location in a short period of time. All of these points must be taken into account by the system if it is to function in an acceptable manner.

If an efficient class scheduling system can be implemented, there are a number of distinct advantages to the user. Being able to generate a minimum-conflict schedule is certainly a strong selling point. The time and effort saved by students, faculty, and administrators will certainly be significant. The system will provide accurate figures on room utilization, and capital expenditure can be better matched with needs. The number of periods necessary in the week can be explicity stated. Many universities will find that Saturday classes are not really necessary. Student section preference will no longer be a significant issue.

With vastly increased amounts of high-speed storage in third-generation computers, class schedule building by computer is not very far in the future. The advantages to be gained will be significant.

REFERENCES

Faulkner, Martin. "Computer Sectioning and Class Scheduling," *Datamation,* June 1965, pp. 35-37.

——. "Some Thoughts on Computer Sectioning at Washington State University," *Proceedings, Tenth College and University Machine Records Conference.* East Lansing: Michigan State University, May 1965, pp. 494-506.

——. "Computer Sectioning—A Second Look," *Proceedings, College and University Machine Records Conference.* Knoxville: University of Tennessee, April 1966.

Murphy, Judith, and Robert Sutter. "School Scheduling by Computer; The Story of GASP" (report). New York: Educational Facilities Laboratories, Inc., 1964.

Schrer, Dan. Registration by Phone at Indiana University," *Proceedings, College and University Machine Records Conference.* Knoxville: University of Tennessee, April 1966.

Simpson, Claude. "The Computer Sectioning Program at Washington State University," *College and University,* Fall 1965, pp. 89-95.

——. "How Washington State Hopes to Register Students at a Cost of 30 Cents Each," *College and University Business,* October 1965, p. 62.

14 an examination of a file structure for personnel and payroll

RICHARD A. KAIMANN

RICHARD A. KAIMANN *expects to receive his PhD from the University of Iowa with a major in Production Management and a minor in Educational Data Processing. He received his MBA in Production Management from Marquette University in 1963, and his BS in Management Engineering from Rensselaer Polytechnic Institute in 1960.*

For the past several years, Mr. Kaimann has served as a senior systems analyst with Allis-Chalmers Mfg. Co., as a lecturer in computer technology at Marquette University, as director of The Educational Data Processing Research Project at Marquette, and as a consultant to business.

His numerous publications include co-authorship of two books: Data Processing in Catholic Educational Administration *(Marquette University Press, 1965); and* Educational Data Processing: New Dimensions and Prospects *(Houghton Mifflin Co., in press 1967).*

Data processing has frequently been applied to the clerical, routine functions of office work in its initial application. Personnel and payroll considerations have been an early procedure on the priority list of activities to be converted to automatic processing. The job, although of a routine nature, is not one to be taken lightly. The design of the file structure itself requires careful consideration. A great deal depends on the use and thoroughness expected of the file.[1]

An extensive investigation into the needs of a personnel and payroll procedure for an educational situation resulted in a need for a surprisingly large record per individual. The maximum number of characters for the tape record was 2,163 characters.

To fully appreciate the magnitude of the problem, input cards were designed. These cards are constructed so as to allow com-

[1] The material reported in this chapter is the result of an intensive study carried out at the Iowa Educational Information Center in Iowa City, Iowa. Combining the efforts of educational specifications and systems analysis, the following members of the IEIC staff justly deserve substantial credit: Dr. G. Richardson, J. Johnston, D. Morgan, J. Perry, R. Sedrel, and R. Kaimann.

plete processing of any data in the payroll and personnel file. Complete flexibility is maintained by providing the potential to manipulate and maintain the file at any time. A series of five programs have been suggested to perform the basic functions of a personnel and payroll procedure. These are as follow:

1. Maintenance
2. Payroll
3. Personnel and payroll folder
4. Contract printing
5. Distribution of expenses

These five programs incorporated with the suggested file will provide an educational institution with the basic information required. To further illustrate the degree of complexity of this procedure, a description of each of the programs and other considerations follows. After those descriptions, a complete, detailed explanation of the necessary input cards as well as the individual record is illustrated. This description contains suggested codes for the input cards, the assigned card columns for each field, field size, and suggested labels to be used in defining the tape file (DTF) for processing purposes. Also included is an indication of field characteristics, that is, where decimal points would occur.

Program: Maintenance

Purpose—The purpose of this program is to create, add records or information to the file, and to delete information or records from the file. Attention will be directed to each applicable segment of the record format with an explanation of what procedures are followed for each.

Card column 1 in each case identifies which input card is being introduced to the procedure. Card columns 2 to 10 in each case represent the Social Security number of the individual that this transaction pertains to.

Card B represents the school number at which this person is assigned. There are four possible for any given person. It is necessary to check to find a blank location, the next successive location, before adding the information to the file. If, for some reason, the number is greater than four, it should be printed out as an error.

The same situation is true of the assignment record segments which are represented by a G in card column 1. There is a separate G card for each assignment. There are 10 possible assignments for each individual. It will be necessary to search the file to find where the next available assignment area is located before adding to a personnel assignment.

The accident record, date, and type of the I card receives a particular type of treatment. It will be necessary to accumulate the accident record by date and type, allowing a possibility of five specific accidents. If this number is exceeded, it is necessary to delete the particular accident which is historically furthest in the past, make an addition to the counter, and then add the new accident to the record. This will then provide a count of the total number of accidents plus the dates and types of the last five accidents.

The account allocation codes which are the L cards are not expected to be updated by the maintenance program, but the provision should be there anyway. These are normally accumulated at the time of payroll generation. The same is true of the flat rate payment accounts, the M cards, as well as the noncontracted SUP compensation, the N cards, and the extra compensation, the O cards. These considerations also apply to the calendar year records, the P card, and the fiscal year records, the Q card.

There is, therefore, an ability to update or correct any of the items on the file, even though many will not receive such attention. In any case, where decimal points appear or apply, they are so indicated on the record format.

As a general consideration for pay procedure, a transaction card, the U card, indicating the number of hours worked, the pay scale per hour and the account to be charged may be submitted at any time. The procedure then is to update the amount unpaid field of the proper account for that individual. This amount unpaid is added to the total dollars paid at the time the payroll is run, and the unpaid field is then to be reduced to zero. This provides the ability to have each or any transaction applied at any given time.

Procedure—It should be necessary to maintain three generations of the file. They should represent monthly file generations where the most recent one is updated at an unspecified number of times during a given month. During this period of time, the transaction register, recording each individual transaction, should be maintained on a three-generation basis as well.

Program: Payroll

The general purpose of the payroll program is to prepare actual warrants, and distribute them, and accumulate the records necessary for the W2 forms, IPERS, FICA, federal and state withholding, and so on. The check is distributed as indicated by the check distribution code. If it is necessary to send it to the bank, the bank address is located in the bank subfield.

The payroll function should examine the gross pay and reduce it by the variety of deductions that are available, and prepare the stub. It also examines the account codes to determine if there are unpaid amounts within them that must be taken care of, and the same is true for flat rate payment, noncontracted supplementary compensation, and extra compensation. In each of the previous cases, if there is an amount unpaid, then as soon as that amount is paid, that amount unpaid field must be reduced to zero. At the time of paying the account codes are credited with the dollar amounts to record year-to-date and quarter-to-date totals.

The deduction amounts for federal and state withholding are found in their respective fields, as are the amounts for the FICA deductions and the IPERS deductions. At the point the warrant is written, it is necessary to update the year-to-date records as well as the quarter-to-date records on both a calendar and a fiscal year basis. It is necessary to note that these two are distinctly separate, with the calendar year running from January through December, and the fiscal year running approximately from September through August.

It is necessary to examine the other deduction fields for credit unions, professional dues, bonds, tax sheltered annuities, life insurance, charities, and the local options 1 and 2, to find if there are additional deductions to be made from the gross pay. In each case, these are recorded on the stub of the check. It is further necessary to examine the sick leave, the other leave, and the additional leave, to determine if there are deductions that should be made from the gross pay on the basis of excess leave.

The payroll option condition applies to the payment of the last period in the academic fiscal year. These must be the ability to pay the person in any of a variety of ways. The conditions describing the situation are as follows:

Code	Description
1	12 month base with balance paid in June
2	11 month base with balance paid in June
3	10 month base with balance paid in June
4	9 month base with balance paid in June
5	12 month base with balance paid during summer
6	11 month base with balance paid during summer
7	10 month base with balance paid during summer
8	9 month base with balance paid during summer

Procedure—Prior to the actual preparation of the warrants, a trial run will be made for checking by the financial officer of the institution. Then, upon approval, the actual transactions, in which the warrants are prepared and a check register is prepared for the financial officer, will be run.

Quarterly, it will be necessary to run an FICA report and an IPERS report. These will take the information from the quarterly totals in the calendar year records. These will then be submitted as required by federal and state law. Once these have been removed from the quarter-to-date records, the quarter-to-date records must be reduced to zero and restarted for the succeeding quarter with the year-to-date record continuing accumulation.

At the end of the year, after the appropriate W2 forms, IPERS reports, and FICA reports, etc., have been prepared, the calendar year-to-date records also are reduced to zero and begun again for the next calendar year. Similar considerations are taken into account in the fiscal year records as dictated by the school. In preparing any of these reports one must keep in mind the maximum limits on the FICA and the IPERS accounts.

Program: Personnel and Payroll Folder

A program will be necessary to print the entire record for an individual on some type of preprinted form. This would fully identify all the information within the individual's file. It will be necessary to design a particular form for this use.

Program: Contract Printing

It will be necessary to provide the capability for preparation of individual contracts.

Program: Distribution of Expenses

It is desired to have the account allocation distribution on a month-to-date, quarter-to-date, and year-to-date basis from the fiscal year records. This entails the sorting of the financial information by accounts and summarizing the information on a month, quarter, or year-to-date basis.

Personnel Considerations

At this time there are few specific requests of the personnel file. One of them pertains to handling the resignation of an individual at the end of the fiscal year, and the subsequent rehiring of that person for the following fiscal year. Since the record cannot be eliminated until after the W2 form is prepared in January, his file is still available, so this creates no problem.

(The following 10 pages carry a detailed explanation of the cards and records of a file structure for personnel and payroll.)

PERSONNEL AND PAYROLL
RECORD FORMAT

CC		DTF NAME		
1	A			
2-10		SSN	Social Security Number (9)	___-__-____
			Name	
11-24		NL	Last (14)	______________
25-34		LF	First (10)	__________
35		NMI	Middle Initial (1)	_
36-49		NMAD	Maiden (14)	______________
			Current Address	
50-64		CAN	Number and Street (15)	_______________
65-74		CACS	City and State (6) (4)	__________
75-79		CAZ	Zip Code (5)	_____
1	B			
2-10	SSN			
			School Number	
11-12		SNC1	County (2)	__
13-16		SND1	District (4)	____
17-19		SNS1	School (3)	___
20-31		SNN1	Name (12)	____________
32-44		SNA1	Address (13)	_____________
45-49		SNZ1	Zip Code (5)	_____
1	B			
2-10	SSN			
			School Number	
11-12		SNC2	County (2)	__
13-16		SND2	District (4)	____
17-19		SNS2	School (3)	___
20-31		SNN2	Name (12)	____________
32-44		SNA2	Address (13)	_____________
45-49		SNZ2	Zip Code (5)	_____
1	B			
2-10	SSN			
			School Number	
11-12		SNC3	County (2)	__
13-16		SND3	District (4)	____
17-19		SNS3	School (3)	___
20-31		SNN3	Name (12)	____________
32-44		SNA3	Address (13)	_____________
45-49		SNZ3	Zip Code (5)	_____
1	B			
2-10	SSN			
			School Number	
11-12		SNC4	County (2)	__
13-16		SND4	District (4)	____
17-19		SNS4	School (3)	___
20-31		SNN4	Name (12)	____________
32-44		SNA4	Address (13)	_____________
45-49		SNZ4	Zip Code (5)	_____
1	C			
2-10	SSN			
			Current Phone	
11-20		CFON	A/C Number (10)	___-___-____
			Permanent Address	
21-35		PAN	Number and Street (15)	_______________
36-45		PACS	City and State (10)	__________
46-50		PAZ	Zip Code (5)	_____
51		MSTAX	Marital Status (and sex) (1)	_
			Name (Spouse)	
52-65		SPNL	Last (14)	______________
66-75		SPNF	First (10)	__________
76		SPNMI	Middle Initial (1)	_
1	D			
2-10	SSN			
			Emergency Phone	
11-20		EFON	A/C and Number (10)	___-___-____

Columns	Code	Description	Entry
21	CITST	Citizenship Status U.S. - Yes - No (1)	_
22-27	DTBRN	Date of Birth MM DD YY (6)	_ _ _ _ _ _
28-33	SFLNM	State folder number (6)	_ _ _ _ _ _
34-39	DTEMPL	Date of beginning employment MM DD YY (6)	_ _ _ _ _ _
40-45	DTPHY	Date Last Physical Exam. MM DD YY (6)	_ _ _ _ _ _
46-51	DTXRAY	Date Last Chest X-Ray MM DD YY (6)	_ _ _ _ _ _
52	EMCLAS	Employee Classifications Professional (1) Non-Professional Sub. Teacher Student	_
53-54	TITLE	Title Code (2)	_ _
55-56	EXPER	Experience (2)	_ _
57-58	EXPTY	Experience-Previous total years (2)	_ _
59	HIDEG	Highest degree held (1)	_
		State and School codes for degrees earned (12)	
60-62	SSD1		_ _ _
63-65	SSD2		_ _ _
66-68	SSD3		_ _ _
69-71	SSD4		_ _ _
72-74	SEMHRU	Total Semester hrs., under grad. (3)	_ _ _
1	E		
2-10	SSN		
		Undergraduate Majors (8)	
11-12	UMAJ1		_ _
13-14	UMAJ2		_ _
15-16	UMAJ3		_ _
17-18	UMAJ4		_ _
		Undergraduate Minors (8)	
19-20	UMIN1		_ _
21-22	UMIN2		_ _
23-24	UMIN3		_ _
25-26	UMIN4		_ _
27-29	SEMHRG	Total Semester hrs., graduate (3)	_ _ _
		Graduate Majors (8)	
30-31	GMAJ1		_ _
32-33	GMAJ2		_ _
34-35	GMAJ3		_ _
36-37	GMAJ4		_ _
		Graduate Minors (8)	
38-39	GMIN1		_ _
40-41	GMIN2		_ _
42-43	GMIN3		_ _
44-45	GMIN4		_ _

Columns	Field	Description	Format
		Approval data (26)	
46-47	APPR1		_ _
48-49	APPR2		_ _
50-51	APPR3		_ _
52-53	APPR4		_ _
54-55	APPR5		_ _
56-57	APPR6		_ _
58-59	APPR7		_ _
60-61	APPR8		_ _
62-63	APPR9		_ _
64-65	APPR10		_ _
66-67	APPR11		_ _
68-69	APPR12		_ _
70-71	APPR13		_ _
1	F		
2-10	SSN		
		Certification Data	
11-12	CDCL1	Class code (2)	_ _
13-14	CDEND1	Endorsement code (2)	_ _
15-18	CDEXR1	Expiration date (4)	_ _ _ _
19-20	CDCL2	Class code (2)	_ _
21-22	CDEND2	Endorsement code (2)	_ _
23-26	CDEXR2	Expiration date (4)	_ _ _ _
27-28	CDCL3	Class code (2)	_ _
29-30	CDEND3	Endorsement code (2)	_ _
31-34	CDEXR3	Expiration date (4)	_ _ _ _
35-36	CDCL4	Class code (2)	_ _
37-38	CDEND4	Endorsement code (2)	_ _
39-42	CDEXR4	Expiration date (4)	_ _ _ _
43-44	CDCL5	Class code (2)	_ _
45-46	CDEND5	Endorsement code (2)	_ _
47-50	CDEXR5	Expiration date (4)	_ _ _ _
1	G		
2-10	SSN		
		Assignment	
11-12	ARES1	Area of Responsibility (2)	_ _
13-14	AACT1	Activity assignment class (2)	_ _
15	ASCP1	Scope (1)	_
16	ALEV1	Level (1)	_
17-19	ASA1	Subject Area (3)	_ _ _
20-33	ASUB1	Subject (4) state code (5) local (3) course sect (2)	_ _ _ _ _ _ _ _ _ _ _ _ _ _
34-35	APYR1	Previous yrs. this assignment (2)	_ _
36-39	ABLD1	Building (school) (3)	_ _ _
40-43	APER1	Percent of time - this assignment (3)	_ . _ _
1	G		
2-10	SSN		
		Assignment	
11-12	ARES2	Area of Responsibility (2)	_ _
13-14	AACT2	Activity assignment class (2)	_ _
15	ASCP2	Scope (1)	_
16	ALEV2	Level (1)	_
17-19	ASA2	Subject Area (3)	_ _ _
20-23	ASUB2	Subject (4) state code (5) local (3) course sect (2)	_ _ _ _ _ _ _ _ _ _ _ _ _ _
34-35	APYR2	Previous yrs. this assignment (2)	_ _
36-39	ABLD2	Building (school) (3)	_ . _ _
40-43	APER2	Percent of time - this assignment (3)	_ . _ _
1	G		
2-10	SSN		
		Assignment	
11-12	ARES3	Area of Responsibility (2)	_ _
13-14	AACT3	Activity assignment class (2)	

Position		Field	Description	Format
				_ _
15		ASCP3	Scope (1)	_
16		ALEV3	Level (1)	_
17-19		ASA3	Subject Area (3)	_ _ _
20-33		ASUB3	Subject (4) state code (5) local (3) course sect (2)	_ _ _ _ _ _ _ _ _ _ _ _ _ _
34-35		APYR3	Previous yrs. this assignment (2)	_ _
36-39		ABLD3	Building (school) (3)	_ _ _
40-43		APER3	Percent of time - this assignment (3)	_ . _ _
1	G			
2-10	SSN			
			Assignment	
11-12		ARES4	Area of Responsibility (2)	_ _
13-14		AACT4	Activity assignment class (2)	_ _
15		ASCP4	Scope (1)	_
16		ALEV4	Level (1)	_
17-19		ASA4	Subject Area (3)	_ _ _
20-33		ASUB4	Subject (4) state code (5) local (3) course sect (2)	_ _ _ _ _ _ _ _ _ _ _ _ _ _
34-35		APYR4	Previous yrs. this assignment (2)	_ _
36-39		ABLD4	Building (school) (3)	_ _ _
40-43		APER4	Percent of time - this assignment (3)	_ . _ _
1	G			
2-10	SSN			
			Assignment	
11-12		ARES5	Area of Responsibility (2)	_ _
13-14		AACT5	Activity assignment class (2)	_ _
15		ASCP5	Scope (1)	_
16		ALEV5	Level (1)	_
17-19		ASA5	Subject Area (3)	_ _ _
20-33		ASUB5	Subject (4) state code (5) local (3) course sect (2)	_ _ _ _ _ _ _ _ _ _ _ _ _ _
34-35		APYR5	Previous yrs. this assignment (2)	_ _
36-39		ABLD5	Building (school) (3)	_ _ _
40-43		APER5	Percent of time - this assignment (3)	_ . _ _
1	G			
2-10	SSN			
			Assignment	
11-12		ARES6	Area of Responsibility (2)	_ _
13-14		AACT6	Activity assignment class (2)	_ _
15		ASCP6	Scope (1)	_
16		ALEV6	Level (1)	_
17-19		ASA6	Subject Area (3)	_ _ _
20-33		ASUB6	Subject (4) state code (5) local (3) course sect (2)	_ _ _ _ _ _ _ _ _ _ _ _ _ _
34-35		APYR6	Previous yrs. this assignment (2)	_ _
36-39		ABLD6	Building (school) (3)	_ _ _
40-43		APER6	Percent of time - this assignment (3)	_ . _ _
1	G			
2-10	SSN			
			Assignment	
11-12		ARES7	Area of Responsibility (2)	_ _
13-14		AACT7	Activity assignment class (2)	_ _
15		ASCP7	Scope (1)	_
16		ALEV7	Level (1)	_
17-19		ASA7	Subject Area (3)	_ _ _
20-33		ASUB7	Subject (4) state code (5) local (3) course sect (2)	_ _ _ _ _ _ _ _ _ _ _ _ _ _
34-35		APYR7	Previous yrs. this assignment (2)	_ _

36-39		ABLD7	Building (school) (3)	_ _ _
40-43		APER7	Percent of time - this assignment (3)	_ . _ _
1	G			
2-10	SSN			
			Assignment	
11-12		ARES8	Area of Responsibility (2)	_ _
13-14		AACT8	Activity assignment class (2)	_ _
15		ASCP8	Scope (1)	_
16		ALEV8	Level (1)	_
17-19		ASA8	Subject Area (3)	_ _ _
20-33		ASUB8	Subject (4) state code (5)	_ _ _ _ _ _ _ _ _
			local (3) course sect (2)	_ _ _ _ _
34-35		APYR8	Previous yrs. this assignment (2)	_ _
36-39		ABLD8	Building (school) (3)	_ _ _
40-43		APER8	Percent of time - this assignment (3)	_ . _ _
1	G			
2-10	SSN			
			Assignment	
11-12		ARES9	Area of Responsibility (2)	_ _
13-14		AACT9	Activity assignment class (2)	_ _
15		ASCP9	Scope (1)	_
16		ALEV9	Level (1)	_
17-19		ASA9	Subject Area (3)	_ _ _
20-33		ASUB9	Subject (4) state code (5)	_ _ _ _ _ _ _ _ _
			local (3) course sect (2)	_ _ _ _ _
34-35		APYR9	Previous yrs. this assignment (2)	_ _
36-39		ABLD9	Building (school) (3)	_ _ _
40-43		APER9	Percent of time - this assignment (3)	_ . _ _
1	G			
2-10	SSN			
			Assignment	
11-12		ARES10	Area of Responsibility (2)	_ _
13-14		AACT10	Activity assignment class (2)	_ _
15		ASCP10	Scope (1)	_
16		ALEV10	Level (1)	_
17-19		ASA10	Subject Area (3)	_ _ _
20-33		ASUB10	Subject (4) state code (5)	_ _ _ _ _ _ _ _ _
			local (3) course sect (2)	_ _ _ _ _
34-35		APYR10	Previous yrs. this assignment (2)	_ _
36-39		ABLD10	Building (school) (3)	_ _ _
40-43		APER10	Percent of time - this assignment (3)	_ . _ _
1	H			
2-10	SSN			
11		OCPYR	Occupation previous year (1)	_
			Related vocational work	
12-13		RVWN1	Number of years (2)	_ _
14-15		RVWT1	Type (2)	_ _
16-17		RVWN2	Number of years (2)	_ _
18-19		RVWT2	Type (2)	_ _
20-21		RVWN3	Number of years (2)	_ _
22-23		RVWT3	Type (2)	_ _
24-25		RVWN4	Number of years (2)	_ _
26-27		RVWT4	Type (2)	_ _
28-29		RVWN5	Number of years (2)	_ _
30-31		RVWT5	Type (2)	_ _
32-33		RVWN6	Number of years (2)	_ _
34-35		RVWT6	Type (2)	_ _

Columns	Record	Field	Description	Format
			In service training record (30)	
36-38		INST1		---
39-41		INST2		---
42-44		INST3		---
45-47		INST4		---
48-50		INST5		---
51-53		INST6		---
54-56		INST7		---
57-59		INST8		---
60-62		INST9		---
63-65		INST10		---

1	I			
2-10	SSN			
			Non-Professional Personnel	
			Chauffeurs license	
11-19		CFLIN	Number (9)	---------
20-25		CFXRD	Expir. Date (6) MM DD YY	------
26-31		CFSDP	State Dr. Permit (6)	------
			Accident Record	
32-38		ARDT1	Date and type (1) (7)	-------
39-45		ARDT2	" " (2) (7)	-------
46-52		ARDT3	" " (3) (7)	-------
53-59		ARDT4	" " (4) (7)	-------
60-66		ARDT5	" " (5) (7)	-------
67-68		ARCTR	Counter (2)	--
			Barrier Status	
69-72		BSBMY	Begin mo. and yr. (4)	----
73-74		BSHRE	Number hrs. earned toward barrier (2)	--
75-77		PERFT	Percent of full time (3)	-.--
78		CKDISC	Check Distribution Code (1)	-
79		POPT	Payroll Options (1)	-
1	J			
2-10	SSN			
			Bank	
11-20		BNKN	Name (10)	----------
21-35		BNKA	Address (15)	---------------
36-40		BNKZ	Zip Code (5)	-----
1	K			
2-10	SSN			
11-15		CONTN	Contract Number (5)	-----
16-18		CWDAS	Contracted Number of working days (3)	---
19-24		LPYDT	Last Pay Date (6) MM DD YY	------
25-31		CONSAL	Contracted Salary (7)	-----.--
32-37		GROSS	Gross Pay Amount (6)	----.--
			Exemptions claimed	
38-39		EXFWH	Federal W/H (2)	--
40-41		EXSWH	State W/H (2)	--
42-47		DEDFED	Deductions (Required) Federal W/H (6)	----.--
48-53		DEDST	Deductions (Required) State W/H (6)	----.--
54-58		DEDFIC	Deductions (Required) FICA (5)	---.--
59-63		DEOIPE	Deductions (required) IPERS (5)	---.--

1	L			
2-10	SSN			
			Account Allocation Code	
11-15		AACAN1	Account Number (5)	_ _ _ _ _
16-17		AACSA1	Subject area (2)	_ _
18-20		AACBC1	Building code (3)	_ _ _
21-27		AACYT1	$ YTD Fiscal (7)	_ _ _ _ _ . _ _
28-34		AACQT1	$ QTD Fiscal (7)	_ _ _ _ _ . _ _
35-37		AACPC1	Percent of gross (3)	_ . _ _
38-43		AACAU1	Amount Unpaid (6)	_ _ _ _ . _ _
44-49		AACMT1	$ MTD Fiscal (6)	_ _ _ _ . _ _
1	L			
2-10	SSN			
11-15		AACAN2	Account Number (5)	_ _ _ _ _
16-17		AACSA2	Subject area (2)	_ _
18-20		AACBC2	Building code (3)	_ _ _
21-27		AACYT2	$ YTD Fiscal (7)	_ _ _ _ _ . _ _
28-34		AACQT2	$ QTD Fiscal (7)	_ _ _ _ _ . _ _
35-37		AACPC2	Percent of gross (3)	_ . _ _
38-43		AACAU2	Amount Unpaid (6)	_ _ _ _ . _ _
44-49		AACMT2	$ MTD Fiscal (6)	_ _ _ _ . _ _
1	L			
2-10	SSN			
11-15		AACAN3	Account Number (5)	_ _ _ _ _
16-17		AACSA3	Subject area (2)	_ _
18-20		AACBC3	Building code (3)	_ _ _
21-27		AACYT3	$ YTD Fiscal (7)	_ _ _ _ _ . _ _
28-34		AACQT3	$ QTD Fiscal (7)	_ _ _ _ _ . _ _
35-37		AACPC3	Percent of gross (3)	_ . _ _
38-43		AACAU3	Amount Unpaid (6)	_ _ _ _ . _ _
44-49		AACMT3	$ MTD Fiscal (6)	_ _ _ _ . _ _
1	L			
2-10	SSN			
11-15		AACAN4	Account Number (5)	_ _ _ _ _
16-17		AACSA4	Subject area (2)	_ _
18-20		AACBC4	Building code (3)	_ _ _
21-27		AACYT4	$ YTD Fiscal (7)	_ _ _ _ _ . _ _
28-34		AACQT4	$ QTD Fiscal (7)	_ _ _ _ _ . _ _
35-37		AACPC4	Percent of gross (3)	_ . _ _
38-49		AACAU4	Amount Unpaid (6)	_ _ _ _ . _ _
44-49		AACMT4	$ MTD Fiscal (6)	_ _ _ _ . _ _
1	L			
2-10	SSN			
11-15		AACAN5	Account Number (5)	_ _ _ _ _
16-17		AACSA5	Subject area (2)	_ _
18-20		AACBC5	Building code (3)	_ _ _
21-27		AACYT5	$ YTD Fiscal (7)	_ _ _ _ _ . _ _
28-34		AACQT5	$ QTD Fiscal (7)	_ _ _ _ _ . _ _
35-37		AACPC5	Percent of gross (3)	_ . _ _
38-43		AACAU5	Amount Unpaid (6)	_ _ _ _ . _ _
44-49		AACMT5	$ MTD Fiscal (6)	_ _ _ _ . _ _
1	L			
2-10	SSN			
11-15		AACAN6	Account Number (5)	_ _ _ _ _
16-17		AACSA6	Subject area (2)	_ _
18-20		AACBC6	Building code (3)	_ _ _
21-27		AACYT6	$ YTD Fiscal (7)	_ _ _ _ _ . _ _
28-34		AACQT6	$ QTD Fiscal (7)	_ _ _ _ _ . _ _
35-37		AACPC6	Percent of gross (3)	_ . _ _
38-43		AACAU6	Amount Unpaid (6)	_ _ _ _ . _ _
44-49		AACMT6	$ MTD Fiscal (6)	_ _ _ _ . _ _
1	M			
2-10	SSN		Flat Rate Payment	
11-16		FLRAU1	Amount unpaid (6)	_ _ _ _ . _ _
17-22		FLRAP1	Amount paid (6)	_ _ _ _ . _ _
23-32		FLRAC1	Account (10)	_ _ _ _ _ _ _ _ _ _
1	M			
2-10	SSN			
11-16		FLRAU2	Amount unpaid (6)	_ _ _ _ . _ _
17-22		FLRAP2	Amount paid (6)	_ _ _ _ . _ _
23-32		FLRAC2	Account (10)	_ _ _ _ _ _ _ _ _ _

1	M			
2-10	SSN			
11-16		FLRAU3	Amount unpaid (6)	----.--
17-22		FLRAP3	Amount paid (6)	----.--
23-32		FLRAC3	Account (10)	----------
1	N			
2-10	SSN		Non-Contracted SUP compensation	
11-16		NCAU1	Amount unpaid (6)	----.--
17-22		NCAP1	Amount paid (6)	----.--
23-32		NCAC1	Account (10)	----------
1	N			
2-10	SSN			
11-16		NCAU2	Amount unpaid (6)	----.--
17-22		NCAP2	Amount paid (6)	----.--
23-32		NCAC2	Account (10)	----------
1	N			
2-10	SSN			
11-16		NCAU3	Amount unpaid (6)	----.--
17-22		NCAP3	Amount paid (6)	----.--
23-32		NCAC3	Account (10)	----------
1	O			
2-10	SSN		Extra Compensation	
11-16		ECAU1	Amount unpaid (6)	----.--
17-22		ECAP1	Amount paid (6)	----.--
23-32		ECAC1	Account (10)	----------
1	O			
2-10	SSN			
11-16		ECAU2	Amount unpaid (6)	----.--
17-22		ECAP2	Amount paid (6)	----.--
23-32		ECAC2	Account (10)	----------
1	O			
2-10	SSN			
11-16		ECAU3	Amount unpaid (6)	----.--
17-22		ECAP3	Amount paid (6)	----.--
23-32		ECAC3	Account (10)	----------
1	P			
2-10	SSN			
			Calendar Year Records (for W-2)	
			Year to Date	
11-17		CYGPY	Gross Payments (7)	-----.--
18-23		CYFWY	Federal W/H (6)	----.--
24-29		CYSWY	State W/H (6)	----.--
30-34		CYFICY	FICA (5)	---.--
35-39		CYIPEY	IPERS (5)	---.--
40-45		CYOTHY	Others (6)	----.--
			Quarter to Date	
46-52		CYGPQ	Gross Payments (7)	-----.--
53-58		CYFWQ	Federal W/H (6)	----.--
59-64		CYSWQ	State W/H (6)	----.--
65-69		CYFICQ	FICA (5)	---.--
70-74		CYIPEQ	IPERS (5)	---.--
75-80		CYOTHQ	Others (6)	----.--
1	Q			
2-10	SSN			
			Fiscal Year Records	
			Year to Date	
11-17		FYGPY	Gross Payments (7)	-----.--
18-23		FYFWY	Federal W/H (6)	-----.-
24-29		FYSWY	State W/H (6)	----.--
30-34		FYFICY	FICA (5)	---.--
35-39		FYIPEY	IPERS (5)	---.--
40-45		FYOTHY	Others (6)	----.--
			Quarter to Date	
46-52		FYGPQ	Gross Payments (7)	-----.--
53-58		FYFWQ	Federal W/H (6)	----.--
59-64		FYSWQ	State W/H (6)	----.--

Columns	Field	Description	Format
65-69	FYFICQ	FICA (5)	___.__
70-74	FYIPEQ	IPERS (5)	___.__
75-80	FYOTHQ	Others (6)	____.__
1	R		
2-10	SSN		
		Deductions (Optional)	
		Credit Union	
11-15	DEDCRS	Savings (5)	___.__
16-20	DEDCRP	Payments (5)	___.__
		Deductions (Optional)	
21-25	DEDPD	Professional dues (5)	___.__
		Deductions (Optional)	
26-31	DEDBND	Bond (6)	____.__
		Deductions (Optional)	
32-37	DEDTSA	Tax sheltered annuities (6)	____.__
38-46	TSAPN	Contract Number (9)	_________
		Deductions (Optional)	
47-51	DEDLIF	Life Insurance (5)	___.__
52-60	LIFPN	Policy Number (9)	_________
		Deductions (Optional)	
61-65	DEDHI	Hospital Insurance (5)	___.__
66-74	HIPN	Policy Number (9)	_________
1	S		
2-10	SSN		
		Calendar Year Deduction Totals	
11-16		Credit Union Savings (6)	____.__
17-22		Credit Union Payment (6)	____.__
23-28		Professional Dues (6)	____.__
29-34		Bonds (6)	____.__
35-40		Tax sheltered annuities (6)	____.__
41-46		Life Insurance (6)	____.__
47-52		Hospital Insurance (6)	____.__
53-58		Charity (6)	____.__
59-64		Local Option 1 (6)	____.__
65-70		Local Option 2 (6)	____.__
1	T		
2-10	SSN		
		Deductions (Optional)	
11-14	DEDCHR	Charity Org. (4)	__.__
		Deduction (Optional)	
15-18	DEDLO1	Local Option 1 (4)	__.__
		Deduction (Optional)	
19-22	DEDLO2	Local Option 2 (4)	__.__
		Sick Leave	
23-26	SLDPY	Days from prior years (4)	__.__
27-30	SLDAY	Days available this fiscal year (4)	__.__
31-34	SLDUY	Days used to date this fiscal year (4)	__.__
		Other Leave	
35-38	OLDPY1	Days from prior years (4)	__.__
39-42	OLDAY1	Days available this fiscal year (4)	__.__
43-46	OLDUY1	Days used to date this fiscal year (4)	__.__
47-50	OLDPY2	Days from prior years (4)	__.__
51-54	OLDAY2	Days available this fiscal year (4)	__.__
55-58	OLDUY2	Days used to date this fiscal year (4)	__.__
		Additional Leave	
59-62	ALDAY1	Days available this fiscal year (4)	__.__
63-66	ALDSY1	Days used this fiscal year (4)	__.__

67-70	ALDAY2	Days available this fiscal year (4)	_ _ . _ _
71-74	ALDSY2	Days used this fiscal year (4)	_ _ . _ _

1	U		
2-10	SSN		
		Pay Transaction Card	
11-20		Account to be charged (5)	_ _ _ _ _
21-25		Number of hours (5)	_ _ _ . _ _
26-29		Rate per hour ($/hr.) (5)	_ _ . _ _

With the preceding formats in mind, it is readily seen that problems surrounding personnel and payroll procedures are not simple. On the contrary, they are quite complex. To properly define, program, and maintain personnel and payroll records is not a simple clerical task to be casually attempted. It requires an in-depth study, careful consideration of anticipated needs, and a great deal of programing effort; although the procedures fall into the category of the clerical and the routine, they must not and can not be taken lightly.

15 test scoring and related reports at the elementary level

MARY ESTHER RAKER

MARY ESTHER RAKER *received her MS in Educational Research and Testing from Florida State University in 1962. Her BS in Mathematics Education was taken at the same institution in 1960.*

While pursuing her graduate studies, she worked as a research assistant at Florida State University, and in 1961 she became coordinator of research with the Hillsborough County Board of Public Instruction. She has served as vice president of the Florida Association of Educational Data Systems, and as secretary-treasurer of the Florida Educational Research Association.

INTRODUCTION

Test scoring in some secondary schools has been done for many years since the introduction of the IBM 805 Test Scoring Machine. It has been given added incentive with the announcement of optical scanners, such as the IBM 1230 and Digitek, but the elementary schools seem to have been forgotten in this age of automated test scoring. With the exception of some scoring of answer sheets for intermediate grade students, teachers in elementary schools have had to continue the clerical chore of hand scoring test booklets, converting raw scores by searching through tables in testing manuals, recording names and other identifying data plus the scores on several lists, recording the data in cumulative or permanent records, and finally, if there were any time or incentive remaining, compiling any statistical data and interpreting the test scores. In the past few years, several school systems have begun projects to alleviate much of the clerical work involved with testing in the elementary school. The medium being used is the mark-sense card.

PROCEDURE

The mark-sense card, as shown in Figure 79, is not to be used as a replacement for the answer sheet, as some systems have done, but rather as a medium for recording raw scores for each subtest. The mark-sense card is designed for the particular test being administered; there are mark-sense positions assigned for each test or subtest raw score to be recorded. The card illustrated in Figure 79 was designed for the *California Short-Form Test of Mental Maturity*, in which there are seven subtests. The field labeled chronological age (C.A.) in months is used to record the additional information needed to convert the scores of this test. Another way to determine the chronological age is to incorporate two fields in the card—

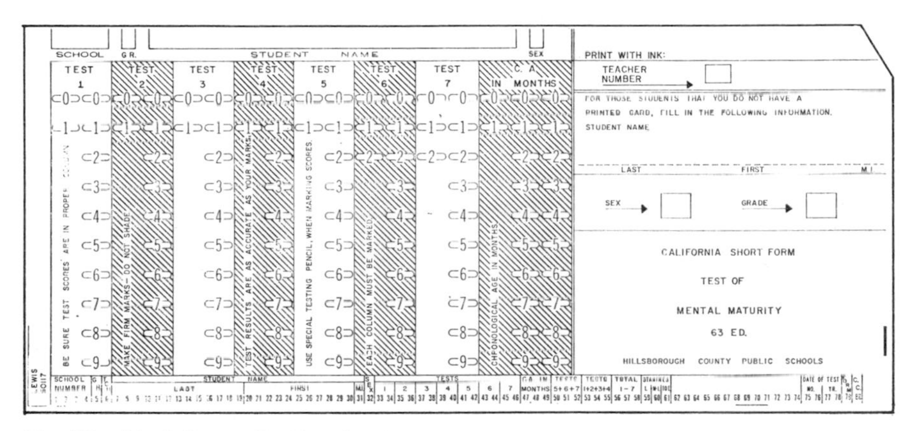
SCHOOL GR. STUDENT NAME SEX
TEST 1 TEST 2 TEST 3 TEST 4 TEST 5 TEST 6 TEST 7 C.A. IN MONTHS
BE SURE TEST SCORES ARE IN PROPER COLUMN
MAKE FIRM MARKS—DO NOT SHADE
TEST RESULTS ARE AS ACCURATE AS YOUR MARKS
USE SPECIAL TESTING PENCIL WHEN MARKING SCORES
EACH COLUMN MUST BE MARKED
CHRONOLOGICAL AGE IN MONTHS
PRINT WITH INK:
TEACHER NUMBER
FOR THOSE STUDENTS THAT YOU DO NOT HAVE A PRINTED CARD, FILL IN THE FOLLOWING INFORMATION.
STUDENT NAME
LAST FIRST M.I.
SEX GRADE
CALIFORNIA SHORT FORM
TEST OF
MENTAL MATURITY
63 ED.
HILLSBOROUGH COUNTY PUBLIC SCHOOLS
SCHOOL NUMBER G. T. STUDENT NAME LAST FIRST M.I. S. TESTS 1 2 3 4 5 6 7 C.A. IN MONTHS TESTS 5+6+7 TESTS 1+2+3+4 TOTAL 1–7 STANINES L N-L TOT. DATE OF TEST MO. YR. N. R. M. C. C.

Fig. 79 — Mark Sense Testing Card.

one for the month of birth, the other for the year. Then, through the use of table look-up routines in the computer program, the teacher's additional clerical task of computing the chronological age in months can be alleviated.

If the school system has recorded (in cards or some other medium) the student's name, sex, grade, and school number, then the mark-sense cards may be pre-punched and interpreted from this data before distribution to the schools. This is particularly applicable should the school system maintain an enrollment or census file. In that instance, the testing cards may be reproduced from the file, as is illustrated in step 1 of Figure 80.

When testing cards are received in schools and distributed to individual teachers, each teacher must insure that he has a card for each of his students. If he does not have a pre-punched and interpreted card for a student, he will have been furnished with extra blank cards on which he must record the identifying data. This is referred to in the flowchart as a "handscribed" card.

After the teacher has administered the particular test in booklet form and has hand-scored the test, he records the raw scores and

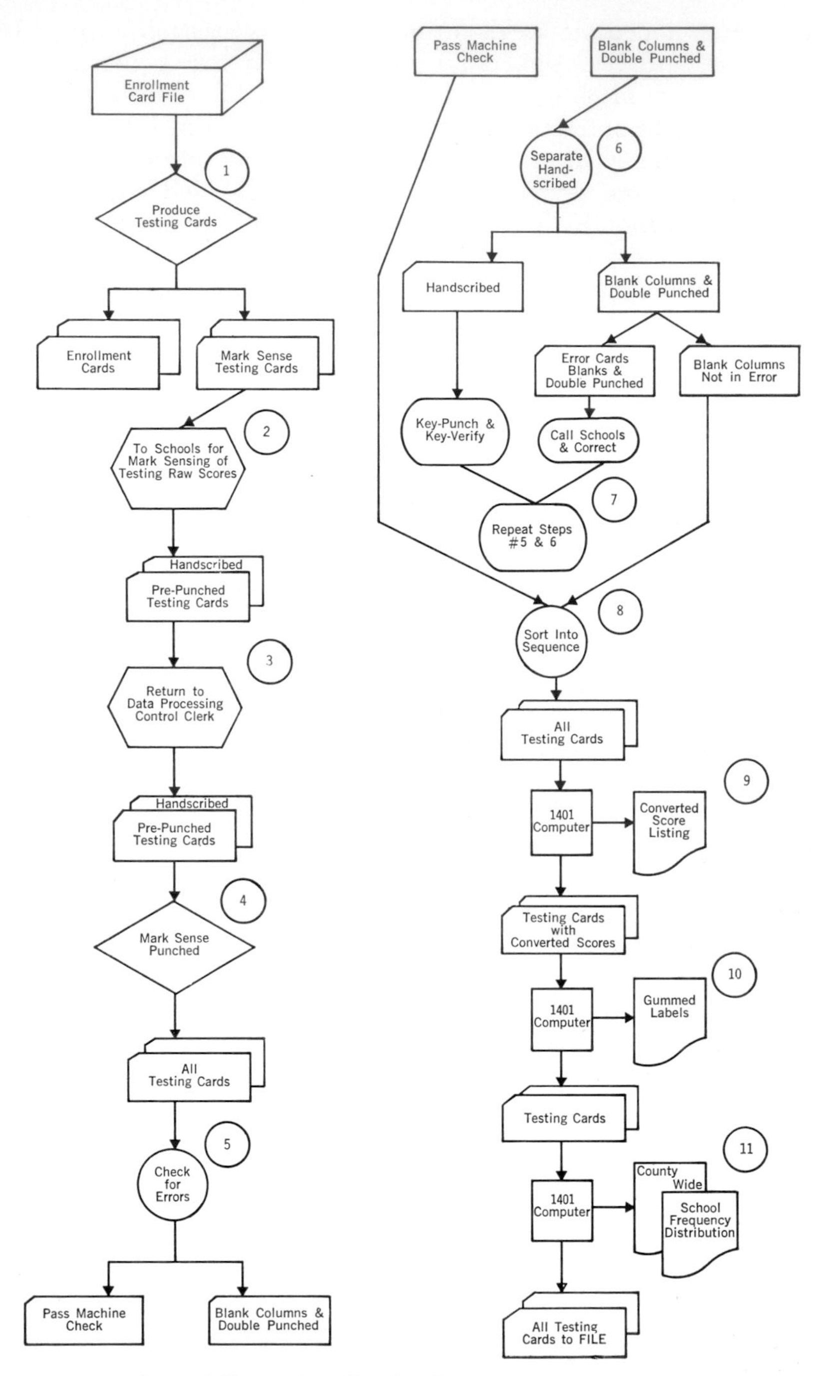

Fig. 80 — Flowchart of Elementary Testing Program.

any other pertinent data, such as the chronological age, on the mark-sense card. The cards are then returned to the data processing center as noted in step 3 of Figure 80.

The first step in processing the cards is to convert mark-sensed information to punched form by using a reproducer, such as the IBM 514 or 519, which has the optional mark-sensing feature. At the same time, the teacher number may be intersperse gang punched into the testing cards from a teacher header card.

Since errors may be made in marking cards (such as two marks in a column or columns left blank), the cards must proceed through an error-checking routine, as noted in step 5 of Figure 80. The check for double-punched or blank columns may be made on the reproducer during mark-sensing of the cards, or the data processing operator's time may be conserved by pulling the error cards on a collator pass. This should be determined in the individual installation.

The flowchart, as detailed in Figure 80, involves the use of a collator at step 5 to pull the cards with double-punches and blank columns. By checking the first position of the student name field, the handscribed cards may be pulled at the same time. Then, at step 6, the handscribed cards are separated from the error cards on a sorter. The handscribed cards are sent to the keypunch section to have the identifying information, such as student name, punched into them.

The error cards must be manually checked to determine the nature of the error and to obtain the correct information from the schools. There may be cards that have been pulled as having blank columns that are not errors. These are cards where the student did not take a particular subtest, and therefore the raw-score columns have been left blank. These cards should be included in the file of cards which passed the machine error check.

After the handscribed cards have been punched and verified and the error cards corrected, steps 5 and 6 should be repeated. This insures that additional errors have not been made during the punching and correcting of errors.

At step 8 of Figure 80, the entire file is sorted into the sequence required for the printed listing of test results. In most instances, this involves sorting the cards into sequence so that each teacher may receive an alphabetical listing of the results for the students in his class. The listing may include the raw scores and converted scores or only the converted scores, as the individual school system chooses.

On a computer, as depicted in step 9 of Figure 80, with a pro-

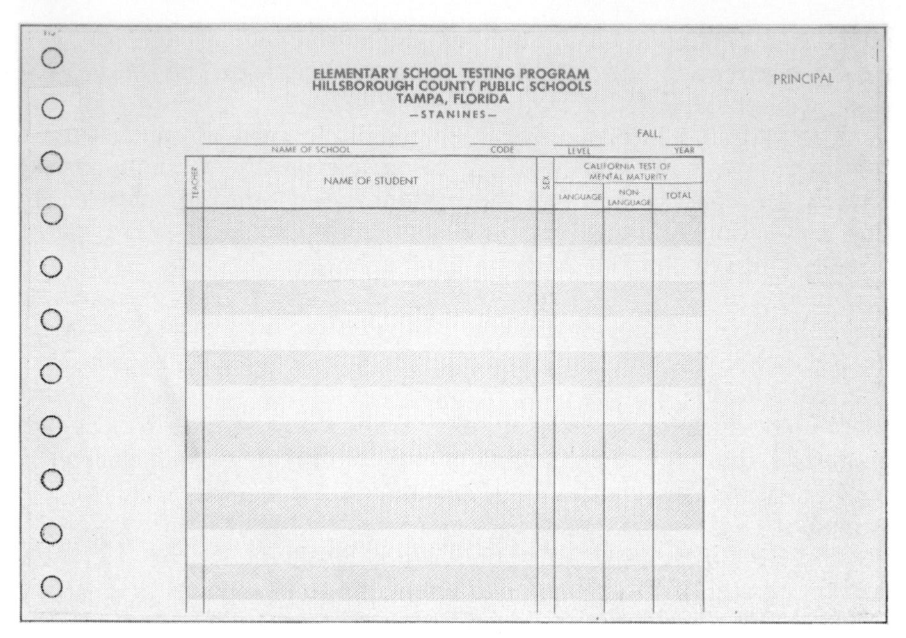

ELEMENTARY SCHOOL TESTING PROGRAM
HILLSBOROUGH COUNTY PUBLIC SCHOOLS
TAMPA, FLORIDA
—STANINES—

PRINCIPAL

FALL

NAME OF SCHOOL | CODE | LEVEL | YEAR

TEACHER	NAME OF STUDENT	SEX	CALIFORNIA TEST OF MENTAL MATURITY		
			LANGUAGE	NON-LANGUAGE	TOTAL

Fig. 81 — Elementary Testing List.

gram involving a table look-up routine, the raw scores recorded in the testing card are converted to the required type of score such as percentile rank, grade equivalent, stanine, etc. At the same time, the results may be punched into the same or another card and a listing printed. An example of multi-part listing is shown in Figure 81, a four-part form with copies for the school principal, school teacher, elementary supervisor, and special services (guidance and testing supervisor). This replaces numerous class lists of results which the teacher formerly completed by hand.

Since the test data is in an automated medium, it is a relatively simple task, as shown in step 10 of Figure 80, to print gummed or pressure sensitive labels for posting cumulative records and/or permanent record cards.

HILLSBOROUGH COUNTY SEVENTH GRADE TESTING PROGRAM — PERCENTILE SCORES
NAME SEX SCHOOL SEC. DATE
FALL, 19

CTMM		METROPOLITAN ACHIEVEMENT TESTS ADVANCED							
LANG.	NON-LANG.	WORD KNOWLEDGE	READING	SPELLING	LANG. TOTAL	LANG. ST. SK.	ARITH. COMP.	ARITH. P. S. & C.	SOC. STUD. ST. SK.

Fig. 82 — Pressure-Sensitive Test-Posting Label.

Figure 82 is an example of the type of gummed label which may be printed. The format of these may vary with individual systems requirements. It is advantageous if the cumulative record or permanent record card has been planned to permit posting of the labels in a specially designed area.

The last function of the testing cards, as noted in step 11 of Figure 80, is the accumulating of statistical data by school and/or

F R E Q U E N C Y   D I S T R I B U T I O N

GRADE 03   T E S T - METRO ACH TEST ELEM   VARIABLE - WORD KNOWLEDGE

DATE 09/65

SCHOOL NAME -   SCHOOL NUMBER -

SCORE	FREQUENCY	CUMULATIVE FREQUENCY	CUMULATIVE PERCENTAGE	CONVERTED SCORE
00	3	3	1.6	1
01	3	6	3.2	1
03	1	7	3.8	2
04	2	9	4.9	2
05	7	16	8.6	2
06	1	17	9.2	3
07	2	19	10.3	3
08	4	23	12.4	3
09	5	28	15.1	3
10	2	30	16.2	4
11	9	39	21.1	4
12	3	42	22.7	4
13	12	54	29.2	4***Q1*
14	12	66	35.7	4
15	7	73	39.5	5
16	9	82	44.3	5
17	16	98	53.0	5***Mdn*
18	7	105	56.8	5
19	7	112	60.5	5
20	10	122	65.9	6
21	1	123	66.5	6
22	5	128	69.2	6
23	2	130	70.3	6
24	5	135	73.0	6
25	3	138	74.6	6
26	8	146	78.9	7***Q3*
27	5	151	81.6	7
28	6	157	84.9	7
29	4	161	87.0	7
30	2	163	88.1	7
31	1	164	88.6	7
32	4	168	90.8	8
33	1	169	91.4	8
34	2	171	92.4	8
35	2	173	93.5	8
36	1	174	94.1	8
37	4	178	96.2	9
38	1	179	96.8	9
39	2	181	97.8	9
40	1	182	98.4	9

Fig. 83 – Frequency Distribution of Test Results.

system. This is by far one of the most valuable reasons for compiling data in automated form. Previously, under manual systems, by the time the teacher had completed all the clerical tasks involved in the testing program, he had little time left to compile statistical data. Also, at the system level, the tremendous amount of data overwhelms manual methods. With data in automated form, the compilation of means, medians, quartiles, standard deviations, frequency distributions, etc., becomes a simple by-product. Figure 83 is an example of such a frequency distribution.

Though this discussion has been oriented around a computer system, the same results may be obtained with an accounting machine oriented system. The basic theory involved in the conversion of test scores is sorting a testing master deck containing the raw and converted scores with the testing cards, and intersperse gang punching the converted scores into the testing cards on a reproducer. Once this procedure has been followed on each subtest, the results are punched cards containing the identifying information, raw scores, and converted scores. Then the various lists, labels, and distributions may be printed on the accounting machine.

SUMMARY

In elementary schools, use of the mark-sense card has resulted in appreciable decreases in the amount of clerical work expected of the teacher. Though teachers must hand-score test booklets, and record raw scores on mark-sense cards, effort from that point on is considerably reduced.

In addition to saving teacher time, the conversion of test scores is more accurate. Errors that occur in hand-converted scores from using the wrong tables or misreading scores are eliminated.

The greatest error reduction is achieved by not hand recording scores on class record sheets and permanent records. The errors in hand transcribing from one source document to another can be numerous in a large school system.

Therefore, by using mark-sense cards, elementary schools may gain their share of data processing services in testing that previously only secondary schools and some intermediate grades have received.

16 high school business data processing curriculum development

MERLE W. WOOD

MERLE W. WOOD *received his MS from Indiana University and his BA from Morningside College (Sioux City, Iowa).*

Mr. Wood was supervisor of business education, Des Moines Public Schools, from 1960 to 1965. His major work has been in the area of business education curriculum development; he has served as consultant on two U.S. Office of Education curriculum projects in the field of business education.

His publications include numerous professional articles; he is co-author of The Receptionist *(McGraw-Hill, 1966). He is a member of several organizations, including the Data Processing Management Association and the Administrative Management Society, and he is vice president of the Society for Automation in Business Education (SABE).*

A PLACE IN THE SCHEDULE

School administrators and boards of education are no longer surprised to find departments requesting the approval of "another course." For the past ten years an already crowded secondary school schedule has had many demands placed upon it. State and local general graduation requirements have taken much of the flexibility from our curriculum structure. The concern of school systems over this strict programing is reflected in the interest and experimentation in the past few years with various schemes of flexible scheduling. One entirely new cluster of vocational courses, data processing, has made its appearance in just the past four years. There is enough evidence already available to indicate that these data processing courses are taking their place in our crowded senior high school schedules.

We can expect continuing pressure to be exerted from the entire range of vocational education courses. Availability of new state and federal funds, the growing re-acceptance of "vocational" programs, demands from business and industry for more trained workers, and a more realistic appraisal of the many "college-bound" students who never get to college, are all going to have an impact on the secondary school curriculum. Finding more usable space in the school program for emerging courses will be a major challenge for school administration in the years immediately ahead.

Some are suggesting that all vocational courses should be held until after students graduate from high school. This is inappropriate and a dodge of the responsibility of the secondary schools. Many students simply cannot afford to wait for an additional year or two after high school in order to develop a salable skill. We *know* that we can teach highly complex vocational skills to secondary students—we have been doing it for years. Business data processing courses need to be considered at the high school level. This may be only one area of many new vocational/technical subjects which conditions will require us to consider housing in our high schools.

WHY OFFER DATA PROCESSING COURSES?

In the past dozen years we have seen automated data handling systems in business change from relatively slow card-processing procedures to sophisticated high-speed computer systems which are literally revolutionizing our way of conducting business and doing research. Other uses of data processing equipment are being developed with alarming speed and rapidity. Public education is often accused (and perhaps rightly so) of taking too long from the time new processes are developed in the world of work until they are incorporated into the curriculum. With the increased speed of these many new developments today, we simply do not have time to wait through our usual process of discovery, investigation, evaluation, installation, re-evaluation, and final acceptance. While our judgments must still be well founded and accurate, there is an increasing need for us to take quicker action based on firm research and sound reasoning. We perhaps need to inject a "calculated risk" into our curriculum work. Only in this way can we hope to keep a reasonable pace with the speedy development of new concepts as they appear in business and industry.

The case of business data processing is an example of what we can do when the need is great. Five years ago the secondary schools offering courses in this discipline numbered fewer than a dozen. Today there are several hundred schools with ongoing programs in some phase of data processing instruction. Hundreds of other schools will follow. At least, this is the present indication.

A recent study conducted by Dr. Fred S. Cook, Wayne State University, presents the status of data processing instruction in our secondary schools.[1] The 2,228 separate high schools which responded to his brief questionnaire represent approximately 10 percent of the high schools in the United States. A few of the results of this survey are important to consider at this point.

1. Larger high schools (1,100 plus ADA) tended to have more data processing equipment, courses, and interest in this field.
2. Over 500 high schools reported that their district had a data processing installation.
3. There were 161 high schools reporting that they had access to the district installation for teaching purposes.
4. Three hundred forty-four high schools reported that they had data processing equipment on the premises.
5. Thirty-six schools reported that they had computers.
6. Active plans to introduce data processing equipment into the schools in the next two years were reported by 322 schools.
7. There were 719 high schools (32.3 percent of the respondents) indicating current offering of some data processing instruction.

One of the interesting points in Dr. Cook's study indicated that only 14.8 percent of the schools reporting have conducted community surveys in order to determine the need for data processing instructional programs. While it has already been suggested that we need to adjust our curriculum quickly to keep pace with technological advances, it is surprising to discover that a basic tool such as the community survey has not been more fully employed in connection with the development of data processing programs.

AN EARLY PROGRAM

One of the early secondary data processing installations was initiated by the Des Moines Public Schools in 1962. This was approached as a pilot project to serve as a guide for other schools as well as a vocational training program to develop employable youth for the many data processing installations in the Des Moines area. This particular center continues to be one of the most complete and comprehensive high school data processing programs in the country. Figure 84 shows the space commitment to this training program in Des Moines Technical High School. It also illustrates the layout of equipment and storage facilities.[2]

TYPES OF PROGRAMS

There appear to be three major directions in curriculum development in data processing at the secondary level. Some districts have

[1] Fred S. Cook, "Status of Data Processing in American Secondary Schools," *The Balance Sheet,* April 1966, pp. 347-50.

[2] Enoch Haga, *Understanding Automation, A Data Processing Curriculum Guide and Reference Text.* Elmhurst, Illinois: The Business Press, 1965.

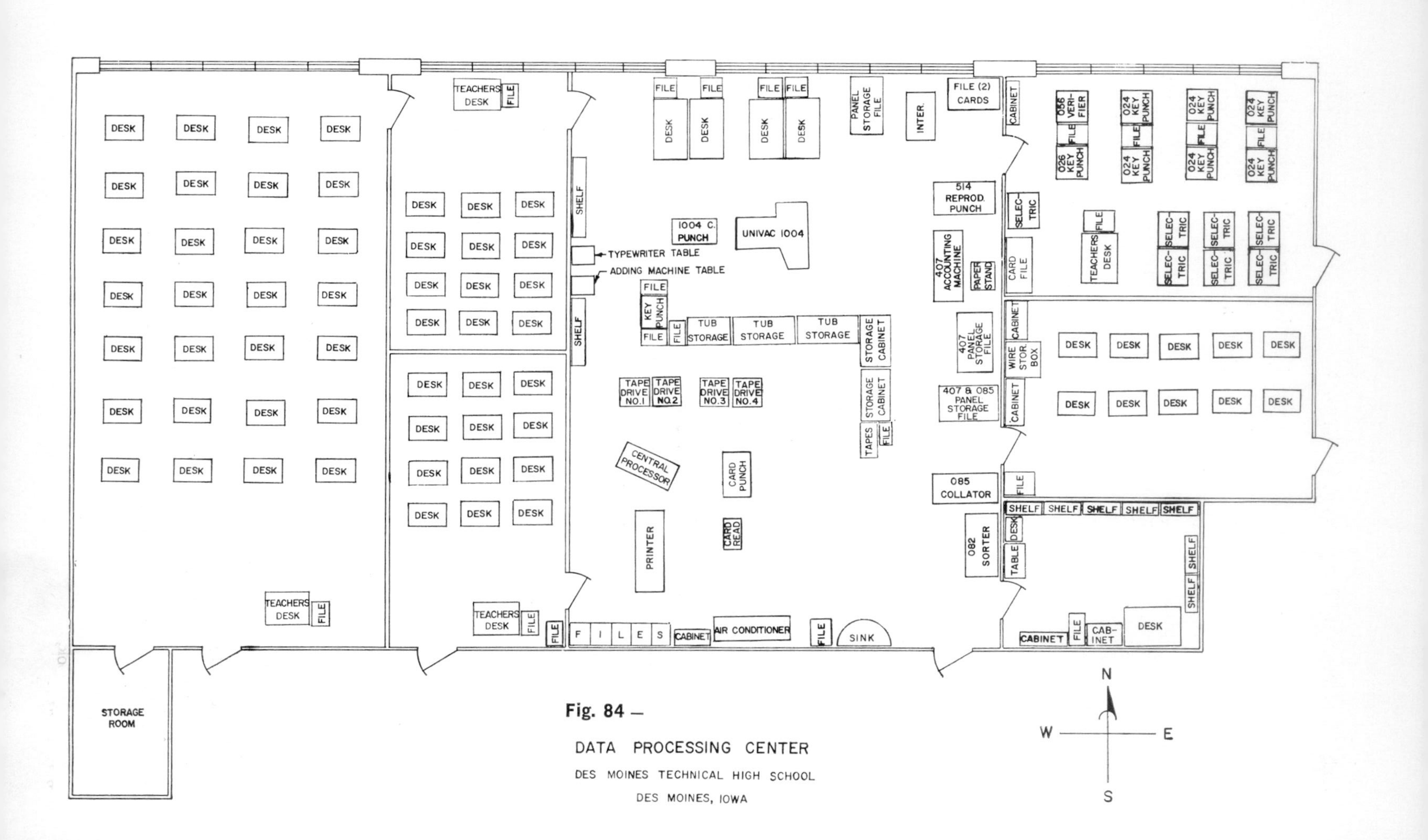

Fig. 84 —

DATA PROCESSING CENTER

DES MOINES TECHNICAL HIGH SCHOOL

DES MOINES, IOWA

equipped a facility with the latest types of high speed computer and card handling equipment. This equipment is supported by considerable storage equipment, air conditioning, heavy attention to supply items, and a low student/teacher ratio. In short, programs such as this demand considerable initial capital outlay with an inherent continuing high cost. However, such installations provide the opportunity to train students for the entire spectrum of data processing jobs.

Another approach has been to concentrate on lower level job training.[3] Courses in keypunch operation and punched card machine operation are becoming more common. At this time little attention is being given to such job titles as tape librarian, console operator, machine operator, coding clerk, etc., although job opportunities exist. The reason for this omission is most likely due to the rigid adherence to the "one-year course" and "one-period-per-day" philosophy. Because vocational competency can be developed in these job titles in much less time than the traditional "one-period-per-day for one year" it is difficult to schedule them into most high school programs.

A third direction is in the development of background and orientation *to* data processing through a specially structured course. This particular course has not been fully developed as yet; however, from attitudes being expressed from various segments within business education it appears that it will ultimately be a one-semester course, and that it will relate to business applications rather than scientific applications. This course, "Introduction to Business Data Processing," is particularly appealing to the small school which cannot justify large expenditures for equipment. The growing demand from America's business community for students to "know something about automated data handling" will probably hasten the development of this important course.

Although the course will be business-oriented, there is no reason why it cannot be an elective for the science-math students who want background in data processing. At this introductory level, much of the logic, systems, and vocabulary are the same for both scientific and business data processing. Besides providing introductory concepts to high school vocational business students, this course will also serve as a base course for the college-bound students who may want to use data processing as a tool for research and study. It can also serve as an exploratory opportunity for students who may want to consider further training in data processing at

[3] *Electronic Business Data Processing Peripheral Equipment Occupations.* U. S. Department of Health, Education, and Welfare, 1964.

the junior college level or in the area-vocational school. When the course is finally developed it now appears that it will follow rather closely the outline presented here.[4]

INTRODUCTION TO BUSINESS DATA PROCESSING

I. Development of Record Systems
  A. Ancient record systems
  B. Early manual systems (1500–1900)
  C. Mechanical accounting systems
  D. Growth and development of electromechanical systems
II. The Need for Automated Data Processing Systems
  A. Expanding demands for services
  B. Uses in decision making
III. Major uses of Data Processing
  A. Business
  B. Government
  C. Military
  D. Scientific
IV. Data Handling
  A. Collection of data
  B. Conversion to input media
  C. Processing
  D. Storage
  E. Output
  F. Uses of output
V. Electromechanical Data Processing
  A. Keypunch
  B. Verifier
  C. Sorter
  D. Reproducing punch
  E. Collator
  F. Interpreter
  G. Tabulator
  H. Calculator
  I. Types of applications
VI. Computer Systems
  A. Computer types
    1. digital
    2. analog
  B. The computer configuration
    1. input equipment
    2. processing

[4] *Business Data Processing Programs in the High School, An Operational Handbook.* Sacramento: California Department of Education, Bureau of Business Education, in press.

3. storage systems
4. output

C. Computer flowcharting
1. general
2. detail

D. Computer language
E. Numbering systems
F. Programing
G. Computer capability
H. Applications

VII. The Data Processing Department
A. Equipment
B. People
C. Problems
D. Functions

VIII. Advanced Training Sources
A. Junior college and area vocational schools
B. College and university
C. Company inservice
D. Machine manufacturers' schools
E. Library and home study

FUNDING THE PROGRAM

Two sources which have been used extensively for funding aid for data processing programs are the National Defense Education Act, Title VIII and the Vocational Education Act of 1963. Each state has its own state plan and its own attitude toward use of these funds. The NDEA funds must be used for technical education in the data processing area. This was pretty well defined as the development of skills which lead to, or relate closely to, computer programing. Schools in some states have been able to use the funds at the secondary level, while other states have restricted the use of NDEA funds to computer programing at the post-secondary level. The amount of financial support to districts has varied from 50 to 100 percent.

Vocational Education Act funds are awarded on a variety of percentages but are usable for courses which are vocational, yet not necessarily technical. Courses such as keypunch operation and punched card machine operation are covered under provision of VEA, while they would tend not to qualify under NDEA, since they are not of a technical nature.

Several of the major data processing equipment manufacturers have special educational discounts applicable for the purchase or lease of equipment to be used primarily for classroom instruction.

The discounts vary considerably and are subject to change without notice. In some cases they are quite substantial, especially when the equipment selected is a type which is being phased out of commercial installations. A great deal of care must be taken in equipment selection since the type of equipment determines to a large extent the kinds of courses which can be effectively offered.

One issue is certain to be raised as districts consider the acquisition of equipment for instructional programs—the question of administrative use of the equipment during noninstructional hours. Most states are encouraging school districts to automate routine school administrative record functions. For this reason, the general attitude of state departments of education will be to approve requests for shared use of equipment. Schools should be cautious, though, not to secure equipment with the primary aim of taking advantage of special state funds, and equipment discounts, under the guise of operating an instructional program, when the real purpose is to process administrative data. If there is to be a sharing of equipment time between instructional and administrative functions, the hours, rules, and procedures should be well defined in advance. Failure to approach this issue honestly at an early date can result in serious internal problems over the availability of equipment.

In each state, the office of the director of vocational education in the state department of education can be contacted for information regarding the availability of funds under either NDEA or VEA 1963. Any district considering a venture into data processing instructional programs should contact this office early in their planning process. Course guides, availability of trained teachers, related research, and other forms of aid are available from this office.

OTHER CURRICULUM RELATED ISSUES

Location of the Equipment

Metropolitan school districts will find it generally impractical and unnecessary to locate complete equipment configurations in each building. In some cases, one centrally located school can house the major units of hardware. In others, it may be necessary to equip several buildings in order to make the facilities available to all students in the district on an equitable basis. It must be decided which buildings can best utilize the equipment, and how students from other buildings can either transfer full-time or be transported daily for a portion of their school schedule. Some courses can be completed in one hour per day for a portion of a semester (keypunch operation, for example). Other courses covering more complicated functions need several full semesters of from one to three periods per day.

Although the availability of the data processing center to students is the prime consideration, there are other factors which need to be considered. The rooms selected for housing the equipment must have access to adequate power. They must have a floor surface which can be kept free of dust. There may be a noise factor in relation to adjoining classes and this must be considered. For some equipment, it is necessary to provide air conditioning in order to control temperature and humidity. If the equipment is going to be used for administrative data processing, it must be located near the administrative offices.

Teacher Selection

Because qualified teachers of data processing continue to be scarce, school districts will usually need to select existing teachers and send them to school for training in this new technology. This should be looked at as a long-term process. It may involve several full summer sessions as well as a good deal of the teachers' time during the school year. Besides the training programs available from the major equipment manufacturers, there are now many colleges and universities offering course work in data processing.

Generally, business teachers with an accounting background tend to be good candidates for this field of work. The teachers selected should be those who are willing to innovate, are eager to experiment, and are highly motivated. Because they will ultimately be making many complex recommendations to administration regarding data processing equipment, curriculum, and supplies, they should have good judgment and be thoroughly trustworthy.

These people will already be qualified teachers. Requesting them to qualify for a new area of instruction can best be justified by paying a stipend during their training period. Amounts which have been paid by districts vary a good deal, but $75 to $100 per week are not rare. Some districts have paid more. It is possible, in some states, for school districts to have a portion of this teacher-training cost refunded by coordinating the project through their state department of vocational education. It is advisable, where possible, to write the teacher-training needs into the original project. This allows state offices to see all district needs in connection with a proposed data processing instructional program.

Maximum Use of Equipment

Because of the heavy outlay of funds in a typical data processing laboratory, it is important for the school district to prepare a proposal which makes full use of the equipment. This would mean a full schedule of secondary students during the school day, use during the late evening and early morning hours for the processing of school district administrative data. Such maximum use can better justify the outlay of the large sums of money which are required to equip a data processing center.

The Advisory Committee

Most states are requiring the appointment and use of lay advisory committees for new vocational and technical programs. This is particularly important in new instructional areas such as data processing. We simply do not have the background necessary to make the many judgments required of us as we establish programs. A half-dozen local professional data processors serving as an advisory group will quickly prove their worth. Not to use this ready source of help runs the risk of many delays, much confusion, and probably a number of unsound judgments. Early in the district's study of the feasibility of establishing an instructional program in data processing, there should be an advisory committee established—and used.

The Changing Field of Data Processing

No school system should go into new program development without the firm assurance that what they propose is appropriate. Signs do indicate that there will be more and more data processing applications in business, industry, government, medicine, and other areas. Early projections indicated that with developing data processing advancements, office jobs would be reduced in number; however, there has been no letup in the demand for qualified office workers.

Some well-meaning voices have suggested that we should not train people for certain types of jobs in the data processing field. This caution has particularly referred to the lower-level jobs, such as keypunch operator and punched card machine operator. The reason for this attitude is that, because of rapid advances in the development of new kinds of equipment, many of the lower-level jobs will be eliminated. This is, of course, a real possibility. We do need to keep abreast of equipment and systems developments. Five years ago there was concern that keypunching was "on its way out." Today there are still shortages of keypunch operators in many sections of the country. We need to concern ourselves with training our students for current job needs and we need to keep sufficiently aware of data processing trends so we can shift our production of vocationally competent graduates to new skills as they are needed by our businesses.

Many of us doubt that we can ever again be confident that we have any of our vocational training areas firmly established. Not only will courses be developed and introduced but others will be eliminated. Within most of the courses which continue, frequent adjustments of content and direction will be needed. If we are to meet our full responsibility to our students, change and flexibility will be rather constant factors in our curriculum structure. Business data processing, as has been mentioned previously, may be only one of a long line of vocational subject areas with which we are obliged to deal.

REFERENCES

Data Processing Courses in Vocational and Secondary Schools. General Information Manual, International Business Machines Corporation, F20-8087.

17 teaching a graduate level university course in methods of computer-assisted instruction

GLORIA M. SILVERN and LEONARD C. SILVERN

DR. GLORIA M. SILVERN *has, in her 20 years of professional experience, been a mathematics teacher; research analyst and head of the statistics department (Sterling-Winthrop Research Institute); senior mathematician, training specialist, and head of customer computer programer training (Bendix Computer Division); senior engineer, and head of a diagnostic programing group (Litton Systems, Inc.); and more recently, senior technical specialist, research specialist, and director of computer programer training (Space & Information Systems Division, North American Aviation, Inc.).*

Dr. Silvern has been active in ACM as chairman of the Special Interest Committee on Digital Computer Programmer Training, as a reviewer for Computing Reviews, *and as business manager of the Los Angeles chapter's* Data-Link. *Recently she completed her second term as president of the American Cryptogram Association.*

With Dr. Leonard C. Silvern she is a co-author of Computer-Assisted Instruction, *soon to be published by Wiley. She has numerous publications to her credit, and has been active in several organizations.*

DR. LEONARD C. SILVERN *was employed by the Department of the Navy in 1939, where for 11 years he was involved in man-machine industrial systems; during this period he also served on combat ships in the Pacific, and at the Naval Research Laboratory (Anacostia, D.C.).*

More recently, Dr. Silvern has been associated with the executive department, division of safety, State of New York; with the RAND Corporation at MIT Lincoln Laboratories; with Hughes Aircraft Co.; and at Norair Division of the Northrop Corp. In 1964, he joined Education and Training Consultants Co. as principal scientist.

In 1965, Dr. Silvern was cited by the National Society for Programmed Instruction for "his significant contributions to instructional technology and the engineering of instruction systems." He is a senior member of the Institute of Electrical and Electronics Engineers, and a member of the American Psychological Association (affiliated with Division 21, Society of Engineering Psychologists), of the National Society for the Study of Education, and of the Society for General Systems Research. His publications are extensive.

THE NEED FOR FORMAL INSTRUCTION ON CAI

The Need Defined

This chapter reports on a particular experience dealing with instructing others about computer-assisted instruction (CAI) rather than with principles, general applications, or research in CAI.[1] It is an extension of an earlier paper presented to the Association for Computing Machinery[2] and an expansion of a more recent one to the Institute of Electrical and Electronics Engineers.[3]

A young girl or boy just graduating from a teachers' college and entering the teaching profession will reach retirement age sometime after the year 2000. If this statement is true, then the teachers' colleges of this nation are now preparing teachers for the kinds of public school instruction we will have in the 21st century! To the best of our knowledge, no teacher-training institution instructs in the methods of CAI, and a good many do not even offer courses on programed instruction. While many voices, both competent and incompetent, are offering to advise and guide CAI projects of the immediate future, there is an accompanying fear by teachers and administrators that they connot distinguish between the experts and the charlatans, and that they would need to comprehend the intricacies of the "giant brain." Consequently, they rationalize that CAI is too expensive, too far out, too far away, or too radical. Many see in the digital computer a disguised form of mathematics; since most Americans have had distasteful educational experiences in math, they tend to shun computing and computers rather than

[1] The authors wish to acknowledge the assistance of individuals and organizations without which the CAI course could not have materialized in the form in which it was given. We express our gratitude to Dr. Charles B. Tompkins, Director, UCLA Computing Facility, and to Vice Chancellor Foster H. Sherwood, UCLA, for their active interest in the CAI course. Our deepest appreciation must go to Mr. Frank M. Fillerup, Head, and Mr. Thomas C. Badger, Mr. William A. Guthrie and Mrs. Marion Sapiro, Business Administration Department, University of California Extension-Los Angeles, for their spiritual and logistical support before, during and after the period of course operation; and to Dr. Robert B. Kindred, Head, Education Extension, for his far-sighted analysis of the use of computers in education.

We acknowledge the assistance of Mr. Carl J. Spring, Data Processing Division, IBM Corporation, for contributing a demonstration session, and of various other IBM and Western Data Processing Center employees for their services. We are particularly indebted to Mr. Frank N. Sass, Manager, Information Processing Center-Los Angeles, General Electric Company, who has been a source of inspiration and encouragement in our development of instructional programs, for affording access to the Phoenix and Los Angeles time-sharing computer facilities. Special thanks are extended to Mr. Wayne F. Dodge and Mr. David H. McMullan, Data Communications Group, General Telephone Company, and their associates, for contributing technical resources and other valuable assistance.

[2] G. M. Silvern and L. C. Silvern, "Computer-Assisted Instruction; Specification of Attributes for CAI Programs and Programmers," *Proceedings,* 21st Annual National Conference, August 1966. New York: Association for Computing Machinery, in press.

[3] G. M. Silvern and L. C. Silvern, "Programmed Instruction and Computer-Assisted Instruction . . . Today and Tomorrow," *Proceedings,* Institute of Electrical and Electronics Engineers, Special Computer Issue, December 1966.

to try to understand and learn about them. Despite this reluctance to come to grips with reality, we are beginning to hear of meetings and symposia dealing with CAI. However, many of these appear to be concerned with the social implications of "automation" rather than with how a CAI system functions and how to write a CAI instructional program.

The CAI course at the University of California was a step toward the formalizing of graduate level, adult continuing education, for those with academic achievement at the bachelor's degree level and higher and with some years of experience in their subject-matter specializations. The course began with the premise that programed instruction is functional and that CAI can be even more effective. With this as a starting point, we were able to bypass lofty academic discussions of its value or its effectiveness compared with other methods of instruction. We were able to concentrate on how it works and how it can be used to optimize real-life solutions to real-life learning problems. This, it was not a course in philosophy but rather a lecture-laboratory experience with computer-assisted instruction.

An Invitation from the University of California, Business Administration Department

The idea of presenting such a course was conceived during a discussion involving the authors and several executives of the Business Administration Department, University of California Extension, Los Angeles, in November 1965. The University invited the authors to consider creating a course on CAI.[4] While a small number of symposia had been conducted since 1961, when the Office of Naval Research conducted a Conference on the Application of Digital Computers to Automated Instruction,[5] no university was on record as offering a formal, for-credit, semester-long course about CAI. One of the authors had been instructing "Teaching Machine and Programed Learning Systems for Business, Industry and Government" at the University since 1963, when he initiated that course,[6] it seemed timely to the Business Administration Department to introduce a new generation of courses dealing with CAI. It should be noted that the University of California Extension is

[4] L. C. Silvern, *Communication,* to M. Sapiro, University of California Extension, Ref: 9.3.1; November 6, 1965. Also, University of California Extension. *Course Proposal,* to L. C. Silvern and G. M. Silvern; November 8, 1965.

[5] J. E. Coulson, *Programmed Learning and Computer-Based Instruction.* New York: Wiley, 1962, pp. 1-291.

[6] L. C. Silvern, "Some Views on the Care and Feeding of Instructional Systems," *Educational Technology,* January 30, 1966, pp. 1-13.

nationally known as ". . .a pacesetter in this fast-expanding sphere of 'continuing education' for adults. . ."[7]

One might expect that, with today's rapidly expanding technology, many private industrial and business organizations would be interested in CAI, either as a product line or for internal employee training. The record shows that only one computer manufacturer has been concentrating of the development of CAI hardware and software. However, although this corporation has an international reputation as a proponent of education and training for product support, no formal customer training programs had been presented on the subject-matter of CAI.[8] A small number of specialists in a few business and educational organizations have been disseminating information in the form of published papers, but not as courses of instruction. Thus, the tasks involved in instructional programing for CAI have been akin to black magic as practiced by conjurers and witches.

As 1966 dawned, nearly all interpersonal communication on CAI was informal, non-structured and sporadic. It was for this reason, in essence, that UC's Business Administration Department decided to offer a course which it identified as "X452.19, Computer-Assisted Instruction (CAI)." Soon after course formulation began, the Education Department added its approval, authorizing students majoring in Education to take the same course under its number, X319.5. It was believed that elementary and secondary school teachers, as well as those in business and industry, should have first-hand knowledge and laboratory experience in preparing CAI.

Approval by the Education Department

It has been our experience, based upon ten years of university adjunct teaching, that graduate students will seek courses of an interdisciplinary nature in other departments or schools within the same university if their major departments do not offer appropriate courses. In less frequent but regular situations, graduate students will take a few specialized courses in nearby universities for transfer credit if it can be shown that their institutions do not have a similar offering. In this case, we believed that while the CAI course was offered in the Business Adminstration Department, enrollment might also be extended to students in the Education Department. Thus, the Business Administration Department invited co-sponsor-

---

[7] "UC Extension Keeps the Pros Up to Date," *Business Week,* March 12, 1966, pp. 196-202.

[8] L. C. Silvern, *Fundamentals of Teaching Machine and Programmed Learning Systems.* Los Angeles: Education and Training Consultants, 1964.

ship by the Education Department, and this was subsequently authorized. It should be noted here that few University of California Extension courses are offered by more than one department. Announcements of the course were made by Business Administration and widely distributed, but the same announcement missed the bulletin deadline for Education, so that those in the education field were largely unaware of the course offering. Despite this disadvantage, 15 percent of the students turned out to be employed in the public school system.

The Co-Instructorship

It was immediately evident that a lecture course might be informative, but not very productive, if a main goal was to be the development of instructional programers. While a lecture-laboratory course would be both informative and productive, it would also require access to one or more computer systems, computer software in the form of CAI compilers, time-sharing capability available at times convenient to the class schedules, several student consoles, logistical support such as keypunching, and a considerable degree of understanding by the regular university faculty and personnel who were not disposed towards an extension course requiring a computer laboratory.

As the course development proceeded, it was necessary to obtain approval for a co-instructorship, both to strengthen the broad range of experience in instructional programing plus computer programing, and to provide assistance in instructional and computer program writing and debugging for a large group of students. The authors, as instructors, performed a job synthesis in order to identify and isolate the behavioral objectives and the skills and knowledge which the students should have upon completion of the course. This course was a "first" and, as often happens in such instances, was apt to become a model to be emulated or to be used as a jumping-off point for developing improved versions. Thus, in addition to the immediacy of the task (90 days from inception to the first class session), there was a strong feeling of long term responsibility to the academic community hanging heavily over the entire project.

DETERMINING CONTENT FOR THE CAI COURSE

Job Synthesis

While job analysis may be defined as *separation* of an existing job or set of tasks, job synthesis is the *combination* of various discrete elements into a new whole or "job." Since there are very few

CAI instructional programers, it is not possible to perform a job analysis. . .the occupation simply does not exist. The alternative is to first produce a job synthesis and, periodically, perform job analyses which will update the data file on this occupation and keep it resonant with actual requirements in real-life.

One must exercise care in examining similar occupations, such as instructional programer for programed texts, hoping to select elements of the job which are also thought to be the same for CAI instructional programer. It becomes increasingly clear that the CAI instructional programer must be more familiar than the text developer with audio-visual methodology dealing with CRT (cathode ray tube) graphic displays, film and filmstrip, since the computer can easily accommodate motion while the printed page embodies a static philosophy. This differentiation may be extended to the need to know about data communications and CAI symbology in contrast with the tasks required in PI text preparation. Of course, we are speaking of a rather broad, supervisor-of-the-future kind of instructional programer rather than one who is being educated or trained just to prepare coding sheets.

The job synthesis produced these course objectives:

1. Impart knowledge of programed instruction by having students work their way through a *programed* course on PI;
2. Have students analyze a task and identify performance standards;
3. Produce a course outline and convert this to computer coding sheets ready for punching on cards or tape;
4. Have those students without experience keypunch their own cards, those with knowledge of keypunching arrange for punching service;
5. Impart knowledge of computing systems through classroom instruction;
6. Have students enter and check out their instructional programs on-line at remote consoles tied by telephone lines to one or more time-sharing computers, debug off-line, manually input program corrections on-line, and iterate until an effective instructional program is developed;
7. Impart sufficient knowledge of data communications, advanced input-output devices, etc., to enable students to make reasonably intelligent cost and effectiveness decisions in their real-life environments;
8. Impart an in-depth understanding of CAI behavioral research at universities and companies; identify societies, journals, and individuals which might serve as data sources for post-course follow-up by interested graduates.

Functions of the CAI Instructional Programer

The instructional programer, also known as lesson planner or author, is responsible for developing the instructional program. The instructional programer may be a team of persons or one senior individual with a staff of specialized assistants. In this chapter, the term "instructional programer" may include one or more persons.

The instructional programer initially performs a job and task analysis. In the more traditional academic subjects, this will probably be quite difficult and may result in major alterations in subject-matter content. Next, he establishes behavioral objectives. These goals are expressed in quantitative as well as qualitative terms. Third, he devises criterion tests which measure these behavioral objectives in quantifiable ways. Today, most criterion tests are of the paper-and-pencil variety and are not actually *performance* tests. Next, the instructional programer develops the course outline to the teaching point level, and then he begins writing steps in the lesson plan. This is a long and tedious enterprise. Finally, the instructional program is completed and the evaluation, debugging, and validation begins. There are a number of iterations of this sequence—program, evaluate, debug, and validate—in which numbers of students representing the actual learner population are used for trying out the course.

The instructional programer writes steps in the form of a lesson plan, bearing in mind the flexibility and the constraints of the particular CAI system with which he is working. These are transformed into statements on a coding sheet. In one CAI system, cards may be keypunched and read in or statements may be entered directly through the keyboard of the instructional programer's console. In another system, the statements may be punched on perforated tape and read in from the console. To indicate the magnitude of a CAI program in terms of number of statements, we may start with an assumption that one typical instructional "step" could consist of from 6 to 20 statements. If a typical learner responds to about one step per minute, one hour of CAI would require the inputting of some 360 to 1200 separate statements. This would be equivalent to approximately 1000 to 2000 punched cards. A 45-hour college course worth three units of credit might consume about 45,000 to 90,000 cards; a high school course meeting daily for 55 minutes during a 20-week semester would take approximately 80,000 to 160,000 cards. This does not include programs for special remedial instruction, information retrieval in connection with out-of-class assignments, etc. One may rapidly convert numbers of cards to feet of perforated tape to appreciate the

```
SEQUENCE   NAME/OP        TEXT                                  PAGE  1

    .9   P001
   1.0         PR       A FORTRAN PROGRAM WILL REQUIRE NUMERICAL INFORMATION TO BE USED IN PERFORMING
                       THE COMPUTATIONS. NOW YOU WILL LEARN HOW NUMBERS ARE REPRESENTED IN FORTRAN.
   1.9   P002
   2.0         QU       NUMERICAL INFORMATION MAY BE CLASSIFIED AS BEING CONSTANT OR VARIABLE. A CONS
                       TANT HAS A SPECIFIC NUMERICAL VALUE WHICH DOES NOT CHANGE. A VARIABLE IS A SY
                       MBOLIC REPRESENTATION OF A VALUE WHICH MAY CHANGE. WHAT DO WE CALL A SPECIFIC
                        NUMERICAL VALUE WHICH DOES NOT CHANGE /
   3.0         CA      A CONSTANT
   4.0         TY       A CONSTANT IS CORRECT.
   5.0         CB      CONSTANT
   6.0         TY       A CONSTANT IS CORRECT.
   7.0         WA      A VARIABLE
   8.0         TY       NO.  A VARIABLE HAS A VALUE WHICH VARIES OR CHANGES.  TRY AGAIN.
   9.0         WB      VARIABLE
  10.0         TY       NO.  A VARIABLE HAS A VALUE WHICH VARIES OR CHANGES.  TRY AGAIN.
  11.0         UN       PLEASE CHECK YOUR SPELLING AND TRY AGAIN.
  12.0         UC       YOUR ANSWER SHOULD HAVE BEEN   A CONSTANT.
  12.9   P003
  13.0         QU       A CONSTANT IS ANY NUMBER USED IN COMPUTATION WHOSE VALUE DOES NOT CHANGE FROM
                       ONE USE TO THE NEXT. IT APPEARS IN ITS ACTUAL NUMERICAL FORM. WHICH OF THE F
                       OLLOWING IS NOT A CONSTANT /        3     12.5     X     3.14159
  14.0         CA      X
  15.0         TY       YES, X REPRESENTS A VARIABLE AND IS NOT A CONSTANT.
```

Fig. 85 — Computer-Generated Listing of a CAI Instructional Program Using Coursewriter Language.
Courtesy of Education and Training Consultants

logistics aspect of instructional programing. However, punched cards and perforated tape are utilized mainly to *enter* the instructional program initially; it is normally stored on magnetic tape or disk files for operating purposes.

Having entered the entire course, several sections or even a few lessons, the instructional programer obtains a listing, such as the one on Figure 85. He then takes the program in the role of a student, as shown in Figure 86; this is done to debug the program as well as to obtain at first hand a feeling of the learner-machine communication flow. Next, the instructional programer uses a larger sample of five to ten individuals from the same student population as his target population. The instructional programer later arranges to conduct one or more larger-scale tryouts under controlled field conditions. Large CAI courses intended for large school populations will require considerable effectiveness testing and have many iterations of tryout, debugging, improving, etc., before final validation.

```
WE HAVE ALREADY REFERRED TO THE INTERSECTION OF THE CROSS-
HAIRS AS THE CIRCLE.  IT IS MORE ACCURATE TO CALL IT:  IRIS

   (NEXT SLIDE --> 48)

BEFORE PRESSING THE LOCK-ON SWITCH, THE PILOT MUST BE SURE
THE TARGET IS INSIDE THE -----.

?CIRCLE
CIRCLE IS CORRECT, BUT IRIS IS A BETTER TERM TO USE.  IT'S
MORE ACCURATE TO SAY:  THE TARGET IS INSIDE THE -----.

?IRIS
YOU'VE GOT YOUR EYE ON THE BALL.  (GET IT?)

THE TARGET APPEARS IN THE IRIS. THE PILOT PRESSES THE LOCK-
ON SWITCH.  THE LASER IS MOUNTED INSIDE A LARGE GYROSCOPE.
AT THIS MOMENT, THE GYRO IS 'UNCAGED'....MEANING IT IS FREE
TO MOVE IN ALL FORWARD-LOOKING DIRECTIONS.  THE LASER IS
LOOKING DIRECTLY AT THE TARGET.  IF THE AIRCRAFT SHOULD
MOVE A LITTLE OFF TARGET, THE LASER WOULD BE LOCKED-ON THE
TARGET AND SWING AS THE AIRCRAFT TURNS AWAY.

SO, YOU CAN SAY THAT THE LASER WILL LOOK AT THE TARGET EVEN
IF THE AIRCRAFT IS LOOKING IN A SLIGHTLY DIFFERENT DIRECTION.
THE LASER, MEANING EYBOL, IS TRACKING THE TARGET.

FOR THE GYRO TO BE 'UNCAGED' AND TRACKING, WHAT ACTION BY
THE PILOT MUST HAVE OCCURRED AN INSTANT BEFORE?

?LOCK-ON
TRUE...THERE IS LOCK-ON, BUT TO OBTAIN IT, WHAT ACTION BY
THE PILOT MUST HAVE OCCURRED AN INSTANT BEFORE?

?HE MUST HAVE DEPRESSED THE LOCK-ON SWITCH
ROGER.

      (NEXT SLIDE --> 49)

WHILE TRACKING WITH EYBOL, THE PILOT IS ALLOWED SOME
VARIATION IN AIRCRAFT ATTITUDE.  WITHIN THESE LIMITS, AND
FOR ANY COMBINATION OF THESE MOVEMENTS, THE LASER WILL
TRACK AND KEEP LOCK-ON.  IF HE EXCEEDS THESE LIMITS, HE WILL
LOSE LOCK-ON.  WHAT WILL HAPPEN IF HE YAWS 3 DEGREES?

?LOSE LOCK-ON
GOOD THINKING.  HE LOSES LOCK-ON.

WHAT WOULD HAPPEN TO HIS LOCK-ON IF HE PITCHES 1 DEG, YAWS
1 DEG, AND ROLLS 1 DEG SIMULTANEOUSLY?

?NOTHING
OKAY.  SINCE HE IS WITHIN 1 DEGREE IN EACH ATTITUDE, HE WILL
REMAIN LOCKED-ON HIS TARGET.

SUPPOSE HE PITCHES 1 DEG, ROLLS 2 DEG, BUT DOES NOT YAW?

?HE WILL LOSE LOCK-ON
BY ROLLING 2 DEG, HE LOSES LOCK-ON.

   (NEXT SLIDE --> 50)

WHICH COMBINATION OF VALUES (IN DEGREES) IS POSSIBLE DURING
LOCK-ON? (TYPE A, B, C, D, E OR F)
```

Fig. 86 — Learner-Computer Communication Flow (The Computer Asks for a Response by Printing and the Instructional Programer in His Role of Learner Types His Reply; the Instructional Program Was Written Using Lyric Language.)

Courtesy of Education and Training Consultants

Establishing and Measuring Behavioral Objectives

With the background of a job synthesis and a fairly precise image of the instructional programer in mind, the next stage was to develop a number of major behavioral objectives. For a "first" course, these were somewhat ambitious, but post-course evaluations revealed that considerable progress had been made in achieving them.

1. Student should be able to describe in detail the various methods of developing programed instruction steps in text format;
2. Student should be conversant with methods of analyzing existing jobs, establishing performance standards, measuring performance, creating course outlines, developing teaching points, creating validation studies and improving materials as the result of practical feedback techniques;
3. Student should be able to produce a job analysis of a mental-manipulative activity from a stimulus consisting of human functions which are either recorded on color film and displayed repetitiously, approximately 25 times, or portrayed in real-life and similarly repeated in a natural manner;
4. Student should be able to produce a simple course outline to the teaching point level for a mental-manipulative job which is to be instructed using CAI;
5. Student should be able to write a CAI program in Coursewriter language, using his previously prepared course outline to the teaching point level;
6. Student should prepare punched cards, have them entered into a computer such as the IBM 1410 CAI time-sharing system, manually take his course on-line as a learner, debug off-line, manually insert modifications on-line, obtain and interpret listings off-line, debug off-line, and iterate until an effective CAI program is produced;
7. Student should be able to describe no fewer than two additional CAI systems, as well as the fundamental specifications for a CAI compiler;
8. Student should be able to explain data communications flow from learner to computer and return.

Having established these behavioral objectives, it was essential that practical instruments be created for measuring them.

The first two objectives were measured by 10 unit self-tests and a post-test in the *Fundamentals of Teaching Machine and Programed Learning Systems* programed course.[9] Chapter Appendix A, Lesson 1.2 and *Notes,* indicate that a progress curve and all scores

[9] *Ibid.*

were to be submitted by the students on or before the eighth class meeting. Students in the CAI class obtained a mean post-test score of 377.1, with 420 equivalent to a perfect score. The range of scores was 319 to 413. This data conforms closely with scores in similar groups.[10,11]

The third objective was measured through the critical examination of student-submitted job analyses. These resulted from direct exposure of the class to an 8mm, endless loop, color film presentation, using the Technicolor 800 Magi-Cartridge projector. For individuals who wished further viewing in motion or in single frame mode, three hand-held ETC Viewers were used advantageously; they could project one single frame of the film for student examination of a small detail, advance frame by frame, or display either forward or backward motion. The subject was a mental-manipulative job, "Writing a Check," taken from the *Basic Analysis* programed course.[12] It was shown at the second class meeting, 23 times repetitively, with each exposure requiring 130 seconds.

The fourth objective was measured through the critical examination, after the third class meeting, of student-submitted COTPs (Course Outline to the Teaching Point Level), Later changes in the COTP resulted from accomplishment of objectives 5 and 6.

Students Required to Write a CAI Program

The fifth and sixth objectives were the most important, since they required each student to write and improve the effectiveness of an actual CAI instructional program. Writing began during the eighth class meeting, and all computer-centered laboratory activities involving student-prepared CAI instructional programs were concluded by the 12th class meeting. Measurement of student performance was accomplished by a combination of critical examinations of instructional programs by the instructors and intrinsic measurement by the students. The latter resulted from feedback in the form of computer diagnostics or hang-up, incorrect output and other error indications obtained from listings, and directly from the computer while on-line during the time the students enacted the roles of "learners" taking their instructional programs.

The last two objectives required proficiency of expression on a

---

[10] L. C. Silvern, *Administrative Factors Guide to the Fundamentals Course.* Los Angeles: Education and Training Consultants, 1964.

[11] *Feedback on Fundamentals.* Los Angeles: Education and Training Consultants, February 1965.

[12] L. C. Silvern, *Basic Analysis.* Los Angeles: Education and Training Consultants, 1965.

variety of system elements. These objectives were not tested, since time had run out at the end of the course for a comprehensive written examination. While it was initially intended to conduct a comprehensive paper-and-pencil examination by the 15th and final meeting, time permitted only a written student evaluation of the course. With a choice of one or the other, the decision made by the instructors was for written feedback.

DEVISING METHODS FOR TEACHING THE COURSE

The Computer Laboratory Philosophy

Instructional programing is one of many activities which is not best learned through lecture or reading methods. The knowledge and skills required for CAI instructional programing are more complex than those required for conventional programed instruction by a factor of 3 to 10. This depends upon the extent of integrated audio-visual media (CRT, slides, microfiche, filmstrip, film, sound film, soundstrip, synchronized audio, etc.) and learner-computer "conversational" interaction. Instructional programers who were successful in developing programed texts may encounter frustration and failure when preparing CAI programs. Much of this may be attributed to the increased care and meticulousness demanded by CAI, since both the instruction and the computer are being programed at the same time. A computer will follow the directions given it by the instructional programer—this is not quite the same as a pencil following the directions of the instructional programer who writes a programed text. Consequently, only those persons who are able to exercise great care while programing can be expected to produce programs that require a minimum of debugging. In some cases, it may be advisable to include an editor on the instructional programing team. There is no substitute for guided experience on-line, and this philosophy was embodied in the "computer laboratory" portion of the course.

Despite some opinions to the contrary, we believe it should be mandatory for the instructional programer to interact on-line with his program as a "learner" during the early phases of programing. While it may appear advisable to break up a long course into units to be assigned to different programers, we feel strongly that more effective programing will result from the efforts of fewer individuals, especially from the interfacing, debugging, and iteration viewpoints.

To meet the behavioral objectives, nonparticipative demonstrations were deemphasized in favor of practical "hands-on" experience with the computer. Programed texts were used wherever feasible; classroom instruction was given on those parts for which programed texts were not available. Tutorial methods, in which both instructors provided guidance and assistance, were used during debugging sessions.

Course Outline for the CAI Course

Three versions of the course outline to the lesson level were developed. The first was published on 16 November 1965 for distribution at the 1965 Fall Joint Computer Conference, Las Vegas, Nevada, for comment by interested educators and computer-oriented individuals.[13] It was revised as the result of feedback and additional conferences with university personnel and manufacturer representatives.[14] The final course outline, further revised after the course ended to reflect changes in content and emphasis during the course, appears in Chapter Appendix A. An expanded version, now in use, appears in Chapter Appendix B.

Classroom Instruction

Classroom instruction in a university course is typically instructor-centered with students taking notes, asking questions, etc. This course followed the same routine except that classroom presentations were accompanied by screen projections using 8mm color motion picture film, slides, overhead transparencies, slide-tape presentations and audio taped presentations. In Lessons 5.1 and 5.8 (see Chapter Appendix A), closed-circuit television with two 23" TV monitors was used in the computer laboratory to enable the class to see the printer-keyboard readout, as shown in Figure 87. However, there was no reason to use CCTV in the classroom presentations, often the conventional application of the medium.

The two instructors contributed their knowledge and services in several ways. Between them, their expertise covered all portions of the course, with enough overlap to insure suitable interfacing. A coordinated outcome was achieved by integrated planning of the shared instruction. One instructor presented the instructional programing and engineering aspects, while the other covered computer programing and computer systems. Also, it was the standard practice for both instructors to be present in class to furnish technical data in response to questions. The diversity of student backgrounds invariably required responses and clarification by both instructors at each session. The major benefit of the co-instructorship, however,

[13] *Class Procedures*. Los Angeles, University of California Extension, Revised Summer 1965, pp. 1-10.

[14] L. C. Silvern, *Communication*, to M. Sapiro, University of California Extension, Ref: 9.3.1.6; May 6, 1966.

Fig. 87 – Closed Circuit Television (CCTV) Was Used in the Computer Laboratory to Enable the Group to See the Printer-Keyboard Readout.
Courtesy of University of California

was in the computer laboratory, where both were available to assist students in debugging, answering questions, etc., while the 20 students took turns interacting with the three consoles.

Computer Laboratory

The first exposure to hardware came in Lesson 3.2 (see Chapter Appendix A). After some introductory material was presented in class, the group was conducted through the Western Data Processing Center in the Graduate School of Business Administration, where special attention was given to the IBM 1410 computer which was later to be used in the course for part of the CAI computer laboratory. The computer operator's console is being explained in Figure 88. While a tour does not provide the most desirable introduction to computers, it does give those unfamiliar with computers a picture of the hardware with which they will be communicating later in the course. Outsides, rather than insides, of the "black boxes" were examined.

In Lesson 5.1, a representative of IBM Data Processing Division demonstrated a special CAI instructional program using the computer in Yorktown Heights, New York, and a 1052 printer-keyboard in the computer laboratory at UCLA. The session lasted for more than an hour, during which long distance telephone circuits were maintained over the 3,200 mile network (see Fig. 89.) While the students were not able to interact with the program at the 1052, CCTV did make every computer printout visible to all attendees, and it was well worth the efforts of the instructors and the computer manufacturer. As may be seen at the end of Chapter Appendix A, graduate students were invited to this demonstration from a nearby institution, the University of Southern California, where one of the instructors had been Adjunct Professor of Education.

For Lesson 5.5, a special instructional program, *Learndo,* was prepared by the instructors, which forced the student at the console to go through and check various switches and switch positions on the keyboard panel and pedestal. This was the first personal exposure to CAI at a console, and it required about 15 minutes to complete. To ease the load during class laboratory sessions, students were encouraged to make appointments to visit the computer laboratory between class sessions to take *Learndo* and become familiar with the 1052 console. It is the view of the instructors that this introduction aided in breaking the tension between man and machine, preparing each student for the moment when he would sit at the same console debugging his instructional program! In Figure 90 is depicted a typical student-machine relationship in the *Learndo* program.

Fig. 88 – The IBM 1410 Computer Used at UCLA for CAI Is Explained During the Tour. *Courtesy of Education and Training Consultants*

Fig. 89 – Demonstration of a CAI Instructional Program Using the IBM Computer in Yorktown Heights, New York, and an IBM 1052 Student Console at UCLA.

Courtesy of University of California

In preparation for entering their instructional programs into the IBM 1410 computer, students converted the teaching points developed in Lessons 2.5 and 2.6 into instructional steps in 5.2 and 5.3. Using Coursewriter, a language developed by IBM for instructional programing, the steps were transformed by the students into Coursewriter statements which were hand-printed on 80-column coding sheets as shown in Figure 91, and than keypunched into 80-column Hollerith cards before Lesson 5.6. Students were encouraged either to keypunch these cards themselves, especially if they had no keypunch exposure, or to have them keypunched at their companies. The Western Data Processing Center was unable to handle keypunching, although an 026 keypunch machine was available for students' use. Cards which had been keypunched were submitted to the console operator before Lesson 5.6 and were read into the computer in time for the computer laboratory session. By the time Lesson 5.6 began, all students had interacted with *Learndo*, were familiar with the operation of the console, and had already registered with the CAI system as students and as in-

```
WHAT IS A SYNONYM FOR 1052?
TYPEWRITER
IT LOOKS AND ACTS LIKE A TYPEWRITER BUT IT ISN'T.  TRY AGAIN.
TYPFWRITER
SORRY ABOUT THAT, CHIEF, TRY AGAIN.
TYPEWRITE
SORRY ABOUT THAT, CHIEF, TRY AGAIN.
STUDENT TERMINAL
THE FIRST SWITCH YOU CHECK IS NOT LOCATED ON THE PANEL.  IT IS LOCATED ON THE
PEDESTAL.  WHICH SWITCH IS IT?
POWER ON POWER OFF
NO. WHILE IT IS LABELED FOR THOSE TWO POSITIONS, IT IS NOT POWER ON POWER OFF.
TRY AGAIN PLEASE.
POWER ON, POWER OFF
NO.  IT IS THE MAIN-LINE SWITCH WHICH YOU EXAMINE TO SEE IF IT IS IN "POWER ON" POSITION.
ONCE THE MAIN-LINE SWITCH IS ENERGIZED, YOU SET THE PANEL SWITCHES.
LOOK AT YOUR PANEL SWITCH LABELED EOB.  WHAT POSITION IS IT IN NOW?
MANUAL
IT SHOULD NOT BE IN "MANUAL"...REACH UP AND MOVE TO "AUTO"
MANUAL
IT SHOULD NOT BE IN "MANUAL"...REACH UP AND MOVE TO "AUTO"
AUTO
LOOK AT THE SWITCH IN THE EXTREME LEFT ON THE PANEL.  THE SYSTEM SWITCH IS IN
WHAT POSITION?
UNATTEND
IF IT IS IN "UNATTEND" THEN MOVE TO "ATTEND"
ATTEND
IN WHAT POSITION DO YOU FIND THE SWITCH JUST TO THE RIGHT OF THE SYSTEM SWITCH...
THE PRINTER 1 SWITCH?
"REC"
INCORRECT.  LOOK AGAIN
"REC"
INCORRECT.  LOOK AGAIN
SEND
INCORRECT.  LOOK AGAIN
HELP
LOOK AT IT ONCE AGAIN.
SEND REC
```

Fig. 90 – Section of Student Readout From **Learndo,** a CAI Instructional Program, to Acquaint Students With the IBM 1052 Printer-Keyboard.

Courtesy of Education and Training Consultants

Fig. 91 – Statements of a CAI Instructional Program Are Handprinted on Coding Sheets.

Courtesy of Education and Training Consultants

structional programers—or "authors" as they are known in the Coursewriter system. Students were assigned to consoles, with scheduling preference given to those who had submitted their decks of punched cards earliest. When a student completed his turn at the console, he moved to a desk for debugging and revising his program, (see Fig. 91) using listings which were obtained from the computer operator. When all those who had working programs were finished with the first phase, students were reassigned to consoles to manually enter the necessary corrections to their programs. This process continued through Lesson 5.7 until all available computer time had been utilized. Regrettably, there was never adequate time for all students to completely debug and revise all instructional programs.

In Lesson 5.8, the students received an introduction to the General Electric time-sharing computer system from the Manager of the Los Angeles Information Processing Center This was followed by a technical discussion of data communications by a member of General Telephone's Data Communications Group and pertinent remarks by the instructors, shown in Figure 92. A major

Fig. 92 – Introduction to the CAI Demonstration Is Presented by the Instructors.
Courtesy of General Telephone Company of California

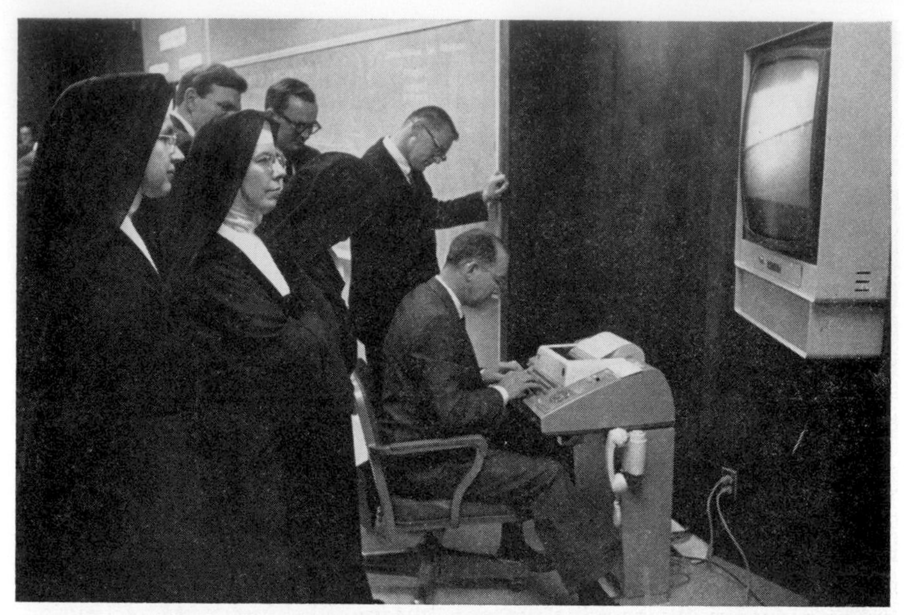

Fig. 93 – Student Interacting With the **Pyros** CAI Instructional Program Using a TT33 Student Console at UCLA Tied by Telephone Lines to the General Electric Time-Sharing Computer System at Phoenix, Arizona.

Courtesy of General Telephone Company of California

part of the class time, more than three hours, was devoted to having students interact with *Pyros*, a CAI instructional program prepared by the instructors in Basic language and stored in the General Electric 265 computer system located at Phoenix, Arizona. Each student took *Pyros* while others watched the printouts on 23″ CCTV monitors, as depicted in Figures 93 and 94. Also, there were many small informal discussion groups in which questions dealing with the instructional and computer programs, computer system and hardware, were answered by the instructors and by General Electric and General Telephone personnel. The computer laboratory phase was concluded with Lesson 5.9.

The instructors believed that the course would progress more smoothly and class discussions would be more meaningful to all students if all received the same problem stimulus in Lesson 2.2, for which they were to develop their CAI programs. While different course outlines were developed (in 2.5-2.6), based upon various instructional programing strategies, the students were all attempting to instruct the same mental-manipulative behaviors, "writing a check." This not only avoided problems involving subject-matter content, it also facilitated instructor assistance in debugging of both the CAI computer programs and the instructional aspects.

Fig. 94 – Student at TT 33 Takes **Pyros** While Instructor (left) Stands by and Student (right) Waits His Turn *Courtesy of General Telephone Company of California*

The actual programs written proved to be quite different from one another; they were named: *Chequit, Xwrite, Chek Reg, DCI, Cullena, Chekit, Rcheckr, Wrtchk, Writeout, Donerite, Chekrite, Ritechek, Chk Wrip,* and *Chktext.* In addition, two special programs, *IRS 1040A* and *IRS 1040B*, were written by two students who had requested that they be allowed to work on a much more complex CAI program for Internal Revenue Service training.

EVALUATING THE COURSE

Student Backgrounds

An examination of the backgrounds of the students is necessary to set the frame of reference for evaluating the course. The academic achievements of the twenty students are described in Table 1, shown below.

TABLE 1.
Academic Achievements of Students

Highest Level of Achievement	Field of Specialization							
	Education			Psych.	Engrg.	Engl.	Philo.	Total
	Instruc. Tech.	Math. Educ.	Educ. Admin.					
Undergraduate				1	4			5
Bachelor's					3	1	1	5
Master's		1	2	2			1	6
Doctor's (Candidate)	2							2
Doctor's				2				2

The variety in fields of specialization might lead one to conclude that the CAI course should be offered in any school of the university except the Business Administration Department! The largest group, constituting one-third of those enrolled, had engineering degrees or undergraduate majors in engineering.

The student group was typical of those found today in programs of continuing education at the graduate level. Mature and serious, they had positions of responsibility in such widely-known technical firms as Astrodata Corporation, Dunlap & Associates, ITT-Gilfillan, Lear-Siegler, National Cash Register, System Development Corporation, and Xerox Corporation. Business and government organizations represented were: Pacific Finance Corporation, Economic Youth Opportunities Agency, the school districts of Beverly Hills, Mira Costa, and Los Virgenes, and several consulting firms. With only three exceptions, all were employed in business or private industry, the others being in public education. Table 2 describes the current occupational activities of the students.

TABLE 2.
Occupational Activities of Students

Current Occupational Level of Responsibility	Psych. Research	Instr. Progmg.	Employee Training	Public Educ.: 10-12 gr.	Comp. Prog.	Comp. Engrg.	Engrg. Communicatn
Managerial	1	2	1	2	2	1	2
Operational	3	1		1	1	1	
Student	1				1		

Only two of the students were female. This ratio conforms closely with our previous experience: we found that, while the number of females in the total work-force in the U.S. was projected at 33.4 percent in 1965, women constituted only about 10 percent of those enrolled in university courses for which the subject-matter was "training" or organized behavior change.[15] The "Fundamentals" course tryout in 1963-64 had an 11.2 percent female population. It appears safe to predict that only about 10 percent of the students who will enroll in CAI courses will be female.

Student Attendance and Attitudes

Attendance was remarkably good. Despite the fact that the course work load and the time required per student was approximately double that expected for a course of 45 hours, the official time assigned to it, the absentee rate for the semester was only 9.3 percent. Five students had no absences during the 15-meeting sequence, several absences were due to a religious holiday, two students were sent on business trips by their employers, and one who was assigned to Washington for a month managed to get himself transferred back to Los Angeles.

In-class attitudes of the group were extremely good. Although there was some grumbling about sessions running overtime, most students were cooperative and appreciated the instructors' efforts to cover the large amount of material—much more than one would normally expect in a 45-hour course. The unusually long out-of-class assignments were also taken in stride.

Student Performance

It is customary to assign mid-semester grades at the University of California; these are based on the A-B-C-E-F system.[16] In this course, three factors were considered: were the assignments completed, what was the quality of the work done, and was it completed on time. Students who satisfied all three factors received A, those who were delinquent in one factor received B, and those delinquent in two factors received C. Grades were assigned independently of attendance records, since students were expected to make up assignments missed during an absence. The grade distribution for mid-semester was: six A's, eight B's, five C's and one N (not-for-credit).

In assigning final grades, the same criteria were applied and the same grade structure was followed. Grade distribution at end-of-course was: seven A's, ten B's and three N's. The improved grades resulted mainly from completion and submission of assignments.

In general, we were satisfied with student performance, con-

---

[15] *Administrative Factors Guide . . ., op. cit.*

[16] *Class Procedures, op. cit.*

sidering that this was a newly created course. However, like most instructors, we feel that there is room for improvement in both method and content. At some future time, prerequisites will probably be established, making introductory courses in programed instruction mandatory. This would alter the entry behaviors of incoming students, so that more sophisticated terminal behaviors would be expected.

Evaluation by the Students

The University requests all students, at the last meeting, to complete anonymously a 28-question "Student-Faculty Reaction Sheet." Anonymity is preserved by having these collected by one student who personally mails them in a single envelope to the Department office. After the semester is over and grades have been submitted, they are usually passed on to the instructors. Of the 28 questions, only four seem to deal with course organization and content evaluation; the others are mainly concerned with clarity of instruction and characteristics of the instructor. Nineteen such student evaluation forms were sent to the instructors by the University. The four most pertinent questions are presented here, together with calibration of the measuring instrument and the range and means of the responses:

4. Is the course as a whole well organized?
   Range: 3 to 5 — 5 4 3 2 1
   Mean: 4.50 — (ORG) (DISORG)

8. Is the speed scale appropriate on each course topic?
   Range: 2 to 5 — 5 4 3 2 1
   Mean 3.38 — (ALWAYS) (NEVER)

17. Are the examinations adequately designed to test the application of your knowledge of this course?
   Range: 3 to 5 — 5 4 3 2 1
   Mean: 4.50 — (ALWAYS) (NEVER)

23. Are the assignments helpful to your understanding of this course?
   Range: 3 to 5 — 5 4 3 2 1
   Mean: 4.50 — (ALWAYS) (NEVER)

One of the greatest problems in the course was time—there simply wasn't enough of it. This is reflected in the lower mean of 3.38 for Question 8 which involves the pace at which various lessons were conducted in the frame of reference of the students' previous knowledge and experience. It is also reflected in the following comments made by the students in response to Question 5, "Recommendations or explanations regarding course organization":

- "too much material in outline to be covered adequately"
- "break course into two or more courses"
- "the course should be expanded to allow more time. . ."

If the instructors' recommendations for an improved version of the course are followed, the additional time should permit a more satisfactory speed scale (see Chapter Appendix B).

RECOMMENDATIONS FOR AN IMPROVED VERSION OF THE CAI COURSE

We believe that several different kinds of CAI courses will be essential in the coming years. At the present time, an organization, be it a school district, a military installation or a business enterprise, cannot simply issue a purchase order for CAI in the same manner that it purchases programed texts! First, a CAI facility is required, which would have to be designed, with compatible compiler software and computer hardware. Developed to satisfy specific needs, the actual installations and implementations might be as varied as the different organizations. Those responsible for designing the CAI facility will require an in-depth understanding of CAI, including the instructional programing aspect. However, they would not have to be instructional programers. Thus, we visualize a course for CAI *managers* which would satisfy the behavioral objectives outlined earlier in this chapter.

Later, a more sophisticated course should be established for the *instructional programer*, with the previous course as a prerequisite. This second course would be confined almost completely to methods of instructional programing in a wide variety of CAI modes, including visual and audio-visual, with little if any reference to programed texts and non-CAI teaching machines. This instruction should be machine-independent; that is, it should not be restricted to programing methods for a particular computer or the computers of any one manufacturer.

The CAI course which has been described in this chapter, and for which recommendations are being presented, is designed to prepare the future CAI supervisor or manager for the task of creating and operating a CAI installation. It is, in other words, a course in CAI *installation management* and, perhaps for that reason, is well suited as an offering in a university's school of business or public administration.

CURRICULUM FOR THE REVISED CAI COURSE

By the end of our CAI course, it was possible to prepare a set of recommendations to the University of California.[17] The reader

[17] *Comm.*, Ref: 9.3.1.6, *op. cit.*

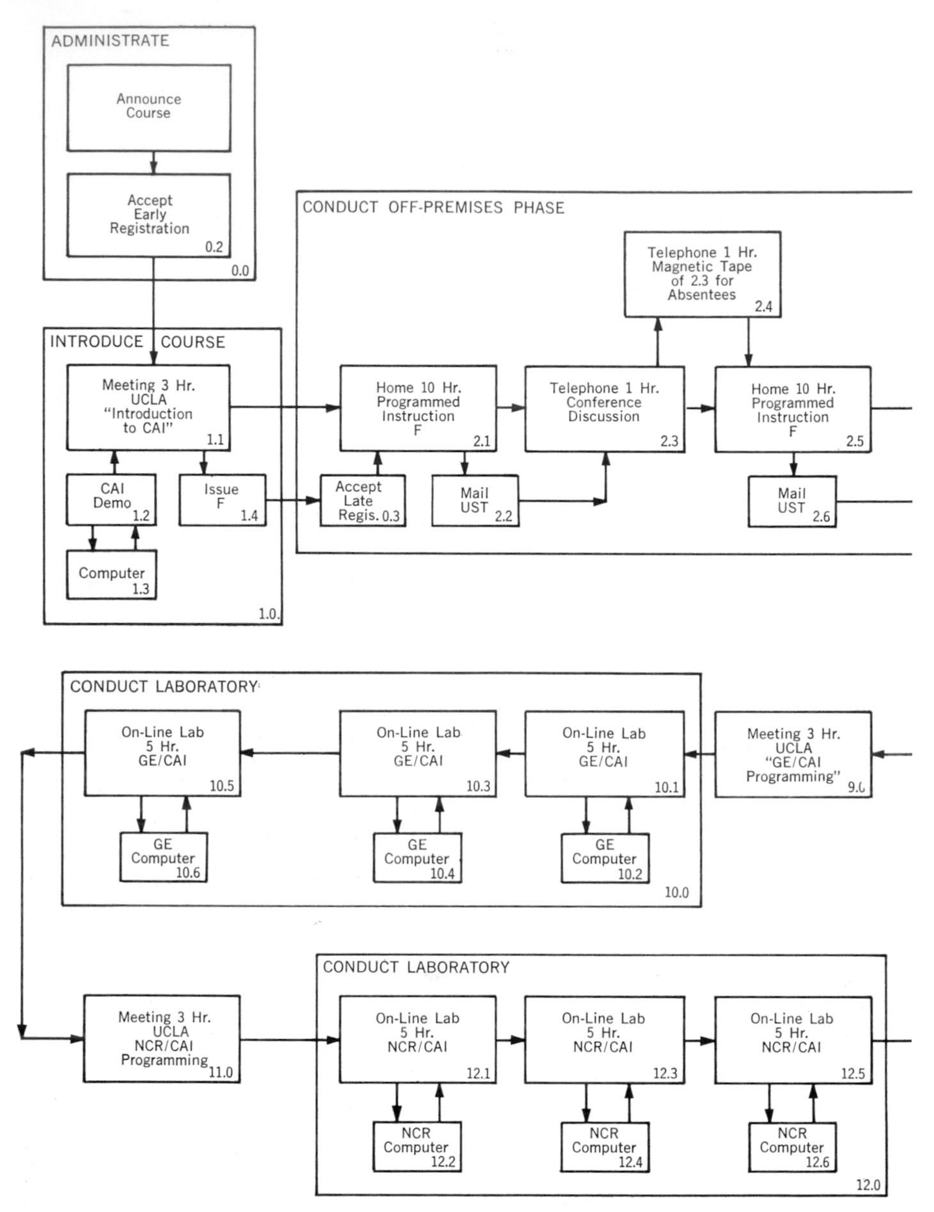

Fig. 95 – Flowchart Depicting Recommended 94-Hour CAI Course.
Courtesy of Education and Training Consultants

is asked to refer now to flowchart, Figure 95 along with the following commentary.

1. The method of instruction should go beyond the lecture-laboratory. 94 hours are recommended, comprised of 33 hours of actual

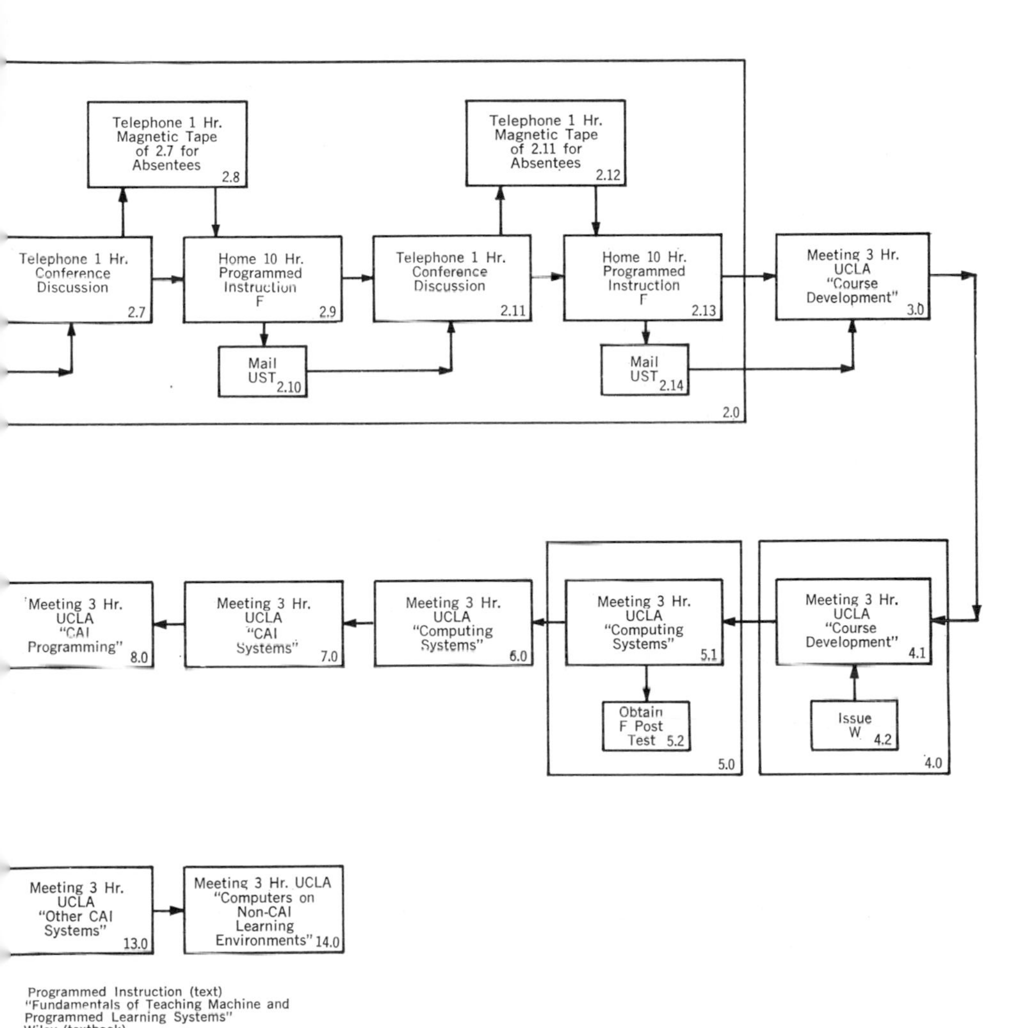

group classroom instruction on campus (four meetings), 18 hours of computer laboratory which may be at non-campus locations where student consoles would be available (six sessions), three one-hour live group discussions by conference telephone, and 40 hours of individualized programed instruction taken at home or office. The programed instruction phase includes mailing of unit self-tests to the instructors. In addition, for those students who wish to review the recorded telephone discussions or who are unable to participate in one or more telephone conference sessions, several hours may be devoted to retrieval by telephone of the recorded group discussions.

2. The official 45-hour time period should be increased to 94 hours, with credit given for that number of hours. Traditional "homework" assignments would be in addition to the 94 hours.
3. The telephone conference network should be supplemented with new and innovative devices, such as the Sylvania Blackboard-by-Wire being produced by General Telephone and Electronics. The wholistic concept of *time-sharing* and the *remote* console, when fully embraced and implemented, should take instruction *to the student rather than require the student to seek out instruction* (and a parking place) at UCLA. This argument holds mainly for adult continuing education in urban and suburban communities where students are less interested in university social activity and more in concentrating their few spare hours on keeping up with their professional fields or acquiring an advanced degree.
4. The major change from the original course would be an *expansion* of time in the computer laboratory. All that is actually needed for the computer laboratory are a number of student consoles remotely located and accessible through an appointment schedule. There seems to be no critical need to tour the computer facility itself. Students should become familiar with punched tape as well as punched card input and output. Each student should have no fewer than three hours of on-line time, the bulk of this as an instructional programer and the rest in the role of a learner.
5. The practice of presenting at least *two* different CAI computing systems, for which approximately equal class and computer laboratory time would be devoted, is strongly recommended.
6. Performance tests should be developed to measure incoming behavior and end-of-course achievement. This would provide a measurement of course effectiveness in acceptable, quantifiable units.

CHAPTER APPENDIX A

BUSINESS ADMINISTRATION X 452.19 & EDUCATION X 319.5

UNIVERSITY OF CALIFORNIA EXTENSION
Los Angeles

"COMPUTER-ASSISTED INSTRUCTION (CAI)"

Spring 1966

Dr. G.M. Silvern
North American Aviation Inc.

and

Dr. L.C. Silvern
Education and Training Consultants Co.

(45 Hours*)

Meeting	Date	Unit		Lesson	Time(min)
1	7 Feb	1.0 Introduction to CAI	1.1	Individual Interests of Students	40
			%@ 1.2	Course Announcements	30
			1.3	Discussion of Course Outline	50
			1.4	Concept of the Systems Engineering of Learning	60
2	14 Feb	2.0 Overview of Programmed Instruction	@ 2.1	Techniques of Basic Analysis	15
			2.2	Selecting and Examining a Mental-Manipulative Job	25
			2.3	Developing the Job and Task Analysis	50
			2.4	Identifying Performance Standards of Tasks	20
			2.5	Producing the Course Outline to the Teaching Point Level (COTP)	70
3	21 Feb		2.6	Complete 2.5 and Evaluate for CAI	80
			2.7	Developing Post-Test and Pre-Test	50
			2.8	Establishing Tryout and Validation Criteria	50
4	28 Feb		2.9	Discussion of Programmed Text and Text-Workbook Design; Examination of Off-the-Shelf Materials	90
			2.10	Review "Systems Engineering of Learning" Sound-Filmstrip, 1.4	46
			2.11	Characteristics of General-Purpose Teaching Machines (Non-CAI); Examination of Machines	40
			2.12	Characteristics of Special-Purpose Teaching Machines (Non-CAI)	20
			2.13	Characteristics of Performance Aids and Communication Aids (Non-Computerized)	30
5	7 Mar	3.0 Overview of Computing Systems	3.1	Introduction to Data Processing and Computing	10
			3.2	Elements of a Computer; Tour UCLA Western Data Processing Center and Examine CAI Computer	65
			3.3	Concepts of Stored Program and Flow Charting	20
			3.4	Steps in the Computer Solution of a Problem	10
			3.5	Programming Languages	25
			3.6	Programming Systems	20
			3.7	Applications of DP in Learning Environments	20
6	14 Mar		3.8	Concept of Time-Sharing	30
			3.9	On-Line Remote Consoles	20
			3.10	Data Flow Between Man and Computer Program	40
			3.11	Languages Used in Data Flow at Interface	40
			3.12	Printer-Keyboard Devices at Interface	50
7	21 Mar		3.13	Keyboard Coupling and Audiovisual Displays and Devices at Interface	30
			3.14	Light Guns and Light Pens as CRT Control Devices	50
		4.0 CAI Instructional Systems	4.1	Concept of the Instructional System	10
			4.2	Large CAI Systems	15
			4.3	Characteristics of Computer Programmers	10
			4.4	Characteristics of CAI Instructional Programmers	15
			4.5	Characteristics of Learner at Learner-Computer Interface	15
			4.6	Introduction to IBM CAI COURSEWRITER (Announced)	70
8	28 Mar	5.0 General-Purpose Teaching Machines (CAI)	$ 5.1	Demonstration IBM CAI COURSEWRITER (Announced) On-Line with Yorktown Heights Computer Using 1052 Console (Computer Laboratory)	80
			5.2	Writing Instructional Programs Using IBM CAI COURSEWRITER (Unofficial version at WDPC)	150
9	4 Apr		5.3	Developing Task Using IBM CAI COURSEWRITER (Unofficial version at WDPC); Using Coding Sheets	200
			# 5.5	(Students take LEARNDØ upon appointment during week; Computer Laboratory)	30
10	11 Apr		# 5.5	LEARNDØ CAI Program Using 3 IBM 1052, Computer Laboratory	40
			# 5.6	First On-Line Entry and Checkout Using 3 IBM 1052, Computer Laboratory; Off-Line Debugging at Desk	140

CHAPTER APPENDIX A (Continued)

Meeting	Date	Unit	Lesson	Time(min)
11	18 Apr		# 5.7 Second On-Line Checkout Using 3 IBM 1052, Computer Laboratory; Off-Line Debugging at Desk	250
12	25 Apr		$ 5.8 Introduction to General Electric Time-Sharing	40
			#$ 5.9 Demonstration PYRØS CAI Program Using GE Time-Sharing Computer and 2 Gen Tel TT 33 Student Consoles On-Line with Phoenix Computer	200
13	2 May		5.10 PYRØS Retention Test #1 (168 hr lapse) and Analysis	15
			5.11 How BASIC Language was Used to Write PYRØS	30
			5.12 Using CATO Language in Plato III; University of Illinois	20
			5.13 Using MENTOR in BB&N CAI System	10
			5.14 Using AUTHOR in SOCRATES System; University of Illinois	10
			5.15 New CAI Languages Being Developed	10
			5.16 Modification of "Systems Engineering of Learning Flowchart" to Incorporate CAI Techniques	95
14	9 May		5.17 PYRØS Retention Test #2 (336 hr lapse) and Analysis	15
			5.18 Completion of 5.16	35
			5.19 CAI at the University of Pittsburgh	15
			5.20 Study of IBM 1500 CAI System (Announced)	85
			5.21 Synthesis; Application of Principles to Writing CAI Steps; Discovery Techniques	40
15	16 May	6.0 Special-Purpose Teaching Machines (CAI)	6.1 Differentiation with General-Purpose T. M.	10
			6.2 Descriptions of Special-Purpose Machine Systems	35
		7.0 Cost/Effectiveness	7.1 Computer Hardware Costs	20
			7.2 Computer Software Costs; Compiler Requirements	30
			7.3 Instructional Software C/E Ratio	40
			7.4 Societies, Journals, and Sources of Research Information	15
		8.0 Home and Family CAI	8.1 Discussion of the Columbia City Project	15
			8.2 Time-Shared Systems for Home CAI Using Telephone Lines and Amateur Radio Communications	20
			8.3 Closing Discussion; Student Written Evaluation of Course for University of California Extension Office	20

Notes:

Page 1: % "Fundamentals of Teaching Machine and Programmed Learning Systems" Course in programmed form. Requires 40 hrs of out-of-class time. Obtain from UCLA Bookstore. Required. Submit curve of progress and scores on or before 28 March (8th meeting).

* official time = 45 hrs; actual time = 90 hrs.

@ "Basic Analysis" Course in programmed form. Optional. Obtain from UCLA Bookstore. No assignments.

Page 2: $ Master's and Doctoral students from University of Southern California, registered in Advanced Instructional Programming invited. Others by invitation only.

Each student assigned to operate on-line for specified period; two Instructors available for debugging assistance.

CHAPTER APPENDIX B

BUSINESS ADMINISTRATION
UNIVERSITY OF CALIFORNIA EXTENSION
Los Angeles

COMPUTER-ASSISTED INSTRUCTION (CAI) SYSTEMS X 481.3 (SEC. 10)
January 9 - June 5, 1967 at UCLA

Drs. G. M. and L. C. Silvern

(94 Hours)
9 units

Type of Meeting	Date	Unit	Lesson	Time(min)
UCLA Classroom	9 Jan	Introduction to CAI	1.1 Course Introduction	20
			1.2 University Announcements	10
			1.3 Discussion of Course Outline	30
			1.4 Overview of CAI, Including Demonstration of "Elements of EYBOL" -- A CAI Program Using GE 265 Time-Sharing System	90
			+1.5 Instructions for 2.1-2.14	20
Out-of-Class	10-13 Jan	Overview of Programmed Instruction and Teaching Machine Technology	2.1 Take "FUNDAMENTALS" * Lesson 1.1.1 (p. 1) to Lesson 1.4.4 (p. 135), inclusive 1.1.1 General Purpose of the Course 1.1.2 Taking the Pre-Selftest 1.1.3 Using this Programmed Text 1.2.1 Man and the Control of Nature 1.2.2 Human Productivity and Human Error 1.2.3 The System Spectrum 1.2.4 Solutions in Business, Industry and Government for Inadequate Performance 1.2.5 Reengineering the Man 1.2.6 Performance Standards 1.2.7 Unit Selftest 1.3.1 Principles of Analysis 1.3.2 Methods of Analysis 1.3.3 Making an Object Analysis 1.3.4 Making an Action Analysis 1.3.5 Making an Information Analysis 1.3.6 Making a Combined Analysis 1.3.7 Unit Selftest 1.4.1 History of Job Analysis 1.4.2 Principles of Job Analysis (DIG) 1.4.3 Methods of Producing a Job Analysis 1.4.4 Unit Selftest	#
Mail	13 Jan		2.2 Mail Unit Selftests 1.2.7 (p. 47), 1.3.7 (p. 86) and 1.4.4 (p. 134) to Instructors	#
Telephone Conference	16 Jan		2.3 Discuss Lessons 1.1.1 to 1.4.4	60 **
Telephone Review	17-23 Jan		2.4 Recorded Conference 2.3 may be Reviewed by Students; Dial Special Telephone Number	
Out-of-Class	16-20 Jan		2.5 Take "FUNDAMENTALS" Lesson 1.5.1 (p. 136) to Lesson 1.7.11 (p. 270), inclusive 1.5.1 The Concept of Measuring a Job 1.5.2 Analyzing the Standard 1.5.3 Calibrating the Instrument 1.5.4 Identifying the Level of Proficiency on the Job Analysis 1.5.5 Unit Selftest 1.6.1 Principles of Course Development 1.6.2 Converting from Job Analysis to Course Outline 1.6.3 Deciding the BIA Cluster 1.6.4 Selecting the Pattern of a Course 1.6.5 Producing the Course Outline to the Teaching Point Level 1.6.6 Unit Selftest	#

+ * #. All symbols explained on last page.

CHAPTER APPENDIX B (Continued)

9.3.1.6.1

Type of Meeting	Date	Unit	Lesson	Time(min)
			1.7.1 The Concept of Lesson 1.7.2 The Make or Buy Decision 1.7.3 The Text or Machine Decision 1.7.4 Programmed Text Decisions 1.7.5 Page Segment Sequential Designs 1.7.6 Page Segment Vertical Designs 1.7.11 Unit Selftest (First Part)	
Mail	20 Jan		2.6 Mail Unit Selftests 1.5.5 (p. 162), 1.6.6 (p. 210) and 1.7.11 (p. 270) to Instructors	#
Telephone Conference	23 Jan		2.7 Discuss Lessons 1.5.1 to 1.7.6	60 **
Telephone Review	24-30 Jan		2.8 Recorded Conference 2.7 may be Reviewed by Students; Dial Special Telephone Number	
Out-of-Class	23-27 Jan		2.9 Take "FUNDAMENTALS" Lesson 1.7.7 (p. 270) to Lesson 1.8.5 (p. 372), inclusive 1.7.7 General-Purpose Teaching Machines; Non-Branching 1.7.8 General-Purpose Teaching Machines; Branching 1.7.9 The Concept of Scoring and Internal Measurement 1.7.10 Logistics of the Lesson 1.7.11 Unit Selftest (Second Part) 1.8.1 The Gap Between Theory and Practice in Learning Psychology 1.8.2 Theories of Learning 1.8.3 Current Human-Instruction Concepts for Adult Learning 1.8.4 Synthesizing a Composite Set of Principles for Adult Learning in Business, Industry and Government Environments 1.8.5 Unit Selftest	#
Mail	27 Jan		2.10 Mail Unit Selftests 1.7.11 (p. 330) and 1.8.5 (p. 372) to Instructors	#
Telephone Conference	30 Jan		2.11 Discuss Lessons 1.7.7 to 1.8.5	60 **
Telephone Review	31 Jan - 6 Feb		2.12 Recorded Conference 2.11 may be Reviewed by Students; Dial Special Telephone Number	
Out-of-Class	30 Jan - 3 Feb		2.13 Take and Complete "FUNDAMENTALS" Lesson 1.9.1 (p. 373) to Lesson 1.11.2 (p. 440), inclusive 1.9.1 The Matrix Method 1.9.2 Deciding the OAI 1.9.3 Writing Written-Completion Steps 1.9.4 Writing Multiple-Choice, Branching Steps 1.9.5 Unit Selftest 1.10.1 Using Pre- and Post-Tests 1.10.2 Evaluating in the Job Environment 1.10.3 Using Feedback to Improve the Course 1.10.4 Using the Course to Predict Job Performance 1.10.5 Unit Selftest 1.11.1 Taking the Post-Selftest 1.11.2 Calculating the Gain of the Course	#
Mail	3 Feb		2.14 Mail Unit Selftests 1.9.5 (p. 415) and 1.10.5 (p. 438; Post-Selftest 1.11.1 (p. 439) to Instructors	#
UCLA Classroom	6 Feb	CAI Course Development	3.1 Discuss Lessons 1.9.1 to 1.11.2; Return Mailed Assignments	40
			3.2 Examine "Systems Engineering of Learning" Flowchart Model	60

18 description of a plato program to teach computer programing

MYRON URETSKY

DR. MYRON URETSKY *received his PhD from The Ohio State University in 1965 with a major in Accounting and other work in Economics and Mathematics. He received his MBA from the same institution in 1962, and his BBA from The City College of New York in 1961. In addition, he became a Certified Public Accountant in Ohio in 1962.*

His professional experience includes work as a senior accountant, as a graduate assistant and assistant instructor in Accounting at Ohio State Universiy, and as an assistant professor in Accountancy at the University of Illinois. Dr. Uretsky has engaged in research on: development of a course in information system simulation, simulation as a means for measuring information system reliability, and design of computer-assisted programed-learning methods for teaching computer programing.

Dr. Uretsky's publications include a manual of instruction for programing Ohio State's 7094 system. He is a member of several professional organizations, including the American Accounting Association, American Institute of Certified Public Accountants, The Operations Research Society of America, The Institute of Management Sciences, and the Society for Industrial and Applied Mathematics.

The parallel development of learning theory and computer technology provides the basis for a fruitful marriage. Indications that machines can be applied to aid in the learning process are not new; Pressey first suggested it back in 1926.[1] Progress in this direction has continually taken place from then to the present. With the advent of large-scale digital computers, the capability for developing a truly flexible teaching machine was finally realizable. An outstanding example of such is Plato, a computer-controlled teaching system developed at the Coordinated Science Laboratory, University of Illinois.

This chapter describes a study of a college course in computer programing using the Fortran II language. Unlike similar

[1] S. Pressey, "A Simple Apparatus which Gives Tests and Scores—and Teaches," *School and Society*, March 1926.

computer programing courses, this one was taught entirely by a computer-based learning program. The purpose here is to provide some observations of the results obtained, together with an indication of the modifications that are currently being made to increase both the scope and effectiveness of the course. No attempt is made to measure the statistical significance of the observation, since the investigation is primarily of an exploratory nature.[2]

THE NEEDS OF MODERN EDUCATION

Before proceeding to describe the Plato system which was used for this study and its application to teaching computer programing, attention is focused on the need for computer-based education. This brief excursion will demonstrate that computer-based education is so flexible that it can always be educationally sound and consistent with current knowledge of the learning process. Indeed, it can be seen that computer-based education sometimes provides advantages over conventional learning situations.

Motivation for a comprehensive study of computer-based education is intially provided by the economics of education. It is apparent that there are increasing numbers of students for every available teacher. This observation does not refer to any particular level of education; it seems valid at the elementary through post-graduate levels.[3] While many plausible explanations have been presented—the baby boom, low teacher salaries, changing relative status of teachers—they are unimportant from the standpoint of this exposition. The fact remains that there are an increasing number of students to be taught at all levels of the educational system.

The implicitly increasing student-teacher ratio is very important since it probably suggests a concurrent decrease in the ability to meet the needs of the individual students. This immobility in meeting needs is very important since both Tolman[4] and Hull[5] have shown that education is part of the need-satisfying process.

---

[2] This work is being supported in part by the Joint Services Electronic Program (U. S. Army, U. S. Navy, and U. S. Air Force) under Contract No.: DA 28 043 AMC 0073 (E) and by the Advanced Research Projects Agency through the Office of Naval Research under Contract No.: Nonr—3985 (08).

[3] There are indications that the original estimate regarding the extent of the teacher shortage on the college level may have been overestimated. See, for example, Cartter, Allan M. *An Assessment of Quality in Graduate Education.* Washington: American Council on Education, 1966, pp. 1-2.

[4] E. C. Tolman, "Operational Behaviorism and Current Trends in Psychology," *Proceedings of the 25th Anniversary Celebrating the Inaugurating Graduate Studies.* Los Angeles: University of Southern California, 1936, pp. 89-102.

[5] C. L. Hull, *Principles of Behavior.* New York: Appleton-Century-Crofts, 1943.

There is thus a relationship between individual differences and student learning. With the increase in the number of students, comes an increase in the number of different situations facing a teacher. The increasing student-teacher ratio thus tends to indicate that there may be a decreasing ability to meet individual student needs.

One of the advantages of small group teaching situations is a built-in ability to facilitate modification of the teaching strategy to meet the needs of the group. An extreme of this situation is the ability to modify the teaching sequence so that it meets the needs of each individual student. Research in this area tends to indicate that there is benefit to be gained from permitting students to control the direction and rate of their educational progress. Early studies in this area yielded conflicting results. See for example: Briggs,[6] Pressey,[7] Thompson and Tom,[8] Anderson,[9] and Gruber and Weitman.[10] These studies concentrated their attention on group methods of instruction. As such they were often criticizable from the standpoint of maintaining inadequate experimental controls. In a more recent study, Campbell used a programed text orientation to show that there were beneficial results from self-directed study in three subject areas—mathematics, global geography, and history.[11] In each of these areas the emphasis was placed upon problem-solving ability, together with the ability to transfer learning to new situations. In one area, mathematics, maximum benefit was found in those instances where coaching in the use of self-directed methods was given to students. Summarizing, Campbell found that the main benefit observed was a reduction in the time needed to comprehend a given set of material. There was no significant difference in the amount of material learned by the student when compared with students in more traditional learning situations.

---

[6] L. J. Briggs, "Intensive Classes for Superior Students," *Journal of Educational Psychology,* April 1947.

[7] S. Pressey, *Educational Acceleration: Appraisals and Basic Problems.* Bureau of Educational Research Report No. 31. Columbus: The Ohio State University Press, 1949.

[8] O. Thompson and F. Tom. "Comparison of Effectiveness of a Pupil Centered vs. a Teacher-Centered Pattern for Teaching Vocational Agriculture," *Journal of Educational Research,* 1957.

[9] R. Anderson, "Learning in Discussion: A Resume of the Authoritarian Democratic Studies," *Readings in the Social Psychology of Education* (W. Charters and N. Gage, eds.). Boston: Allyn & Bacon, 1963.

[10] H. Gruber and M. Weitman. *Self-Directed Study: Experiments in Higher Education.* Report No. 19. Boulder: University of Colorado Behavior Research Laboratory, April 1962.

[11] V. N. Campbell, *Self-Direction and Programmed Instruction for Five Types of Learning Objectives.* Technical Report No. AIR-D10-12/63-TR(b). Palo Alto, California: American Institute for Research, December 1963.

A significant segment of the value associated with an individualized relationship between the teacher and the pupil is derived from the speed and variability of the feedback that is provided to both the teacher and the pupil. In this sense, the term "feedback" is being used to indicate the stimuli being presented as a result of past actions. Stolurow points out that feedback provides four critical functions needed in the learning process.[12] These four functions are its ability to shift attention, change subject matter cues, change task responses, and alter motivation. Individual students have different needs to be met and different means by which they attempt to satisfy them. It is thus not surprising that a given feedback item or method will influence different students in different ways.

Programed Teaching Devices

As a possible solution to the problems mentioned above, considerable attention has been paid to the use of programed teaching devices. These techniques recognize that most complex tasks can be dissected into a series of simpler tasks. Similarly, the learning of complex tasks can be broken into the problems associated with the learning of a series of simpler tasks. Classical learning theory has viewed this as a simple process of reinforcing correct responses and, perhaps, imposing penalties on incorrect responses.

In the simplest of the programed learning approaches, each student is expected to progress through all of the steps in the learning program. This approach was first proposed by Skinner.[13] It provides the student with a *linear* program that is unable to meet the needs of the individual students. Since all students vary, it is not surprising that some of the students find these programs boringly slow, while others find them excessively rapid.[14]

Another approach to programed learning requires that the student be given alternatives at each point in the program. The next frame presented is always determined by the response provided by the student. This permits increased adaptability to individual student needs. *Intrinsic* programing, first proposed by Crowder, is thus able to use selective reinforcement and punishment

---

[12] L. M. Stolurow, *Teaching by Machine.* Cooperative Research Monograph No. 6. Washington: Office of Education, 1961, pp. 4-5.

[13] B. F. Skinner, *The Behavior of Organisms: An Experimental Analysis.* New York: Appleton-Century-Crofts, 1938.

[14] J. C. Holland, "Teaching Psychology by a Teaching Machine Program." Unpublished report for the Harvard University Department of Psychology, 1960.

to more effectively meet student needs.[15] Even so, this minimally adaptive strategy makes no use of prior information about the needs of individual students, nor does it make use of any information regarding responses prior to the one under consideration.

Contrasted with intrinsic programing is *adaptive* programing, which attempts to make use of all relevant prior information regarding a student's performance.[16] This information includes items such as aptitude, personality test scores, as well as an analysis of past responses in the program. Based upon this information, a student may be required to repeat, remedy, skip, or decelerate. There are indications that an approach such as this is needed to make programed teaching adapt to the needs of individual students. All students do not react similarly to alternative teaching strategies. For example, Briggs found that superior college students learned factual material better when a correction procedure was used within a set of frames.[17] Contrasted with this is the finding by Irion and Briggs, that a prompting method was more effective than a correcting procedure in teaching high school boys map symbols.[18]

Applicability of Computers

There are few alternatives to using a computer as the basis for an effective automated teaching system. It offers advantages over other forms of teaching devices in meeting the needs of both students and educators. This section briefly examines some of these advantages.

The success of a teaching device is intimately related to its ability to meet the needs of students. However, it has already been shown that there is no consistency in these needs. Even when one considers the students taking a single course, their backgrounds and motivations combine to create different sets of needs to be satisfied. Since each of the students has his own unique needs, the teaching strategy should ideally be varied accordingly. In an ideal situation, a class of 30 students would be taught by using 30 differentiated strategies simultaneously. An option such as this is not

---

[15] N. A. Crowder, "Automatic Tutoring by Intrinsic Programming," *Teaching Machines and Programmed Learning* (Lumsdaine and Glaser, eds.). Washington: National Education Association, 1960.

[16] L. M. Stolurow, *op. cit.*

[17] L. J. Briggs, "The Development and Appraisal of Special Procedures for Superior Students and An Analysis of the Effects of Knowledge of Results." Unpublished Doctoral Dissertation, The Ohio State University, 1949.

[18] Irion, A. L. and L. J. Briggs. *Learning Task and Mode of Operation Variables in Use of the Subject-Matter Trainer.* AFPTRC-TR-8. Lowry Air Force Base, Colorado; AF Personnel and Training Center, 1957.

usually feasible, therefore compromises are usually made in an attempt to maximize the benefits, subject to existing constraints and limited resources. These compromises include items such as group lectures and the use of fixed-response formats in teaching machines that can be mass produced.

The advent of the large-scale computer brings with it a possible solution to some of the problems which necessitate extensive compromises. A large-scale computer may be used to guide the lessons of many students simultaneously. By guiding the lesson, it is meant that both the learning sequences and the components of the sequences may be modified to meet the needs of the individual students. Once the computer has been provided with a set of rules enabling it to differentiate between various sets of needs, its computing ability may be utilized to provide individualized teaching. An extreme of this situation would be the case where the student determined his own learning sequence. An example of such a program is described in the paper by Easley, Gelder, and Golden, describing a computer program for teaching students the essence of mathematical proofs.[19] In this case, the sole guidance for the student is provided by presenting him with a set of axioms, rules of logic, and proofs to be derived.

Closely related with the ability to permit the student to control his learning progress, is the ability to handle the scoring of student responses. In this respect, only the computer provides the ability to score and analyze relatively free-form responses. For example, in the Easley, Gelder, and Golden paper, the student responses are graded on the basis of consistency with the rules of logic and prior proofs by the individual student. This same capacity creates the potential for evaluating student responses to determine trends of individual difficulties.

One of the least mentioned advantages for using a computer in this area is its potential as a monitoring device. The ability to measure student reactions as they are taking place goes far beyond a simple tabulation of response types. It conceptually extends to an examination of items such as response rates and patterns of responses. With all the progress indicated in the literature of learning theory, the surface problems have barely been scratched. This powerful device thus provides the ability to maintain previously unavailable records for use in testing various hypotheses. These records provide the researcher with the capability both for examining

---

[19] J. A. Easley, Jr., H. M. Gelder and W. M. Golden. *A Plato Program for Instruction and Data Collection in Mathematical Problem Solving*. CSL Report R-185. Urbana: University of Illinois Coordinated Science Laboratory, 1964.

student reactions and for developing models simulating student performance under varying conditions.

In the remainder of this chapter attention is focused on the Plato system at the University of Illinois. This system possesses all of the requirements for meeting the above specified needs for individualized teaching. It is shown that where limitations do exist, they are due to factors other than current technology constraints.

THE PLATO SYSTEM

The Plato system is a computer-controlled teaching mechanism developed at the Coordinated Science Laboratory of the University of Illinois. This system is currently in its third generation. Earlier models consisted of a single student station connected to a medium size computer,[20] and a two-station version designed to study the problems associated with a multiple-station system.[21] The current version has 20 operating student stations and uses a CDC 1604 computer.[22] For certain very simple learning programs, it is probable that the computer facility can handle up to 1000 student stations.

Organization

The organization of the Plato system is very straightforward. Each of the 20 students is assigned to a student station like that shown in Figure 96. It can be seen from this illustration that the student stations are isolated from each other by a partition, thus providing the ability to obtain separation needed for the maintenance of adequate experimental controls.

Individual student stations consist of a keyset together with a TV display and storage device. Figure 97 illustrates the organization of these stations. In addition to the keyset, TV display, and storage device, all of the student stations share access to a slide selector and the central computer.

Basic to the entire Plato concept are the teaching programs contained in the computer. These programs may be divided into two groups, inquiry logics and tutorial logics. The inquiry logic provides the student with a series of problems together with a syntax for

[20] D. Bitzer, W. Lichtenberger and P. Braunfeld, "PLATO: An Automatic Teaching Device," *IRE Transactions on Education E-4.* 1961, pp. 157-61.

[21] D. Bitzer, W. Lichtenberger and P. Braunfeld, "PLATO II: A Multiple-Student Computer-Controlled Teaching Machine," Programmed Learning and Computer-Based Instruction (J. E. Coulter, ed.). New York: Wiley, 1962, pp. 205-16.

[22] D. L. Bitzer, E. R. Lyman and J. A. Easley, Jr. *The Uses of Plato: A Computer-Controlled Teaching System.* CSL Report R-268. Urbana: University of Illinois Coordinated Science Laboratory, 1965.

Fig. 96 – A Plato Student Station, Showing the Keyset Together With the TV Display.

requesting additional, pre-stored, or simulated information from the computer. Primary emphasis of this self-directed logic is placed upon the student's ability to perceive and organize relevant data-problem relationships.[23]

[23] *Ibid.*

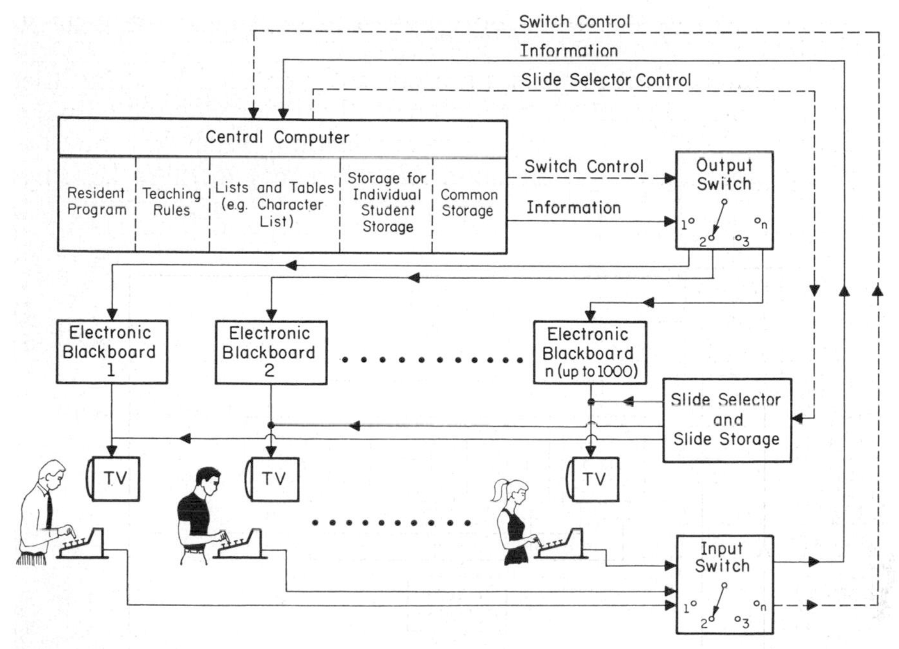

Fig. 97 – Organization of the Plato System.

The currently described investigation makes use of a tutorial logic. These logics lead the student through a learning sequence by presenting him with material, analyzing his response, and then taking action on the basis of this analysis. Since many readers may be unfamiliar with this particular logic, a brief description follows. A more complete description is found in *The Uses of Plato: A Computer-Controlled Teaching System.*[24] The sequence of operations being described, together with the options available, are illustrated in Figure 98. It will be helpful for the reader to refer to this illustration while reading the following description.

Information is provided to the students by one of two methods. First, each student station shares access to a central slide selector which provides random access to 122 slides. The actions taken at the student stations are independent, thus the 20 stations may simultaneously be using the same or different slides. In many investigations these slides contain frames in the learning sequence, analogous to the contents of programed text frames. Second, the individual storage devices provide the capability to plot information on the TV displays. There are no restrictions placed on this plotted material; it may be new material, the student's answer, the re-

[24] *Ibid.*

sulting analysis of the student's response, or anything else deemed useful by the programer.

All of the student responses are currently entered by using the keyset, although investigations are currently under way which may make possible other modes of communication. Each key on the keyset possesses a unique number. All references to these keys by

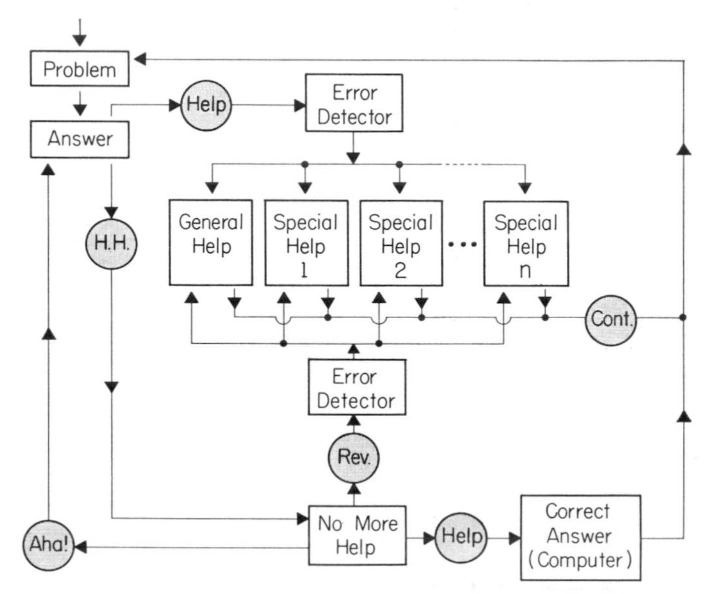

Fig. 98 – Student Response Sequence Together With Available Options.

the computer are made by using these numbers. At the same time, students know the keys by the characters that are printed on them. This provides the possibility for using removable caps on the keys, to meet the needs of different experiments. At various times these caps have corresponded to the keys on an ordinary typewriter keyboard, contained mathematical symbols, or contained words and symbols for paired-associate tests.

In the tutorial logic, the keyset performs two basic functions, *viz.*, it provides a means for students to enter their responses and it provides the students with the ability to control their own progress through the learning program. The sequence of steps followed at this point, is illustrated in Figures 99 and 100. When the student feels that he is satisfied with his answer, he presses the button labeled "judge," which transfers control to a subroutine designed to analyze his answer. This subroutine may simply perform a character-by-character comparison between his responses and those previously

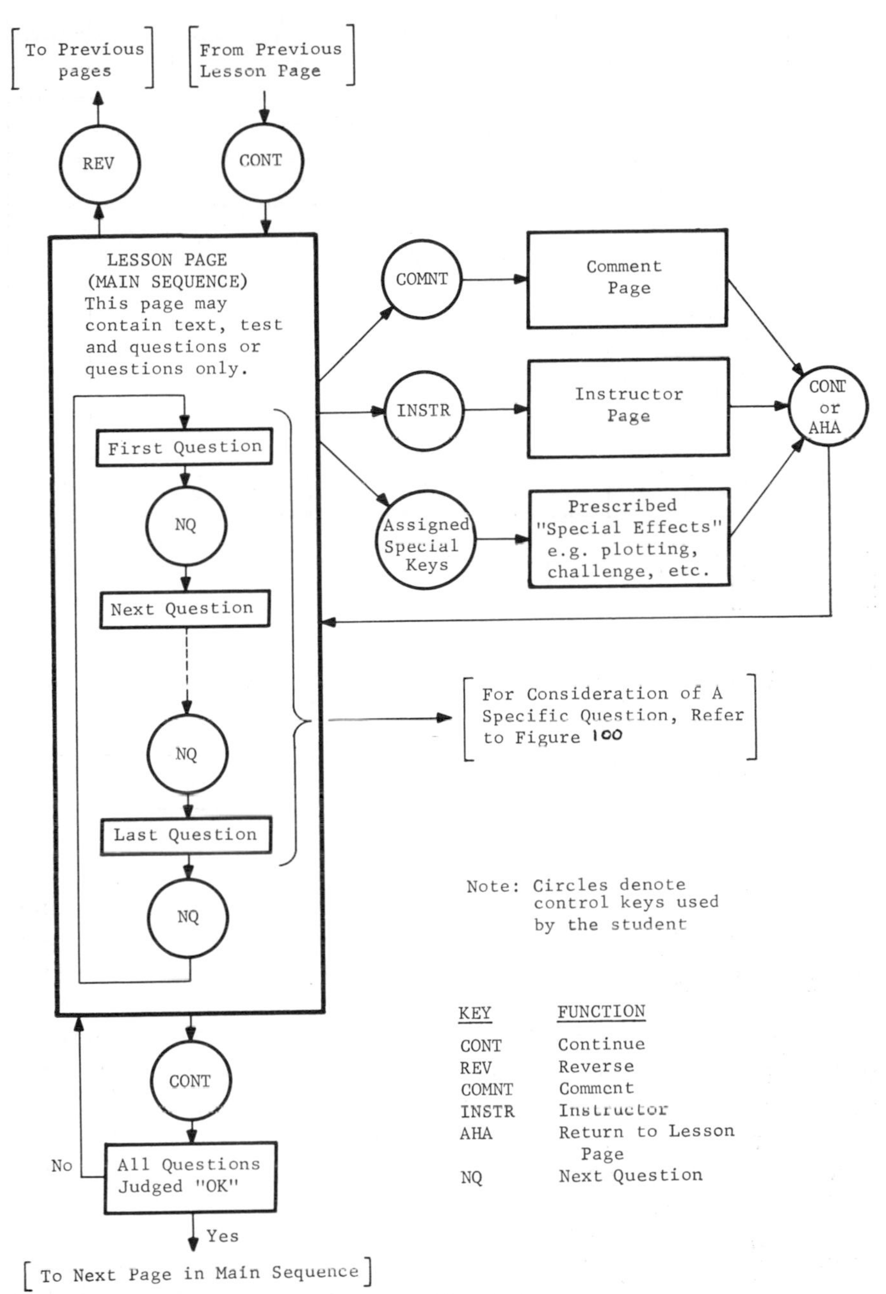

Fig. 99 – Flow Diagram of a Plato Teaching Logic.

stored by the programer, or it may perform some more sophisticated analysis. An example of the latter case is found in the frames of

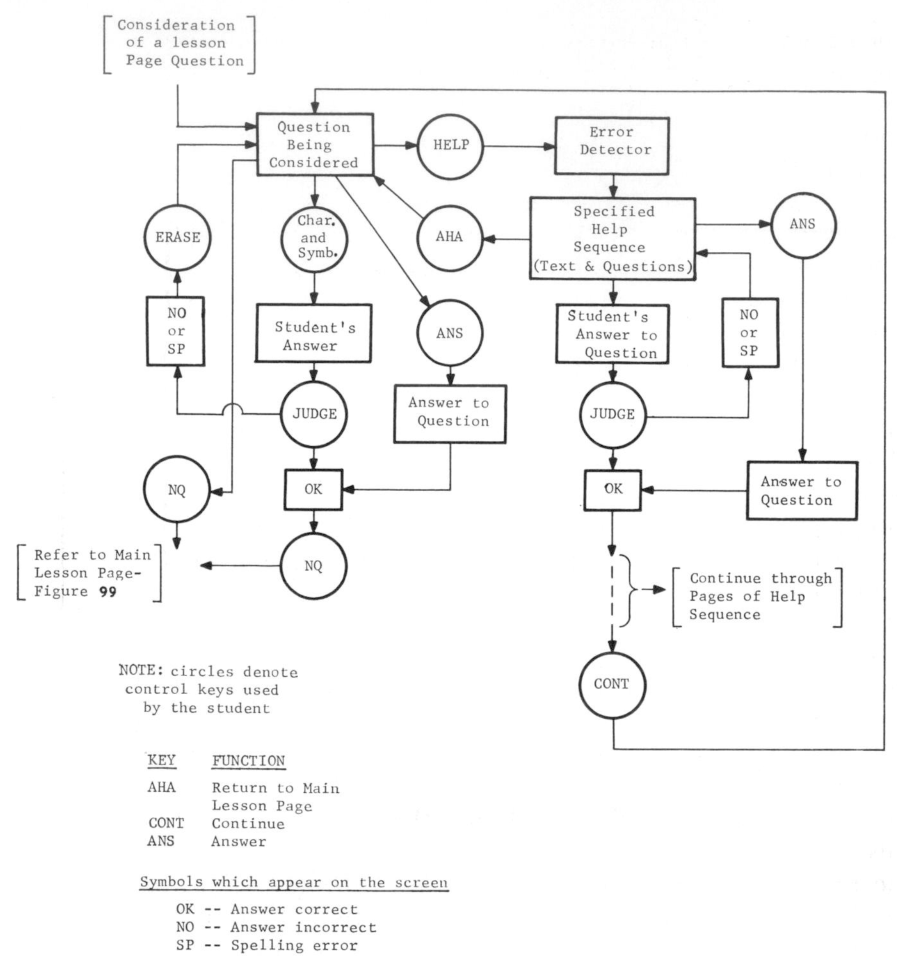

Fig. 100 – Flow Diagram of a Plato Teaching Logic, Continued.

the Fortran experiment which require the student to construct a valid arithmetic expression. In response to this request, the judging subroutine analyzes the student response for agreement with the relevant rules of the Fortran language. Similarly, a judging subroutine is available which checks the validity of the spelling in the student responses.

The more common judging subroutines normally result in one of three indications, *viz.*, that the response was correct, incorrect, or correct except for spelling. More sophisticated judgers such as those described in the previous paragraph are easily written. Thus the student may obtain an indication regarding the validity of his answer together with remedial material or clues to the reason for his error. At the author's option only, the correct response may permit the student to progress to the next step in the program by pressing the "continue" button. Until the student receives an indication that his response was correct, the "continue" button is inoperative.

More than one problem may be placed on a single slide. Thus students can be provided with problems meeting their individual needs. Also, the development of increased problem-solving capability is possible, since the problems may be varied with respect to material tested and degree of difficulty.

Additional help is provided to meet individual student needs. In the current version of the teaching logic this help is not automatically given, but must be explicitly requested by the student. The help sequences may consist of additional material, additional examples, or additional problems and drills. At the option of the programer, special help sequences may be prepared to remedy errors detected in the student responses. Several alternative special help sequences may be provided, with the choice dependent upon the nature of the error(s) detected.

The slides in the scanner may contain one or more "lessons." Students are informed that they have reached the end of a lesson by having the computer plot the words "END OF LESSON" on the TV display. A lesson may be less than or more than a single session. Where a lesson is longer than a single session, or where a student feels that he has had enough for the day, the computer stores his stopping point, so that he may begin at this same place when he returns for the next session. There is a provision to enable the student to review previously completed frames.

One of the most powerful provisions in the teaching logic concerns the ability to have students enter their comments into the computer. By first pressing the "comment" key, the student can temporarily leave the teaching mode to enter a comment for the programer. These comments typically refer to their reactions to the lesson, or to items that they feel are not presented adequately. Experience indicates that students are more prone to make comments in this situation than in the usual group-teaching situation. A possible explanation is that they feel less restricted by the influence of group pressures under these circumstances.

The Computer Program

The computer program used in the Fortran experiment is a very general program operating in two separate modes, a student mode and an author mode. The program may operate in these

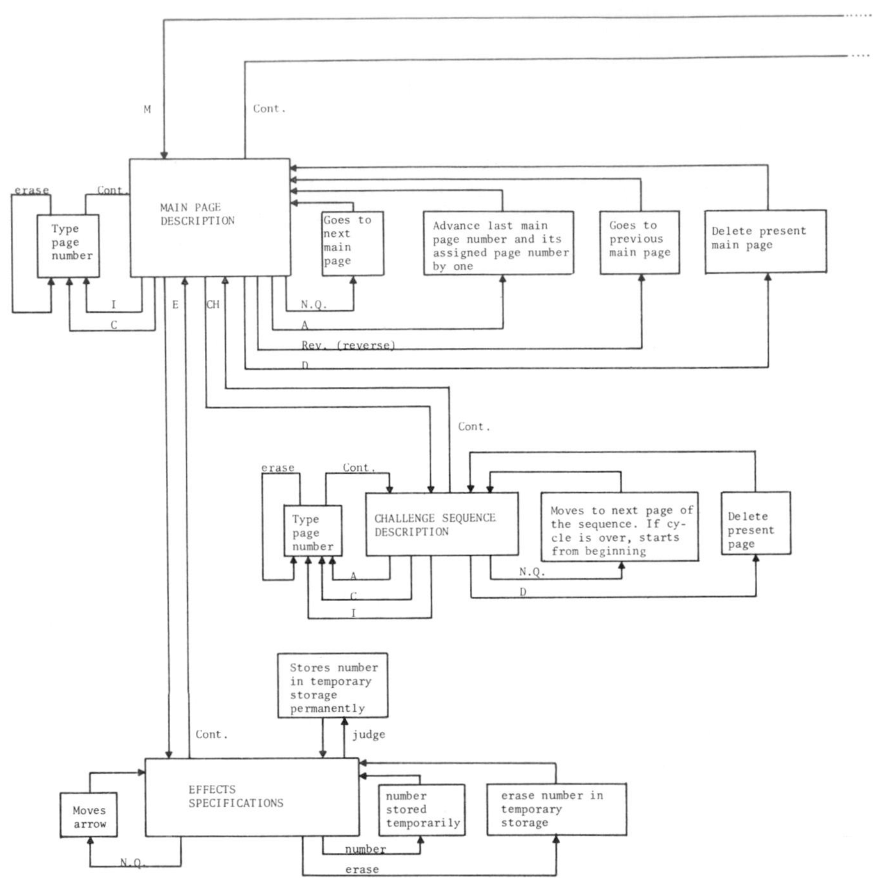

Fig. 101 – Flowchart of Process Used in Assigning Page Numbers to Frames in the Teaching Program.

modes separately or simultaneously. In the student mode the program performs in the manner described previously, leading the student through an individual sequence of steps designed to teach some selected material. When the program is operating in the author mode, the programer can insert additional material, alter existing material, or make modifications in the teaching program. Since it is possible to operate in this mode while the students are using the program, modifications may be made to meet the needs that were not foreseen at the time the program was written.

Figures 101 and 102 show a flowchart illustrating the capabilities available in the author mode. Any student station can double as an author's station. The conversion takes place as a result of simultaneously depressing a predetermined set of keys. While this

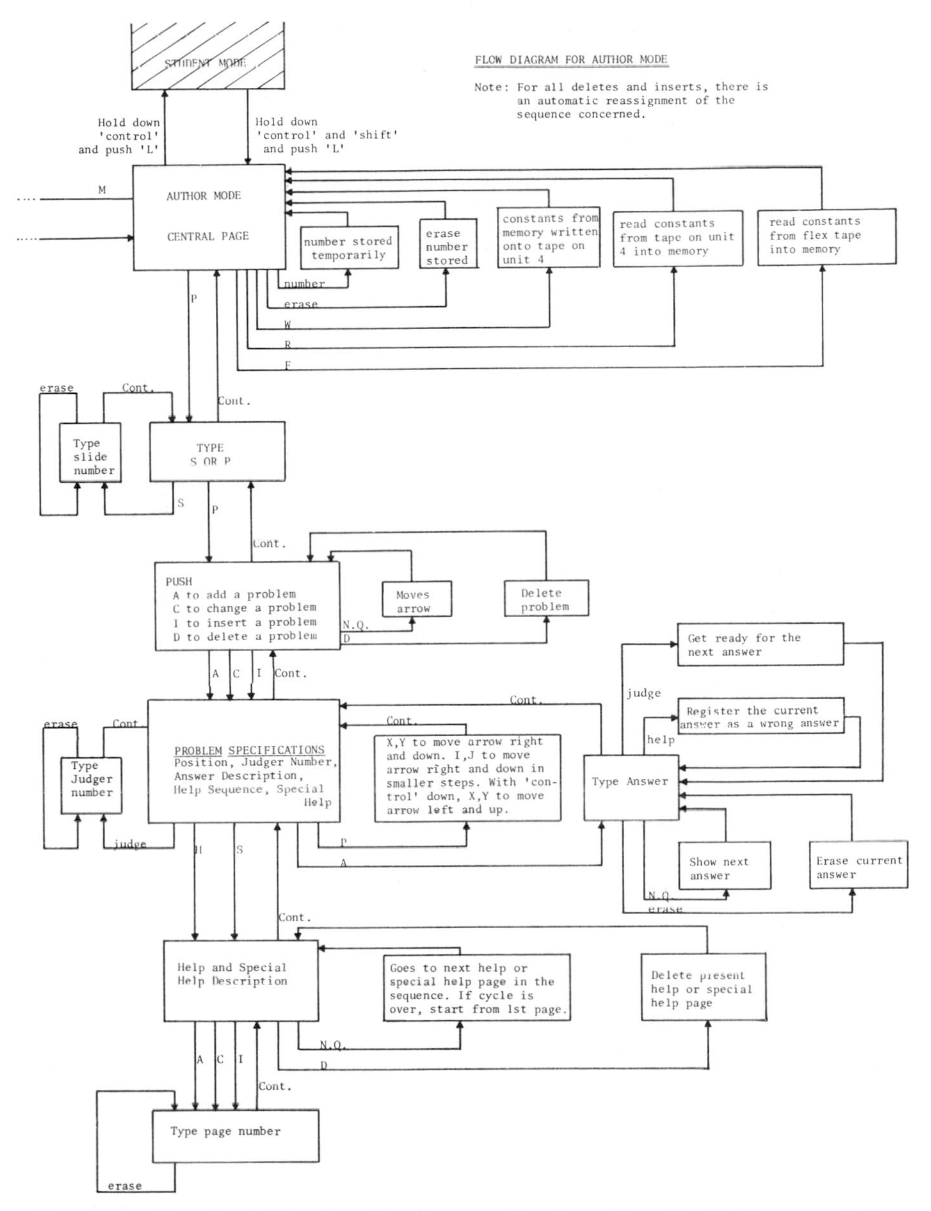

Fig. 102 – Flowchart Showing the Process Used to Specify Problems and the Methods Used for Judging Them.

does admit the possibility of having a student accidentally enter into the author mode, the combination of keys to be pressed makes it highly unlikely. It is probable that a student entering into this mode would recognize the difference in the frames presented.

There are two separate phases associated with the author mode, dealing with the individual slides and the page assignments respectively. In the first phase (shown in Fig. 100), the author deals only with the individual slides. Each position in the slide scanner is assigned a unique reference number, which must be referred to by the author when dealing with the slide in that position. When the author types a slide number, the slide in that position is immediately shown to him on a TV display. His next objective is to provide the computer with all of the information needed to tack actions associated with the slide in question. This information consists of the locations of the problems on the slide, specification of the judger(s) to be used in analyzing the student's response(s), providing a list of alternative student responses (if required by the judging subroutines), and providing for help and special help sequences.

Once the information specified above has been provided for each slide, it only remains to determine the sequence in which the students will see the slides. The sequence of steps needed for this purpose is shown in Figure 101. In this process, each slide is assigned a page number. These page numbers are then assigned a "main page" number, indicating their positions in the learning sequence. A given slide may be used in connection with several different "main pages." Although this process may seem somewhat tedious, recognition should be taken of the fact that in most instances the page and main page numbers increase simultaneously by a unitary amount. For this reason, provision has been made for simultaneously increasing the numbers associated with both of these items. In addition, provision has been made for the addition and deletion of pages from the main page sequence. In this latter case, all of the other page assignments are automatically adjusted accordingly.

Part of the task associated with the determination of the learning sequence involves the specification of special effects. Provision has been made for making selected keys on the keyboard illegal (inoperative), for giving the students graph plotting capabilities, and for specifying the end of the assigned lesson. One of the very important functions provided by this latter effect is to make it impossible for the students to reach certain parts of the program, as in the case where the author is making modifications while the students are taking a lesson.

Development of this teaching program is truly significant as a contribution to research in automated education. Its value lies not in the ability to teach a student any given course, but in its generality. Nothing has been said about the requirements of specific subject matter areas because this information is irrelevant. The teaching logic is easily modifiable with respect to both teaching strategies and response evaluation. Indeed, the program was originally developed for use in an electrical engineering course, but required only the addition of several judging subroutines to make it applicable for the current experiment. At various times, this program has been used to teach courses dealing with electrical engineering, library science, braille, arithmetic, mathematical logic, and computer programing.

Monitoring

The essence of good teaching is the availability and use of feedback relating to student behavior. The effective teacher comes to class prepared with not only a teaching strategy, but also the ability and willingness to react to the needs of individuals comprising the class. It is in this area that one can make the most cogent arguments criticizing the lectures that are used to teach large numbers of students in lecture and TV courses.

The Plato system provides considerable flexibility in making available and using various forms of feedback. A typical Plato lesson is run without any instructor present in the room. It is not even necessary to have someone in the room to answer questions regarding the use of the Plato equipment, since this information is generally provided to the students as the first part of the programed learning sequence. This information is always available for review purposes.

Students are monitored in two ways, by a remote console and by the use of a "dope" tape. Real-time monitoring of student activities takes place by using a remote console that is capable of duplicating any one of the student consoles. Using this console, it is possible to observe the performance of the individual students. It is also possible to determine when immediate modification of the program is needed to meet unforeseen circumstances. In addition, each student keyset possesses an "instructor" button which permits the student to communicate directly with the person at the remote console.

Every time a key is pressed at a student station, a record of this action is placed on magnetic tape. This record contains an indication of the station number, the key pressed, and the time that it was pressed. It is thus possible to analyze this tape to determine the performance of the students and the learning program. Using this information, it is possible to find out how many students make particular kinds of errors, just as it is possible to obtain a clear image of individual student behavior.

In the past few pages, an attempt has been made to provide the reader with a general description of the tutorial logic implemented on the Plato system at the University of Illinois. It has been shown that this is a very general system that is capable of teaching many students at a time. The computer program described was a very general one, permitting adaptation to most semilinear learning programs. The remainder of this chapter describes one of the experiments that is being performed on this system.

THE FORTRAN EXPERIMENT

The ability to program computers requires the mastery of two separate areas, *viz.*, the rules of a programing language and the ability to apply this knowledge to obtain the solution to a problem. Certainly, the first of these areas lends itself to programed learning in a straightforward manner. The readily apparent adaptability of the system, combined with the severe shortage of capable teachers, provides strong motivation for further investigation of computer-based teaching of computer programing. Additional motivation for this study was provided by the recognition of the need to have all business students able to use the computer as a research and learning tool. As a result, it was decided to investigate this problem further, using the Plato system. This investigation had two symbiotic objectives of examining the problems associated with teaching computer programing, and at the same time, examining the kinds of problems that students have when learning computer programing. In short, the investigation was focused upon studying the problems of computer programing and the problems of teaching computer programing.

The Sample

Subjects for the experiment were drawn from four accounting classes being taught at the University of Illinois. There were a total of 20 students involved over the course of two semesters. At any one time there were 10 students taking the program, since the Plato system was not yet expanded to the point where it could simultaneously process 20 students.

The student subjects were all currently taking an elementary accounting course at the University. This fact alone does not necessarily bias the sample, since the course is required of all students in the business curriculum. All of the students used were volunteers. They were interviewed to determine why they had volunteered. It was found that there was no consistency in the answers to this question. The stated reasons ranged from intellectual curiosity, to recognition of the importance of programing, to an attempt to impress their teachers.

A control group of students was provided by a class currently taking a business administration course which included computer programing. The lectures given to this class were programed, i.e., they were essentially verbal duplicates of the programed frames shown to the experimental group.

The reader is cautioned against attempting to associate any degree of statistical significance with the observations presented here. Indeed, numerical bases for the stated observations have been intentionally omitted to avoid this temptation, however unintentional. The sample upon which the observations are based is far too small for valid conclusions. Of the initial 20 students, three must be eliminated from further consideration because they failed to complete the entire program. The stated reason for their leaving was the pressure of final examinations at a time when grades are becoming increasingly important. In addition to these deletions, it must be observed that it is doubtful whether any degree of validity may be associated with the overall results obtained from the first of the two groups. This group served to debug the program. In conclusion then, the observations that will be presented are based upon numerical relationships and upon comments made by students. While these observations have dubious statistical validity, they do serve to indicate the type of situations that did and may continue to arise.

Format of Experiment

The group was told that their performance in the experiment would take three forms: (1) responding to problems contained in the learning program, (2) programing computer problems for solution on a computer (an IBM 1620), and (3) completing objective examinations. They were not told that measurements of their performance were being made, nor were they told what criteria would be used for analyzing their performance. This apparent lack of information was intended to permit the students to seek their own optimum combination of speed and accuracy.

Students in the experimental group were introduced to the Plato system by showing them the location of the student stations. No further instructions were provided since the beginning frames in the first lesson provided a programed introduction to both programed learning and the use of the Plato equipment.

The Fortran program was organized around a series of concentric modules. It was decided that the primary objective of the early lessons was to overcome a feeling that there was something mysterious about computer programing. This was to be accomplished by getting the students to run a successful program as soon as possible. To implement this objective, the first module was designed to provide the students with the concept of a computer program, together with the administrative details needed for processing a program. This concept was easily implemented by providing the students with *basic* rules regarding input-output, format and end statements, together with the rules for naming variables. It should be emphasized that at this point the students were provided with only very basic—and sometimes oversimplified rules. For example, after being told that a punched card contains 80 columns, the students were told that a description (format) of the card must contain a description about *all* of the 80 columns. This is obviously not necessary from the computer programing standpoint, but it was decided not to burden the students with exceptions at this early point in the learning process.

Subsequent modules were built around the background described in the previous paragraph. They gradually added to the student's repertoire of statements. In each case, additional statements were added to meet the needs of specific problems, or because they provided a convenient simplification of previously learned material.

The learning program was semilinear since all of the students were required to process all of the main frames. In addition, branching was provided to meet the needs of the individual students. While working with each frame, the students could request additional help when they wished. If this help was requested after the student had already responded incorrectly, the kind of help provided was dependent upon the kind of error that was made. As one example, a student incorrectly identifying the name *Adolph* as an integer variable would be led through a sequence of steps (1) asking for valid beginning letters for integer names, (2) providing additional examples, and (3) requesting the completion of several examples.

One of the objects of a program such as this was to condition the students to react to relatively weak stimuli. At the same time it must be recognized that part of the power of a programing language such as Fortran comes from the ability to permit the programer considerable freedom in the construction of statements and their components. Testing responses of this kind can prove troublesome in printed texts, since the author's sample solution may or may not be able to provide an adequate judge of the student's response. In this program, however, it was only necessary to construct a judging subroutine which analyzed the student's response for consistency with the relevant rules of Fortran. Thus frames requesting unstructured responses were used frequently and satisfactorily.

After completing each learning module, both the experimental and control groups were given an objective test and programing problem. Both groups were required to solve the programing problem and then run it on an IBM 1620. This requirement was established to allow the students to see the interaction between the statements comprising a complete program. A time limit was established for the successful completion of each program. This time limit forced the students to complete the problem before beginning a new learning module.

Results

Having presented the format of the study, it is now possible to draw some tentative observations. These observations constitute hypotheses subject to further validation.

1. Based upon follow-up interviews with members of the experimental group, it was found that there were no instances where they would have preferred some other mode of teaching. There was some feeling that the pace of the program needed modification, but these criticisms were evenly divided between students in favor of speeding up the program and those in favor of slowing it up.
2. Students in the experimental group completed modules in approximately 65 percent of the time required by students in the lecture sections. A possible explanation of these results is provided by observing that all of the students in a lecture section had to adhere to the time required for every question asked. This was not the case in the programed sections, since the time devoted to help was individually determined and independent of actions taken at all other student stations.
3. There was no noticeable difference between groups with respect to performance on the objective tests.
4. As the course progressed, two related observations became noticeable. First, students in the experimental group began making an increasing number of typing errors. Second, these same students began complaining about an increasing number of keypunching errors. An analysis of these phenomena indicated that this difficulty was due to a difference between the arrangement of the keys on the Plato keysets and the keypunch keysets.
5. After adjusting for the difficulties mentioned above, an analysis of

the performance in computer programing indicated that students in the experimental group were able to get their programs running in approximately 80 percent of the time required by the control group. Closely related is the observation that students in the experimental group tended to ask for less outside assistance during the actual writing of programs.

In summary, it was found that the students in both groups were able to achieve the same level of proficiency. However, the students in the experimental group managed to reach this level in considerably less time than students in the control group. There is inconclusive evidence that the free-format responses permitted in the Plato program helped to increase the students' facility for problem solving. This observation, if proven correct, would tend to indicate that programed-learning can be profitably applied to complex problem-solving situations. The ability to implement such a program will probably rest heavily upon the ability to implement flexible programs in computer-controlled systems.

A judging subroutine is being developed which will permit the students to compile and run entire programs from their individual student stations. This complex judger will analyze each of the individual statements for correctness. Where errors are detected, the students will immediately be provided with remedial material. When a grammatically error-free program is achieved, the computer will interpretively execute it. As a by-product, the availability of this judging subroutine should eliminate the difficulties that students experience when rotating between Plato and keypunch keysets.

In subsequent iterations of the experiment two versions of the program will be used. One of the versions will be essentially a programed text, with none of the flexibility provided by a computer system. The second version will be the same program together with the flexible judgers. Comparison of the results obtained should shed some light on the relative advantages of computer-based flexibility.

SUMMARY

The Plato system at the University of Illinois is a computer-based teaching system capable of adapting to many different subject areas. As a computer-based system, it provides considerable flexibility in design and execution of learning programs that adapt to the needs of individual students. Research by others has indicated that this flexibility is necessary to obtain the maximum efficiency in the learning process.

An investigation of a learning program designed to teach Fortran has indicated that there is a considerable benefit to be achieved from the use of a computer-based teaching program. These benefits come from more rapid learning, and possibly more effective learning of problem-solving techniques. Future experiments are planned to examine this possibility.

REFERENCES

Filby, Y. "Teaching Machines," *Nordisk Psykologi.* 1961.

Frase, L. T. *The Effects of Social Reinformers in a Programmed Learning Task.* Technical Report No. 11. Urbana: University of Illinois Training Research Laboratory, September 1963.

Klaus, D. J., and A. A. Lumsdaine. *Self-Instructional Supplements for a Television Physics Course.* Palo Alto, California: American Institute for Research, 1960.

Lumsdaine, A. A., and R. Glaser (eds.). *Teaching Machines and Programmed Learning.* Washington: National Education Association, 1960.

Porter, D. "Some Effects of Year-Long Teaching Machine Instruction," *Automatic Teaching: The State of the Art* (E. Galenter, ed.). New York: John Wiley & Sons, 1959.

Skinner, B. F. "The Science of Learning and the Art of Teaching," *Harvard Educational Review,* Spring, 1954.

Stolurow, L. M. *A Model and Cybernetic System for Research on the Teaching-Learning Process.* Technical Report No. 4. Urbana: University of Illinois Training Research Laboratory, September 1964.

INDEX

L

M

N

O

P